Two Centuries of

LIFE

in

DOWN

1600 — 1800

John   Stevenson

The White Row Press

First published 1920
This edition published 1990
by the White Row Press Ltd.
135 Cumberland Road, Dundonald
Belfast BT16 0BB

Introduction copyright © Ian Wilson
This book has received financial assistance under the Cultural
Traditions Programme

Cover: Lagan Village, County Down, c.1790,
from a watercolour by G. Morland, Ulster Museum, Belfast

Printed by the Guernsey Press Company Ltd.

British Library Cataloguing in Publication Data
Stevenson, John, ca.1850-1932
Two centuries of life in Down, 1600-1800.
1. (County) Down, history
I. Title
941.65

ISBN 1 870132 30 0

FOREWORD

Two Centuries of Life in Down first appeared in 1920 published in Belfast by McCaw, Stevenson and Orr, in which John Stevenson was a partner. This fine new edition of what has long been a collector's item arrives at a time when interest in local studies has never been greater, a phenomenon that would have delighted Stevenson, whose books seem only with difficulty to have reached publication and then sold sparsely. The years have not dated this, his *magnum opus,* however. It is as fresh today as when written and the secret of its success is its use of primary sources. Stevenson had nothing but contempt for the notion of history as "a valley of dry bones". He believed that to work, it had to be a living thing, and so wherever possible he lets his characters speak for themselves, through diaries, letters, inventories, accounts and other manuscripts, a method which gives the text a tremendous vitality. Stevenson promised to avoid previously published material, and scarcely a page passes without direct transcript from powerful land-owners, aristocratic ladies, grasping land agents, diligent Presbyterian ministers and a host of others. The author leaves the stage to his characters, appearing from the wings to outline the context and link the narrative. It is "the grace and favour of the old word", that he wishes his readers to hear, being especially grateful on behalf of posterity to the diary writers, who, he surmises, could not be spared as readily as historians!

This approach to local studies, which gives the book a timeless quality, was ahead of its era, as indeed could be said of some of Stevenson's other work. He translated de la Tocnaye's *A Frenchman's Walk through Ireland,* now recognised as a unique account of the country on the eve of the 1798 rebellion, but it was turned down by eleven publishers before his own firm published it in 1917, in an edition that sold only two hundred copies before being remaindered in 1929 to Belfast bookseller Hugh Greer!

Stevenson published three other works:- *Pat McCarty, His Rhymes* (London, Edward Arnold, 1903); *A Boy in the Country* (same publishers, 1912) and *Bab of the Percivals* (London, Wells, Gardner, Darton, 1926) but only the first sold even moderately well. It is his best fictional work, worth searching for, a collection of a hundred poems purporting to be a Co. Antrim farmer reflecting on the daily round, the changing seasons, birth and death in the townlands. Stevenson succeeds in entering the mental universe of Pat McCarty, an achievement that he replicated on a much grander scale in *Two Centuries of Life in Down*. *A Boy in the Country* appears to be a heavily autobiographical account of a city boy holidaying in Co. Antrim, which underlines again Stevenson's championing of the classes then neglected by historians - "the people of the corners and corridors".

His eclectic contribution to the cultural life of the community was recognised by the award of an Honorary M.A. by Queen's University in 1926. Interestingly, the University halls of residence stand on the former site of his home, "Coolavin", 78 Malone Road, Belfast, which was demolished about 1964.

Stevenson's forebears came from the Ards Peninsula, apparently the Kircubbin area. Little is known of the author beyond the fact he was a self-made man whose father was an employee of the Linfield Mill in Belfast. Some autobiographical detail in the introduction refers to the impact on his youthful mind of Bangor Abbey (where he later carried out the fruitless archaeological 'dig' described in Chapter One) and archaeological travels in Egypt and Peru. Stevenson had varied interests. A letter of 1889 from Edward Harland survives in the Public Record Office, politely declining to involve the shipyard in Stevenson's concept for communication by under-water sound waves, while another of Stevenson's theories - no doubt unique to him - postulated that character was revealed by the initial letter of the Christian name (the strongly built 'B' is superior to the shaky 'V' ...) Worthy indeed of Flann O'Brien's indefatigable polymath, de Selby! Stevenson died in 1932 and a collection of his papers is held by the Public Record Office of Northern Ireland.

In *Two Centuries of Life in Down* his Scots planter background does not make Stevenson's appraisal less steady as he is scathing, for instance, about Presbyterian intolerance in the excellent chapters on the Kirk and mocking about bad popular literature. He was also fastidious about strong language and this forbade him to repeat "the verb describing the bird's action" when the bare head of one of his characters is bombed!

The original dust jacket of *Two Centuries of Life in Down* boldly proclaimed: "The book contains an immense amount of most interesting material, hitherto unpublished." Clearly engaged on a labour of love, Stevenson delved into records some of which are now lost to us. The preservation in print of the galaxy of sources is more significant now than ever, therefore, and this handsome new edition is an apt and overdue tribute to John Stevenson's immense talent and industry.

Ian Wilson

ILLUSTRATIONS

Publisher's note: not all of the portraits which appeared in the 1920 edition were of reproducable quality. After taking advice we have omitted five and retained twelve, re-photographing four of these. We would ask the reader to make allowance for their age and poor condition.

CONTENTS

INTRODUCTORY

Two
Centuries
of
Life in
Down

NORMALLY the prefatory statement in a book finds place before the table of contents. For this work it is desirable that it should stand immediately before, and be read as part of, the first chapter.

History we know too often as a valley of dry bones. The shapes of the past it exposes are but skeletons, more or less bleached or broken as the time to which they belong is far away or near. What corresponds to mass, form, colour, and movement of living bodies,—the intimate, infinite detail of the life of long ago,—is missing. If the land of the life is our land, its long dead our forefathers, then, for sight of dry bones,—records of battles in field or trials in law-courts, of grants of acres and titles,—we crave the touch of beings in whom is " the heat of life." We long to get close to the old folk in their daily round,—to know them as they ate, drank, married or were given in marriage, as they worked, talked, thought, prayed, loved or hated ;—in their sweet contents and vexing disappointments. We wish, in short, to see them alive,—and the vision comes but seldom by way of history.

In the following pages an attempt is made to bring again the fair show of life to the skeleton of bookish story. The story is that of the first successful Plantation in Ireland ; the life is the life of its settlers and their descendants ; the scene, broadly, the territory in North Down granted by James the First to James Hamilton and Hugh Montgomery ; the period, that beginning with the arrival of the adventurers in 1605-6, and ending with the dawn of the industrial era in the first decade of the 19th century,—a round two hundred years.

The introduction of the personal note will help to clearer understanding of what a reader may expect to find if he adventures further. In the beginning, this book was a boy's awed contemplation of a rudely-cut monument built into the wall of the old church of Bangor in Down.

HEIR·LYES·BELOVE·A·VE·LEARVED·AVD
REVERAVD·FATHER·IN·GODES·CHVRCH
MESTER·IHON·GIBSON·SEИCE·REFOR
MACIOИ·FROM·POPARY·THE·FIREST
ДEAVE·OF·DOVИE·SEИD·BYHIS·MAIES
·TIE·IИTOTHIS·KIИGDOM·AИD·RECEVED

BY·MY·LORD·CLANEBOYE·TO·BE·PREAC
HER·AT·BANGOR·AT·HIS·EИTRY·HAD·XI
COMMVИICAИTES·AИD·AT·HIS·ДEPAR
TOVR·THIS·LYF·23·OF·IVИII·1623·LEFT·1500
BEIИG·OF·AGE·63·YEARS·SO·CHRYST·VAS
HIS·ADVAИTAGE·BOTHE·IИ·LYFE·AИD·ДEATH

As what Ruskin calls "the hereditary instinct for antiquity" is not an acquirement by study,—is, indeed, a thing of which we may say, as of the wind, "we cannot

tell whence it cometh,"—I may, without immodesty, claim
its possession. Since the instinct woke to life at sight of this
old stone, it has busied itself with the old work of human
hands from Egypt to Peru ; but, always, has returned with
special interest and pleasure to the place of its awakening,
to occupy itself with things of the country and time of the
old Dean's activities.

Every phrase, every word, I might say, of "Mester" John
Gibson's record appealed to the very young boy, hearing the
call of the past for the first time. "Ane learned and reverand
father in Gode's Chvrch " had a grand sonority, and took
fast grip of the mind—to say the words was to see visions of
cathedral aisles. It was with the feeling of transportation
to the Bangor of Stuart times that, long years afterwards,
I found the same form of words on a stone in the Cathedral
of S. Benigne at Dijon. " His Maiestie " and " My Lord
Claneboye " filled the pews with shades of old nobility. The
evocative power of a word is not the same for every breast ;—
Claneboye, for the boy, caused emotions strange and romantic,
—not to be explained by words.

Later, with opportunity to wander any day, or every
day, in the churchyard, I found many memorial stones of
the early Scots. The great Lord Claneboye must have seen
them many times,—he came nearer with the thought. One
to the memory of Beatrix Hamilton, who died in 1627, aged
only 27, had a worn inscription, its metrical portion beginning
with the lines—

" The Bodie of Beatrix heer below
In hope of Glorie doth now sweetly rest."

Beatrix was a beautiful name, and that mysterious influence
of initial of which I have, elsewhere, elaborated a theory
made her a beautiful person. Very tender and pathetic
are the words addressed to her husband. Speaking of the
heavenly city, with its " jasper wals and Ports of Peerrless
Pearl," she says, or is represented as saying—

> " Thither I goe,—she said,—this Bodie fraile
> Shall shortly in my Cofin Sweetly rest.
> Onse sweet to thee bot now to Christ,—Farewell,
> Wel meet I fully have whom I love best."

Most of these early 17th-century stones are heavy oblong slabs with lettering in relief. The statement of name, with description of the commemorated and date of death, begins at one corner of the stone, and is carried round the margin to finish at the starting point, the centre space being devoted to heraldry and doggerel,—pious, affectionate, or appreciative. A man drowned in 1629, certified by the marginal inscription to have been " a worthy Gentleman," William Stevnstone,— perhaps one of my own people, for they were of the Ards,— is thus made to express his hope in a joyful resurrection :—

> " This Corps I left on Walter Shore,
> My Soule now bathes in Flodes of Glor,
> No Tempests tose no Deeps can droune,
> No Death can Reave that purchased Crovne,
> I died in Chryst with Chryst I rest.
> Chryst was my Hope my Gaine,
> My Bodie heir in Grave doth lye,
> In Grave not to remaine."

Many other old stones there were, with verse of like quality and quaintness, setting forth the virtues of deceased Esquires, Provosts, and Merchants,—all such monuments now, I believe, housed, for their preservation, in the disused church ; but in the days of which I write, lying against the church walls in the open : and there, with a very ancient sound,—the cawing of rooks,—in my ears, I spent much time with the old people, and, in a manner, saw them.

I could not be so much on this sacred ground without learning of those who knew it far earlier than the Scots,— the monks of Bangor's once famous Abbey,—and of religious and social activities of which this was the scene for a thousand

years before My Lord Claneboye and his settlers landed.
Eagerly I read Ware, Harris, Reeves,—every book or paper
I could find which had anything to tell of the old monastic
life,—and sadly found it, all put together, to be very little.
Perhaps the story of the Abbey lay underground.

The search for relics on this old, old site was, by stress
of life-work, delayed for long ; but just as soon as circumstances permitted, I made an effort to lay bare what earth
might hide of remains of Bangor's once great Church and
School.   The story of the quest and its disappointing result
is told at length in the first chapter.

While directing the work of excavating, the maps made
for Lord Claneboye in 1625 were used ; study of these revived
interest in the fortunes of the Scots, and, gradually, the
design of this book took shape. What the work contains
of value is derived from unpublished documents, relating
to Down, discovered in the collections of the British Museum,
the Bodleian Library, Oxford, and the Advocates' Library,
Edinburgh ; and from a vast number of letters and manuscripts of various kinds, which, as result of systematic search
for a number of years, have been found in the houses of old
county families.

Many books have been read for this study, and extracts
from some of the rarer have been used; but reading of printed
matter has been, in the main, with intention that the already-
published should not be reproduced.   Something of historical
setting is, however, required by the plan of the book, and
this, for the greater part, has been supplied by the Hamilton
and Montgomery Manuscripts. The writers of both were
members of the families whose fortunes they chronicled, their
writings were completed in the century which saw the Settlements, and what they record is contemporary and first-hand
knowledge.   Secretary Hamilton may have seen and talked
to Lord Claneboye,—certainly he knew his son and grandson,
and from them learned what, in his story, did not come
within his observation.   The connection of William

Montgomery, the chronicler, with the Lords Montgomery
of the Ards and Mount-Alexander, and their fortunes, was
even more intimate. He was a boy at Newtown School in
the lifetime of the masterful Hugh Montgomery, who founded
it. When he went to Utrecht to complete his studies, he was
visited by the chief of his family, the banished third Lord, for
whom he had unbounded admiration. On a slight staging,
constructed principally of material supplied by these two, the
Ancients are allowed to appear and speak for themselves, so
that what is knowable of their state, surroundings, character,
manners, and habits, is learned from their own words.

From what is stated above, the reader will know that
he is not to expect to find here reasoned and connected
accounts of political and military movements affecting Down
with other parts of Ulster. These have cursory attention
where desirable, or come under notice when the old people
like to talk of them; but, by the plan of the book, the large
things of the public, amply treated by a hundred authors,
are put aside in favour of the things which concern the family
or individual. It is in these that we find ourselves of kin
with the sleeping of centuries ago, be they our forefathers
or people of another race. Jehoram may muster his forces
and call the king of Judah to help in the chastisement of
Moab, defaulter in tribute of the wool of one hundred thousand
lambs and one hundred thousand rams,—the tale leaves us
cold; it is of a land that is very far off. But we read the
touching little story of a family of his subjects, as told in
II Kings IV. 18-20—

> " And when the child was grown, it fell on a day, that he went
> out to his father to the reapers. And he said unto his father,
> My head, my head. And he said to a lad, Carry him to his
> mother. And when he had taken him, and brought him to
> his mother, he sat on her knees till noon, and then died."

—and, straightway, we are at home in Israel.

There are those who profess to be bored by extracts, and
these may think that the work had been better done by digest.

True, the digest is easier to read, but in it the grace and savour of the old word are lost, and, inevitably, something which was not in the old has been acquired. Re-casting of old documentary matter is, indeed, to be likened to that manner of " restoration " of an old church which is effected by demolishing it, and rebuilding. The stones may be numbered and re-set in nearly the old position, but the dignity, the identity, the mysterious life of the building, have been destroyed ; and when an old setting of words is modernised in spelling and arrangement, it suffers like disaster.

To spare the reader the weariness to eye and brain of heavily annotated pages, I have made references to authority only where absolutely necessary, and, then, in the text. But I beg him to understand that there is, in the writing, no futile imaginative matter ;—every phrase of statement outside the extracts can be justified. Varied in character as are the old documents used,—and they comprise letters of love, of friendship, of business, of gossip ;—letters by soldiers, lawyers, clergymen, physicians ;—letters of agents, bailiffs, and domestics,—it is not to be expected that every phase of the life of old Down can be by them illuminated. Nevertheless, the temptation to supplement, by assumption, what they may tell has been resisted, and where a subject has appeared to lack enlivening through shortage of reference in the manu-scripts, the deficiency has been made good by extracts from old printed matter, with full acknowledgment.

To the realizing of any representation by pigment,—the best is but suggestion,—the beholder contributes as much as the artist. Unconsciously he transforms a stretch of blue paint into clear air, and changes to daisied field a patch of speckled green. If the reader will do for this word-picture what, involuntarily, he does for the painting, then, I am hopeful, that, for him, the hands will go back on the dial of time,—he will see the old people of Down move and hear them speak.

John Stevenson.

Coolavin,
   Belfast.

CHAPTER I.

A Famous Christian Settlement

BEFORE we live for a time with the Scots, our fathers, let us cast a glance at the land of their adoption as it was in the old time before them.

The great Map of the World in Hereford Cathedral represents the earth as flat and circular, its central point the City of Jerusalem. The disc breaks into raggedness round its circumference,—entirely detached portions being the islands of the earth. On one of these, divided in two parts by a wide river, and having, in outline, no resemblance to Ireland, are figured, on the northern half, two cities— Bangor and Armagh.

The map, with its errors of form and placement of territory, and with its grotesque drawings of men, one-eyed, one-footed, or headless, supposed to inhabit the wild places of the earth, is testimony at once to the ignorance of the monkish cartographer, and to the ancient celebrity of the places he has named. That celebrity, in the case of Bangor, was due to the existence of the famous Monastery and School, founded by Comgall the missionary in 558,—a Christian

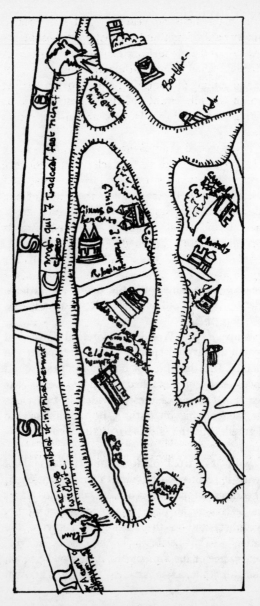

IRELAND ON A
MONKISH MAP
OFTHEMIDDLE
AGES. From
the great Map
of the World
in Hereford
Cathedral;
date 1314. The
long island to
left, divided
by a broad
river, is Ire-
land. One of
the places
marked in the
upper portion
is Bangor, the
other Armagh.
In the lower
half the two
towns shown
are Dublin and
Kildare. The
broad river
dividing the
island in two
is the Bann,
the river in
the south is
the Shannon.
England has
twenty-six
towns, Wales
four, and Scot-
land six.

settlement which, in its thousand years of existence, became the parent of many educational and monastic establishments in Ireland, Scotland, and on the Continent. The history of Down occupations begins here, although, doubtless, for centuries before the coming of Comgall, the land of his settling was well known to the inhabitants of the opposite shore as a place for raiding and trading. Houses are visible across the sea on a clear day.

For nearly two hundred years Bangor Abbey and Schools enjoyed great prosperity ; students and clerics in residence at one time being numbered by thousands. The first half of the 9th century saw the beginning of the raids of the sea-rovers, Danes and Norwegians, and these affected disastrously the fortunes of the settlement. The Irish Annals continue through the 9th, 10th, and 11th centuries to chronicle the deaths of Abbots, but the glory had declined. Under Malachy O'Morgair (early 12th century) there was a revival of activity, which for a time brought fame to the old Church, but later, with the Anglo-Romanisation of the Irish Church, Bangor's influence again declined. The next century saw this decline accelerated.

" An enactment of the Anglo-Irish Parliament, held in Kilkenny A.D. 1367, decreed that no mere Irishman should be allowed to make his profession in a religious house situated amongst the English. This enactment extended to the Abbey of Bangor, and, after it, the race to which Comgall, Columbanus, and Gall belonged, was to be excluded from the cloisters they had sanctified, and the rich endowments which the piety of the Irish had consecrated to religion were given to foreigners." (O'Laverty.)

The long career of the famous abbey and college closed with the suppression of the monasteries by Henry VIII. Nominally the vast possessions of Bangor then fell to the Crown ;—really they came into the hands of neighbouring chiefs, who held them until the coming of the Scots.

We know far more about the Egyptians of 5,000 years ago than we do of Bangor teachers and students. The

Antiphonarium Benchorense, now in the Ambrosian Library
at Milan, a collection of hymns, collects, prayers, and
anthems, is the most important—almost the only important—
relic of the great establishment.   One of its religious
poems commemorates, in dignified language, the rule of
the first fifteen abbots, and their names and the order of
their appearing agree, in the main, with references in the
Irish Annals.

Records containing material for the reconstruction of
the domestic life of the great community are not known to
exist.   In the early centuries members were probably housed
in little huts of wood or wattle, covered with thatch ;   the
church,—probably of stone from the beginning,—in the
centre of the settlement.   Provision of food was, partly, by
collection—the juniors scouring the country daily for gifts,—
and partly by cultivation of farms and gardens around and
through the settlement.   The only known portion of the
writings of Comgall the founder, coming to us, indicates that
farm work was familiar to him.   The fragment is preserved
in the works of his disciple Columbanus, and reads—

> " If the cultivator of the land and husbandman, when preparing
> the soil to commit to it the seed, does not consider his work
> all done when he has broken up the earth with the strong share,
> and by the action of the plough has reduced the stubborn soil,
> but further endeavours to cleanse the ground of unfruitful
> weeds, to clear it of injurious rubbish, the spreading shoots of
> thorns and brambles, fully persuaded that his land will never
> produce a good crop unless it be reclaimed from mischievous
> plants, . . .   how much more does it behove us, who believe
> the hope of our fruits to be laid up, not on earth, but in heaven,
> to cleanse from vicious passions the field of our heart."

Corn-mills were necessities to these great communities,
and Bangor had one.   The old *Life of S. Comgall* says that
the founder of the Abbey was accustomed, every night, as
penitential exercise, to remain a long time immersed in the
stream which turned the Bangor mill ;   but this is probably

a pious invention of later times, when Comgall the practical
had become Comgall the saint.

Of stone, or other material, on the ancient site there
are no remains of magnitude commensurate with the fame
of the abbey. A wall about ninety feet in length, sixteen feet
in height, and three feet thick,—probably a part of Malachy
O'Morgair's 12th-century church,—is all that is visible.
Bearing in mind the Irish custom of marking the burial-
places of eminent ecclesiastics by richly-carved crosses, it
is almost incredible that there is visible so little material
evidence of the living and dying here of such a vast number
of persons through a thousand years.

No record of search for such evidence is known to the
author ; and, believing that, spite of all the burnings, demoli-
tions, and disasters chronicled by the Irish annalists, much
of interest must lie underground, he undertook, in the year
1895, the exploration of the ancient site.

Where excavation should begin was a question difficult
to decide. The Bangor communities were, at certain periods,
very large, and the various constructions required for living
in, for working, for teaching, and for worship, being, in earlier
ages, of one storey, would occupy a very large space. It is
probably correct to give to the occupied area a sort of creep-
ing motion. As buildings became unfit for their purpose
through decay or disaster, new constructions would be erected,
not on the sites of the old, but beside them. In this way, in
centuries, the area of occupation would slowly shift position.

Land maps of the time of native Irish occupation never
existed,—the earliest to be looked for would date from the
time of the Scottish settlement. That one of the early acts
of Sir James Hamilton would be the mapping of his lately-
acquired estate seemed probable, and, happily, the conjecture
as to existence of such survey was justified by the finding,
at Bangor Castle, of a complete series of maps of the planted
lands. This survey was made in 1625 ; that is to say within
a score of years of the coming of the Scots.

On the section occupied by Bangor appear, on the map
of the Abbey site, certain sketches of buildings not now in
existence. To find the foundations of these, and, from them,
ascertain their plan and use, and probable date of their
erection, incidentally unearthing worked or inscribed stones
and articles of domestic use, was the object of the first series
of excavations.

The assistance of Mr. (later, Sir) Thomas Drew, the
eminent antiquary and authority in matters of ancient Irish
architecture, was sought and readily obtained. It was
apparent that, provided the old surveyor had worked exactly
to scale, a transparent copy of his map, harmonised with
scale of the Ordnance Sheet and placed on the top of the
latter, would, at once, locate position of the objects drawn
on the old map. A certain point of anchorage was the tower
of the old church appearing in both surveys.

Mr. Drew kindly undertook the task of bringing the
old work into scale harmony with the Ordnance Survey.
The result proved the reliability of the work of Raven, James
Hamilton's surveyor of 1625-6, and disclosed some very
interesting facts. One of these was that, as anticipated,
the ancient burying-ground extended far beyond the limits
of the enclosure in which the old church now stands. It
included the ground which has been, for very many years,
the rectory garden. No tradition existed among old Bangor
people of this garden having been ever part of a graveyard.
An old man, whose ancestors for 150 years had been sextons
of the church, had never heard of the graveyard occupying
larger or other ground than at present. Yet the accuracy
of the old Raven survey was established by the first spade
work, which laid bare skulls and bones on the site indicated
by the map, at a spot far away from what is known as the old
churchyard.

The first series of trenches was cut in the neighbourhood
of the above-mentioned old wall, which is marked on Ordnance
Map as " Ruins of Abbey." The trenches varied in width

from two to four feet,—digging was always continued until
virgin soil was reached. This unmoved earth was never
more than five feet from the surface, and was sometimes
reached at a depth of three feet. It was assumed that the
ground level was much above that of ancient days, and this
assumption was supported by the appearance of a recessed
arch in the old wall, the spring of the arch being near the
ground. The underground portion of the building was here
laid bare, but only to find rough boulders of the wall's foundation, lying on bright red sand, at less than three feet from
surface level.

The results of the excavations were most disappointing.
Everywhere over the wide area treated were found bones ;
everywhere the friable black earth indicated ground used
for interments over a long period, and everywhere the outstanding characteristic of the worked ground was its poverty
in stone, wrought or unwrought.

Mr. Drew, at Dublin, during the progress of the work,
was supplied with maps and tracings showing the lines of
trenches cut, and from time to time he made suggestions.
as to direction of these, his advice being accepted in every
case. To his and the author's surprise and regret, the
carefully planned and fairly extensive excavations failed to
discover anything of the slightest importance.

The conclusions drawn from observations during the
search are these. The ground level, instead of being higher
than that of ancient times, as is invariable in the case of
undisturbed burial-ground in use for a lengthy period, is
considerably lower. The Scots found a wide range of ruined
buildings on the abbey site, and a hummocky waste which
had been burying-ground for nigh on a thousand years, filled
with monumental stone, some of it richly carved. They
levelled the waste and made building stone of the monuments
for their new church, built against an ancient tower. And
as this church, become old, was rebuilt in the last century,
and the dead lie close around its walls, a search here for the

venerable monuments of the great church and schools of
Bangor is out of the question. Only one fragment of a
sculptured cross has survived the Scots. This was discovered
doing duty as step to a door in the churchyard wall, many
years ago, by the late Marquis of Dufferin and Ava, and was
by him removed to the chapel of Clandeboye House.

And, doubtless, the ancient walls, of which the small
remains appear on Raven's map, were used as quarries to
furnish stone for the house of James Hamilton and the church
of his settlers.

CHAPTER II.

Down before the Coming of the Scots

AFTER the Danes the Norman English. When Pope
Adrian IV.,

> " for the purpose of extending the limits of the Church, checking
> the torrent of wickedness, reforming evil manners, sowing seeds
> of virtue, and increasing the Christian religion,"

and in consideration of a payment of one penny per house
per annum, gave Ireland to the arms of Henry II., much of
the land of Leinster quickly became spoil for the King's
Knights and their successors. Conquests in West and South
quickly followed, but Ulster the difficult remained untouched
until 1177, when John de Courcy, under licence from the
King to conquer the northern province, entered Down,
defeated the Irish at Downpatrick, and paid his followers
by large estates in the land of the rolling hills. So came
to settle in the East and North of Down the Jordans,
Chamberlains, Savages, Copelands, Martels, Ridals, and
others. Though they built strong castles, they were not
able to withstand the persistent attacks of the Irish and the
ill-treatment of English kings and their deputies through

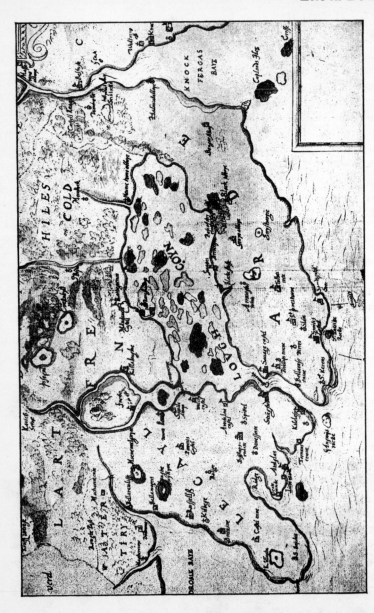

Supposed to be the earliest MAP of COUNTY DOWN. Original in Public Record Office, Chancery Lane, London. Described in Dunlop's Catalogue of XVIth Century Maps of Ireland as "Anonymous of about 1500. Size 19" × 14½". Much used by Burghley."

four centuries, and by the time of Elizabeth, most of these
families had disappeared and English influence had declined
nearly to vanishing point. The Savages held out longer
than others, as they had been by far the most powerful of the
Anglo-Norman families in Down. Their possessions, which
extended to neighbouring counties, were perhaps greatest
about the middle of the fifteenth century, when the head of
the house was almost in the position of an independent prince.
There is a story told of one of the family, a certain Sir Robert
Savage, who, before going out to battle with the Irish near
Antrim, prepared a great supper, which was to serve for his
enemies if they defeated him, or for himself and his friends
if he returned victorious. He slew on that day—it is said—
3,000 Irishmen, and returned, giving God thanks for his
success, to eat his supper.

Threatened incessantly by the Irish,—attacked sometimes by neighbours of his own race,—left to fight the King's
battles if it did not suit the policy of the Lord Deputy to defend
him against the King's enemies, and treated as a rebel if he
made war without authority, the lot of the head of one of
these old English families in Down in the early centuries was
an unenviable one. The wonder is, not that the English
had declined greatly in power and wealth after four hundred
years, battling against overwhelming odds, but that any of
them remained at all and remained loyal to the English
king. Many adopted Irish manners and dress and conformed
to Irish custom,—some found it their interest to side with
the Irish in order to preserve their territories from the
encroachments of adventurers like Essex.

Although one Ulster chief burned the English patent
for his lands, scorning to hold by parchment from Elizabeth
what he had won by the sword, others discerned the growing
power of England and made terms with the English ruler.
Among these were the O'Neills of Claneboye, who fortified
themselves by a grant from the Crown of the territory which
included the Northern and Eastern parts of Down, soon to

fall to the hands of the Scots. But although the chief knew English manners, and professed allegiance, nominal at least, to the English Crown, and although conformity to English law and land custom was involved in the acceptance of such grants, the Irish tribal system and custom of living under it were but little changed. According to the custom of Tanistry, the chieftainship of a tribe passed not by regular descent, nor by will, but by election,—only relatives of the chief being eligible. This custom allowed the people to give the leadership to the man of the family esteemed strong,— a brother or cousin or an uncle of the chief being preferred to a son physically or mentally weak. By this custom the territory with which this book is mainly concerned passed, about 1589, from Sir Con McNiell Oge O'Neill to his cousin Con McBrien Fertagh O'Neill,—the last chief of the Claneboye branch.

As this book deals less with historic event than with the life of the common people, it is proper here to say a word or two about the life of these and of their relationship to their elected chief, before the coming of the Scots.

Irish land belonged, not to a king, but to the people, who, in the lifetime of a chief, elected the Tanist to succeed him. The chief's ownership was not absolute,—he held the tribal lands merely as trustee for his people. These disliked at all times fixed or set payments, although always recognising their duty to support their lord, and willing indeed to submit to his unreasonable exactions. The irregular gifts of people to chief were mostly in kind, and these equivalents of rents were never for set measurements of land, but were calculated by the size of the flocks and herds owned by the rentpayer. Rents for measured lands as understood to-day were not possible, seeing that the cattle in search of pasture were driven anywhere or everywhere through the possessions of the tribe. Arable land was divided among the free men every few years.

The chiefs lived in stone castles—that of Con O'Neill,

who lost the greater part of his territory to the Scots, was situated on the Castlereagh Hills, a few miles from Belfast, with a glorious view over the great bay of Carrickfergus. At times, however, the chief had to be content with a house of clay. His people lived, for the most part, in huts made of branches stuck in the ground and bending inwards, with wattle interwoven and built round with sods. Of these folk, their appearance, possessions, beliefs, and manner of living before Plantation times, there is an interesting account in Eachard's *Exact Description of Ireland* (1691). He says of the " natural Wild Irish "—

" they are of a middle Stature, strong of body, of an hotter and moister nature than many other nations, of wonderful soft skins, and by reason of the tenderness of their Muscles, they excell in nimbleness and flexibility of all parts of the body ; they are reckoned of a quick Wit, (though besotted to many follies) prodigal and careless of their lives, enduring Travel, Cold and Hunger ; given to fleshly lusts, light of belief, kind and courteous to strangers, constant in Love, impatient of abuse, and injury, in enmity implacable, and in all affections most vehement and passionate. They are very much delighted with Musick, but especially with the harp and Bagpipe; at the first many of them are very Skilful.

" As for their Diet, they feed very much upon Herbs especially water-cresses ; upon Mushrooms, Shamroots and Roots. They delight also in Butter tempered with Oatmeal ; also in Milk, Whey, Beef-Broth, and Flesh ofttimes without any Bread at all. As for their Corn, they lay it up for their horses, for whom they are very careful; when they are Hunger-bitten in time of dearth, they disdain not to eat raw flesh, after they have pressed out the blood thereof : and for to concoct it they will drink down very large quantities of Usquebah or Aqua-Vitae, draught after draught. They also let their Kine blood, which when is grown to a Jelly, and strewed over with Butter, they eat with a very good Appetite.

" As for their Attire, they commonly wear little Jackets of Woollen, and those very short ; Breeches most plain and close to their Thighs ; over these they commonly wear a Mantle of Shag Rugg deeply fringed, and well set out with many colours, within which they often lap themselves, and sleep on the very ground. They go for the most part bare headed, unless it be when they put on an headpiece. They wear their Hair long, and count it the greatest ornament. The Women also make a great esteem of their Hair, especially if it be golden colour and long withal, for they lay it out in a full length plated in a bravery : they rather load than adorn their heads with great quantities of fine linnen, rolled up in Wreaths.

" Their way of Living is after a very odd sort, having no great imployments ; for they are given to idleness above measure, and count it the greatest riches to take no pains, and the most pleasure to enjoy their Liberty. Their Cows and Cattle are the chiefest Wealth they have, and in greatest esteem. They count it no shame or infamy to commit Robberies, which they very frequently use with great cruelty ; when they go to rob they make prayers to God that they may meet with a booty ; and they suppose it was sent them from God as a Gift. They also suppose that Violence and Murder are no ways of displeasing to God, for if it were a sin, he would not present them with that opportunity ; and they count it a sin not to make use of a fair opportunity ; further they say that this sort of Life was left to them, and that they only walk in their Fathers steps, that it would be a disgrace to their Nobility to forbear such Facts and get their living by Labour.

" When they go out in a Morning to do any business, they mark him they met first ; if they be prosperous they endeavour to meet him oft, if not they are as careful to avoid them. Before they Sow their Corn, the good Wife or Mistress of the house sendeth Salt to the said Field. In the Towns, when any Magistrate entreth first upon his Office, the Wives and Daughters along the Streets, and out of the Windows, bestrew them and their Followers with Wheat and Salt. At every third word it is ordinary with them to rap out an Oath, as by The Trinity, by Christ, by St. Patrick, by St. Brigid, by their Baptism, by their Godfathers hand and such like. When they take never so solemn Oaths they will be forsworn upon every occasion, but if they sware by any great Man and be forsworn, they forfeit a great Sum of Money or Cattle to that same person whose name they used.

" They are of Opinion, that if their Butter be Stolen, 'twill soon after be restored again if they take away any of the

Thatch that hang over the Door, and cast it into the Fire.
They believe, that the Kite will not take away their Chickens,
if they hang up the Egg-shels out of which they were Hatched
in some place of the Rough of the House. If any praise an
Horse, or any other of their Beasts, before they have said, God
Save him, or have Spit upon them ; if any harm befal that
Beast within three days after, they seek out him that praised
him, and then mumble the Lords Prayer in his right Ear. They
fully believe, that to set a green Bough of a Tree before their
House on May-day, will cause them to have abundance of Milk
all Summer long. They have besides these, many other Follies,
which for shortness sake, I shall now forbear to mention.

" When they first see the Moon after the Change, commonly
they bow the Knee, and say the Lords Prayer, and then speak
to the Moon with a loud Voice, Leave us as whole and as sound
as thou hast found us. They use to look through the Shoulder-
Blade-Bone of a Sheep, when the Flesh is clean taken from it ;
if they see any dark or duskish spot in it, when they look through,
they say that some Course shall shortly be carried out of the
House. They pray for Wolves, and wish them well, and then
they are not afraid to be hurt by them. They count it unlawful
to rub down, or curry their Horses, or to gather Grass for their
Meat on Saturdays. When an Horse is dead, they hang up his
feet and legs in the House ; yea, the very hoofs are esteemed
as a hallowed and sacred Relick. They count her a wicked
Woman or a Witch that cometh to fetch Fire from 'em on
May-Day ; neither will they give any Fire then, but unto a Sick
Body, and that also with a Curse.

" When anyone lies a Dying, Women hired on purpose stand
in Crossways, calling upon him with great Out-Crys, and abundance of rediculous Expostulations, why he should depart from
so many Advantages. After he is Dead, they keep a Mourning
with lowd Howlings and clapping of Hands together. When
the Corps go forth they follow it with such a Peal of Out-Crys,
that a Man would think the quick, as well as the Dead, were
past all Recovery. Neither do they Mourn less for those that
are slain in Battel, or by Robbing, though they affirm such to
have an easier Death, yet they will rail on their Enemies with
Spiteful Words, and continue for a long time a deadly Hatred
against all of that Kindred. They suppose that the Souls of
the Deceased go into the company of certain Men, famous in

those Places, of whom they still retain strange Fables and Songs, as of Giants of great Renown, which they say they ofttimes see by Illusion.

"Their Warefare consists of Horsemen, of Soldiers set in the Rere-guard, whom they call Galloglasses, who fight with sharp Hatchets ; and of light-armed Footmen called Kernes. whose service is with Darts and Skeanes. To give a shout to every Man going out of a Gate, is counted fortunate. They commonly use the Bagpipe instead of a Trumpet : they carry about them Amulets ; they recite certain Prayers and in joyning Battel, they cry as loud as they can, Pharroh, with this perswasion, that he who cryeth not so loud as the rest, shall suddenly be taken from the Ground, and carried along the Air, into certain desart Valleys, where he eateth Grass, lappeth Water, hath some use of Reason, but not of Speech : But at last by the help of Hounds and Hunters shall be brought home again.

"In matters of Religion they are Roman Catholicks, in some things very devout, mortifying and keeping under their Bodies, very much, watching and praying, fasting every Wednesday and Saturday ; some of 'em fast on St. Catharine's Day and also on Christmas Day, though they be never so sick. In matters of Divine Service they are very slovenly, the vestments are so foul and nasty, that they would make one cast up his Stomach : The Altar portable. and by some abuse or other polluted ; the Mass-Book all torn, the Chalice of Lead without a Cover to it, and the small Vessels for Wine made of Horn. The Priests themselves are very poor, and mind nothing but gathering of Goods. They make a great shew of the Canon-Law but have never a jot of Learning."

Of the land he says—

"It produces a vast number of goodly Flocks of Sheep, which they share twice a year. Here are likewise exceilent good Horses, (which we call Hobies) which have not the same pace with others, but a soft and round Amble, setting one Leg before another very finely. As for Cattle, here are infinite numbers, being indeed the principal Wealth of the Inhabitants : (it is said, they will give no Milk if their Calves be not by them, or their Skins stuffed with Straw or Hay ; For Bees, they have such numbers, that they are found not only in Hives, but also in the Bodies of Trees, and holes of the Earth. It

is very much troubled with Wolves, but has no Snake or vene-
mous Creature whatsoever, neither will any live here. It has
variety of all sorts of wild and tame Fowls ; and vast quantities
of Fish, especially Salmon and Herrings. All living Creatures,
besides Men, Women and Greyhounds, are smaller than ours
in England.

" The principal Riches and Commodities of this Kingdom
are Cattel, Hides, Tallow, Suet, great Store of Butter and Cheese,
Wood, Salt, Honey, Wax, Furs, Hemp, Linnen Cloth, Pipe
Staves, great quantities of Wool, of which they make Cloth and
Freezes, with those course Rugs, or shag Mantles, which are
vented into Foreign Countries ; Variety of Fish and Fowl and
also several Metals, as Lead, Tin and Iron ; in a word there is
nothing wanting either for Pleasure and Profit, every thing
being extraordinary cheap and plentiful ; and of late times
the Industry of the Inhabitants has not been so much wanting,
and by reason of the great Converse with the English, are more
Civilized then formerly ; both Trade and Learning flourishing
in such a measure, that were it not for these unhappy Broils,
it might well have been counted as Beautiful and Sweet a
Country as any under Heaven."

Given large tracts of fertile land, well wooded and
watered, in possession of a primitive, semi-barbarous people
such as Eachard describes, in close proximity to a much more
civilised race hungering for land, a change of occupancy is
inevitable. The situation in Down at the close of Elizabeth's
reign may be considered as not unlike that of an Indian
reservation in the United States of America when the wave
of industrial population has touched its boundaries. From
1570 until the Scots' Settlement, hungry eyes were turned
to Down. Elizabeth might recognise an Irish chief's rights
to territory and even give him a title, but that did not prevent
her granting the same lands to a favourite. Brian McFelim
O'Neill, Chief of Southern Claneboye, possessor of 30,000
beeves and of other herds innumerable, was recognised by
the English and knighted in 1567. Yet, in 1571, the Queen
granted to her secretary, Sir Thomas Smith, and to his son,
with other lands, the whole of Sir Brian's territory. The

grant conveyed not merely lands, tenements, forests, quarries, manors, lordships, rents, services, advowsons of churches, tithes, etc., etc., but " natives, male and female." According to the writer of the *Life of Sir Thomas Smith, Knight*, published in London in 1698, the " good design " of the projected Colony in Down was that the half-barbarous people there " might be taught some civility." In the vulgar modern tongue of the territory granted, to " larn people to be civil "

EAST DOWN in 1572. From a map supposed to have been engraved for Sir Thomas Smith.

is to punish them very severely for their impudence ; and although the sense of the seventeenth-century phrase is, of course, to teach civilisation, the seventeenth-century operation had on its objects the effect expressed by the modern vulgar phrase. It meant for them the removal of their chief's authority, the ousting of them from their lands, and, generally, changes in the conditions of existence to which the natives could not adapt themselves.

The enraged Sir Brian, after ineffective protest to the Queen and her advisers, took the field and wasted the territory to prevent the English from finding shelter or sustenance. Smith the younger held out for a year, when he was shot by a wild Irishman, and all the fine regulations for the ordering of his Colony in the Ards became inoperative. Strange to say, a new grant from the Queen conveyed to her favourite, the Earl of Essex, part of the lands just granted to the Smiths. Sir Thomas consented to an arrangement by which he abandoned a part of his lands, and endeavoured for a short time to maintain his hold on the remainder of the territory, but was unable to fulfil the conditions of the grant, and after his failure and that of Essex to settle the country, the old Claneboye territory in North Down fell again into native Irish hands and old tribal ways. In 1586 the Chief, Sir Con McNeill Oge, made formal surrender of his lands to Queen Elizabeth, and next year, as a submissive and loyal subject, received them back under Letters Patent. His Tanist and successor was the Con O'Neill of ignoble memory from whose grasp the main portion of the territory passed to the Scots, never again to know the easy rule and ancient customs of the " Wild Irish."

The effects of the troubles of the last quarter of the sixteenth century were, in North Down, disastrous to people and to land. Sir Brian in revolt burned every remaining building of monasteries or churches.

" Scarce and starving—a country without happiness and without religion," was the comment of a traveller in the Ards in Queen Elizabeth's time ; and when the first of Montgomery's Scotsmen came, says the writer of the Montgomery MSS.,

> " In three parishes could not be found thirty cabins nor any stone walls but ruined roofless churches and a few vaults at Gray Abbey, and a stump of an Old Castle in Newton in each of which some gentlemen sheltered themselves at their first coming over."

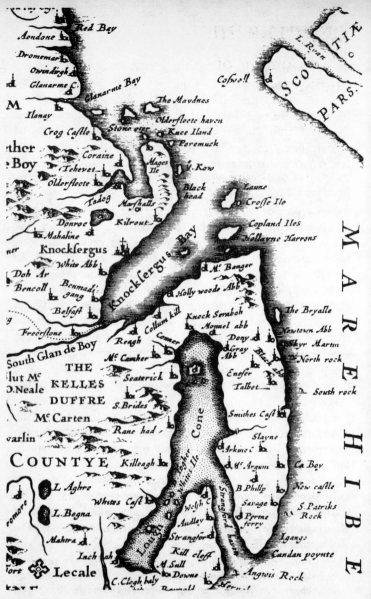

From a 17th Century MAP OF IRELAND, printed at Amsterdam.
Original at Orangefield, Belfast.

CHAPTER III.

The Coming of the Scots

In his grey castle on the low range of hills overlooking Belfast on the southern side, the last Lord of Southern Claneboye, a degenerate son of the O'Neills—" a drunken, sluggish man " the writer of the Montgomery MSS. calls him,—and pensioner of the English Crown, saw the old order change, and the stern-faced, hard-working Presbyterian Scot, over the greater part of his territory, take the place of the " vehement, passionate, prodigal, careless Irish " of Eachard's description.

The occasion of the momentous change which was to have such far-reaching effects was absurdly trivial. A change of occupancy was, perhaps, inevitable and desirable, but one could wish that the manner of effecting it had been different. According to the writer of the Montgomery MSS., Con O'Neill, a few months before the death of Queen Elizabeth, being then with his brothers, friends, and followers at Castle-reagh, " in great debauch " sent some of his servants into Belfast with small casks, for wine. They, returning drunk, encountered some soldiers who treated them badly and took the wine from them. In a scuffle which followed, one of the soldiers received a wound from which he died in the night following.

This trumpery affair was magnified by the powers into "levying war against the Queen," and Con was promptly clapped into prison at Carrickfergus. The stringency of his captivity appears to have been relaxed after the accession of James I., for the prisoner was allowed to walk the streets in the day-time, and even to entertain his friends in victualling houses ; only a single sentinel having him in custody. Now appears on the scene one of the winning Scots,—evidently on the watch for opportunity to get a transfer of Irish-held lands in return for services, real or imaginary, rendered to his King and countryman. All that happened is evidence that Montgomery and Hamilton, sharers in the Claneboye lands, and perhaps other waiting and watching Scots, knew that transactions affecting lands held by improvident Irish were imminent, and were on the alert to profit thereby. The fine situation of North Down and its proximity to Scotland must have made the territory of Con O'Neill an object of special attention.

According to the story, Hugh Montgomery, Laird of Braidstane, and in favour with King James, employed a Thomas Montgomery, the owner of a vessel trading to Carrickfergus, to kidnap and carry off Con O'Neill. This Thomas, to execute the plan, made love to the daughter of the Town Marshal, and gained her consent to marriage with him. Using the opportunity gained by his favour with the girl and her parents, he captured the willing Con, took him over to Scotland, and thence to London,—Hugh Montgomery undertaking to get for his prisoner a free pardon from King James, on condition of the transference to the Scotchman of half of the great territory of South Claneboye. Hugh Montgomery had powerful friends at court,—George, his brother, was Dean of Norwich, and had been the medium of communication from the watchful Hugh to the King, of information about the state of affairs in the North of Ireland.

The Earl of Eglinton, in great favour with the King, himself
a Montgomery, was ready to act in his kinsman's interest.
It is not surprising, therefore, that success attended the
enterprise, and that King James, for no serious consideration,
light-heartedly made over the vast area of South Claneboye
to Montgomery, who was bound to re-convey to the pardoned
O'Neill one half of his ancient lands.

But another waiting and watching Scot had eyes on
North Down. James Hamilton, eldest son of the Minister
of Dunlop, Ayrshire, with a comrade, James Fullerton, had
started a school for teaching Latin in Dublin in 1587. They
became Fellows of Trinity on the establishment of that College
five years later. Whether they went to Dublin, definitely
with intention to serve the interest of James VI. of Scotland,
or whether, being there, they saw prospect of greater profit
in the King's service than in teaching, and so became political
agents, is a debated point. What is certain is that they
did become such agents. Letters in the State Paper Office,
partly in cipher, show them as active Scottish agents, with
no lack of enemies, engaged in the political intrigues of Queen
Elizabeth's last days. In the secret communications of the
time, Hamilton is represented by the sign

and Fullerton by " No. 88." A letter of George Nicholson
to Sir Robert Cecil, the Queen's Principal Secretary of State,
dated from Edinburgh, 7th February, 1600, contains the
following notes (cipher translated) :—

> " Mr James Hamilton is in great hatred, some say for Your
> Honor. Mr James Fullerton is presently out of taste. yet not
> charged with offence, as they do and intend to do Mr James
> Hamilton. Sir Thomas Erskine hath wrought this . . . .
> I grieve to see Erskine work Hamilton disgrace by charging
> him with overmuch familiarity with Your Honor and with
> £100 per annum, etc."

With James on the throne of England there was no longer need for Hamilton and Fullerton to stay at Dublin. The year 1603 finds them at London, honoured by knighthood, and, doubtless, seeking substantial reward for services rendered. Fullerton " had the King's ear," and easily persuaded His Majesty that the grant made to Montgomery was far too large for one person, and suggested that Hamilton should receive part. James promptly replaced the agreement with Montgomery by one entirely in the name of Sir James Hamilton, who was bound to convey one-third of the lands to Montgomery and one-third to Con O'Neill, retaining a third for himself. Montgomery, naturally, was displeased and angry, but as the gift was still magnificent, he wisely refrained from serious protest, and the tripartite division of the Claneboye territory was completed.

It is no part of the design of this book to follow closely the fortunes of the adventurers and their families, nor to deal with the effect of the transaction on the unfortunate O'Neill, and therefore a very short statement of successions in ownership is here needed.

The weak and improvident Chief of South Claneboye soon disappears from the scene. He appears to have parted, on unfavourable terms, with portion after portion of his lands to Hamilton, Montgomery, Sir Moyses Hill, ancestor of the Downshire family, and others, and to have died in poverty. Montgomery prevailed on him to execute a deed binding him not to alienate his lands without the knowledge of the Scotsman, a covenant not observed by the Irishman, for, in 1616, he conveyed to Hamilton and Hill his ancestral property at Castlereagh and a large part—perhaps the last part remaining to him—of his lands. Con's son, Daniel, a minor at the time of these transactions, became Protestant, entered the English Army, and came to be in favour at the Courts of Charles I. and Charles II. Many years after his father's death he petitioned the Lords of the High Court of Parliament to set aside grants by which had been

Signature from a document
in Trinity College, Dublin.

"I knew that thou wert an hard man" might have been
said with truth by contemporaries who had dealings with
JAMES HAMILTON, first Grantee of Down Plantation lands.
Knighted on the accession of James I.; created Viscount
Claneboye in 1622; died 1643-4.   Portrait at Castle Ward.

"Managed according to his genius, and not much thwarted or overdriven" (*Hamilton MSS.*). JAMES, SECOND VISCOUNT CLANEBOYE, FIRST EARL OF CLANBRASSIL. Lost in struggle with the Parliamentary Army much of the vast property bequeathed to him. "Became corpulent, scorbutic, hydropsic, and . . . . . died in June 1659." Portrait at Castle Ward.

alienated from his family the " lands, mannors, tenements
and heredetaments in the Upper Claneboys and the Great
Ardes." He charges Hamilton and Montgomery with having
worked

> " on the weakness and inexperience of the said Conn in the lawes
> of the Kingdom, (and) made him beleeve that he had committed
> some capital offence against the Crowne."

Montgomery is charged with having taken from Con eight
townlands " to the value of £15,000 . . . for and upon
the only consideracion of £317," and Hamilton and Sir Moyses
Hill are said, " by many undue practices, insinuacions and
circumvencions," to have procured from the petitioner's
father, 66,000 acres, " upon the onlie consideracion of £60
fine then paid, and the yearly rent of £160 Sterling." The
petition was unsuccessful,—the O'Neill territory in Down
had passed for ever from O'Neills. Daniel, " in understanding
much superior to the whole nation of the old Irish" (*Clarendon*),
married the Countess of Chesterfield and died without issue.
Of him Charles II., writing to the Duchess of Orleans on 24th
October, 1669, says :—

> " Poore O'Neale died this afternoon of an ulcer in his gutts ; he
> was as honest a man as ever lived : I am sure I have lost a
> very good servant."

Hamilton—knighted on the accession of King James, and
created Viscount Claneboye in 1622—died, aged 84, in 1643-4.
Within thirty-five years after his death, his vast estates had
passed out of direct succession, and about the year 1679,
after long litigation, came to be unequally divided among
the representatives of the adventurer's brothers.

It was the fate of the Montgomery estates to pass, also,
somewhat quickly from the holding of representatives in
direct succession. Hugh Montgomery, later Sir Hugh, was
created Viscount Montgomery of the Ards. His grandson
was created Earl of Mount-Alexander in 1661, and in the
circumstances described in Chapter V., his son, the second

Earl, in 1675, sold a large part of the estates to the Colvil family. This part was afterwards re-sold by them to Alexander Stewart, ancestor of Lord Londonderry, the present proprietor. Such small remainder of the original possessions as remained with the Mount-Alexander family fell into the hands of the childless widow of the last Earl of the name, in 1757, and were by her bequeathed to her nephews, Samuel De la Cherois and Nicholas Crommelin, who, by descendants, are still represented on the Plantation lands of the Montgomerys.

Of the two men thus rewarded by the lordship of princely territories for political service, Hamilton was certainly the more polished. A teacher of Latin, a Fellow of Trinity, he had a mind enlarged by study of the Classics. One who met him frequently in England on visits made necessary by quarrels with his neighbouring planter, Sir Hugh, says that he

" observed him a wise and discreet man and much better tempered
than the other."

The family chronicler speaks of him as " one of the greatest scholars and most hopeful wits of his time," and, later, summing his labours and characteristics, says :—

" As he was very learned, wise, laborious, noble, (especially to
strangers and scholars), so there is great ground to judge he
was truly pious, as he was certainly well-principled."

He was certainly astute, for we know, from the writer just quoted, that he made great use of the services of his brothers and his nephews, " as also of some other very fine gentlemen," and obliged them to dependence on him all his life, by reserving the bulk of their rewards for disposition by his Will. As this Will was never signed, the reward of the presumptive legatees " proved," as the family historian states, " too late for them." The Viscount and his friends must indeed have been " laborious," for the maps of the great property drawn by Raven for the noble Lord within twenty years of the time of the Wild Irish, indicate a well-ordered and well-planted estate.

Montgomery had been a soldier in Holland under the Prince of Orange. The ruse of making love to a custodian's daughter practised by his envoy in the matter of the taking of Con O'Neill, was one Montgomery had made use of, on occasion, in Holland. He had the soldier's temper, and showed it in his dealings with his fellow-planter in the matter of boundaries. His letters and actions indicate that the Scotch adjective " canny," used to characterise his sayings and doings, is not misplaced. The writer of the Montgomery Manuscripts, anxious to glorify the record of the founder of his house, has to mention that his Lordship furnished the six churches he had built, or repaired, with large Bibles and with Common Prayer Books—

> " both sorts being in folio, and fair Dutch print, and all having
> his Lordship's Coat of Arms as Laird of Braidstane stamped
> on the covers with leaf gold."

—not a notable giving from a man who had gained the lands of a principality for small political services.

That the two men foresaw the possibility of attaining wealth and honour through the acquisition of Irish forfeited lands, and watched and waited and worked for such acquisition, is not a matter of surmise. That they looked for their fortune in Ireland is stated by one of the family. And Montgomery of the Manuscripts, who said of himself, " I never courted any advancemt . . . els I might have been a Knt and a Barrt too," makes it clear that the titles bestowed on the adventurers had been angled for:

> " But to speak freely of both Braidstane (Montgomery) and Mr.
> James Hamilton, I believe neither of them had been Lords
> if they had not sought to be so."

In the Denmylne collection in the Advocates' Library at Edinburgh, are letters dated 6th December, 1614, from the Earl of Abercorn to his friends at Court—Fullerton and

Murray—reminding them that "his Ma/ did diverse tymes
promeis . . . to creat for me these two barronnis in
Ireland." Both letters contain the names of Hamilton and
Montgomery. That to Murray is only a covering letter:

> "This few lynis ar onlye to accompany Sir Hew Montgomerye
> and Sir James Hamilton's lettiris desyreing yor freyndlye ayde
> and assistance wt his Ma/ in their favouris."

No doubt the adventurers became wealthy,—whether
happiness came with riches and honours is questionable.
The favour of princes is difficult to hold, and James I., who
gave, easily and ignorantly, large rewards to favourites, was
very ready to reduce his bounty if pains were taken to make
him understand the real magnitude of his gifts. The family
chronicler represents Hamilton as "once at the point of ruin
as to the King's esteem," and in Wentworth's time "he had
much ado to keep himself from ruin." The circumstances
of the time, when large imperfectly-surveyed tracts of forfeited lands were granted by the Crown, bred a race of
examiners of titles, or 'Discoverers' as they were called.
These made it their business to search for technical flaws
in the titles of the grantees, and such were sufficiently
numerous to make 'discovering' a very good trade. These
men were rewarded for a find by a grant of land or money at
the expense of the person whose title was adjudged defective.
The Crown countenanced the somewhat disreputable proceedings of these gentry, as they often made it possible to
force the possessors of lands to accept new grants at advanced
rents. There is plenty of evidence that Montgomery and
Hamilton suffered from the attentions of the 'discoverers.'
In a letter dated 6th December, 1614, the Earl of Abercorn
begs his "loweing cusigne," Sir James Fullerton, to insist
with His Majesty that Sir James Hamilton and Sir Hugh
Montgomery be not farther questioned for the Black Abbey,
to which they have so just a title. Montgomery, who wrote
in pure Scots, and filled his letters to friends at Court with

phrases expressive of devotion to His Majesty's interests,
and descriptive of his own hard case, appears to be dealing
with one of these title difficulties in a letter dated 25th
January,—the year not stated, but certainly more than ten
years after the first grants,—and addressed " To his honn^{ble}
and his approvid good friend Mr Ione Murray gentilman of
his Mat^{es} prevei purce of bedchalmer." He says :—

> " Now Sir for the second part of his Ma^{tes} propositioune conserning the passing of my estat to me *it being now funde woyd* " (void).

Montgomery is apparently at London at the time, for he
groans over the expense of his journey. He might, he says,

> " 'hef stayit at hom' and had the matter rectified at an expense
> of ' a fifte or a threiskor of punds ' . . quhar as now 1400 lb
> (£) will not karie me hom agen to my greit ouirthraw."

He explains that he has planted the lands with under-tenants,
and is " bound to mak all thaer estats good." He deplores
the mistrust of him, and, he continues,

> " Wth all reverence I spik it will be thocht an evill rewarde for
> my serveic and especially quhar as I am com heir to attend and
> consume my self onle to his Mat^e servic, . . quha hes
> bein evir funde willing and fathfull to serf his Mat^e and that
> to the uttirmost that my persoune, puer or credit could strich."

He points out that the failure to confirm him in his position
will be to the damage of the King's interests,

> " and the hinder of his Mat^{es} most necissarie serveic intendit
> by me if that his Mat^e out of his Mat^{es} most princely and
> accustomat bontefull considerahoune help me not : that to
> this hour notwithstanding of my grivous burdeings hes nathir
> soocht help nor put his Mat^e to a penny chargis."

The wordy letter winds up with a plea for despatch in dealing
with his petition, and gives as reason for writing, when he
had conversed with his friend only the day before,

> " I thocht good to wrayt unto rathir nor to fach you wth long and
> oftin trubilsom spichis,"

and he subscribes as " Yours evir or his awin nevir."

Hamilton had also to defend two important suits instituted
by the Crown,—one charging him with " having usurped all
the liberties and franchises granted to him by his several
patents, etc." In this case he had judgment against the
Crown. In the second he appears also to have been successful, except in the matter of the Admiralty's claim of rights
at Groomsport.

In addition to the troubles arising out of difficulties
with the Crown, the settlers suffered much loss of money
and peace of mind because of their mutual enmity. Montgomery never forgave Hamilton for his interference with
the former's agreement with O'Neill, and his cancellation
of the King's first grant, and the lives of the two were
embittered by quarrels about boundaries, which quarrels
were not settled by ensuing " tedious and chargeable lawsuits," for in 1614, as a result of arbitration, Montgomery
gained from his neighbour extensive additions to his estates,
especially of Abbey lands, but not enough to content him.
Both adventurers suffered much through proceedings at law,—
Hamilton had a lawsuit, said to have been " in some respects
worse than all," with the widow of his brother William, and
both estates were threatened by an action taken by the
descendants of Sir Thomas Smith, and by that instituted
by Daniel O'Neill.

While the Crown rents payable by the planters were
very small, allowance must be made for necessarily heavy
disbursements of the early years of the Plantation. In all
probability the removal expenses of the Scots and English
brought over, were borne entirely by the undertakers. And
there is evidence in letters of the Earl of Abercorn in the
Denmylne Collection, that the King, on occasion, expected
and called for special contributions from his planters in
Ireland. The Earl, himself a planter at Strabane, addressed
to Mr. Ione Murray, " of his sacred Ma/ bed-Chalmer," a letter
dated Bangor, 3rd of October, 1614, which letter is interesting
and for various reasons should be quoted in full.

" Maist loving cousing having spent thir thre wekis passit in
trying and clering all maters questionabill betwixt my cousing
Sir James Hamilton & Sir Hew Montgomere als weill in the
marchis of thair landis as vtherwayis quhairin I thank God
I have maid ane guid progres as I hope to bring it to ane happe
end for thame boithe and to many gentilmen of gud faschion
duelling vnder thame in this Kyngdome quhair thai have above
2000 habill Scottis men weill armit heir rady for his Ma/ service
as thai sall be comandit thir many I will certefe zou I had at
on dayis hunting with myself sence my heir cuming quhilk I
most confes did incourage me the les to spare my travellis to
put thame and hald thame in concorde vtherwayis foirseing
ruyne to thameseltis by discord not without greit hinderans to
his Ma/ service and I beleve his Ma/ being trewle informit of
my procedingis sall think I do him no lytill service heirin for
beleve me thir gentilmen leving in concord as I trust now thai
sall, being favored and allowit by his Ma/ in gud and civill
coursis altho thai be mene gentilmen his Ma/ may assuredle
expect grait service of thame in this Kyngdome and besydis
thame be assurit thair ar no corner in the northe quhairin thair
is not gud numbers of our nation & quhat I have at Straban I
will not tak notice myself leving it to vtheris.   Thair is cravit
throch this Kyngdome by derection frome the Lord Depute &
Counsall alsweill frome the vndertakers as vthers ane voluntar
supple & fre gift as thai call it to his Ma/ quhairin it feiris me
thai do muche wronge his Ma/ I resavit ane letter frome Sir
Tobe Oafeild for this effect to quhom I have answarit that geve
I souild have occasionn to be at any publik meting for that
bissines I waild maist willingle explaine my affection to my
gratious Maisters service having nothing bot that quhilk I
acknawlage to be his and frome him.   And to the berar of his
letter & my answer quhilk was Mr Hare Acheson I said vnto
him geve his Ma/ souild have occasioun to crave anything of
me in that faschion in this Kyngdome I couild never mak offer
of les then one zeirs rent at leist this I gave out of purpois to
make vthers the moir fre & that vthers souild not take advantage
of me & honest men of our nation in this Kyngdome & certefe
his Ma/ as I have said I have nothing in this woirld quhilk I
will not be rady to lay doun at his sacred feit & myself with
all to be deposit vpon at his Royall plesour. & quhat I say for
my self I do in lyk sort for all thois quhome of I sall have power

& credit and spetialle I gave this assurance for Sir James and
Sir Hew heir present with me. Quhairfoir geve it pleis his
Ma/ quho out of his grait wisdome considers the hardnes of our
beginnings in this Kyngdome to desyre quhat is ours we desyre
to vnderstand his sacred Ma/ gratious plesour & notwithstanding
of our poverte his Ma/ sall have profe of our love & radines &
that we sall as we ar bund of all dewte prefer his strait to our
awin meseries. Sir Hew Montgomere is in building ane fyn
housse at the Newton quhair of ane quarter is almost compleit
& Sir James Hamilton hes buildit at Killilenche ane vere stronge
Castell the lyk is not in the Northe. After I have put an end
to thair questionis & clerit thair quhole marchis I purpois to
go to Straban quhilk I think sall be about the 6 of this instant.
It is thocht the parliament sall go fordwart heir the 11 of this
instant befoir quhilk tyme I purpois to have my brother Sir
Claud at Dublin quha now is at Straban taking ordour for his
buildingis I hope ze will acquent his sacred Ma/ with my desyre
to know his plesour & in all diligence lat me be certefeit thairof.
quhilk I will expect in this Kyngdome befoir the 24 of this instant
this I trust ze will tak in gud pairt as no service I sall be habill
to do zow can be trubelsum to me I wisse ze souild wrete to my
lord Secretar of Scotlland to derect zour answar in all diligence
to my bedfallow at Paslay quha thairefter in all haist will not
faill to derect the same to me.

"Thus my most loving dewte remeberit to zour self & zour
most woirthe lady I rest

Zour most loving
cousing

Bangor the
3 of October 1614

It may pleis zou to present my most humble service to his
sacred Ma/

To my most loving cousing Mr Ione Murray on of his sacred
Ma/ bed-Chalmer

At court with spede and in his absence to his Lady & Sir James
Fullerton."

This communication, which, at first glance, seems to be made in simple, unconsidered language, is really a very artful statement. The King wanted money for Irish purposes,—what more natural than that he should ask from the adventurers so richly benefited by the Royal bounty? It is clear from the letter that these feared a very large assessment. The Earl, under guise of simple narration, dwells on his endeavours to compose the differences of Hamilton and Montgomery in the King's interest. He informs the Royal personage for whose eyes or ears the flattering sentences are penned, that the undertakers in Down had provided over 2,000 able Scots, armed and ready for the King's service,—that they are engaged in costly building enterprises, necessary for the defence of His Majesty's newly-planted lands, or for the honour and comfort of his servants who were spending themselves and their fortunes in turning the lands of roaming Wild Irish into civilised territory. In dealing with the call for money, the writer is careful to designate what is to be given " a voluntar, supple and fre gift," and he and his friends hope, by an assumption that one year's income would be considered extraordinarily generous and far beyond what the King might expect, to limit their contributions to that extent. The letter was probably successful in its object. James had surely not the heart to tell his undertakers, who were wearing themselves out in his service, that the (in their estimation) rich gifts, which with such flattering words they were " rady to lay down at his sacred feit," were inadequate, and would have to be increased.

With enemies, secret, cunning, and envious, at Court, open and violent in Ireland, the situation of the Down planters was beset with difficulties. But they endured and succeeded, for the descendants of the men they planted on the wasted lands yet till the farms of the rolling hills, and still over a great part of their settled territory the tongue of the people is the tongue of the lowland Scot.

CHAPTER IV.

The Scots at Work

As we look at the rude carving and quaint spelling on the tombs of the early Scots in the old churches and church-yards of Down, we take, unconsciously, an impression of primitive and quiet life, and straightway proceed to transfer the impression to the minds of our ancestors themselves. Counting them happy in their freedom from the stress and strain of modern life, we, thoughtlessly, attribute to them knowledge of their good fortune in this respect.

But far away from these were thoughts of primitives and peace. Their traditional time of the quiet life lay back in the pre-Columbus years. For them the world was no more the disc of the Hereford priest, Jerusalem its centre,— the world had suddenly grown larger. The men who came with Hamilton and Montgomery had lived through Elizabeth's reign,—even the illiterate of them had heard of the travels of Raleigh, and the deeds of Hawkins and Drake and Dudley and Cumberland in the seas and lands of the golden West. Movement and change were everywhere, the crowns of England and Scotland had been joined, and great events

were happening in Ireland. There the Scots found within
a few hours from their shores an America of new land, where
for roaming Red Indian lurked the Wild Irish in woods and
morasses. ' Quaint,' ' quiet,' ' early,' ' primitive,'--the words
had no application to their time in the minds of the Down
Scots,--they saw themselves in the glow of a hot modernity.

The spring of 1606 witnessed the beginning of the Settlements, and the work proceeded apace. At enmity with each
other, the planters did not allow their quarrel to interfere
with their land surveying and allotment,--perhaps by reason
of it they worked with the greater strenuousness. Hamilton
established himself at Bangor, and took his younger brother
William into his service. Montgomery made his headquarters
at Newtownards, where he roughly repaired portions of an
old Castle to provide shelter for himself and friends. He
brought with him the Shaws, uncle and brother of his wife,
Patrick Montgomery, brother-in-law, and Hugh Montgomery,
a cadet of the planter's family. With him also, or following
quickly, came members of allied families, Boyd, Nevin, Moore,
Neil, Catherwood, and many others. To these were given
large tracts of land in freehold, and other holdings by lease,
laying the foundation for the status of minor gentry of the
county in the centuries to come. In turn the grantees let
their lands, sometimes in very small parcels of two, three,
or four acres at the rent of a boll of barley per acre. Hamilton
and Montgomery's undertenants and those of their friends
were certainly of better character and standing than the bulk
of small occupiers in later settled Ulster counties. Still it
was Stewart of Donaghadee who wrote of incoming settlers
from Scotland and England as

> " generally the scum of both nations, who, for debt, or breaking
> and fleeing from justice, or seeking shelter, came hither, hoping
> to be without fear of man's justice in a land where there was
> nothing, or but little, as yet, of the fear of God."

New settlements have more than their share of the
adventure-seeking violent and godless, and these and their

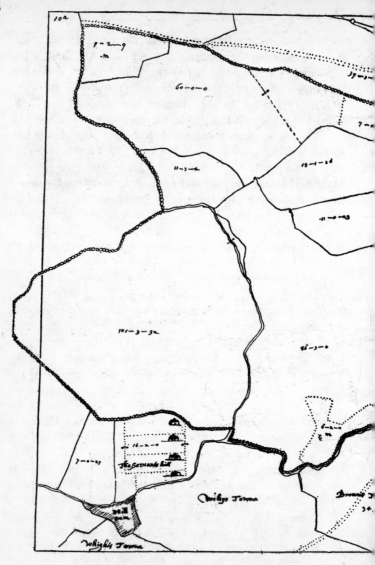

EARLY DAYS OF THE PLANTATION. BANGOR and neighbourh
(near ' The Crosshill ') mentioned in the Plantation Comm
Original at Bangor Castle.

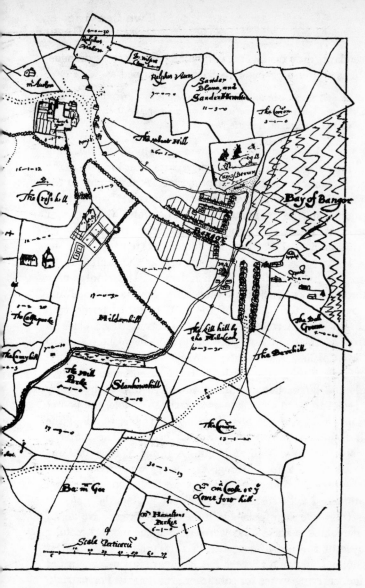

n 1625. The surveyor has sketched the "fayre stone house"
ers' Report as having been built by Hamilton (see p. 49).

descendants may trouble the community for years. Edmonds,
Customs waiter at Bangor in 1637, is described as

> " of evil fame, debauched and dangerous . . . having, it is
> known, offered violence to his own mother and drawn her blood
> to the danger of her life."

But from the beginning there were spare-living, God-fearing
folk, and the good harvests of a few years later brought many
of good character and men of property. A testimony to the
rapid improvement in manners and morals at Bangor is to
be found on the monument to gentle John Gibson, first
Protestant Dean of Down,—the reader is referred to its
inscription copied in the introductory statement. On the
poor lands some of the Irish remained as Canaanites to be
thorns in the side of the Scottish Israel. The Montgomery
historian speaks of them as Gibeonites, hewers of wood and
drawers of water. Some of the settlers made terms with
natives who preferred any service to leaving their place of
birth, but they did not learn to love their masters. Lord
Deputy Chichester, writing to Lord Salisbury on 3rd October,
1610, says " they (the Irish) hate the Scottyshe deadly."
While the larger holders under Hamilton and Montgomery
proceeded to build stone houses as fast as possible, the poorer
men in a wild and houseless land had, perforce, to adopt the
Irish fashion and construct wattled booths. The material
for construction was all at hand. A frame of trees or large
branches was set up,—through the beams was woven under-
wood,—outside, and against this were built sods,—the roof
was thatched with rushes. In such rude shelters did many of
the settlers live their first days in the new America. No doubt
the hardships of these days were endured the more cheerfully
because of the nearness of friends in Scotland. By 1607 it
was not uncommon for Scotch folk in days of favouring weather
to ride, carrying wares for sale from Stranraer to Portpatrick,
leave their horses there, cross the Channel, hire horses at
Donaghadee, ride to Newtownards, sell their produce, and,

reversing the journey, reach homes round Loch Ryan by bedtime.

In the towns of Bangor, Newtownards, and Donaghadee the houses were, from the first, of stone or clay. In Bangor, clay building, now a lost art, would seem to have prevailed if we are to take as true the statement in a letter written a century after the time of Hamilton. In 1740 a certain Michael Echlin, wishing to sell some houses, wrote to a likely purchaser telling him that " the houses are built with stone and ruff-casted, not built with Mudd like the rest of Bangor houses." These mud or clay houses, well roofed, roughcast on outer wall surfaces and lime-washed within, were warm and durable, and the beginning of the 20th century sees many still occupied.

It was a wild country in which the settlers raised their first shelters. In the great woods deer were numerous, the wild boar saw the century waning before it disappeared, and the author of the Montgomery MSS. mentions wolves in the list of animals hunted by the first Viscount Montgomery, who, soldier-like, " delighted little in soft recreations " and sought his pleasure in the field with horse and hawk and hound.

Their tenants fairly housed, the two men set themselves to build dwellings of comfort and dignity befitting the state of great landowners who were Knights, and hoped to become Lords. The Plantation Commissioners visiting Bangor in 1611 reported :—

> " Sir James Hamylton, Knight, hath buylded a fayre stone house at the towne of Bangor, in the Upper Clandeboye, within the Countie aforesaid, about 60 foote longe and 22 foote broade ; the towne consists of 80 newe houses, all inhabited with Scotyshmen and Englishmen. And hath brought out of England 20 artificers, who are makinge materialles of tymber, bricke, and stone, for another house there.
>
> " The sd. Sir James Hamylton is p.paring to buyld another house at Holly Woode, three mylles from Bangor, and two hundred thowsand of brickes with other materialles ready at the place, where there are some 20 houses inhabited with English and Scottes."

All whose tastes incline them to seek intimate knowledge
of the places or persons of a past, know how great is the
longing to exchange modern description for representation
of the studied in contemporary map or picture. The craving
can be gratified in respect of the first of our planters and
his territory. Hamilton lives in the portrait preserved at
Castle Ward, and, fortunately, the surveys of his vast estates
made by Raven in 1625, as the land became settled, have
survived the dangers of three hundred years, and from these—
some of which are here reproduced for the first time—we can
see what the eyes of the settlers saw in the streets of the
little old-new towns and land divisions of the first twenty
Plantation years. The map sections, of which there are
many, measure about 19 in. by 14½ in. and are coloured. They
indicate farming, land divisions with the name of the holders,
roads, houses, mills, mosses, woods,—if a solitary tree grows
near a boundary it is named ' Whitethorn,' ' Crabtre,' etc.
The title-page to the Bangor section (p. 51) gives the ' quarters '
about the house, " the Towne and Demesnes." The " newe
house of Bangor" of this document is the " fayre stone house—
about 60 foote longe and 22 foote broade " of the Plantation
Commissioners' report, and the surveyor's little sketch, reproduced in the reduced plan (pp. 46, 47), shows a plain
house of two storeys set in a garden ; a kiln and barn in
neighbouring field. This house was, later, altered to, or was
replaced by, what the late Marquis of Dufferin and Ava
called " a Horace Walpolian sort of house," which was demolished when the present Castle of Bangor was erected.
The " 80 newe houses " of the little town are shown,
the main street being the way over which, for a thousand
years before Hamilton's time, had passed the traffic from the
port to monastery and church. The drawings of the little
towns of Holywood (p. 52) and Groomsport (pp. 54, 55) are
here reproduced, each with its indication of the " cuney
burrow " or rabbit warren, which seems to have been in
each case an ordered and bounded area. It is interesting to

note that a may-pole is indicated on the old plan at the inter-
section of the main roads of Holywood, where, ever since,
a successor of that drawn by Raven has been maintained.

Great as was the grant to him by James I., it was not
great enough for the ambition of Hamilton, who proceeded

TITLE-PAGE of the Maps of Bangor Manor, made for
James, first Lord Claneboye, 1625.

Original at Bangor Castle.

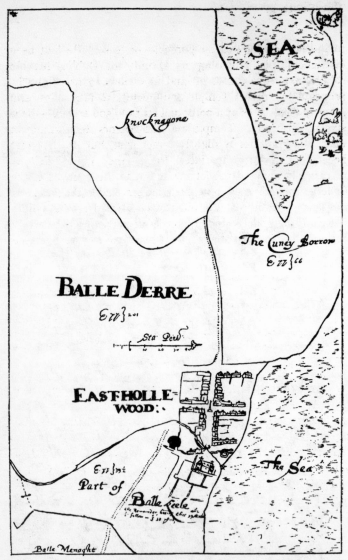

HOLYWOOD, Co. Down, from one of a series of maps made
in 1625 for James, first Lord Claneboye.

Original at Bangor Castle.

to increase his estates by purchase or lease. He had been instrumental in procuring for Trinity of Dublin, his old college, extensive grants of land in various counties, and he proposed to Provost Temple and Fellows to take a fee-farm grant of these lands at a perpetual rent of £500 a year,—about sixpence per acre. Temple and the Seniors were willing to make the grant for a slightly larger sum, but, to the great benefit of Trinity in later times, the Junior Fellows successfully opposed the letting as not in the interests of the College, the proposed rent being much under the value of the lands. Hamilton was much disappointed at this failure to secure the College lands in perpetuity. Somewhat naïvely he tells the Provost and Fellows that they were breaking faith with him, and that

> " if he were to inform his friends at Court of this treatment of
> him by the College, and through them, or from himself, the
> King should be informed that the reason which influenced the
> College in this matter is some dislike they have of the Scottish
> people, the College will hazard the loss of the King's favour,
> provoke the displeasure of the Scotch, and risk the discontinuance
> of their annual pension from the Crown."

An interesting letter, preserved at Trinity, and here printed, well exhibits Hamilton's grasping character. In it he claims credit for Herculean effort to enrich the hospital by gifts of escheated lands from the King. He paints in red the difficulties and dangers of undertaking, from all of which he will relieve the College authorities if only they will make over to him in perpetuity their lands at a profit rent of ninepence per acre. The artful letter is worth reading.

> " Sr. I have receaved your letter from mr Ware, your Colledge
> affaires I am myndfull of, wch for the Proceedings have receaved
> some alterations, But yit I hope we shall bring all to that issue
> that shall give you Contentment / whereof you shal be shortlie
> advertysed, when I can have obtayned a warrant wch I am about
> for you, & wch I will not speak nor wryt of, untill it be gott, &
> then it shall define it self unto you. In the mean tyme I am

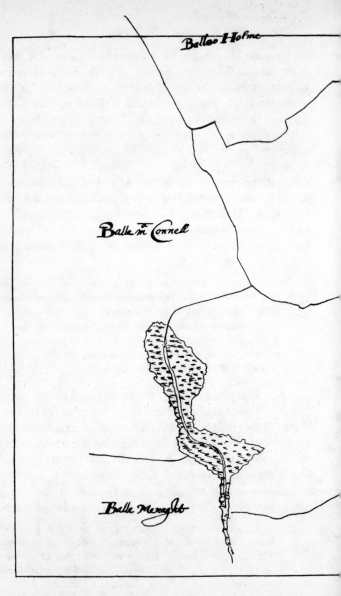

Balleo Holme

Balle m Connell

Balle Menaghb

Original at Bangor Castle.

ROOMSPORT and neighbourhood in 1625.

passing under the great seall of England so much land as is
allowed unto you out of these Escheted lands . The Particular
is now a drawing up for the same. You have wyn me in, into a
peece of service that is full of Danger & difficulties, for your
land is to be Planted under the same reservations & conditions
& bulding of the lyk castles & howses & planting of tenents in
the lyk forme as other the undertakers, and for Performance
of thit I am Pressed to give bonds, into wch if I shall enter, it
will amount to nere three thousand pounds that I must be bound
in, to performe such articles as I perfctlie see will not be performed wthin the tyme limited for the same, I will by the next
send you the Particulars of youre lands. The Abundance of
lands now lett at the kings rate of penny half penny an acre,
doth clogg us heavilie, together with the burthen of the said
Conditions, and every undertaker is a seeking tenents all that
he can, Because they would have help to perform their conditions
and agreements, every of them even he that is best monyed, The
lands in the north certanelie in tyme will doe well, but they
will drowne for the present the man that undertakes & is not
well furnished and stocked to performe what the land may
requyre, to advance the goodnes of it. your land is scattered
some in Armagh wch is the best, some in fermanagh some in
Tirconnell, The best must make good the worst. If you will
have me to undertake your land now gott, I will undertake it,
good, & bad, neir, and remote, and all at the Rate wch we then
agreed upon when you were here, wch was six fold the kyngs
rent over and above the kyngs Rent to hold it the same sort
& in fee farme from you as you do from the king, I will bear the
chardges of all your Patents & of all other things for the setling
of it for you, for wch purpose I will directlie build upon speciall
places of danger in every of the severall lands & so lett the lands
& the houses together. This will be very chardgeable unto me
at first But will well bring it self in afterwards, And myn owne
lands in the north upon the sea syd being much sought for, I
would lett more ther to men of wealth but to such as should
plant me one peece or other of yours, The King doth give five
yeares of freedome frome the Rent, if I do deall wth you, you
shall give but two to me, and yet I will give fower yeares freedome
to whome I shall build no houses & three & two at least to them
to whom I shall give houses, and all both freeholders and under-
tenents and all persones of yeres that shall resyd upon your land

shal be bond to take the oathes of Alleageance, supremacie, &
to Mantayne the Religion now by the lawes of this Realme
established. Consider of these things w^h your selves, and if I
can do you good, or if this be a good bargan for you, I will
performe it, whatsoever it cost me, Otherwys lett me tell you
(And kep it with your self (I pray you) untill it appear hereafter)
That my frends & I have as we think obtayned sixteen thousand
acres of land by esteem, in the Countie of Cavan w^h will cheiflie
rest upon me to see order taken for the Planting of, if you see
a better Bargan, I do wishe it with all my hart, & will do for
you whatsoever I can besyds, If you will have me that I do
undertake your lands I will bring & send over tenents and worke-
men frome hence & out of Scotland before I com from hence,
And when you have receaved the Particuler wch is now drawing
up, & wherwith also you shall receave Articles of Agremet betwen
us, if you lyk them, pfite them under your hands & Colledge
seall, that I may have a warrant to be for my dealings & to
shewe to such as I shall deall with all. Comend me kyndlie
to m^r Alvie & m^r Temple whose letter I hope shortlie to answer
with effect of doing somewhat But I dare not motion all that,
wch he desyreth for I am sure to be rejected, But I will go as
far as I can & the busines of the Colledge shall goe in front w'^h
myn owne, if m^r Temple will be advised by me he shall take
some of your lands in Armagh though but fyve hundreth acres,
and he shall nether be chardged with any of the Remote lands,
nor pay a dearer rent. You are much beholden to Sr James
fullerton who hath been very zealous of your good & is your
great sollicit^r in this business, And if your lands could be lett
as he doth wishe & my self, you should make a sound rate/
But now we are wooing of People to Com thether, who if they
have any Competent being here, are loath to remove from hence,
And if they be beggers & lean people without money, they ar
not fitt for us/ But indeed there is non that is more sought
unto by any, then my self for one of my place and I think I shall
plant the most of my lands w^h Englishe Tradismen/ This I
have written unto you that you might befour the Particuler
com, debate of it wi^h yor selves, and then more spedilie send
me an answer I could lett some of your lands, to some great
men here, and to some Captens there, But I had rather lett it
to such honest men of meaner Ranck, who if they do not pay me
their Rent shall, whether they will or not, pmit me to fetch

away their distresse, then to deall wth such Monsuers who being
our tenents we must petition onto, & entreat for our rent ffor
the Poor Colledge must know no thing but certaintie & freedom
from Truble, And albeit I know you ar much worn, yet take
Comfort, for by the grace of the Almighti God, we will have a
Continued certaintie for it within les than a year, that it shall
have good means to be still a Colledge wch the Lord make riche
in all good learning and pietie, And so Comending me to you
all & to mr Usher & mr Richardson.

I am ever to every of you

28 Mai   Yours assuredlie

1610   James hamiltone."

Although he failed to secure a fee-farm grant on his
own terms, he obtained, later, possession of a large portion
of the College lands on a lease for twenty-one years. Then,
finding that he had undertaken too much, or, despairing
of making a profit in such short time, he sublet the lands to
Sir James Carroll, a speculator who was unable to meet his
obligations, and, to the benefit of the College, the lease was
broken.

Raven's survey also shows Hamilton as owner of much
of the land which had formed part of Con O'Neill's third,—
the improvident Irishman having made rapid progress in
the alienation of his property.

And, in 1610, " for a good valuable consideration," from
the family of Whyte (Le Blanc), Hamilton became possessor
of the Duffryn territory. with

> " 10 castles, 1,000 messuages, 1,600 cottages, 200 tofts, 10 water-
> mills, 1,000 gardens, 15,000 acres of arable land, 1,000 acres of
> meadow, 1,000 acres of pasture, 10,000 acres of wood, 1,000
> acres of moor, 1,000 acres of heath and furze, etc., etc."

This made him master of Killileagh on Lough Cone (Strangford Lough), of which Raven's map of 1625 is here reproduced
(pp. 62, 63). The castle here shown is the " vera stronge
castell, the lyk not in the North " of Abercorn's letter quoted
in a preceding chapter, and its magnificence has so impressed

the surveyor that he has made a drawing of it, on larger
scale, outside the map, explaining that this is

> " THE CASTELL OF KILLELEAGH AT LARGE w^c ye smalnes
> of Rome ther woud not Suffer."

Deer are indicated in the extensive park.

Hamilton's " good valuable consideration " to the Whytes
did not buy their goodwill.   Indeed, it would seem that goodwill did not go with any large sale of lands in 17th-century
Down, for Con O'Neill's son felt himself defrauded through
the bargains weakly made by his father with the Scots ; and
when it came to sale from Scot to Scot, ill-feeling went to the
purchaser with his new lands.   The second Earl Mount-
Alexander sold a great part of his estates to Sir Robert Colvil,
and the Clarendon letters (Clarendon to Lord Mount-
Alexander, June 26, 1686, and others) show that he made
to the Lord Lieutenant insinuations of his purchaser's disloyalty.   Hamilton's plaint that the Whytes did not love
him for buying them out of Duffryn, notwithstanding his
" lardge bounties," is found in a letter to the Marquis of
Ormonde, and dated 28th November, 1643, many years
after the purchase.

> " It may please your Lordship to know that one Christopher
> Whyte of Marshall Wrath in the Countie of Louth, (from whose
> grandfather and father I had purchased many yeares agoe, this
> Territory of Duffrin, for great summes of money, and had granted
> to them and to him as the heire of that Family, a yearly annuity,
> which was still thankfully payd, with many free and lardge
> bounties given to his brothers and sisters towardes their prefer-
> mentes from time to time, and to him every yeare once or twice
> besides the Anuitye). This Christopher Whyte I say, (not-
> withstanding the love and liberalitie which I had used him
> withall) came downe into this countye soone after the first
> rupture of the rebellion, . . .   with two waggons of Armes
> and Ammunition, and joined himselfe in rebellion with Colonel
> Constantine O'Neale, the leader of the O'Neales in the Countie
> of Downe. . . .   The said Whyte raised . . . by means
> of his kinsfolkes, which his ancestors had left tennantes in the

territory of the Duffrin, under me, as well all his said kindred,
as all the Irish septes in the said territorie, and who joining
with the others committed many inhumane barbarous murthers
upon the poore Brittaines here, and thereby have made exceeding
many Widowes and Fatherles Children."

The indignant lord goes on to say that this Christopher
Whyte has appeared again on his ancestors' territory,

" this Christopher Whyte who had wrought this bloudy murther
upon the poore people here, . . . is come downe here by
way of the enemy, his former confederates, . . . & sent
me word that he had your Lordship's passe, (without which
voice noe money could have saved his life) I caused bring it
to me and found it obtained within seaven dayes after the
Agreement of the Cessation."

Lord Claneboye proceeds to tell the Marquis that he
was forced to set a strong guard on Whyte,—

" to keep him from the fury of the people who were all in an
uproare to pull him to pieces after they knew he was here, and
who at all Centinells & outgates of the towne have layd men
to kill him." (Carte MSS., Bodleian Library, Oxford.)

He assumes that Ormonde had not knowledge of Whyte's
rebellion, else the safe conduct had not been given. He
will not be answerable for the man's life, sends him under
good guard to the Marquis, and prays his Lordship to direct
Whyte to keep within his own quarters, where he was at the
day and hour of the Agreement, etc., etc.

A letter of Charles II. to the Lord Chancellor in 1661,
sheds a light on Hamilton's claim to have been very generous
in his dealings with the Whytes. He paid, he says, " great
summes of money " for the Dufferin territory, and ' granted '
a yearly annuity to the family. The King's letters called
on the Chancellor to restore to Whyte's widow and children
the rent charges of £40 and £60, and arrears thereof, payable
out of the Clanbrassil estate, funds of which they had been
deprived since the taking of Drogheda, " by the late Usurper
by whose party he (Whyte) was barbarously murthered."

The ' generosity ' of the purchase terms disappears in the
cold light of the statement to the Chancellor. This speaks
of Whyte's father as

> " seized of a great Estate in Ulster called the Druffen, (now valued
> to be worth two thousand pounds per annum and upwards)
> the which he sold to Sir James Hamilton, since Viscount Clana-
> boy, for a very small consideracion, reserving onely to him &
> his heires a Rent-charge of Fourty pounds per annum, . . .
> & sixty pounds per annum more in consideracion of part of the
> purchase money yet unsatisfied."

Forty pounds per annum rent charge, as part of the bargain,
and sixty pounds per annum interest on money unpaid, do
not give occasion for much pluming on ' generosity.' Of
course there are still the part of purchase money actually
paid and the " many free and lardge bounties given to his
Brothers and Sisters," but one can hardly refrain from dis-
counting the latter after reading the Hamilton-Ormonde and
the King-Chancellor letters together.

Although the Abercorn letter speaks of Killileagh Castle
as ' buildet ' by Sir James Hamilton, it is believed that the
core of the structure had been standing for at least 400 years
before his time. Taken and partly demolished by General
Monk in 1648, it was restored by Henry, Earl of Clanbrassil,
in 1666. In modern times the Castle was renovated (1850)
under direction of Sir Charles Lanyon, architect, and in 1859,
the Gatehouse section, which had formed a separate residence
for a branch of the family for 200 years, was rebuilt by the
late Marquis of Dufferin and Ava, and by him given to the
brother of Lady Dufferin, Mr. Gawen R. Hamilton ; reserving
the right to a rent, annually, of " a red rose to the Lady, or
a pair of gilt spurs to the Master of Clandeboye."

What Montgomery's house was like in elevation is
impossible to indicate, as maps of his estates corresponding
to those made by Raven for Lord Claneboye have not been
discovered. The Montgomerys were very unfortunate in
the matter of fires, in which, it may be presumed, all early

EARLY DAYS OF THE PLANTATION. KILLILEAGH in 1625.
still standing, and is now balanced by one of similar desi
Original at Bangor Castle.   second E

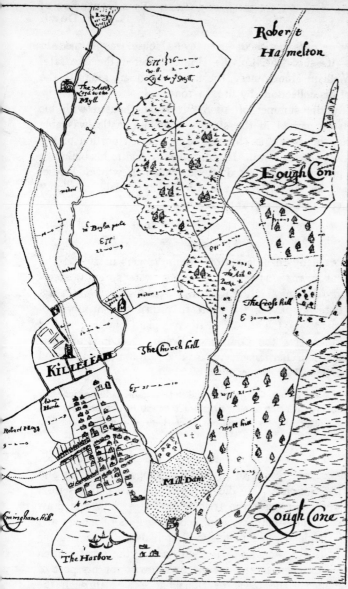

Robert Hamelton

Lough Con

The lands lyeth to the Myll

The Boylea parke

medow

medow

medow

KILLELEAH

Robert Hog3

Eminghams hill

The Church hill

Mill-Dam

Myll hill

The Crosse hill

The Ash Parke

Lough Cone

The Harbor

er, to left in drawing of the castle, which is very ancient, is
he right-hand corner. This was erected in 1666 by Henry,
lanbrassil.

family records perished. Newtown House was burned in
1664,—its successor, Colville House, suffered the like fate,
and William Montgomery, the family historian, refers to the
loss of his collections by fire, in 1695.

By the summer of 1608, Sir Hugh, housed with his
friends on arrival in the stump of an old castle, was able
to bring his wife and children to a repaired portion of the
old priory of Newtown. He continued to add to his buildings
here until the completed work, called Newtown House,
justified his historian's appellation of " princely mansion."
The houses of his servants rose near—

> " a good towne of a hundred houses or thereaboutes, all peopled
> with Scottes,"

as reported by the Plantation Commissioners in 1611. The
principal towns on both plantations were speedily incorporated,—Bangor, Killileagh, and Newtownards in 1613,
each borough having the right to return two members of
Parliament. In the same year the two planters were returned
as members for the County of Down, receiving for their
attendance in Parliament the sum of £198 13s. 4d., levied
by the Sheriff of the county.

> " Yet among all this care and indefatigable industry for their
> families, a place of God's honour to dwell in was not forgotten
> nor neglected, for indeed our forefathers were more pious than
> ourselves."

With these words the author of the Montgomery MSS.
introduces the record of his chief's doings in building and
repairing churches. He did not withdraw his planters from
their work, but made the Irish ' Gibeonites ' hew and draw
timber for the sanctuary, and, accepting gifts of money and
labour, made the old monastic church decently serviceable
as a house of worship. He built also " the great church
and bell-tower near the mount and town " of his port of
Donaghadee. The tower of Donaghadee was, through the
greater part of the nineteenth century, a stump, and clearly

had never been carried far in stone, until a member of the De la Cherois family, in the nineteenth century, raised the now existing belfry. Yet the family historian speaks of the ' bell-tower,' and the crude map of the town made in 1780 and reproduced for this work (chap. X.) shows a tapering steeple. The explanation may be that the ancient stump had borne, more than once, erections in wood, which lasted until destroyed by fires. Hamilton and his settlers built or rebuilt the church of Bangor, using, it is believed, the ancient monuments and remains of buildings as quarry materials, and, probably, repairing the still existing tower which is indicated in Raven's drawing, and which is much too massive to be the work of poor men in the early years of their settlement. Other churches on the estates, some, as at Holywood, of great antiquity, were repaired, and chaplains for them were provided.

Evidences of the " indefatigable industry " of the two knights are plentiful. A letter, printed in the notes to Lowry's edition of the Hamilton Manuscripts, which shows Sir James, lord of many castles and innumerable acres, as a merchant dealing with the prosaic details of transactions in oats, is, at the same time, an example of his masterful severity in dealing with the relatives in his service. His brother William has been slack in making a bargain, and has failed to collect money due. Hamilton is too angry with him to use the conventional courtesy in address,—

> " 9th July 1619.
> William,—I have written lately to you by Patrick Shawe, but in good trueth not so much as I thinke. I will write no more than that if there be not greater care had, things will fall out that you and I both will be sorry for it."

Unlike Montgomery, Hamilton had little wifely aid in the early days of the Plantation. He was married three times ; " his first two ladies proved but little comfortable to him " says the writer of the Hamilton story,—who adds,

> " his putting away of his second lady was not with general satisfaction to his friends and contemporaries."

There is a mystery about the putting away of this lady, who was a daughter of Lord Brabazon of Ardee. The writer of the family story is concerned to glorify the career of the great head of his house, yet he admits that Hamilton's putting away of the lady was not pleasing to his friends. From this it would seem that there was no breach of conjugal fidelity on the lady's part. No record of divorce proceedings can be found among the records of Dublin Courts, and yet the legitimacy of the son born of the third wife in the lifetime of the second appears never to have been questioned.

More fortunate in his first marriage, Montgomery had, in Elizabeth Shaw, a helper to whose wisdom and energy much of the success of his settlement was due. While Sir Hugh attended to legal matters and the general interests of his colony, his practical wife managed his domestic affairs with the skill of the virtuous wife of Proverbs xxxi., and withal found time for much work in the development of the estates. Of her labours the Montgomery historian has to say :—

> " This . . . gave occasion to Sir Hugh's Lady to build water-mills in all the parishes, to the great advantage of her house, which was numerous in servants, of whom she stood in need, in working about her gardens, carriages etc. having then no duty days' works from tenants, or very few as exacted, they being sufficiently employed in their proper labour and the publique. The millers also prevented the necessity of bringing meal from Scotland, and grinding with quairn stones (as the Irish did to make their graddon) both which inconveniencys the people, at their first coming, were forced to undergo. . . .
>
> " Her ladyship had also her farms at Greyabbey and Coiner, (Comber) as well as at Newtown, both to supply new-comers and her house ; and she easily got men for plough and barn, for many came over who had not stocks to plant and take leases of land, but had brought a cow or two and a few sheep, for which she gave them grass and so much grain per annum, and an house and garden-plot to live on, and some land for flax and potatoes, as they agreed on for doing their work, and there be at this day many such poor labourers amongst us ; and this was but part

of her good management, for she set up and encouraged linen
and woollen manufactory, which soon brought down the prices
of ye breakens and narrow cloths of both sorts."

Looking back three-quarters of a century to the Colony's
early days, the writer casts an admiring glance at the capable
lady, ordering well her household, and the larger household
of the settlement ; and, forgetting for the moment dangers
and distresses of the time, sees through a golden haze the
happy results of Lady Montgomery's rule.

" Now everybody minded their trades, and the ploughs, and the
    spade, building, and setting fruit trees, etc. in orchards and
    gardens, and by ditching in their grounds. The old women
    spun, and the young girls plyed their nimble fingers at knitting,
    and everybody was innocently busy. Now the Golden peacable
    age renewed, no strife, contention, querulous lawyers, or Scottish
    or Irish feuds, between clanns and families, and sirnames, dis-
    turbing the tranquillity of those times ; and the towns and
    temples were erected, with other great works."

Strangely, the Montgomery MSS., while proceeding to
tell of the Viscount's second marriage, omit any record of
the death of the busy lady. It would appear that his Lordship's widowhood was not long. He went over to Scotland
for distraction, consolation, and to look after business, having
much conversation with his chief, the Earl of Eglinton,
on matters of heraldry. While there he married the Viscountess of Wigton, who " proved but little comfortable to
him," for, after a residence of only a few months at Newtownards, she returned to Scotland and point blank refused
to set foot on Ireland again.

The Town Book of Belfast, and Historical Records of
Old Belfast (R. M. Young), should be studied by those who
wish to understand the conditions of life in abutting English-
ruled districts during the early years of the Scottish Plantation
in Down. Sir Arthur Chichester was in power at Carrickfergus, in sight of Hamilton's territory. According to writers
on the Irish side, he was a monster of cruelty and insatiable

4

o 7 - 51

The Church hill

c M Austin

Quimbins hill
18 — 0 — 28

Thom
Lela
1 —

The Church yrie

The Denns hill
10 — 1 — 10

Brimgans hill
48 — 2 — 25

The waist

Ralphes Modow
4 — 0 — 36

Alex: Blare
1 — 1 — 22

- 3 - 0
John Wilson

The Wheat hill
26 — 1 — 0

Ralphes Acars

Camels hill
16 — 3 — 24

Comon
16 — 0 — 5

Sander Blare & Sander Hameltons parkes
11 — 3 —

5 — 3 — 17
M C ... Gvill

Comon
4 — 2 — 2

Daued 5 — — 27
Mongumre

Stilles hill

Comon
6 — 1 — 0

John Wilsons Parke
6 — 2 —

The great forbe hill
54 — 1 — 3

Steuensons Parkes
16 — 2 — 0

THE BAY OF BANGOR

Original at Bangor Castle.

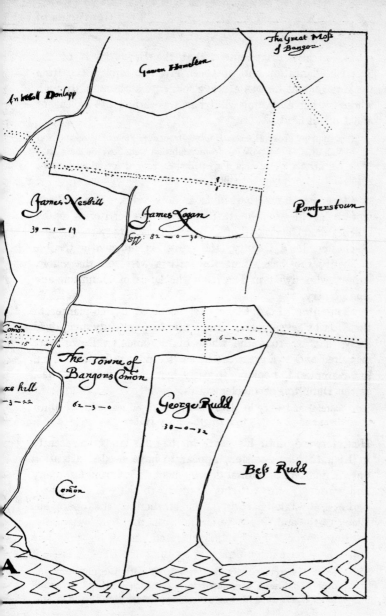

The Great Moss
of Bangor

Gawen Hamelton

An Ketall DonLapp

James Nesbitt

39 — 1 — 19

James Logan

Ew 82 — 0 — 36

Pomferstoun

Comon

— 15

The Towne of
Bangons Comon

xs hill

— 3 — 22

62 — 3 — 0

George Rudd

38 — 0 — 32

6 — 2 — 22

Comon

Bess Rudd

A

RMS in the Manor of Bangor, 1625.

greed,—greatly disappointed that the Down lands of the
Scottish Plantation had not been given to him. Seen from
the English side he was a brave soldier, a statesman through
whose wisdom a howling wilderness was turned into a pleasant
and fruitful land,—

> " a man of great Honour, Piety, Prudence, Justice, Bounty and
> Valour, . . . so far from Ambition and Covetousness that
> he, neither by friends nor of himself, moved for advancement,
> Military or Civil, but still it was conferred on him unsought."

It is necessary to read from both sides. The midway
picture of life in the disturbed Ulster territories under
Chichester, Governor of Carrickfergus (1597-1604), and
Chichester, Lord Deputy (1604-1615), is sufficiently terrible
to justify the belief that the settlers were, on the whole,
happy, who dwelt in Down on the lands of Hamilton and
Montgomery.

Hamilton, Lord Claneboye, out-lived his co-planter of
the Ards by seven years. The estate maps already mentioned
show that by 1625 the whole of his lands in Down were
measured and to a great extent let (see pp. 67, 68 and 72, 73,
for examples). Looking to early increase in value, he was,
as the Hamilton chronicler states,

> " careful and wary in giving inheritances or leases above three
> lives and . . . that length with very few."

Henceforward, until his death in 1643, his lands, so recently
in Irish tribal possession, appear to have needed attention
only in matters of normal development. But troubles, many
and various, were with his Lordship to the end. He had,
perforce, to take part in administration of the obnoxious
Black Oath, and, Presbyterian in sympathy, had, outwardly,
to countenance the Laudian persecution of his ministers
and others for nonconformity. At the same time, it is said,

> " he had secret friendly correspondence with the ministers and
> others that were persecuted for conscience sake, yea, some hid
> in his house when his warrant and constables were abroad looking
> for them,"

and although the troubles of 1641 affected the Ards but little, they must have caused the old lord many anxieties.

Montgomery, Viscount Ards, died in 1636, unreconciled to his great rival. His burial in the church of Newtownards was made the occasion of one of those great displays of pomp and heraldry of which Scotsmen of the time were so fond.

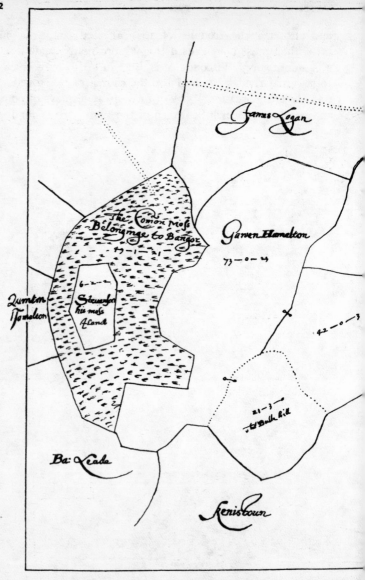

Original at Bangor Castle.

Ach the Doons hill
10—1—26

The Church
Yard

Thomas m
Lelan
5—1—34

Quintins hill
18—0—26

Mᶜ Austin

Alexander m
Lelan
19—3—17

Erche

Mouett
3—1—4

John foe fild
1—1—37

The Church
Hill
39—1—4

Gabriell
Pollock
3—2—0

65—2—

Mᶜ Austin

John m Lelan
35—1—19

Andrew
Linsey his
Bulle hill
29—1—31

Demesne

Nicholᵃᵇ mᶜ Lelan
34—2—0

The bogmedow
3—2—7

Cⁿⁿ Hameltons hill
35—2—5

Cranhill

Boleys hall

s in the Manor of Bangor, 1625.

CHAPTER V.

The Time of the Troubles

DECAY of the Hamilton family fortunes set in with the passing of the first Lord Claneboye. Long and laborious as had been his career,—the exciting years of acquisition, years of great anxiety,—he knew the solace of success. The Dublin schoolmaster had become the head of a family, the ennobled owner of vast estates, with limitless possibilities of wealth for his descendants. But his only son, as the records show, was not a lad of parts. The boy's limited capacity for acquirement accounts, it may be assumed, for his father's direction to a tutor

> " that he should be managed according to his genius, and not much thwarted or overdriven in the prosecution of learning and other improvements,"

and his saying that

> " he would not lose the substance for gaining of accidents and would rather have no scholar than no son."

A sense of the youth's very moderate attainment is suggested

by the qualified form of appreciation made use of by the
family chronicler when he said

> " he returned (from the journey to Rome with his tutor) with
> great improvements in such things whereunto his genius allowed
> or agreed unto."

Copied in the notes of Lowry's edition of the Hamilton
Manuscripts, is a letter written to his mother by the boy,
on tour in France.   It is a short, dry communication of nine
lines in print, in which his mother is addressed as " your
Ladyship " five times.   Making due allowance for the formality
of the period in addressing relatives, it is a poor production
for a nobleman's son, far from the country home and out to
see the great world.

But even had he possessed ability equal to that of the
founder of the family, it would have been impossible for
him to avert many of the disasters of his troubled life.   The
civil war, which had commenced in 1641, was still young at
the time of the death of first Lord Claneboye, and, for ten
years after that event, the troubles were to continue.
Commander of forces raised among friends and tenantry,
the second Viscount engaged in the war against the Irish,
" being therein," as the Hamilton chronicler records, " very
laborious, with a very good measure of dexterity and courage,"
a statement in which is apparent the qualified character of
praise noted already in connection with the young man's
scholarship.   Fat, phlegmatic, easy-going, James, second Lord
Claneboye, first Earl of Clanbrassil, was quite unfit to hold,
in such difficult times, what the strong hand of his father
had gained.   One is helped in picturing the man by the story
of his adventure with a brownie at Newtownards.   The
family feud was not perpetuated by the sons of the first
Viscounts, and after reconciliation of the families brought
about by the common dangers of the wars, the heads were
accustomed to meet at each other's houses and to take counsel
together.   In this way, James, second Lord Claneboye,
being at the house of his friend Viscount Montgomery, at

Newtownards, having spent a pleasant evening, remained for the night. According to the record he had taken " medicine for fleabitings," which means that his Lordship had taken "as much as was good for him," and while he slept a wicked brownie cut away his shirt, leaving on his fat person only the neck and wristbands. What a great ' to-do' there was in the morning when the Lord Montgomery came to see why his friend tarried in his bedroom, and how the bulk of the missing garment was found, later, where it had no business to be, is told by the author of the Montgomery Manuscripts.

The great cost to him of his military operations, and the generous support he rendered to Protestants fleeing from the disturbed districts, greatly burdened his estate, even before his disastrous defeat by the Parliamentarians in 1649,—when he had sided against them and in favour of Ormonde. He was made prisoner, his estate was sequestrated for six years, pending payment of a fine of, according to one account, £9,000, and according to another, £10,000. It is believed that he compounded by payment of half the fine, and to meet demands made on him he had to contract a great deal of debt, and so lived with his family on a scale much lower than that of his father's establishment. He had married, in his father's lifetime, Anne, daughter of the Earl of Monmouth, a good and able woman. She it was who conducted successfully the negotiations with Oliver Cromwell for mitigation of the penalties incurred by her husband by siding with Ormonde,—an additional proof that the Earl's mentality was not of a high order. Of this marriage was issue three sons, and a daughter who died in infancy. James, the eldest son, died, aged 15, in 1658. Grief at his son's death and anxieties due to his losses depressed and dispirited Clanbrassil,

> " brought him low in his disposition of mind comparatively with himself in former times ; he became corpulent, scorbutic, hydropsic, and so decayed gradually till at length he died in June 1659,"

after making a will in which it was provided that, should
his sons die without heirs, his estate should be divided into
five equal parts,

> " amongst the Eldest Sons, or Issue Male of my five Uncles, as
> the Lands can be laid out in the most Equal and just divisions,"

a will which gave occasion to disputes and lawsuits extending
over many years.

His contemporary of the Ards, Hugh, second Viscount
Montgomery, married in 1623, Jean, eldest daughter of Sir
William Alexander, King's Secretary for Scotland. His
father built for the young couple a house at Comber, on a
gentle elevation, called Mount-Alexander out of compliment
to the lady. Not much is known of the second Viscount,
as the records concerning him made by William Montgomery
have been, unfortunately, lost. On the outbreak of the
rebellion he received a commission from the Irish Government, and soon after from the King, to be Colonel of 1,000
foot and five troops of horse, finding, himself, the greater
part of the money for their equipment and support for a year.
His son, Hugh, on his travels on the Continent, returned
hurriedly to England on first news of the rebellion, and there
received a letter from his father urging a speedy journey
home, as he feared the development of a "drowsy distemper"
which had fastened on him. The second Viscount's fears
were justified, for he died suddenly on the 15th November,
1642, being only 45 years of age.

The life-story of Hugh, third Viscount, and most like-
able of the Montgomerys, is a long record of misfortunes.
As a child he had fallen and so hurt the ribs of the left side
that a large abscess formed. Ultimately this healed, leaving a
wide opening over which a plate was worn, and through which
it was popularly believed the movement of the lungs could
be seen. He had been attended for this trouble by a Doctor
Maxwell, who, in 1642, was acting as physician to Charles I.
Called home by his father's letter, the young man paid a visit
at Oxford to his old doctor, who was pleased to find the

delicate boy grown into a strong and healthy man. He
mentioned the curious case to the King, who asked the celebrated Dr. William Harvey to report on it. Harvey found
that what others supposed to be the lung, was really the
heart, the movement of which was clearly seen,—nature
having provided a protecting integument for the apex.
Instead of making a verbal report to His Majesty, Harvey
took the youth to the King, who received him kindly and
kept him at Court for a few days.

Arrived at Newtownards, he saw his father die, and
immediately took command of the forces raised by the second
Viscount. Under General Munro he headed the British
forces in the fight at Benburb in 1646, and "warmly charging—
being coldly seconded," was taken prisoner by the Irish under
Owen Roe O'Neill, and clapped into Cloughwooter Castle,
a stronghold " on an island scarce bigger than its foundation."
There he remained for two full years, endeavouring to relieve
the tedium of his confinement by study. Released in exchange
for a prisoner of O'Neill's party, he devoted his time and
means to the furtherance of Royalist interests. A bright
interlude in the sadly developing drama is the young Viscount's
marriage to Mary Moore,—sister of Henry, first Viscount
Moore,—in December 1648. The girl was only seventeen, and
when she appeared on the home-coming at Newtownards
with a younger sister and two young brothers, there were
great rejoicings. Montgomery, with his grandfather's love
of heraldry and romance, organised a tournament and sports
which lasted several days—producing sights " never beheld
by any of the Ladies or any of the attendants before that
time." The days of rejoicing were quickly brought to an
end. Montgomery, in communication with the King at
Breda, accepted from him the appointment of general of the
royalist forces in Ulster, and quickly took the field against
the Parliamentarians. A momentary gleam of royalist
success encouraged the Scots of Down to declare Charles II.
king, at Newtownards, in 1649. Claret, "catched in hats or

bowls by who cou'd or wou'd," flowed from the spouts of
Newtownards market cross, to the accompaniment of the
sound of trumpets, drums, and guns, with bonfires in the
streets and illuminated windows in the houses at night.
But not for eleven years yet was Charles II. to succeed to the
throne. Cromwell, after settling with the English royalists,
made short work of the Irish, and at Lisnastrain, on 6th
December, 1649, Montgomery, defeated, fled to join the King's
chief servant, the Marquis of Ormonde. In April 1650,
Montgomery with others went to Clonmel, and there submitted
to Cromwell.

This done, he was allowed to return to Newtownards,
pending settlement of a composition to be paid by him to
Parliament for permission to administer his estates. As
more active than his neighbour Clanbrassil, he was more
harshly treated. After a short stay with his young wife,—
seeing his daughter Jean, then three months old, for the
first time,—he was summoned to London to appear before a
Committee of Parliament, by whom he was banished to
Holland, under bond to refrain from any communication
with Charles Stuart, to keep out of Scotland or the Spanish
Netherlands, and not to return to England or Ireland without
the license of the Council of State.

In Holland the young Viscount wearied and worried,—
thinking of his girl wife and daughter in the great house at
Newtownards, the failure of the King's cause, the ruin of his
fortunes. It was of the policy of the Parliament to reduce
the royalists of Down by fines and forced expenses,—indeed,
for a time, a scheme to expatriate the men who had turned
desolate Down into fruitful fields found favour. It was
proposed to move the hard-working Scots and their leaders,
and to replant them in the South and West, where, being far
from Scotland, " they could do no harm." Fortunately for
Down and for Ireland, the proposed removal was never
effected.

The man who was to write lovingly of the Montgomerys

half a century later,—who had been a boy at school in
Newtownards at the time of the wedding tournament,—was
now a student at Leyden, and, to the great joy of his heart,
" the Viscount came to see him."

> " His loᴾ was then an unwilling traveller, to his great cost in that
> dear country . . . His expense was that wʰ his enemies
> always partly aimed at . . . But all the entertainment wʰ
> travel gave his Loᴾ was full of pain and throes, for he cou'd
> have no comfort (or but very little), till he was delivered from
> that captivity in that Babilon of religions and nations. His
> earthly treasure was in Ireland and his heart was there also."

Out of the fifty-year-later report of doings in the
captivity in Holland, still bubble the enthusiastic love and
devotion of the young Leyden student for his family chief.
An example is found in the story of a meal at a Dutch inn.
The practice of making great persons pay a great deal more
than was paid by common folk for the same service, was
widespread in the seventeenth century. Evelyn, speaking
of the action of Cromwell and his partisans in seizing and
shutting up a place of entertainment and refreshment, speaks
of Mulberry Garden as

> " now the onely place of refreshment about the towne for persons
> of the best quality to be exceedingly cheated at."

Montgomery, for the purpose of avoiding extortionate
charges, did not disclose his rank, but the landlady of an
obscure Dutch inn saw the nobility that " sprang out of his
(Montgomery's) eyes, features and presence," and charged
accordingly, to the disgust and indignation of the student
kinsman, who is here allowed to tell the story in his own
words.

> " It was very lucky I had the happiness to see his Loᴾ . . .
> bound to my studies . . . but this once I accompanied
> him to any village or town. When we were at Hunsterdyke
> and general-wheres, he kept himself so as to pass for a Gentᵐ,
> and we strove to do so in this dorp. Ensign Simeon
> Erskin was then his Loᴾ'ˢ only servant, Lᵗ. Col. Geo. Stewart,
> Capt. Hugh Montgomery, and myself had that afternoon

"He had humane prudence which might stock an able statesman" (*Montgomery MSS.*). SIR JAMES MONTGOMERY, of Rosemount, Greyabbey, Co. Down ; second son of Hugh, first Viscount Montgomery.

Portrait in the possession of descendants at Auckland, New Zealand.

REV. JOHN MCBRIDE (1678-1718), champion of Presbyterianism against Episcopacy in Belfast ; called derisively by the Vicar " the great Professor, Mr. McBride." The original of this portrait, with a sword-stab made by a soldier disappointed of arresting the minister, is preserved in the session-room of the First Presbyterian Church, Belfast.

walked from the Hague with his Lo^P, as if we had been
fellows.   We went to a tavern in Hunsterdyke afores^d, and we
had all got an appetite for victuals ; so after two or three stoops
of Rhenish (without distinction of hats or any extraordinary
deference one to another) Simeon and I were dispatched for meat;
we had a cold veal py but did not price it.   This gave but small
suspicion that there was any Lord in company, yet for all the
restraint that was on us all that we should not drop one word
or action w^h might discover that there was a Nobleman amongst
us, yet this hausfrau watched like cats, peeped and perceived it.
I did (and so did the rest) wonder at it, yet the matter was not
so difficult to know, for notwithstanding that settled melancholy
w^h was in his Lo^{P's} heart, yet the rays of his noble soul often
broke the prison and sprang out at his eyes, features and presence,
which were always (and when unafflicted) seen in his Lo^{P's}
generous countenance ; and so we lost our labour of conversing
in mascarade.   In short, the landlady brought in all to . . .
bill (without paper), ag^t w^h we objected : for it was five times
the price of the Wine (w^h we drank liberally and wherein we
agreed).   Then the covetous, imperious, wretched woman put
into the scale (to make the bill relevant) the py, then the bread,
butter, chees, small beer, spitting in the room, smoaking, her
pictures and attendance, and chiefly she urged there was a great
Lord there ; bidding us in plain Dutch words be content and
pay willingly, for if the Prince of Orange was there ' she would
not abate one doit.' "

At the end of a winter in Holland, Montgomery petitioned
Oliver Cromwell to be allowed to return home, and, after
some formalities, and an appearance before the Council at
Whitehall, his plea was granted, and he was permitted to
compound for his real and personal estate for a fine of £3,000.
Business in connection with his composition took him up to
Dublin. Taking his wife and children with him, he settled
them at Mellifont at the house of his brother-in-law, Lord
Viscount Moore, but the Commissioners of Government under
Parliament objected to this residence with a relative as
giving opportunity to plot, and the harassed Lord of the
Ards had to move to lodgings near Dublin Castle. His
chronicler charges the Commissioners with increasing the

expenses of Montgomery of deliberate intention,—they, or
some of them, made no secret of their unfriendly feeling,
Corbett telling the Viscount that he hoped to see his head off.
Amelioration came with permission to move to Howth Castle
" on warranty to be forthcoming when called for," but this
improvement did not last long.

> " I do believe the usurpers had it for a necessary maxim to
> impoverise the Royal Party, pinching them by considerable
> crooked serpentine ways, . . . and by their composition
> money and intolerable taxes on their lands, whereof their rents
> must answer near to the half, having no consideration of
> creditors ; but that they might take the other half moiety, and
> so starve the family, and also by trying them to all attendencies
> as afore^sd."

The ' attendencies ' were so numerous that the family
were soon back in lodgings in Dublin, and there the young
wife—the girl bride of the tournament at Newtownards
of seven years before—died. A few words by the writer of
the Montgomery Manuscripts may tell the story of this
second removal to Dublin.

> " The inactive manner of living at Mellifont and Howth, and
> the temptation of a bottle of wine which in the city was often
> offered and accepted f^m the loyalists to remove heaviness of
> heart, to forget poverty, and to remember misery no more, made
> his Lo^P corpulent and unhealthy : Yet this infirmity of his
> body was not regarded by Corbett and his gang, but his Lo^P
> was enjoyned to present himself at their council door twice a
> week, and dance attendance there until word was sent out that
> he sh^d come in or might retire himself : which dancing, (without
> music) being troublesome and costly, and his Lady falling sickly
> at Howth, necessitated his Lo^P to remove her with his family
> to dwell in Dublin, where (her Lad^P's distemper increasing upon
> her) she died and was buried as the times would allow ; and his
> Lo^P expressed his grief and her worth in an excellent elogy of
> his own composure."

The bereavement of the still young Viscount (he was
at the time only 35 years of age) did not move the hearts
of the Commissioners in the direction of lenient treatment

of their victim.   He was soon sent as prisoner to Kilkenny,—
falling ill there, was allowed to go to Naas—then to Leixlip.
Again he was imprisoned in Dublin, but released on account
of ill-health,—he engaging not to leave Dublin and not to act
in any way prejudicial to the Government.   Spies were
sent to watch his movements,—the unfriendly Commissioners
placing him

> " in slippery places that he might slide and fall into the pitts they
> had digged, . . . Thus his LoP continued in Dublin (as
> it were on the brink of perdition), soliciting liberty to attend
> his affairs in the country, and to provide payment of his com-
> position money."

At last on bail he was suffered to return to the desolate house
at Newtownards, and then

> " after watering his couch with his sorrowful tears for some nights
> he was persweaded to reside with his mother at Mt Alexander."

His mother was now wife to Major-General Monro,—who, at
this time, was a prisoner in the Tower of London, but soon
afterwards regained liberty.

Two letters of Montgomery—addressed to his stepfather, Major-General Monro, and belonging to this time—
have been strangely preserved.   They were found, in August
1917, in the library of Portaferry House, bound as end leaves
of a book of instructions for Justices of the Peace.   This
book was printed, probably, about 1635 (the title-page is
missing), and at an unknown date, later than 1657 and prior
to 1692, it was re-bound, apparently by an amateur who
used family correspondence and other documents as fly leaves
and end papers.

These letters confirm what is stated in the Montgomery
Manuscripts about the distressful state of the Viscount's
fortunes at this time.

The references to corn, to remittances from " Mr. Charry
and Dunkan," and to bad money, find explanation in another
of the old documents so oddly preserved.   This sets out
the " Instructions given by the Lady Jean Viscountesse

Montgomerie and the Lady Viscountesse Marie Montgomerie
to Ihon Duncan concerning the Corne Milnes in the
manors of Donnadie, Neutoune, Cumber and Cuningburne."
The Viscount's estate was at this time sequestrated, and the
opening lines of the Statement explain that " the statt
(State) hath been pleased to allow unto us all advantages
and profitts of the corne milnes afforesaid and . . . that
portion of maintaince allowed for use and the subsistance
of our severall families and my Lord's brother and sisters."

The ladies Jean and Marie Montgomerie, of these instructions, were respectively mother and wife of the writer of the
letters here following. The young lady must have been dead
at the date of these letters, as the Viscount does not in them
mention her, while he speaks of the " dear children who
have been a greate comfort to mee att this tyme." The
first of these letters is dated 13th January, 1656-7. The ' lb.'
sign of the letters is, of course, ' £.'

" Right Honrbl.
        Yors of the 2 being the first I . . . many moneths
. . . . the post I received yeasterday.
I hope you have received letters sent 3 weekes sinc directed
to James McGill and on (one) tenn dayes agoe sent by Maj^r.
Rawdon, by all which as by this itt may apeare to you thatt
I am in extreme want for I am indebted one way or other thatt
I must presently pay about 80 lb and have not now 3 lb in the
world itt is a greate presse to mee thatt my de . . . who
have been soe carefull and by God's blissing soe miraculously
successefull . . . my children's dyett should bee Alys
(always) unsatisfied, soe as Charles must at least send me on
100 lb and you whatt . . . gott but lett nott him know
whatt . . . have. As for Mr. Charie or any who are
negligent I must intreat you to bee . . . and make them
understand theire duty I hope Mr. Charie has given you all
corne hee could spare, according my former commands. As
for the 20 lb you borrowd . . . itt hadd been 2000 lb for
yor service. I know I owe you more money than it came indorse
itt upon the back off on (one) off thee bills I remember you
hadd long sinc off me upon acounts at Neutown : My dear

children who have been a greate comfort to mee att this tyme are all extreme well ; I am proceedinge withall speed to the setting tyme whereoff I doutt nott to give you a . . . . .

(Here several lines are missing, part of the letter having been cut away in trimming the book after re-binding.)

. . . for his lott elsewhere in Conocht . . . I was a little mistaken in my last soe now both these are doon in on (one) act off parlament, my cousin Will wrights he has good hopes butt his petition was nott then read but was to be last Saturday. I feare my sister is in a deep consumption and that shee must necessarily com heere this Spring to bee cured if that shall bee possible. You shall heare more fully by Capt. McGill shortly from

> Yor most faithfull friend
> and Servant
> Montgomerie."

The beginning of the second letter has been cut away in the re-binding.

" I punctually received I am . . . . . . ly busie about the finash of my composition thatt I have hardly tyme to write this (my mother I hope will pardoun my sylence att this tyme) and itt forceth me abroad in such badd weather and late houres thatt itt is god's grate mercie I grow nott ill again and indeed I wold not undergoe itt but that I had noe desyre to live butt the good of my poore children and waning health serve nott thatt end I doe nott value itt, and I thank god I finde nott any hurt as yett by my staying. Next week I am confident to make a full and I beleeve a good end ; and after I hope wee shall bee in a condition to . . . or servants know themselves i till then beg Charles Camball sent me 6o lb and I ow 1 . . (100) att least heere I have not been able to . . . from Debts (thatt wold not admitt any delay) to pay off all you and hee both sent me. In the 22 lbs you sent me there was 26 badd . . . I pray you bee extreme carefull in receiving money and lett Mr. Charry and Dunkan have warning off itt at theire perrill. I cannot have tyme untill my composition bee over to peruse the accounts you sent me. I am indeed glad to heare thatt my deare Sister is reco . . . what is desyred is sent by the bearer. I earnestly desyred to have an exact account off her condition least her disease prove exelerated and nott cured ; and my physition has admirable skill loves mee intyrely. The wyndes have been soe crosse that wee have nott harde from Ingland these 3 weekes ; itt will bee towards the end off Aprill before I dare venture to ryde doun, and then I heare . . . . . . progresse soe as . . . . .

(Here part of the letter is cut away. What follows is written along the side of foregoing, but each line of this side-writing is cut at both ends causing loss of words or parts of words.)

. . . I pray you desyre Girsell that I may have a small Quantitie off . . . such as may be of a good stealnesse (staleness) by that tyme. My little ones are ex . . . and I am, Yor faithfull friend and Servant

Montgomerie.

. . . att Mrs. Ken her house
. . . John's Lane Febry 5, 1656. remember me most kindely to honest Mr. Gill."

Systematic persecution of the royalists ceased with the coming of Henry Cromwell to Ireland. His policy was to conciliate all parties. He made an effort to find a common working ground for Presbyterians, Independents, and Anabaptists,

" but to no purpose for these parties cou'd not be twisted together more than a rope can be made of sand."

The great change in the attitude of the rulers of Ireland induced Montgomery to go to Dublin to pay his respects to his Excellency. There he had an

" attack of sickness which did cast him into a deep palsy that seized all one side of him,"

but after many weeks he recovered and returned to Newtownards, there to enjoy the company of his grandmother, mother, sister, brother, and " honest kind Major Genl. Monro," now released.

December 1659 saw the last of Montgomery's troubles from Parliamentarians. On the 29th day of May, 1660, Charles II. became King. Montgomery, who had been active in his interest, hurried to Whitehall to kiss his

Majesty's hand. Honours many were showered on him; he
was created Earl in 1661, taking the name of the house at
Comber, Mount-Alexander, for title,—receiving a grant of
lands in County of Kildare (to be revoked later); received
appointment as Master of the Ordnance and Military stores
for Ireland; married for second wife " a very good lady,"
the widow of Sir William Parsons,—a union which seems to
have been a happy one.

And now, for three short years, happiness and the promise
of tranquillity seem to have come to the troubled Earl.
Arrangements had been made for the settlement of his debts,.
by gales from the rents of his estate, within five years; all
of this income retained by him in this period not to exceed
£500 per annum for the maintenance, at boarding-schools
in Dublin, of his daughter and two sons of his first marriage.
His lady's jointure furnished means for housekeeping, his
pay supplied him in clothes and coaches (which were splendid),
and he had a round yearly sum to spare. But,—and he was
under 40 years of age,—" his body being grown unwieldy and
bulksome," a fatal lethargy attacked him—the drowsy
distemper of his father,—and on a hurried journey from Mount-
Alexander to Dublin, this best of the Montgomerys died at
Dromore, 15th September, 1663,—the poor heart bared to the
curiosity of a king, now " wissened and shrivelled to less than
it should be," ceased to beat. He was buried by torchlight
in the church his grandfather had restored,—the procession,
with great pomp and heraldic display, being ordered by the
nan who loved him,—the sometime student at Leyden,—
ıis chronicler to be, who says :—

> " With what fortitude, discretion, Christian patience, affyance on
> God, prudence and pity on men and foresight on affairs he made
> his way through the different passages of his life . . . .
> his very enemys found his Christian forgiveness and generosity
> . . . his devotion pure and unmixed, being done for duty's
> sake and not to serve secular ends . . . his was the heart
> of oak for honesty and fidelity in right principles. . . . I
> write affectionately and without flattery."

To return to the Hamiltons. Although James, second Lord Claneboye,—first Earl of Clanbrassil,—had not been nearly so active in the royalist interest as his friend Montgomery, he had suffered much loss from the wars, and the exactions of the Parliamentary party when success came to their hands. His young heir, at the time of his father's death, was at Oxford, whence he was hurriedly recalled, and there were family hopes and purposes for a marriage which would bring a handsome dowry to make good the wastages of estate in the wars. But the young man would not be guided for his welfare, " being very much drawn to idleness and low companionship." He saw a wife to please him in Lady Alice Moore, daughter of the Earl of Drogheda, a lady admittedly " very handsome, witty and well bred," but

> " giving too much opportunity and access to noblemen and gentlemen reputed vitious,"

portionless, yet prodigal, and

> " to the great grief of his mother and trouble of all his relatives "

he married his charmer. Her extravagances added so much to the burdens of debt on the estate that her husband had to sell a considerable portion of his lands. The grim old Castle of Killileagh was too dull for her Ladyship, who liked to be much abroad—in the city of Dublin—and afterwards at the Court of England. There is a reference to her in the Rawdon letters which is not to the witty lady's credit—" she thinks to trip up Nell Gwin's heels."

One child was born of the marriage, but survived only two months, and now her Ladyship began to press her husband to set aside the disposition of the estates made by his father, and to settle the properties upon herself and her heirs. Such a proposition from a young wife to a young husband was certainly startling, and called forth the opposition of Clanbrassil's friends. His mother's warning was emphatic :—

> " Son, expect that within three months after you perfect such deeds you must lodge with your grandfather and father in the tomb of Bangor."

As a youth, "very much drawn to idleness and low
companionship" (*Hamilton MSS.*). HENRY, SECOND
EARL OF CLANBRASSIL. Through incompetence and
extravagance the reduced estate he inherited was still
further wasted. Died without issue, Jan. 12, 1675-6.
Portrait at Castle Ward.

JAMES HAMILTON of Tollymore; one of the five
cousins of Henry, second Earl of Clanbrassil, accused,
with his namesake of Bangor, of securing an undue
advantage in the division of the Claneboye-Clanbrassil
Estates.   Portrait at Tollymore.

But this Delilah wore her Samson to her will,—his Lordship

> " wanted not sense of his misfortunes by his Lady but strength
> to restrain them,"

and signed a will appointing his wife sole executor, and
making her heiress to all his property, after payment of one
poor legacy of £10 to the poor of Bangor, and with only one
condition,—that, " at or before her death " his dear and loving
wife was to leave £500 per annum to some one of her husband's
name and relation, as she should think fit.   Delilah had won,
and it fell out as the poor Earl's mother had foretold.

> " Within three months after, under very suspicious circumstances,
> he died suddenly ; was emboweled within five hours after, and
> privately (I say not secretly) buried in Christ's Church in Dublin,
> and soon after his corpse was lifted and sent to be privately
> intombed in Bangor."

So ended, in three lives, the line of Lords Claneboye-
Clanbrassil ; such part of the founder's vast territories as
remained at the death of the third Lord passing into the
hands of an unscrupulous woman.

Here is not place to tell the long story of the lawsuits
following.   The five cousins of the deceased Earl immediately
instituted proceedings to recover the estates, which they
claimed under the will of the first Earl.   Two of the five,
James Hamilton, of Tollymore, and James Hamilton, called
at the time, ' of Newcastle,' were empowered to pursue the
suit at joint expense of all, and these two were, later, accused of betraying their trust, and buying out, in their own
interest, the Moore claims for £2,400.   The indignation of
the three was great, but it does not appear that they were
able to obtain a remedy.   All that was left to them was to
accept such things as the defaulting two chose to give ; plus
their undisputed right to shares in the jointure of the first
Earl's widow.

The flighty Countess died before the termination of the
lawsuit.   In the year after the death of her husband she
married another Hamilton, Lord Bargeny, whose assistance,

advisory and financial, she counted on for maintaining her hold on the Clanbrassil estates. But this husband was not as pliable as the first,—

> " he straitened her so very much for money that she could neither live to her mind nor gratify her friends nor defray small debts."

A fire in their house consumed £4,000 worth of furniture and apparel.

> " She could not get herself recruited to that splendour she designed, being thus disappointed and also under great distemper of body, she fell under a high fever and rage and distraction by it . . . regretted the infamy and misery she had brought herself to, and the sad state of her soul thereby, and so died . . . her own friends neglecting her (tho' they kept her papers and what else she had) her servants took course to have body sent to Bangor privately, and so buried without any the least solemnity."

In the division of the property by the two cousins accused of betrayal of their friends, Bangor and the " fayre stone house " of the planter James of 1606, fell to James Hamilton, grandson of William, brother of the first Lord Claneboye, known first as ' of Newcastle,' but, after the settlement, as James Hamilton of Bangor.

For a little longer Montgomerys of the direct line were to live on the settlement, but with a gradually decreasing hold on the land. Hugh, second Earl of Mount-Alexander, was only 13 years of age when his father died. While yet a minor, misfortune came to him through the burning of Newtown House with all its contents. His interests were well looked after by the family chronicler, who spent much labour and many days in London in the interest of the minor, and who succeeded in obtaining for his charge a grant of lands in lieu of St. Wolstan's in Kildare, which had been granted to his father, and then withdrawn—by Charles II. Attaining his majority, the young Earl came to live at Newtownards in the gatehouse of the burned mansion, and soon after married for love, Catherine, daughter of Carey Dillon, who brought him no portion " except goodness, colmlyness and good

breeding,"—a good dower, but not of value in clearing an estate of debt. The young wife's beauty did not long adorn the gatehouse,—she died in the year after her marriage. Interest had not been paid on old debts, and these were now such a burden that, in November 1675, the young Earl sold to Sir Robert Colvil the whole parish of Newtownards for the sum of £10,640. Later in the same month another slice of the estate was sold to the same buyer for £3,000. Temporarily relieved from the pressure of debt, the Earl went to England and took for second wife Elinor Berkley—daughter of Lord Fitzharding, "who brought his Lordship very little money—yet run him into further debt." This Fitzharding is the Sir Charles Berkley of Pepy's Diary,—a worthless scamp, and panderer to the vices of Charles II. No good could come to the young Earl or his fortunes from such a union. In a very few years it became necessary to sacrifice more of the estate. A bit of common gossip at the little country town at the Earl's gates is found in a letter dated 1680, from Rev. James Gordon, sometime Presbyterian minister at Comber, to his daughter Jean at Edinburgh.

> "Receiv herewith some of myne own & brethren's principles which I did communicat some 2 years agoe unto my poore Earle of Mount-Alex^r. His English Lady and highlie Episcopall has moved him to fall off his estat almost, and its very like at her father lord Fitts harding his coming over to Ireland she'll move him next to goe live in England."

In a very few years it became necessary to sacrifice more of the estate, and, this time, in 1679, the manor and lordship of Mount-Alexander went to Sir Robert Colvil for the sum of £9,780,—the Earl reserving only the Manor house and farm buildings, gardens, orchards, and demesnes, with certain townlands, tithes, etc. This Montgomery seems to have passed his time in struggles to be free from debt, and struggles for preferment, pleading for this his father's losses in the service of the State ; losses which had necessitated the sale of two-thirds of what his father had left him. When he

died in 1716, without issue, the title and such small part
of the estate as remained fell to his brother Henry, who had
been living the quiet life of a country gentleman at Rogerstown
near Dublin.

His sorrows and distractions notwithstanding, the second
Earl did not neglect full development of his powers. The
picture here given of the attainments and accomplishments
of this gentleman of Down, is taken from the Montgomery
Manuscripts :—

> " The remarks I have made in ye 2d Earle of Mount Alexander,
> in w^h he resembles his most worthy patern and parent, the late
> Earle, I observe to bee these.
>
> " Imprimis. His upright justice, in paying his fathers and
> his own creditors. So the late Lord sold all his lands in Scotl^d
> to defray his fathers and grandfathers debts, with use upon use
> (called the annualls, and the custom in Scotland so to charge
> debtors) and the principall debt, and the charges of sending out
> men to the warrs according to his lands. In all which, his late
> Lo^p was imposed upon neatly by his receavers and agents (they
> are called factors and doers in Scotland) both here and ther
> when ye accounts of many years came to be taken of the estate
> for and during ye warrs of Ireland. So this present Earle acted
> good and suffered loss on ye like account as his father did for
> justice sake.

2dly. His frugality, and yet he kept a gentile table in his adver-
sitys.

3dly. His Christian fortitude, in bearing crosses, vulgarly called
misfortunes.

4thly. His liberality in his former prosperitys.

5thly. His being a beneficiall true friend seasonably, and in the
best manner.

6thly. His penning letters gentilely, as to ye reason and succinctly
as to the words of them.

7thly. His doeing devotion and alms, withoutt a trumpett or
any ostentation.

8thly. His constant adherence to ye lawful Church wherein he
was christened and bredd.

9thly. His right martiall way commanding and governing the royall fort at Charlemont; his s^d company and troops towards which he was carefull and kind; wth his faithfulness in his present imploym^t over the artillery to save charges to the King, as well as his former prudent and assidious endeavours and struglings ag^t ye Irish.

10thly. His goodness to servants, in preferring them to places, or enabling them otherwise to live comfortably and creditably.

11th. His complacency and winning behavior in conversation, and generous hospitality.

12th. His great ingenuity in poesy, which will appeare, when his modesty will permitt him to show to others the pieces of his composure; some of which I have read with an approveing admiration.

13th. His ability for Council and speech at ye Board and on the Earles Bench, wch doth also appear in his next qualification, to wit:

14th. His judgem^t in positive and polemic learning, and his apposite ready expressions of his sentim^ts therein, and on all subjects, as well occasional as premeditated, is beyond most of those who have studyed or dared to be teachers in pulpits.

" In all these premises (at least) with skill in riding, fenceing, danceing, musick, ye French tongue and mathematics (which are endowments gained by God's blessing, on his endeavour to acquire and make them habitual virtues or accomplishments;) I say, in all these, and, as I believe, in more things, his Lo^p doth truely patrizare, according to the old proverb, viz. patrem sequitur sua proles, which is the same with our common saying, as the old cock crows the young cock learns.

" Besides and over the aforesaid lovely resemblances, our present Earle hath an excellent hand in faire writing and true orthography for spelling words, and ingraving coats of arms, cyphers and flourishes on copper, brass, silver, or gold;

" As his Lo^p is a skillfull artist in miniature, with pen, pencil and Crayoon; his Lo^p is likewise a (scarce matchable) artist at violin, flute, recorder, cornet, hautboys, and the huntsman's musical instrum^t, playing on them all, not by help of his nice well tuned eare only, but by ye diversity of their propper sett noats also, with wonderful skill and dexterity, to ye extraordinary satisfaction of discerning hearers.

" All which utensills for ye ey and eare are laid aside or hung up and slighted (like as the Jewish harps were at Babilon) or are with his neglected recreations with ye muses, thrown into unseen places, ever since council board, parliament, assizes, and session business, were his avocations from those painting and musical divertisements of his melancholy.

" Furthermore, at his own or a friend's house, and before a select company (in the time of his retired condition) he did condescend (sometimes) to show some rare fates of legerdumain, and did act the mimick, both which he did to admiration, but in the latter of these he personated a drunken man, and so lively counterfeited one, that a person of quality who knew his temperance (coming unexpected) wondered extreamely and believed him really fudled to the last degree ; wee hunored ye mistake till his Lo^P reeled to ye window and rubbing his face of a sudden returned to ye table as sober as he was at his rare showes, which were hushed up at ye news of the incomers being come to visit his Lop.

" His Lo^P's recreations abroad are now (mostly) doeing the K. and country service, and tending ye affaires of his grand mastership, and so they are at home ; but at leizure times, in the neighbourhood and in and about doores, he entertains himself with requisite visits, or in angling, or in using the setters for partridge, etc or by walking to take fresh aire, or in viewing his orchards and plantations and stables, or discoursing with visitants, or perusing books, or trying experiments and problems in the mathematicks, or doeing private bussynes for himself or friends.

" As for meate, drink and sleep (in which is Lo^P is temperate to a miracle) and a few of ye last named actions, they are the refreshm^t and recruiters of his natural, vital, and animal spirits, when exhausted by h s sedulity in the affaires of his stat on."

CHAPTER VI.

The Last of the Montgomerys.

THE record of the Montgomerys has hereafter no concern with military exploit or Court appearance ; it is a story of quiet country life. When Hugh, fourth Viscount Montgomery, second Earl of Mount-Alexander, died without issue, his brother, Henry, a kind, easy-tempered man, with no stomach for politics or military service, inherited the title and reduced estates. Coming north from Rogerstown, Co. Dublin, with his two sons, Hugh and Thomas, he took up his abode at Mount-Alexander, and for the remainder of his life devoted himself to farming. When his younger son, Thomas, fell in love with, and married a Huguenot girl,—the young widow of Phillip Grueber, a London merchant,—he did not set up a separate establishment, but brought his bride to his father's house. The lady was Marie Angelique De la Cherois, daughter of Daniel De la Cherois, of Lisburn, whose fatherly love and fine character shine in the letters he sent to his daughter and her husband in London. The spelling and grammar of these communications vary very much, for the old man had become blind, and could not always secure the services of the same amanuensis. One of these letters, in which he gives the young couple good advice and warns them against trying to grow rich too soon, is here given.

" Lisburn 20 March 1719/20

" Mes tres cher enfans,

J'ay recue votre lettre du 11 passé dans un temps ou j'estoit dans une rude attaque de goutte plus forte que je ne laye encore eue de ma vie & quy a eté aux deux pieds & mesme au genoux. Dieu mercy je suis quitte de toute douleurs. Il me reste beaucoup de foiblesse & ne puis encore marcher Je voy avec beaucoup de satisfaction comme vous pariossez contant l'un de l'autre. Je souhaite de tout mon cœur que cela continue jusque que a la fyn de vos jours pour nostre mutuelle satisfaction. Pour ce que vous souhaittez que je me rends aupres de vous il y a peue d'aparance que je le puisse faire veue l'etat ou je suis tant de la goutte que de ma povre veue quy est presque eteinte en sorte que je ne conois plus personne que par a voix. Quant au voyage que vous avez resolue de faire en France & revenir par la Holande je laprouve fort & prie Dieu de tout mon cœur de vous y conduire & ramener heureuse. Je suis tres obligé a mon beaufrere Couilliete de ce qu'i vous offre sy honetement sa maison. Vous trouverez de bons parans. Faite leurs bien des amitiez de ma part & n'oubliez de voir vostre cousine a Leyden & afyn que elle vous puisse mieux reconaitre porte avec vous la boîte & la bague pour luy faire voir & faite luy bien des amities. Vous devez voir ausy tous les autres parans. J'ecry aujourdhuy a Mons Vanderduyne tuteur de ma niece que vous devez dans peue aller a Leyden pour le voir & vostre cousine   Vous le saluerez de ma part comme tous les parans de ce pays la. Je suis persuadé que vous y recevrez bien de l'amitie. Je voy avec beaucoup de plaisir que Mons Grueber fait de bonnes affaires. Je le prie & l'exhorte sur tout a s'atacher a en faire de solide & de se garder sur touttes choses de ces negoces dangereux ou pour un quy reheusy il y en a cents quy se ruine   Garde vous sur toutes choses de vouloir devenir trop tost riche & n'entreprinez rien sans consulter d'habile negosiants & sur tout Mons vostre pere, que je salue. Reponde aux bonté que on a pour vous afyn que on vous la continue & avant vostre depart ne manque pas de m'envoyer la descharge que je vous aye demandé & que me promettez par vostre letter.

" He is of a sweet temper and disposition, affable, curteous and complacent" (*Montgomery MSS.*). HENRY, THIRD EARL OF MOUNT-ALEXANDER. Lived at Rogerstown, Co. Dublin, until 1716, when he inherited title. Lived afterwards at Mount-Alexander, Comber.

Portrait at the Manor House, Donaghadee.

Mary Montgomery

MARIE ANGÉLIQUE MONTGOMERY, née De la Cherois, who became Countess of Mount-Alexander. She survived her husband, and, dying without issue, what remained of the once great Montgomery estates passed by her will to her cousins, De la Cherois and Crommelin.

Portrait at the Manor House, Donaghadee.

Vos tantes vous remercye de vostre souvenir & vous asseurent
de leurs amitie comme font tous les parans & amis quy vous
saluent. Vostre cousine Daniel est accouchée avant heir d'un
garson mais quy est venu mort au monde   Elle est passablement
bien pour son etat. Il ne me reste que de vous asseurer de ma
tendre amitie puis que je suis & serez toute ma vie mes tres
chers enfans.

Vostre tres affectioné pere

D. De la Cherois

Saluez de ma part Mons & Madame Grueber la famille de Mons
Pigon & tous les amis que se souviene de moy Acheminé l'incluse."

Freely translated this reads :—

" My very dear children,

I received your letter of 11th ult. at a time when I
was laid up by a severe attack of gout, worse than I ever
had in my life before, and which affected both feet, and
even my knees. God be thanked I am now free from pain,
although still very weak and unable to walk.

"I see with great pleasure that you are pleased with
each other, and I wish, with all my heart, for our mutual
satisfaction, that you may continue in the same mind to
the end of your days. As to your wish that I should pay
you a visit, it is, I fear, little likely that I shall be able to
travel, remembering what I suffer from gout, and that my
poor sight is so nearly lost, that now I know people only
by their voices.

"For the journey which you have decided to make in
France, returning by Holland, I have nothing but approval,
and pray God with all my heart to take charge of you
and bring you back safely.

"I am much obliged to my brother-in-law, Couilliete,
that he opens his house to you so kindly. You will find
good kinsfolk. Remember me kindly to them, and don't
forget to see your cousin at Leyden. That she may recognise you the better, take with you, and let her see the box
and the ring, and give her my best love. You should see

also all the other relations. I am writing to-day to Mr.
Vanderduyne, guardian of my niece, that you are shortly
going to Leyden to see him and your cousin. Greet him
and all the other relations of that neighbourhood from me,—
you will be well received.

"I am glad to see that Mr. Grueber is doing well in
business. I pray and exhort him above all things to hold
to safe trade, and to avoid risky transactions, of which,
for one that succeeds, there are hundreds that spell ruin.
Keep yourselves, above all, free from the desire to become
rich too soon, and undertake nothing without consultation
with able merchants, and especially your father, to whom
I wish to be remembered. Be grateful for the kindness
shown to you, so that it may continue, and before you
leave, do not forget to send me the receipt which I have
asked for, and which is promised by your letter. Your
aunts thank you for your remembrance and assure you of
their love, as do all the relations and friends here.

"Your cousin Danielle gave birth the day before
yesterday to a boy, still-born. She is fairly well in the
circumstances. It remains to me now only to assure you
of my tender love, and that I am, and shall be, all my
life, my very dear children,

Your very affectionate father,

D. De la Cherois."

P.S.

"Kind remembrances to Mr. and Mrs. Grueber, the
family of Mr. Pigon, and to all the friends who remember
me. Forward the enclosed."

This letter is dated March 1720, and the end of his
daughter's married life in London is fixed by the date—25th
May, 1723—of a letter of condolence on the death of her
husband. Two years later the young widow became a lady
of Down by marrying the heir to the Mount-Alexander title
and estates. Much of Thomas Montgomery's time in the

early years of his marriage seems to have been spent in Dublin, on business connected with lawsuits—the Mount-Alexanders seem ever to have been occupied in consultations with lawyers and appearances before judges, wasting thereby much time and money. The young man's letters to his father, when not dealing with farming matters, are stilted and formal in the extreme.

" July 18 1729.

" The clover must be cutt and made very carefully up. Dictionarium Rusticum can direct y^r Lord^p how to use it."

The kind old gentleman of the Manor House portrait surely did not relish the strained artificiality of such a letter as this :—

" Dublin, Sept 23, 1729.

" The Pleasure of receiving your Lord^{p}'s Letter last Monday gives me allways a new reviving spirit in my confinement in this towne, wch to me is much more dismal than a realy confinemt, having not the pleasure of seeing the pure nature in its Lustre, mainly the green feilds, and the full satisfaction of y^r Lord^{ps} company, the wanting of wch is the greatest regret to me Imaginable, not only considering the filiale duty I am by nature obliged too, but the many other tyes you have obliged me in."

A letter to his wife, at home at Mount-Alexander, is quite free from such unnatural expression. He is at Donaghadee, to see Major Hamilton, who is " waiting for a wind."

" Donadee feb 6 1727.

" My Dearest Molly,

The People comes in soe very slow am afraid I shall not get home this night but will God Willing be home tomorrow by dinner, you Cannot Imagine what a vexation tis to me to be from you Considering the short time I have to stay with you and may he who is the occasion of my Journey suffer in the flesh Maj^r Hamilton is still here waiting for a wind but goes off this day my Duty to my Lord and believe me allways to be for ever

Yr

Tho : Montgomery."

The words, " the short time I have to stay with you," are
prompted by the thought that he is to go to Dublin again
on the never-ending legal business. He is there a month
later, and his Lady has a shrewd suspicion that he is in Dublin
oftener and longer than strictly necessary, and enjoys himself
there mightily. She has expressed her suspicion, wondering
if he really deserves " the name of dear Tom," and wounded
love replies :—

" Dublin, March 9th 1727.

" My Dearest Life,

How can you in yr last to me mention I doe not deserve the
Name of Dr Tom from you since I am very punctual of giving
you all the demonstrations of all the truth, and Sincerity of all
my inward Intentions to you, you cannot Imagine what uneasyness the Indifferent style in yr last to me thinking by it
you thought I was entirely given over to Pleasures and
neglected my return home wch I am sure I never gave you any
Reason to think soe, but will attribute all to too much fondness
of me People at a Distance may Imagine business is to be done
whenever they come to Dublin am sorry you think in the least
I should impose on you of soe much Reason and I of soe little
to make you believe Black is White, I will not answer all the
daring speeches in yr last to me noe farther than I will be home
as soon as I possibly can Striving all in my power to end my
affairs here I wish you had come up in my place you having more
prudence to guide you, and Judgmt to see duty and matters
more expeditiously done than lies in my power tho' neither
ashamed nor afraid to any I have to doe wth. I was with
Mr. Stevenson last night att James Blackwoods where wee
discoursed the affair of William Johnson over and as there is
noe subsheriff as yett named must take farther advice how to
have the execution executed and hopes by next post to have it
Ready.

" I imagined you had wrote to Mrs Caldwell to have yr shoes
bought ready made but finds by yr last tis only the Laces you
want wch I will buy myself and not trouble her wth it this day
I bought the Sugar, nuttmegs, mace, and sagoe and will observe
everything in my power you have desired me to doe I gave my
Lord by some posts agoe an acct that I gave you an acct in my
letter what proposale my Lord of Howth made and referred him

to your Letter to know whether twas Pleasing to him or not
soe hopes his anger will be appased Beef gives a very great
Price in Dublin soe woud if you think convenient tell now what
Bullocks you think you can spare you may make Robt McCully.
by chance tell some of Butchers that there are some Cattle at
M^t.Alexandr to be sold.

"My Captn tells me he lost the other night att the Groom
Porter 6o moydores and a Cash note of 38—and is dayly Losing
money att the Liuats he gives you his sarvice and to my Lord
and Birkie the Bishop of Limerick, make my Duty acceptable
to my Lord and the above named Ladies I hope you have lately
heard from my Father Lacherois and hope he has got his strength
again Mr. Crommelin need be under noe uneasyness for there is
noe division made as yett between the heirs I will add no more
but will leave you to Judge the uneasyness you have & doe
now leave me in by the stifness of your last letter but will allway
have the same sincerely for my Dr Molly wch is and ever shall
remain in the Bosom

of y^r ever

Tho. Montgomery."

The very interesting letters which follow are written
by the lady, who has, evidently, accompanied her husband
to Dublin at times to supervise his work and hasten the
progress of the legal proceedings. With the Frenchwoman's
vivacity she had the Frenchwoman's ability in conducting
business, and doubtless the legal matters requiring attention
at Dublin moved more quickly and satisfactorily for her
presence. She never quite mastered the tongue of her
adopted country, as will be seen by the letters which have
been copied from the originals in the Manor House of
Donaghadee. These little epistles in broken English help
us to get a glimpse of the Mount-Alexander household in
being. The ' Janny ' or ' Jenny ' of the correspondence was
Miss Jane Montgomery, sister of Thomas, who appears to
have acted as housekeeper for her father during her sister-
in-law's absence.

And now that the troubled story of the Montgomerys

is drawing to an end, it is pleasant to come to " domestick
affaires " with the mistress of Mount-Alexander, and to the
living word, mentally heard, in her lively letters.

" Dr Janny,—I received yours, and am glad my letters comes
to you even after delays, it luckly there noe secrets in them
it is a great satisfaction to me to hear my father continues to
be better   I believe you begunne to emagine that I am settled
here for good & I am almost of the oppinion too for I cant
tell yet when we be home, but can assure you sincerely ther
nothing I wish for more, & that I am continually teezing Mr.
Montgomery to make all the hast possible : and besides the
pleasure of seeing you all I regret every fine day I loos, or att
least but half enjoys in towne

for my part that dont look on God marcyfull with a lover eye.
I thing (think) it was very rude of him to leave the country
without takeing his leave of you, tho it seems you give a more
favourable enterpretasion : but to leave off triffling, and come
to domestick affaires, you must certainly be mistaken when
you say there is but one bullock fatt.   I cant remember exactly
how many ther was when I came away, till I see the account
I have at home ; but I fancy there must be more.   If ther is
not, you must look amonst the dry cows if ther is any fit to sell,
& use them, and if ther is not, let me know it : the 16 of next
month Rachell time is out, so please to give her warning against
then.   I wod a done it before, but still flattered myself of been
home, for I will not be plagued with her any longer, so let her
provide for herself   It is now full time to begin to stil : as for
the rok water you know how that made : for the milk (?) water
the herbs that are in it is mint, angelica baum, cardus, worm-
wood and merigold.   polly shaw knows the quantity ther must
be of each herb, and how the still must be manege, so recommend
it to her care.   there nothing worth writing here, so must end
in desiring you to give our humble duty to my Lord, and assure
his lordship we long extremely for the pleasure of been with him
the squire and the bishop give their service to you, and believe,
sincerely, Dr Jenny, your friend,

                                             Mary Montgomery.

Kiss pet lin and nest for me a thousand times.
              June 19th (? 1729), (presumably from Dublin).
Mrs Jane Montgomery, at mountaliexander, near belfast."

" 30th June (? 1729).

" Dr Janny,

Next to the pleasure of been att home nothing gives me more the hearing my lord and you are well I thought when I left you last it wod not be for so long nor doe I know yet when we will come but hope it will be soon you say I have been long in this expecttasion but I can only repait it is against my will.

I am very glad the coals are safe in but hears ther no lock on them which is very wrong david tel me that that was one the mans old room wont doe ther none here so you must send for one a munday to bellfast charge the post to bring a good one you get it for two sh I send half a crowne as for brewing you may get the malt ready and then brew it will be the better to stand some days ground let the post enquire if he can here of a tub of good butter & let me know the beef dont look as if the wer falling away let me know john oppinion about them Mr. Montgomery assure me the not the worst as yet so much for domestick affairs I walked to portevo a thursday to see mis ross I have noe news nor if did wod writ them to you since you are so ungreatfull as no to think me for acquainting you with that of Mrs. forresters death which I hear since is certain Mr. Montgomery gives his service to you & we desire you assure my lord of your most humble duty & that you believe me sincerly dear Janny your friend

M. M.

the squire is hurrying me to bed pray tel the post to send the letters here for tho directed to my lord the are for Mr. Montgomery & delays may be of concequence in business you know 9^{br} ye 30 (presumably from Donaghadee).

I have sent a crowne

pray send by andrew a p^r of sheets & 2 pillow casis som mould candles & other bigg ones 2 pecks of meal & order mould candles to be made & send table clothes if there be any clean."

" Dear Jeanny,

I had the pleasure of yours, and 1 am very glad that you are well, and evry thing goine so, but could wish and desires you to give me a more pertuculer accounte spacilly of the gardens, how the new gardener behaves, and he dus lords improving, and if ther is much frute ; if ther be pray send some as offen as you can and comberes to mrs mecartney. I hope by this

time that the cows is come for the people ; I need not recommend
you to manage them to the best advantage. I can assure you
I long to be home more than you to have us, and is sore against
my will I am here, and am teasin Mr. Montgomery evry day to
goe, but he cant as yet fix a time. as for news I suppose you
have heard by this time of the surprisen way of the king death,
which will occion a uneversel morning for a year, but it is not
yet know what the leaders will take. since I wrot you last I
was at hoath to see this new lord, where I saw molly Stephney
how (who) I like extremely, she seems to be an agreeable good-
natured geal ; she inquire very much after you. hoath is a
pretty place if it was improved. I did not stay all night. you
wer saeing you wer sorey you was not here when my lord died,
but you not heved seen him, for he wold not see no dody (body),
and refused to see my lord and lord Montgomery. my lord is
at rogerstowne. Mr. Montgomery gives his service to you. I
saw the last letter you rowt to him. I am surprise you give
attention or take notice of what megie says. pray order the
horse to be turned of the grond, for he was to take ameditatlly
away. as for hinds I wonder you shold emagine I was angry
att his goine away, since it was by my consent and order. let
me hear from you as soon as possible. pray let me know how
the pigoins thryiv, and believe me, your

                                         Mary Montgomery.

June ye 24 (? 1729), (from Dublin).

To Mrs Jane Montgomery, at Mt Alexander, near Belfast."

" dr Jeany,

    I received the pleasure of your tow letters, and has a great
one to hear you are perfectly recovered of your indisposition
I flatter myself that you wod be glad on evry account we were
home. I give you my word none can wish it more than I. It
very easy for one people that dont know one business to wonder
why we don't come home to try the coals. I find that ournot
coming when we have so menney calls is a sure proof we cant ;
as for my part that I am not encline to flater my self, the sayeing
that he has found a coper mine gives my noe joy, and he assure,
he was here last week, if it be true it well be a agreeable dis-
appointment. I well tell you a piece of news well surprise you
if you have not heard, I am sure it did me, which is that cozin
nancy crommelin came here yesterday, with cozin sam ; you

may believe a littel transported to see Dublin. it been what she so ardently wish for, tho I fear it will not answer her high rased expectasion, for besides that things seldom dus, the towne is allmos emtey, so of consequence but littel divertsion more then that. I hope our stay will be short. I am resolved not to tale one word of rachel in this, and cant forbear laughing, tho it wont become for the future, for I have this day lost one of my fore teeth, which is no small affliction to me, and yet as I say I cant forbear when I think rachel has been a consent subject with us in every letter; but domestic affaires must be minded. I believe it is cheper to buy vessels then to have them made, considering we must feed the man. I hope Mrs Meredeth well leave us a good legece if she deys, I am sure she aught. I am concerned my lord is so melancholy he certainly has a dull time of it, but I hope we soon meet. Since the secret is out and you know I have a monkey, I must tell you his perfectsions first, for his person I wod only wrong it to describe it for it is past my doeing, and to give you a idee of his wit or ingenuity, as you please to call it, I must tell you he washes all the china, and I designe he shall save a servant by putting him in tom place; I am sure nether lenny nor eu will preserve ther . . . in your good graice when you see him. Ill (I'll) buy your missling. I need not tell you after haveing wrot all this trash that had any thing here that could have furnished me with the plasure of entertaining you, I wod a wrot it you, so after desire you to present my most humble duty to my lord, giving you the service of all here named, I conclude. I assure I am Dr Janny, your assured friend,

Mary Montgomery.

July ~, (?1729) " (from Dublin).

" Dear Jenny,

By the date of your letter I aught to have got it a munday, but received but a wedenday. Considering how maney is lost, it well one gets tham a tall In your one before that, you mention a maid, which, by the character you had, you think her quallifide for our service. I wish you had writ me where she had lived; we could better guise (guess) what she can doe. I think to wait till I come home, which time I cant yet fixt, for I have disappointed you so offen that I wont pretend to say it til I am certain of it. Noe dody wish for it I am sure much as

Dr Janny

*j receiv'd all the things but robin mcculla
how often make mistakes has instead of the double refined
suger has sent powd' suger j have sent it back I
desire you send it back & yet the double for it which
i am charge for he may give it to this post a munday
the now j think on it you may send it by david low
must come a munday with a dozen of wine pray take
care it be well packed up send also two fat ducks if
ther is anny ther is 13 shirts so dont be uneasy if you
wont find the number
j hope you be mistaken in your conjectters for mr
montgomery assure me that we be home before then
but if j see noe appearances of it j will send
for you to have the pleasure of passing it you
mis ron was not here yet but j expect her tomorrow.
your capt dinned here yisterday I enquird for you
my lord dont ballk of goeing home ther nothing
worth mantionen here all give ther service to you
& j assure you j am as usale sencerly your
friend
mary Montgomery*

xbre ye 6

The writing of Marie Angélique Montgomery (née De la
Cherois), whose husband became last Earl of Mount-
Alexander. She had the Frenchwoman's genius for
economical housekeeping.

Dr janny

if robon hat thaugth fit to get
the things att marguessin janrery as j
had desired you to order him the mistake
wod not have hapened but it is now over
as for bruing j will have but one bow
bruced been yet uncertain when we come
home ther furs enougth to the fireing
no experce & as for ther trouble that not
to be much consedered you must have
a baril of ale made d if the malt be
good it will draw allso two barrel of
small beer j have sent a pd j haf of
hopp'j 3 dorn of emty botels pray
have their put up them you sent yesturn
came very safe j we shall be sure to
drink your halth in the oranye wine
if you were here we shoud j believe
joyne to it your friend that we gennud
drink in that liquor j believe you
were surprised to see the squire he
was home in very good time hed all
here give the servier to you M ry

The lady's home was at Donaghadee and at Comber.
The original letters are preserved at the Manor House,
Donaghadee.

my self. I am pleased and sorry that the harvest is in, for it amused my lord hows time is, I believe, dull at present. It vext me extreamely to here you say he had not gott a letter from me this month, for one honour I writ tow, which I had the honour to myself. By this post I promised you some time agoe to give you some news of your aunt stepney and her family. They are all well except molly, that has hurt her brest to that degree that the fear it will turn to a cancer. The are strangely divided amonst them self. I don't know for what reasons ; but charls has left his mother, and betty is gone to live with her upon some deferances the have had that is all I can learn of it. My lord and lady carteret are expected every moment, soe that the towne will soon be gay, of which I shant partake much till then. I have noe news. I hear lady conway and the joung ladys are gone for England, but not my lord. Pray let me know if it true, for ther is so meany lees wan don't know what to believe. I alsoe am told for a sure thing that mr. blackwood is soon to be marryd to mrs. grace mecartney, which wod give me a great deal of pleasure, for, besides that, I believet wod be very hapy. She wod be a very agreable nebour. I should wrot you this news from here, tho' in returne you writ me a thing that should a passed here, which I heard nothing of before, of crack (?) haveing made a young lady make a fauls step. He is not un-likely to doe such a thing, but if it is it has made no noise. I have enquired for musling. It is chaper to buy it from the pedlars. As for the apples, what the room wont hold the must be put in the cider house. I know of no other place. Mr. cromelin leave this tomorrow, and cozin delacherois only wait for a wind to goe for England. Nanny stays til I goe. She gives her service to you, as due the sqrire and the bishop, and believe me, as usual Dr Jenny, your sincere friend,

Mary Montgomery.

7^{ber} 11th, 1729 (from Dublin).

Pray take care of the preys for seed.

Mrs. Jane Montgomery."

The following letter appears to have been written from Donaghadee :—

" Dr Janny,

Pray let robin mecully bring to morrow from Belfast half pd of green tea the same as the last half a pd of tea the same of the last if the have no green of the same sorte let him enquire where the good & bring it for y have none he must allso bring two pd of rice & two pd of bearly one pd of singel refined suger those things he must get at sanders andrew must come home with them a friday morning He must allso bring two pd of duble refined suger let it the best patrick is in great hast to be gone for to take care of the horses so can add no more only I am sincerely

Yours friend

all give ther service to you I send a guinea send me my change by andrew be sure send to me candead a peack of meal the bread is so small that to compaire them let robin bring four loaves two brown & two white which andrew will bring let them be fresh backed 4 pennesons.

M. M.

X^{bre} 11th.

you had best defer the brueing til saterday then Mrs. english well be home & save you the trouble or help you."

Mrs. Montgomery's father, Daniel De la Cherois, died in 1729. He had been followed to Lisburn by two sisters, Louise and Judith, who escaped from France with great difficulty. Travelling on horseback by night, hiding in the woods by day, attended only by a faithful page,—their gold and jewels concealed about them,—they succeeded, after great hardships, in reaching Leyden in safety. Louise died in 1723, but Judith survived her brother for many years, dying, in the end, at 113 years of age, not from senile weakness, but from indigestion brought on by eating too freely of goose stuffed with onions, at supper on Michaelmas night, 1765. She never learned English—having been laughed at for mistakes she abandoned the study. For over thirty years she spent her time with her nieces, Mrs. Crommelin and Mrs. Montgomery (later Countess of Mount-Alexander), at Comber and Donaghadee.

She is the ' Mrs. Lasherway,' 105 years old, at the time Harris wrote his History of the County Down. Her grand-nephew, Nicholas De la Cherois, used to describe her as

" a little, active, sprightly old lady, who delighted in teaching little children."

The new lady of Mount-Alexander seems to have retained the affection of her sister-in-law in London, Mary Grueber, as will be seen from two letters preserved at Donaghadee and here copied at full length.

" London, 2nd December, 1726.

" Dear Sister,

You will be surprised to see so short a letter from one that so often writs epistles more to be caled by that name then Letters. but I can assure you it is owing to the want of time not of inclination we are so lately come to town that our life is in a perpetual hurry as you can imagine. but to come to the purpose att last your platt is Shipt on Board the Renard Thomas Moore Master directed to James Wilkison Esqr; I hope Dear Sister after so long a delay it may come safe to your Dear self pray be so kind as to enquier when you receive this Letter if it is got safe att that Dear Ireland where I wish to be with all my heart but am strongly in immagination you will think if I tell you what trouble it as given me that it would be beging a Compliment but be assured that if I could have sent soonner I should with much pleasure Mr. Magin had promised to have taken it but was not so good as his word but I believe the charges wont amount to a great deal and no obligation to the afforsaid Gentleman I believe their is no occasion to send you a Catalogue of what has bin sent nott doubting but you know it already I have seen the Bills of Lading that Mr Vigne intends to send to Mr. Wilkison. we came in town last Tuseday very much fatigued but judge how glad your bitty was, especially when I think I can receive your Letters a Day soonner than I could at Feversham which is much more to my satisfaction the same night I had the pleasure of my good Neighbours Mis Fauquiers which bears the affliction of losing their father with all the Patience immaginable they— themselves more than ever but continue their sivility very much to me and will I hope we are as much together as usual frank fauquier learns to play on the french horn so their is an increase of fortune to the Daughters So weak a constitution as he is that has a continual horsness to this Day and I believe will have as long as he lives Jack Walton and gatine was here and played at Omber with me for between frends I am the rake of the family

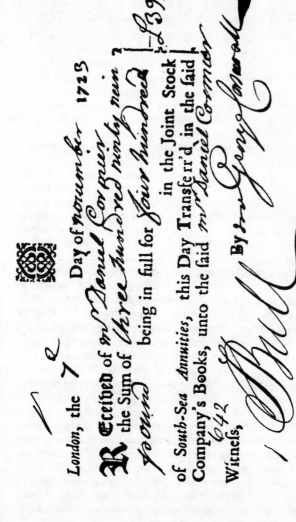

London, the

Day of November 1723

Received of mr Daniel Corquin
the Sum of three hundred ninety nine
pounds being in full for four hundred £399

in the Joint Stock
of South-Sea Annuities, this Day Transferr'd in the said
Company's Books, unto the said mr Daniel Corquin

Witness,
642

By mr George Caswell

The South-Sea Bubble. Receipt for stock taken by a member of the Huguenot colony.
Original at the Manor House, Donaghadee.

the first has bin given over by all the phisicians no body expected
his life of a Malignant fever but is pretty well recovered I have
not seen my Aunt Chevenix but am in hopes I shall one Day
of next weak and I am determind to know where her Son Daniel
is if he is above ground I shall find him out one way or another
for I will have what he owes me Gatine tells me some says he
is Maried to that Lady I have mentioned to you and that he is
att London pray God he me that I may be revenged of him I
own Dear Sister it is a little improper to allway's entertain you
with my distres but I hope as you are one of my most Dear
frends you will excuse it and take it from one that has never
found out so real a frend as your Dear self that I could have
any trust in I expect an answer not only to this but to my last
in perticular their is a very good prospect of getting mony for
us ever body is of the opinion that their will be undoubtedly a
War if so it will be well for the Powder Makers tho we whould
pray for the peace att home I have no time to writ you any
news for I am anxious that this Letter may goe without further
delay.—you me be fully satisfied that your Plate is gone I hope
you may abtain it without any deficulty since it is old Platte
pray Dear Sister My Most humble Service to Mr. Montgomery
if I can serve you in anything no body I am satisfied can do it
with more pleasure I must leave of tho with Reluctancy if I was
to follow my inclination I could set up all night since I think
no time is better spent then in writing to one that one loves so
tenderly as I love my Dear bitty which I beg—you would be
fully persuaded, and be ashurd of the unspeakable senserity
that nothing can efface the love that proceeds from

> Dear Sister
> Your Most humble Ser^t
> and affectionatte Sister till Death

December the 2nd 1726."   Mary Grueber.

" Dear Sister,

I am very much surprised of your long delay in not answering
3 Letters I have done myself the pleasure to writ to you nothing
vexes me more I do asure you then my not hearing from one
that I vallue and esteem as I do your Dear self I hope I have
never given you any reason to reject our coresponcy which to
me was most agreable if the fault lays of my side I am very
willing to own myself guilty and endeavour to make all things

easy as much as lays in my power tho I have examined all my
actions and proceedings in regard to you and may say for myself
cannot find the any thing that could deprive me from not hearin
from you I was always in hopes we should a continued writing
to one another since it was not my luk to live near you and by
that means being as great friends as ever tho the more I think
of you the greater love I have and shall to my last minut? I
flatter my self I have had the misfortune to have some of my
Letters miscary it would be to great a mortification to me was
I to indulge my self in the thought of your neglect the last letter
I had the pleasure to writ to you was directed att your country
seat for as you had never writ to me since you was att Dublin
I did not know your direction tho I asked my father that told
me you lodged att Mr. Colvils in stafford street I did not neglect
writing to you there but both my Letters have bin lost to my
sorrow for I had intrusted you with a great many things that I
should be very sorry any body but your self should be acquainted
with but as I have a great deal of confidence in you makes me
so presumtious. I suppose you have received my last letter
wherein I acquainted you of my sisters going to be tied in the
holly State of matrimony to her great joy and all the famillys
especially for your humble servant so dont intend to make any
further description of the Gentlemans because I fancy you know
it already by my last. I am just come from Wanstead where
I had bin these three Weeks last past att Mrs. Fauquiers they
have procured me all the pleasure immaginable as Dancing at
the assembly where there is a resort of the best Company in
England every munday you may asure your self I was not
bakward of going there the last munday I was there I had for
partner Lord Castlemain that Dances in perfection and I think
the most civil and polite Gentleman I ever spoke to so I was
very hapy for you know I love Dancing of all things we was at
his house two days before to see my Lady but unluckily she was
gone out we walked about the Gardens which are much improved
since I had the pleasure of going there with you the young Lady
went with me att a great many other fine houses and Gardens
to tedious to mention besides I am afraid my Letter would grouth
tiersom as I have not heard from you this great while att lest
this five months your mind may be altered and I should be
inwilling to do any thing—please to so intend to make an end
as soon as I have concluded the favour that must beg leave to

desire to grant Dear Madam that is to let me know your mind
if I shall cease being troublesome to you with my Letters or
continue as usial your proceedings with me makes me dubious
as to that affair tho—must tell you if you deny the thing in the
World that does me the most intrinsick I also desire you would
let me know if you intend I should remit you the remainder of
your—tikets ore put that mony out at use these things I most
hartelly wish to know speadelly to put me out of doubt and to
know if your health as also of your Dear spouse that I beg my
humble service may be acceptable to him in case you wont be
so good as to answer the Letter pray bid some body of your
acquaintance to do it that I may know my fatte which would
vex me of all things was I to hear a furbidance of my Letters
but I flatter my self to the contrery and . . . wont be so
cruel to deprive me of a thing I . . . great a vallue on pray
let things go on as the will grant me the favour of you innestim-
able that is so precious to me mine is not of so great a vallue to
you but is as sincere to the full and shall be to my last minute
your most humble servant and affectinate sister till Death,
                                                     Mary Grueber.
pray direct my Letter for me att Captain Burtons in fenchurch
street near the London tavern for fear of mistake i'll attempt
this way to see if I shall have better Luck.
                              August 26th 1727.

I hope you have received the fan I hope you will except tho the
present is not worthy of that favour but be asured if it was in
my power to have given any more no body should have done it
soonner but pray take the will for Dead Mrs Carmical was to
send it to you pray excuse the liberty it is only to put you in
mind of your bitty that loves you dearly."

On the death of the third Earl in 1731, his son Hugh
inherited the title and estates. Dying in 1744, he was succeeded by his brother, Thomas Montgomery, fifth and last
Earl of Mount-Alexander. For the last sixteen years of his
life his residence appears to have been at Donaghadee. The
Countess survived her husband, and as the couple died childless, the remnant of the once great Montgomery estates passed
to members of families of French extraction, relations of the
Countess, Samuel De la Cherois, and Nicholas Crommelin.

CHAPTER VII.

The Kirk in Down—I.

ONE of the ostensible reasons for Jacobean grants of Irish land to planters was the advancement of religion in the territories to be settled. The first Scottish planters were not neglectful of the spiritual needs of their followers and tenants ; they provided and supported ministers for the various parishes of their estates. These were generally men of high character and considerable attainment. Blair, brought to Bangor by Lord Claneboye, had been a professor in the College at Glasgow. Livingstone, settled at Killinchy on the western side of Strangford Lough, a great-grandson of Lord Livingstone, guardian of Mary, Queen of Scots, translated the Old Testament into Latin. He was skilled not only in Greek, Latin, Hebrew, and Chaldaic, but had also knowledge of French, Italian, German, Spanish, and Dutch. Cunningham at Holywood, on the southern shore of Belfast Lough, a man of saintly character, had been preacher to the Earl of Buccleuch's Regiment in Holland. Hamilton of Ballywalter was nephew of Lord Claneboye, and abandoned a promising secular career to care for the souls of the dwellers

in a little fishing hamlet of the Ards peninsula. Apostolic
in spirit and in the abundance of their labours, these, and
others like them, wrought marvels of reclamation among
the settlers, who, in part,

> " were such as either poverty or scandalous lives, or, at best,
> seeking better accommodation did set forward that way." (Adair).

If these teachers had a weakness, it was their forgetting that
they were not sinners above many on whom the tower in
Siloam fell. Readers of their lives may recall instances of
trouble coming to these good men that is treated as the
chastisement of a loving Father, while a like disaster happening to others is sin's punishment by an angry God.

The position of the early ministers of Down was peculiar,
in that, while Presbyterian in doctrine and principle, they
were admitted by the bishops to the parish churches and
received tithes. Nominally subject to prelatic rule, they
refused to conform, even in minor matters, to Episcopal
Church practice. Blair felt that he had wounded his conscience when he consented to allow Lord Claneboye and his
wife to communicate, kneeling in their own pew. Under the
influence of Laud this happy tolerant state of affairs came to
an end. Bishop Echlin, who had admitted Blair to Bangor—
asking to be present with Cunningham and others as " a
presbyter among presbyters,"—now showed a changed countenance, and began, in 1631, to press for conformity to the
practice of the Episcopal Church and subscription to its
articles. Blair, and others, refused, and were suspended.
On appeal to the Primate (Ussher) the suspension was
cancelled, but Echlin, supported by Laud, effected his purpose
later, and between 1632 and 1636 the non-conforming ministers
of Down were obliged to leave their churches. In the latter
year, Bishop Leslie—successor to Echlin—met a number of
his clergy at Belfast, requiring them to sign agreement with
the new Canons approving the Thirty-nine Articles. Cunningham and Hamilton, who had been unmolested by the

earlier proceedings, refused to sign, and with Ridge, Calvert, and Brice of Co. Antrim, were promptly silenced. Among the Wodrow MSS. in the Advocates' Library, Edinburgh, there is a report which contains the opening part of Mr. Cunningham's speech before the Bishop. It reads like S. Paul's farewell address to the elders of Ephesus. After hearing of the sentence upon Mr. Hamilton and Mr. Ridge, Mr. C. (Cunningham) spoke to this effect :—

" I have now lived this 20 yeirs among you in this kingdome serving the Lord in his holie ministrie and thot so to have spent out of the rest of my days (which cannot be long for my bodie is verie crushed) in the same imployment my doctrine & lyf for y^t tyme ar knowne to the most who are heir present I apeal to al ther consciences if they can say anything against me in ay^r of them ze I evir keiped me close to the comissione of my Lord, bot now I am required to receau impositions upon my ministrie which ar against my conscience I rather lay downe my ministrie at the feit of my Lord & Saviour Christ of q^m I did receave it, than to lieu w^t ane eivil conscience in the frie libertie at whos words most of y^m who was present declaired the greife of ther herts by ther sad countinance & divers burst out in weiping not being able to continow themselfs, bot the Bp. replyed to the purpose Mr C. I confes your lyf & doctrine haith both beine good bot I most say to you that which was said to a certaine man at rome who was to be put to death for inimitie some pleided for his lyf aledging he had done good serwice to the comone wealth & could noe mair erterwaird bot on of the counsal replyed ' *non opus est discere qui parere nescit,*' and so say I to you the church haith noe neid of thos who cannot tel how to obey which wt that he speidilie rose up & went away whil Mr. C was adressing himself to speik who much grieud y^t he was never hard " (Wodrow MSS., Vol. 25, No. 22, p. 15.)

A bishop might silence their ministers, but could not turn the hearts of the people from their principles, nor quench the love they held for their persecuted guides. The ejected ministers remained for a time in their parishes, and by private conversation and meetings of small numbers in convenient places, endeavoured unobtrusively to carry on their work.

How true the people, in the main, were to their deposed teachers, is evidenced by the fact that, when Livingstone accepted a call to Stranraer, some of his hearers followed and settled there ; and twice a year a large company—in one case five hundred persons—travelled to Donaghadee, and braved the risks and annoyances of a stormy passage in the small boats of the time, in order that they might attend the Communion service presided over by their loved minister. On one day he baptised twenty-eight children brought from the scene of his labours in Down.

It is outside the sphere of this book to attempt a connected story of the varying fortunes of the Presbyterian and Episcopal Churches in North Ireland. Such story, at great length, from the Presbyterian point of view, is told in the pages of Adair's *True Narrative*, Reid's *History of the Presbyterian Church in Ireland*, and other works. Here is only space to indicate, by a few extracts from manuscripts or books, the attitude of the two religious bodies to each other.

The author of the *Conduct of the Dissenters* may be allowed to state the case against Dissent. The writing dates from 1712. The Dissenters, it appears, had the audacity to ask from Parliament—

    " 1st   That, by a *Bill of Inaulgence*, a full security for the free Exercise of Religion according to their consciences might be given them.

    2ndly   That there be no such clauses annexed to it as may disable them from serving their King and Country."

The author says—

    " Upon this occasion of mentioning a toleration with the Test clause, their great champion, Mr. Boyse was employed, and did at this time very audaciously Address the Parliament with the case of the Protestant Dissenters of Ireland,—the desire of the Dissenters being stated in the two Propositions foregoing."

The author is horrified at the boldness of these requests, and continues :—

" Their (the Dissenters) Demands are no less than the Repeal of
Laws, necessary for the Preservation of our Constitution ; and
they are founded upon the plausible pretence of *Untainted
Loyalty in all Turns of Government.* Tis certain, their clamours
rais'd from this pretence of Merit, have prevail'd upon too many
honest Churchmen, and extorted their consent to admit them
into Places of Trust and Profit. . . . I have undertaken
to shew, that such their Demands are founded upon claims
notoriously False and Unjust."

Viscount Montgomery (third Viscount, first Earl of Mount-
Alexander) had foregathered with Dissenters to his cost, and
knew how evil were their thoughts and deeds. Referring
to the commission of King Charles II. to Hugh, Lord Viscount Montgomery of Ards, the writer proceeds :—

" His Lordp thought it necessary to signifie to His Majesty's Subjects of Ulster his Investiture with this Commission and accordingly published a Declaration Dated July the 4th, 1649, the
Original whereof I have seen amongst his Lordship's Papers,.
from whence the following Paragraph is transcribed *verbatim*—
The King our Most Hopeful and Undoubted Sovereign, having
by this Gracious and Ample Commission been pleased to appoint
me Commander in Chief of the Forces within this Province of
Ulster, etc., I do foresee and already have great cause to believe
that I shall thereby become the Butt and Mark, whereatall those
judgments and Affections are biased either by Envy, Malice or
Ignorance, will shoot their sharpest arrows ; and that even this
Honour and Authority, with which His Majesty has been pleased
to cloath me and which, till these worst of times, in all places
wherever either Religion or Civility were professed and practised,
did not only protect men from Injuries, but did procure Respect
and Obedience unto them, is now in the opinion of some misled
or mistaken People, become a sufficient ground to load even
Men of Honour and Integrity with all the Reproaches and
Injuries, which distempered Brains can invent, loose Tongues
utter, or rash Hands' act.

" It seems that this Noble Lord was perfectly apprized of the
Temper and Dispositions of the North at that time. For in
three days after this Declaration was Published, his Prophecy
was fulfilled to a tittle.

" A Presbytery was hereupon conven'd at Bangor near Belfast,.

July the 7th 1649, in which a Declaration was drawn up with
many scurrilous and groundless Personal Reflections upon his
Lordship, happy in the Scandal of such Infamous Tongues and
Pens, whose Encomiums would have been the keenest Satyr ;
as their Reproaches are the most exalted Panegyrick, and prove
the best Foyle to illustrate the Untainted Loyalty and Heroick
Virtues of that Noble Lord, in those Times of Tryal.

" In this Declaration his Lordship is taxed by the Presbytery
with these following Particulars :

1st   For lifting up himself against them . . . becoming
       the Principal Instrument to ruin them—if the Lord
       restrain him not.

2ndly for betraying the Covenant.

3rdly for owning King Charles II.

4thly for cloathing himself with a Commission from the King "
       (etc., etc., up to 9thly).

The insolent behaviour of the Dissenters, the writer
says, is equalled by their hypocrisy.   They have the indecency
to talk of establishing the Kingdom of Christ.

" By their assuming and insolent Behaviour about this time they
gave great occasion to make men judge they had not sought
only for the Preservation of their Lives and Fortunes but in a
Prospect of Establishing what they call *the Kingdom of Christ.*
After this they began to boast of their great Merit from the
Publick, their Rescuing the Nation from Popery and Slavery.
This was in the mouths of all their Agitators and Undertakers
nor wanted they powerful Abettors to urge their Merit so far
that they quickly obtained a Repeal of the *Oath of Supremacy*
which before had excluded them from Places of Trust and power,
and was the only Barrier against them at that time to preserve
our corporations in the hands of the Conformists."

The Bishop of Waterford (Thomas Mills) would have
no conversation with Dissenters.   He marvelled at their
impudence in building a meeting-house near his Cathedral.
Addressing his clergy at Waterford on one occasion, he said :

" As for Dissenters, they were the most inexcusable schismatics
in the world, and they should have no conversation with them
nor read their books and particularly none of Mr. Boyse's . . .
but confine themselves to the study of the fathers.   He was

> dissatisfied with them for conversing with the dissenting ministers.
> He wondered at the boldness of the Dissenters for building a
> meeting-house in that place so near the Cathedral   .   .   .   he
> saw not how in conscience they could read the burial service over
> dissenters, etc., etc."

Let now Dissent take up its parable against Episcopacy.
The (Episcopal) persecutors when they had the power were
unspeakably mean and cruel.   The saintly Cunningham
of Holywood, who spoke of his body as " verie crushed," at
the time of his ejection by Bishop Leslie, did not long survive
that event.   He died at Irvine in 1637.

> " Five weeks after his death, a summons was issued for him to
> appear before the High Commissioner at Dublin, and a fine of
> twenty pounds was imposed because he failed to obey—although
> information of his death had been given to the court.   To crown
> all, the officers seized upon the cows and horses of his widow,
> who had no other property remaining for the support of herself
> and her eight fatherless children, and kept them till security for
> payment was given to the amount of forty pounds."   Latimer
> (from Wodrow MSS., vol. lxii.)

> " At the suggestion of Charles, Wentworth determined, in 1639,
> to compel the Ulster Scots who were above sixteen years of age,
> to swear that they would obey all the King's ' royal commands.'
> This declaration was known as the BLACK OATH.   Commissions
> were issued to the northern magistrates to administer it in their
> districts.   It was to be publicly read to the people, who were
> to take it on their knees.   Scots who professed to be Roman
> Catholics were exempted.   But troops, sent to compel Presby-
> terians to swear, executed their orders with ruthless severity.
> Even Lord Claneboy deserted the principles of his youth, and
> became a persecutor himself."

(It is fair to Lord Claneboye to state, on authority of the
writer of the Hamilton MSS., that while his constables with
warrants were out to arrest persons who refused to take the
Oath, he had secret friendly correspondence with non-
conforming ministers and hid some of the persecuted in his
house).

" The Ulster colonists, horrified at the idea of declaring they would
obey commands, which were certain to be contrary to the laws
of God, and injurious to the liberties of the country, refused
obedience at the risk of being committed to prison. Many were
seized and brought to Dublin, where some were kept for years in
confinement. A man named Henry Stewart was fined in five
thousand pounds, his wife in the same amount, and his daughters
and servant in two thousand pounds each. Unable to pay the
fines they were committed to prison. Many thousands of
Presbyterians then fled to Scotland, and, although they felt
banishment grievous, they afterwards blessed God for permitting
them to be driven out of a country where, had they remained,
they might have perished in the great rebellion." (Latimer.)

Episcopacy in power discriminated against Presbyterians
in enforcement of laws.

" During the period of Episcopal ascendancy, it was the practice
to press with full force against Presbyterians the penal laws
seldom enforced against Catholics. The Papist was pardoned,
and the Presbyterian punished for violating the provisions
of the same enactment." (Latimer.)

The Episcopal party were willing to join with any sect
in order to persecute Presbyterians.

" About this time some Baptist ministers came to Ireland, and
˖divided the sectarian interest with the Independents. These
preachers were exceedingly ignorant and overbearing, but they
did not make much impression. The old Episcopal party,
however, joined with them to strive to maintain the persecution
of Presbyterians." (Latimer.)

The Bishops grudged to the Presbyterian ministry the
miserable little State allowance of £1,200 per annum (rather
less than £10 per annum per person) which had been theirs,
with certain defaults of payment, from the days of Charles II.,
and regularly paid from 1690.

" Year after year the Bishops attacked it (the grant) and urged the
Government to put an end to it. In 1711 we find the House of
Lords (made up largely of bishops) petitioning against this
grant, and at last they were successful." (Woodburn : *The
Ulster Scot.*)

Writers on the Episcopal side did not hesitate to aver
that the grant was not genuinely applied to the support of
ministers. It was used as a

> " Fund to plant and propagate their Schism in places where the
> numbers and Wealth of the Dissenters have not been sufficient
> to form a Conventicle or support a Teacher." (*Conduct of the
> Dissenters.*)

These notes apply to a period of, roughly, three-quarters
of a century. Such extracts taken from writings on both
sides could be multiplied indefinitely.

During the years of the period indicated, the influence
of the two parties alternately waxed and waned. Episcopacy
gained the upper hand in Down when Blair, Livingstone,
Cunningham, and others were ejected in the years 1634-
1636 ; and held it while Wentworth pursued his policy of
forcing all the Scots of the Northern Plantations under the
Episcopal form of Divine service. Presbyterian fortunes
revived with Wentworth's recall and the re-establishment of
religious liberty under the Lords Justices, Parsons and
Borlase. They flourished exceedingly from the days of the
landing of the Scottish Army in 1642, with their Presbyterian
chaplains, and the influx of civilian Scots which followed.
Presbyterian congregations with properly constituted sessions
were established in Down at Bangor, Ballywalter, Comber,
Donaghadee, Holywood, Killileagh, and Portaferry. The
year 1644 saw the signing of the Covenant—" to root out
prelacy, popery, superstition and profaneness." In 1645-6
another Presbyterian congregation was formed in Down (that
of Dundonald), and throughout Ulster thirty Presbyterian
ministers were preaching, without let or hindrance, to settled
congregations. A temporary reverse came with the accession
to power of the Independents, who began to persecute such
as were unwilling to sign the ' Engagement ' to be faithful
to the Commonwealth of England. Presbyterian ministers
refused to sign, and were banished as a consequence. Again
the flocks so numerous and prosperous found themselves

shepherdless, but not for long. Oliver Cromwell granted
the banished permission to return, with full freedom to preach.
Under his son Henry, as ruler of Ireland, favour followed
liberty, and the not illiberal provision of £100 per annum
was made for all Presbyterian ministers who cared to apply
for it. Now began a new and great immigration from Scotland which so strengthened the Church that, in 1660, the
year of the Restoration, the Presbyterian ministers of Ireland (thirty in 1647) had increased in number to seventy,
ministering in eighty congregations to nearly 100,000 people.

With the accession of Charles II. power reverted to
Episcopacy. When the King was practically a prisoner in
Scotland, he had been compelled to sign the Covenant,—
compelled, too, to listen while he was lectured in public for
his vice and frivolity. The dislike he then acquired for the
stern morality of Presbyterians accounts for the passing of
Acts of Parliament against Dissenters. Again the storm
beat upon the house of Presbyterianism. Nearly all the
ministers were ejected—Jeremy Taylor, in one day, accounted
for thirty-six of them ; and again the silenced ministered to
their people in woods and fields. The old trick of making
it appear that the ministers of Presbyterianism were disloyal
was resorted to. Writing to the Duke of Ormonde the
bishop says :—

> " May it please your grace, the perpetual and universal complaint
> of all my clergy, and generally of the honest part of the people,
> being so great against the permission of these pretended ministers
> to abide amongst them, and now every man being awakened
> with the late rebellion, and we being sure that many things are
> true which we cannot prove . . . I thought it my duty
> to propound the whole affair to your grace's consideration,
> etc., etc." (Mont. MSS., p. 248.)

Under pretence of complicity in the Blood conspiracy
to seize the Duke of Ormonde, Lord Lieutenant, and Dublin
Castle, many Presbyterian ministers were seized and imprisoned—those in the diocese of the implacable Bishop

Leslie, for six years. Belief in the untruth of the accusation
gradually spread, and, by 1668, the people began to build
' meeting-houses ' in which their banished ministers were
emboldened to preach, and observe publicly, the ordinances
of the Church. Most of these old houses have disappeared
or have been altered out of recognition. Those in Down
were thatched buildings, and were cruciform, or of the kind
called ' triple aisle '—represented in plan by the letter T.
The former had a door, and in some cases a gallery, at end of
each arm of the cross, access to these galleries being from the
outside by flights of stone steps. Again Presbyterianism
held up its head. With permission to worship in freedom,
the masses deserted the churches of the Establishment, and
filled the ' meeting-houses,' and the number of Presbyterian
adherents was greatly increased by the families fleeing from
Scotland to escape the persecution now raging there.

The Revocation of the Edict of Nantes resulted in an
accession of numbers to Presbyterianism. The bitter writer
of the *Conduct of the Dissenters* rails at the ingratitude of the
refugees in forsaking Episcopacy.

> " Before the late Revolution the French Protestant Refugees
> were received into the bosom of the Established Church of
> Ireland, with all possible Marks of Tenderness and Christian
> Charity. They had a Church appointed for them, a salary of
> Fifty Pounds per Ann was fixed upon the Establishment for the
> support of a French Minister Episcopally Ordained, they all Con-
> formed to the Doctrine, Discipline and Liturgy of the established
> Church by Advice of the most Eminent Foreign Divines who were
> consulted. The Government presented the Congregation with
> a considerable number of French Common Prayer Books, etc."

This kindness notwithstanding, the Huguenots had the
bad taste to join the Presbyterians. They

> " had chosen Presbyterian Teachers and erected Schismatical
> Conventicles."

In the long struggle for ascendancy between Episcopacy
and Presbyterianism it cannot be said that either side won.
Compulsion, and attraction (by opening the way to places

of honour or profit) at the hands of the Established Church,
alike failed to turn the Scots or their descendants in appreciable
numbers from their attachment to Presbyterian doctrine
and practice. To this day the territories of the Hamilton
and Montgomery settlements in Down are overwhelmingly
Presbyterian. On the other hand, Episcopal control of the
Irish Parliament succeeded in placing and holding the faithful
Presbyterian under great disabilities. It seems incredible
that the men who by their bravery at Derry saved the Episcopal Church in Ireland were soon, by the action of the leaders
of that Church," deprived of even the humblest public office."
It roused the ire of Daniel Defoe that the Defenders of
Protestantism should be so scurvily treated. It roused the
ire of the Champion of Episcopacy—author of the *Conduct*—
that Defoe should so far forget himself as to claim for Dissenters
equal rights with Conformists. What is the use of enacting
these salutary laws if they are to be eluded ?—" scandalously
eluded " is his expression.

> " There is one thing which I take to be matter of great consequence
> and which seems to have its Effect in their general Scheme of
> this Monopoly of Trade And that is That the Act of Parliament
> *Excluding Dissenters from Places of Trust* is Scandalously eluded
> in a matter of the last Consequence. For it is so contrived that
> Gentlemen who have never officiated nor can be supposed to
> intend it, have Presbyterian Deputies to act as Post-Masters
> who never so much as Occasionally Conformed. And farther
> that in some Instances Post Masters of Inferior Towns have been
> made Presbyterian Substitutes in Towns of much Greater Conse-
> quence. The latter is the present case of Belfast as the former
> is of Antrim, Ardmagh, etc. I desire to know whether any
> Instance can be given of this Nature in any Nation that the whole
> Business, Secrets and Correspondence of those who are Conform-
> able to the Establishment should be left in the power of such
> who are Dissenters from that Establishment. Is it reasonable
> that . . . the Secrets and Business of Persons who by the
> Laws of our Nation are only Qualified for Publick Trusts, should
> be left in the Power of those who by the same Laws are excluded
> from any share in that Trust."

Doubtless the provisions of the obnoxious Acts were
' eluded ' much and often ; nevertheless, the injustice of such
laws produced on the Presbyterian side a deep feeling of
resentment, while, by the other side, these discriminating
laws were made the ground for an assumption of social
superiority which expressed itself in unlovely ways long after
the Acts were removed from the Statute Book. Even in
the last quarter of the nineteenth century, a clergyman
of the Church of Ireland, quoting from the writings of a
Presbyterian Minister, refused him the courtesy title of
' Reverend,' and referred to him as $A *****B**** P.M.$
(Presbyterian Minister).

A century of wrongs at the hands of Episcopacy, with
occasional periods of supremacy of Dissent, bred in some of
the later Presbyterian ministers a temper less fine than that
of their predecessors in Down.   The rôle of the Hebrew prophet
was too readily assumed by the successors of Blair and
Livingstone, and old judgments on Egypt, Babylon, and
Nineveh were re-thundered against the Prelatic oppressor
of an Irish Israel.   Men of the prophetic denunciatory tongue
were hardly likely to lead their own flocks " where streams
of living water flow," and it would appear that the preaching
of this time to which the term ' faithful ' is applied, was
modelled too closely on the style of the Old Testament
prophetic utterances, and had little of the Gospel's power of
drawing with the cords of love.   In an old manuscript book
in the possession of the Presbyterian Historical Society at
Belfast, there is copied a sermon delivered at a Communion
service (date probably about 1675) which evidently has been
considered worthy of careful preservation. Part of it is
here given. Note the recurrence of ' stife neck.'

" Take this home with you from the Communion of Coyner that
Christ will bide in britain & Ireland and in testimony of it we
get a heart to pray for it & ye will not . . .   him alone till
he bide with you and if ye wold have him bideing : put to the
door everything that takes him to the door with your worldli-

ness to the door with your Carnality & Careless hearing of the
word to the door with all your Idols if you would have him
bideing : next they are a stife people what lies here   It is the
Case that they are in and Moses is very sensible of it the Case
is a stife neck ye may see 3 things wysts here.   1 Long in the
wilderness and yet stife necked many a cross is gone over our
head and yet stife necked 2 many wandere in the wilderness and
yet stife necked.   It is within fourty years since Ireland was a
wilderness yet many a mercy have we goten since and yet stife
necked Irland.   3rdly. Take notice of this a stife necked people
will meet with anger from God for there is ay an ill turn in their
hand that will meet wt anger 4thly. Take notice of this a swaying
body will   . . .   a stife necked people upon the hand of it
and the   . . .   of God upon its hand & Lord go with upon its
Hand to all at once when ever we go to   . . .   a stifenecked
people looke us in the face wrath lookes us in the face yet we will
not give over this Lord go with us.   Now Sirs wold ye think
of this thour he's a   . . .   full case upon they hand & a sinful
land upon they hand and when ever thou goes to prayer the
sinfullness of Irland turns like a gyant upon thy hand yet I will
make a argument of the stifeneckedness of Irland & plead with
God about it where in lythes this stifeneckedness.   There is
five peices of it and I appeal to your own consciences if ye be
not guilty 1 peice of stifeneckedness for all that came upon them
yet they and their lusts never parted Lord pitty the North of
Ireland O if our eyes that are ministers wells of tears to rune
down upon this account O Ireland Ireland for all that is come and
gone ye are not parted with your lusts 2 piece of stifeneckedness
they never submitted to God submission to the will of God they
never wan too that but when ever God began to Rubb upon their
Shins then they spake against God alace where is submission to
God where is a taking one (on) his yoke 3 piece of stifeneckedness
when ever God yoked with them they cryed down what God had
done for them & cryed down their present case and cryed up the
case they were in formerly above all many says woes is us since
we left off playing at the football on the Sabbath Day we will
not say that our parishes will say this but some old bodyes among
you will say many wea that ever Reformation was in the 3 Lands
we Reform ye better & will hear tell of it they cry ay one against
God when he begins to Rubb upon them they cry down the bonie
land of Canaan and cryes up Egypt they wold rather be wining

the flesh potes in Egypt with two or three onions than be in the pleasant land of Canaan nixt this stife neckedness appears by the many noes that the word gets   And though ye say not noe to the word yet we will let it alone till the morrow and maybe till tuesday and let me tell you it is the plague of the parishes of Ireland that they stricke not the iron when it is hot when the word warmes thy heart pray to God men & women that he would help you to hold to it, etc."

This use of the recurring word was apparently characteristic of the preaching of a section of Presbyterian ministers, and is perhaps what John Evelyn refers to when he speaks of ' repetitions ' as a fault of Presbyterian preaching. The convention appears to have affected sermon form for many years. The following short extracts are from manuscript copies in possession of the Presbyterian Historical Society at Belfast. All the sermons were preached in 1704.

Recurrent word ' LOVE.'   " Wee must not look upon the chastisment he lays one (on) his people as evidence of his wrath but as the mark of his love and that he will not sufer them to go one in their sins for every son he loveth he chastneth. O when God cheks us for our Sins we must not take that as a mark of his displesure but as a mark of his love not to let us go on in our Sins. All that are the objects of his love O the estem they have of him. By the sinceritie of our love to Christ we may disern his love to us O how ought wee to admire and wonder at his love to uss—gro not proude under the manifestations of his love to us but be humble and return love for love as Christ has true mutual love to believers, so believers have a true heart love to him."— *Mr. James Bruce, at Communion Service, Belfast, August 20th,* 1704.

Recurrent word ' CONSCIENCE.'   " The apostle exhorts timothy to keep the mistery in a pure concience while I recomend to you the keeping of a good concience it has the keeping of it selfe and uss too our Conciences while wee are here are but enlightned and wee see but darkle David a man after Gods own heart no doubt had a sanctified Concience Yet by diping his hand in the dish did wofuly defile his Concience a weak concience may be a good

concience and it flows from the weakness of knoledge by which it
is directed as a man may be a weak man and a good man so
concience may be a weak one and a good one too."—*Mr. John
McBride, Belfast,* 1704.

Recurrent word ' ALTERATION.' " What think ye of this the third
allteratione that a little time preduceth and first it is in the 11th
and 12th of exodus in the 11th chapter Pharoah commands moses
Sir let me never see your face again and if ever I see your face
again your head shall not stick upon your craig weet or ever
midnight Moses and aron and all ye children of Iserail is all
dismised out of eygpt that is an unknown allteratione in a
sudent . . . nere the end of the 14th chapter all the children
of Iserail is all weeping in the face of a read sea being pursheud
by enemies and having a rock on every hand in the begining of
the chapter they are singing over all ther sorowful songs in
triumph of victorie the songs of Joy that is a great allteratione
in a verie suden ther is a fifth great allteratione that ye wil find
in the book of Ester when ye see a living haman one day and a
hanged haman the next day Great is the allteratione."—*Mr.
Michael Bruce (preached in Scotland).*

Another example may be taken from the preaching of
Mr. McCracken of Lisburn. It is but just to say that the
report comes from the writings of an enemy to Presbyterianism.
The text was Galatians v. 1.

" His method of speaking to it was. *First,* He enlarged upon the
Slavery of the Jewish Yoke of Ceremonies ; *Next,* he descended
to the Popish Yoke ; then fell to a *Third* Yoke, in the manner
following, viz. There is, (says he), another Yoke as bad as any
of the former, I mean the Yoke of Common Prayer, of Kneeling,
of the Sign of the Cross, of the Surplice, etc. That is the Devil's
Yoke and they that bear it are in the way to Hell."

Not by such arid stuff did Livingstone turn many to
righteousness, and draw hundreds of his old parishioners
twice a year, over many miles of land and sea, that they
might hear the words of truth in love. Truly these,—the
spiritual children of the self-sacrificing type of Presbyterian
minister,—did not offer to the Lord service which cost them
nothing. When the Word could not be brought to them

they were willing to travel far to it ;—when it could not
be preached to them under roof by day, they would hear it
in field or wood by night.

It cannot be denied that Presbyterianism in Down (and
elsewhere in the North of Ireland) was, in the second half
of the seventeenth century, as intolerant as was the Church
established. The Conception of Presbytery as the only Israel
of God called for denunciation of, and war against, all outside
the bounds of the Western Holy Land. " We hold," says
Rutherford of St. Andrews, " that

> " toleration of all religions is not farre from blasphemy . . .
> if wolves be permitted to teach what is right in their own errone-
> ous conscience . . . then godlinesse and all that concerns
> the first Table of the Law must be marred."

In the hands of a certain section of the ministers of Dissent
at this time Fright and Force were the instruments for the
saving of men : the terrors of the law to frighten the sheep
into the fold and the rod of discipline to keep them there.
The rod of the magistrate was desirable for those who refused
to submit to discipline, but this never came into the hands
of Presbytery. Admit that these men were narrow, hard,
mistaken,—a tribute to their honesty and self-sacrifice
cannot be withheld. The outstanding fact their story tells,
is, that they were not in the priesthood for a morsel of bread.
When their incomes were suddenly removed, they lived hardly
and scantily, and ceased not, while free, by night and day,
to ride over large areas to perform the duties of their calling
for their scattered flocks. Few, very few, were they who
bought sustenance and freedom from harassing anxieties
by Conformity. Compare with their spirit that of the
Independents invited by Oliver Cromwell to come from New
England and settle in Ireland, where he wished their influence
to be paramount. Their reply was that they would come,
' If '

> " 1. he (O.C.) would establish their worship and Church Govern-
> ment as they were in New England.

2. would give them houses and lands in a healthy part of the country.

3. would enable their people to come with them.

4. would give them the right to choose the Governor of their Settlement.

5. would exempt them from taxes for several years."

Not so did the old ministers of the Kirk in Down count the cost and value their lives.

The intolerant spirit does not appear to have dominated Presbyterianism for a very long time. True, when William III. came to the throne, there were Presbyterians who became 'non-jurors,' for that, when the Papists were in the power of his troops after the Battle of the Boyne, he had failed to execute the vengeance of the Lord on them ; and for this, that while he was a pillar of Calvinism on the Continent, in England he placed himself at the head of a prelatic church,— and prelacy, by the Covenant, was " damnable, idolatrous and soul-destroying." But the majority were content to pray the King only for religious liberty, with a very moderate bounty from the State. The change of tone came with the knowledge that the Israel of God camps in fields wider than any that can be seen from one standpoint.

Even when the Kirk saw Babylon where Bishops ruled, the hearts of many of her ministers were certainly more charitable than their tongues, else would not have existed for them that lively affection which held the children of the Kirk of the Scots true to her against every inducement.

And what of the men who ministered in the parish churches for a hundred years after Blair, Livingstone, and Cunningham were cast out ? It is not uncharitable to say that they were undistinguished, unworthy Their indolence and mediocrity are easily accounted for. The parish church, with the old non-conforming clergy gone, was not the church of the Scots—the church of the people. The hearers, there-fore, were very few in number,—in some cases the buildings were nearly empty. The church was the church of the small ruling caste ; the incumbent, with greater security of tenure than the Presbyterian minister enjoyed, had far less incentive to work—far less demand for ghostly counsel and advice. Only a man on fire with zeal for men's souls could flourish in such a situation,—a zealot would not have pleased the Lord of the Soil. In such circumstances it is not to be wondered at if the incumbent became indolent, and sought the favour of his patron by becoming for him a sort of interested representative—a superior bailiff. Whom my Lord loveth he will love, with whom my Lord is displeased he will not parley. In the Castle Ward collection are various letters from Rev. James Clewlow, incumbent of Bangor (1730-1748), addressed to his patron. Not in any one is there an expression breathing interest in the spiritual welfare of his charge. He is My Lord's manager—indeed, he signs himself " a manager yt will observe your directions." He takes his instructions for the holding of vestries from his patron, who, it may be explained, is not pleased with the conduct of Mr. Blackwood of Ballyleidy (now Clandeboye), and the manager knows it.

" My Lord,

I observ'd yr direction in not holding ye last Michaelmas vestry, as yu desir'd me ; since wch time ye great Mr Blackwood had not looked me straight in ye face, I beg yt ye lease for ye new meeting-house may not be perfected till after our next Easter Vestry."

If " ye great Mr. Blackwood " will not comport himself to the satisfaction of my Lord's manager, he shall not have the lease of the meeting-house.

" Bangor, February y 19th, 1738-9.

" I would not have troubled yu wth any letter of mine, till priviledged had not it been for a discourse yt happened att Mr. Blackwood's table, last Wednesday. I was present. Captain Rose then complained heavily of the ill-usage he received from ye family, in being lately debarred from his right to his burying-

place in this Church ; says his mother-in-law, old Mrs Rose,
cannot live long, ye cancer encreasing so fast upon her face.
He declared when she dyes, he will have her buried here : says
if he is denyed entrance he will break open ye Church door.   Mr
Blackwood joyned him in ye justness of his complaint   Now,
this is to beg the favour of yr Lordship, to give me yr directions
how I shall conduct myself in case matters open as they threatened, and to send me such a letter as soon as possible, yt I may
shew, in my own vindication, shoud there be occasion.

" The cant is, if this be a Parish Church, whoever has a burying
place in it has a right to bury there.   If it be no Parish Church,
the Parish shall no longer contribute to the repair of it.   So at
next vestry I expect to meet with opposition.   Nay, I am
threatened to have my small dues taken from me.   This is but
a bad introduction for a lease of a new Meeting-house.

.   .   .   .

" As Easter Monday will be ye 30 instant, be pleased my Lord
to lett me know before yᵘ go your circuit, what money yᵘ will
demand of yᵉ Parish for yᵉ repair of yᵉ bells & steeple att this
time : I have some reason to believe yᵗ we shall meet with some
opposition, att yᵉ vestry about this : but I beg your Lordᵖ will
not grant a lease of yᵉ meeting-house till yᵉ vestry is over & yᵉ
shall have an account of our proceedings as soon as yu return :
they are now going to pull down yᵉ old meeting-house, I have
appointed overseers and a Treasurer. Old John Luke dyed
last friday without yᵉ least sickness, but a pure decay of nature.
The living of Portaferry is now vacant by yᵉ death of Mr. Rogers
of Lisburn & I beg yᵘ would be pleased to prevail wᵗʰ yᵉ
Bishop of Derry to joyn with yu in soliciting yᵉ Bishop of Down
for yᵗ living for me, be pleased to make use of my Lord Limerick's
name to yᵉ Bishop of Derry.

Yʳ dutiful servᵗ

Jas. Clewlow.

Bangor, Jan. ye 24ᵗʰ 1740."

His lordship is well advised to keep out of the way and
allow his capable manager to handle the stubborn Presbyterians.

" My Lord,

Last Tuesday we held a Vestry & yᵉ parishioners were very
unanimous in giving all their six days labour next year to yᵉ

donaghadee road ; but I took care to except ye corporation, in
ye act of Vestry.   I never saw so numerous a vestry since I came
here ;   But then there was great care taken, both by Captain
Ross & Mr Blackwood, to make their people attend it ; & ye
preacher in ye meeting-house recommended their attendance
from ye pulpitt : Mr Echlin, by y^r directions, desired to know
of ye vestry wither ye Parish wou'd be willing to keep up y^e
schoolhouse, att their own cost as usuall, & pay ye expense, now
due for ye repair of it ; & they declared against it : upon w^{ch}
I made no motion for ye repair of bells wch I am very confident
ye Parish meerly thro' ye Influence of Ross and Blackwood will
not be brought into without a lawsuit : But next Easter if I
live I will try y^m once more ; unless yr Lordship has a mind y^t
a vestry shoud be called before y^t time.   Your Lordship never
showed more judgement, in any small affair, than by not coming
to Bangor last Michaelmas ; y^r temper I believe has been pritty
well tryed at Castleward by ye tennants, from hence, but I am
persuaded it wou'd have been better tryed had y^u been here :
But by pursueing ye same measures one year more y^t y^u have
done this, yu will be pritty lasy for ye time to come ; & y^u have
a manager, y^t will observe y^r directions :

Y^r dutiful serv^t

Jas. Clewlow.

Bangor, Octer ye 10th. 1741."

The references to persons and places so well known by
Down men are justification for quoting the worldly Clewlow
at such length.

Another reason for the inferiority of the Episcopal
clergy is found in the unsettled state of the country for so
many years.   A man of good reputation and fair abilities
was not likely to leave a populous parish in England to
minister to a handful among prelacy-hating Presbyterians
or rebellious Catholics.   Therefore, until settled times in
the later 18th century, such was the dearth of good clergymen
that the incapable or discredited had easy entry.   The
difficulty of quality belonged to the higher ranks as well
as to the lower.   The evidence here presented applies not
exclusively to Down.

Clarendon, Lord Lieutenant in the time of James II.,
a member of the Church Episcopal and Established, no censor
of morals, has rarely a good word to say of the clergy. Writing
to Lord Sunderland on March 2, 1685-6, he says of Dr. Manby,
Dean of Derry :—

> " I could entertain your lordship with a great deal more of
> this dean ; how, in the two times he was with me, I catched him
> in several lies ; but think I have been too tedious already."

To the Lord Treasurer, in the same year he writes of one,
Jones, who had pleaded for preferment :—

> " There is one Jones in England, who was chaplain to my Lord
> of Arran, and by him made dean of Lismore : he has been in
> England near a year, gaping for preferment. I know, he is
> recommended to the king for his loyalty, as his majesty told
> me himself. I took liberty to tell the king, I could not object
> against his loyalty ; that I knew he was bred a clerk in the
> stables at the Mews, since his Majesty's restauration ; that he
> had wit ; but that I thought, by what I had seen myself, he did
> not live, as a man of his coat and calling ought to do. When
> he came to me at London to bespeak my kindness, I wished him
> to go with me into Ireland, and reside upon his deanery ; which
> would be a good inducement for me to recommend him for
> better preferment. His answer, in plain terms, was : that he
> would not go into Ireland, till he knew, what would be done for
> him. I tell you this story, in hopes, that you will take some care,
> that this man might not be imposed upon me at this time ;
> which he would look upon as a triumph."

And when a Bishop of Down (Thomas Hackett), after
six years' absence from his diocese, applied for license to
remain yet longer in England, Clarendon's reproof was severe.
His letter is dated from Dublin, May 25, 1686.

> " My Lord,
>   I have received your lordship's of the 12th of the last month
> by Sir Robert Hamilton ; and I had another before, quickly
> after my arrival in this Kingdom. I am very glad to find by
> your Lordship's last, that you are in so hopeful a way of recovery
> from your great and long continued distempers. Your lordship
> will give me leave to wonder, that you should in the very same

letter, wherein you wish to be permitted to enjoy the air of
England for some little time for the confirming and establishing
your strength, before you adventure on a journey, or the change
of air ; that you should, I say in the same letter desire me to
renew your license of absence for a year ; which I take to be
more than some little time. My lord, it may not perhaps become
me to go about to instruct a person of your lordship's rank, and
knowledge in your duty to the church ; it being more proper,
I confess, for me to learn mine from your lordship . but, considering the station the king has thought fit to put me in here,
your lordship will pardon me, if I put you in mind, that it is
now six years, since you have been from your diocese ; and that
the king by his instructions commands me to take care that
the clergy keep strict residence. Though your lordship has
several worthy persons among the clergy of your two dioceses,
who do their duties very well ; yet, by the accounts they give
me of the affairs of the church in those parts, I find an unspeakable
want of the bishop's presence there ; many of the clergy being
absent from their cures, and leaving them to mean and ignorant
curates, such as will serve cheapest ; which gives a grievous
advantage to the adversaries of our religion   and I should think
myself guilty of unpardonable failings, if I did not endeavour
all that lies in me, to redress those irregularities ; which would
not be very difficult, if your lordship were upon the place.

" Sometime since your agent applied to me to renew your
licence of absence for six months ; but I told your chancellor,
Mr. Lovell, that your former licence would expire the 14th of
this month ; that six months longer would expire the 14th of
November next, which, being just at the entrance upon winter,
I thought would be an ill time for your Lordship to begin your
journey, and therefore I granted your licence for three months.
I would earnestly request your lordship not to lose the benefit
of this fine season ; when the weather, as well as the ways, are
good : and if you will set out in July, by as easy journeys as
you can desire to take, you may be here before the 14th of
August ; which will be the best time for you to come hither.
I am sure, I need not dictate to your lordship the blessing as
well as the comfort, which always attend a man in doing his
duty.

" As for what your lordship mentions, and seems desirous that
I should do, to appoint you a coadjutor, I doubt not the legality

of it ; but it is a matter of great consequence, and requires to
be better considered of, than I have yet had time to do. But,
I hope, your lordship will speedily tell me, that you are on your
way hitherwards : and then that expedient need not be made
use of. I doubt not, but your lordship will have an account of
the death of Mr Robert Maxwell from other hands : he enjoyed
as I am informed, to the value of £900 per annum in church
preferments, most of them in your dioceses. He never resided
upon any."

The scandal of the ill service of the church by the Bishop
was so deeply felt by the Earl, that he wrote to the Archbishop
of Canterbury on the subject.

" To the Archbishop of Canterbury.

                                        Dublin Castle, May 25, 1686.
My Lord,
        I would not make any ill reflections upon greater and wiser
men, who have filled this place before me ; but certainly it is
impossible to help thinking, there have been great omissions
somewhere, when I see the deplorable condition of the church
affairs here throughout. The ruinous state of the fabrick of
most churches is very melancholy : very few of the clergy
reside on their cures, but employ pitiful curates ; which necessi-
tates the people to look after a romish priest, or nonconformist
preacher : and there are plenty of both. I find it is an ordinary
thing here for a minister to have five, or six or more cures of
souls, and to get them supplied by those who will do it cheapest :
and by this means some hold five, six, nay nine hundred pounds
per annum in ecclesiastical preferments, get them all served
for £150 per annum, and not preach once a year themselves
When I discourse with my lords the bishops upon these things,
I confess, I have not satisfactory answers ; but yet, by your
grace's advice and assistance for my support, I do not despair
of doing some good : for many things may be redressed without
any other difficulty. than men's doing their duties   . . .
that which has most entangled me is the bishop of Downe and
Connor ; who has now been absent from his charge six years.
Quickly after my being here he writ me a very civil letter, and
desired me to renew his licence ; which I refused to do longer
than for three months after the 14th of this month, when his
former expired ; after which I received another letter from him,

a copy whereof I take the liberty to send to your grace. I doubt, with submission to your grace's better judgment, whether this be a fit time to make coadjutors; but sure I am it is not fit to do it of my own head, nor by his advice, who desires it. I would humbly beg your grace to let the Bishop of Downe know, what he ought to do : for really it is a shame to think, how his dioceses lie. The dean of Downe is a very honest good man, and does his duty ; but he can do no more."

Primate Boulter finds it necessary to protest against sending him a Bishop from the Bench in England. He says (January 2, 1726), " I hope we shall not have one sent for being troublesome or good for nothing there."

A clergyman without knowledge of the language of the people in the place of his rule may be appointed to a Deanery—if " well affected to his Majesty." The following is from a letter by the Primate, addressed to the Bishop of London :—

" My Lord,   " Dublin, Sept. 6, 1726.

The bearer is Mr. Abbadie, Dean of Killaloo, one who for many years has made a figure in the world, by the writings he has published : I find upon enquiry, he was by King William recommended to the government here for somewhat considerable and would have had the deanery of St. Patrick's, which fell soon after, but that *having no knowledge of our language*, it was thought improper to place him in the greatest preferment in this city : However it was then fixed that he should have the next deanery that fell, which happened to be that of Killaloo, which was given him with one or two little things to make him amends for its falling short of the other deanery."

The Primate to the Duke of Dorset :—

" My Lord,   " Dublin, Feb. 20, 1734.

Your Grace would be pleased to order Mr George Palmer to be presented to the said Rectories. Mr Palmer is a clergyman of a *very fair character* in my diocese,

. . . .

" A deplorable account of the paucity and incompetency of the Protestant clergy is given by Henry Lesley, the Bishop of Down, who asserts that divine service had not been performed in many

of the parish churches for years together ; and by an inquisition
taken in 1657, it appeared, that only seventeen churches in the
diocese were in good, or tolerable repair, whilst another report
informs us, that of one hundred and twelve churches, all but
ten were in ruins." (Knox.)

At the time of the Revolution, Queen Mary pronounced
the Irish Episcopal clergy to be the worst in Christendom ;
and although capable men like Primate Boulter effected
much improvement, the clergy's care of some parishes must
have been deplorable as late as 1745, to have permitted the
celebrated Mrs. Delany to write to Mrs. Granville and Mrs.
Dewes on the appointment of her husband to the Deanery
of Down :—

> " It is very strange, but the poor have been so neglected here,
> they say they never saw a clergyman in their lives but when
> they went to church. . . . Never did any flock want more
> the presence and assistance of a shepherd than this Deanery,
> where there has been a most shameful neglect ; and I trust in
> God it will be a very happy thing for the poor people that D.D.
> is come amongst them. The church of Down is very large,
> but it is not a quarter filled with people ; the Curate has been
> so negligent as never to visit any of the poor of the parish, and a
> *very diligent and watchful dissenting preacher has visited them
> on all occasions of sickness and distress*, and by that means gained
> great numbers to the meeting. D. D. has already visited a
> great number, when he has been with all the Protestants he
> designs to go to the Presbyterians, and then to the Papists ;
> they bless him and pray for him wherever he goes, and say he
> has done more good already than all his predecessors ; *the last
> Dean was here but two days in six years ! "*

While the Established Church clergy in Ireland were,
thus, for long, unlearned, indolent, absentee, incompetent,
or of doubtful character—and the testimony above quoted
is that of their bishops and members of their own church—
the Presbyterian preparation for the teaching office was
ordered and severe, and none who did not stand the prescribed
tests received license.

The rules for education, trial, ordination, and settlement of candidates for the Presbyterian ministry, were drawn up by the General Committee of Clerical delegates from all Presbyteries met at Benburb in 1672 ; and became the law of the church.

> "These rules provided for the private education of candidates for the ministry under supervision of the meetings. Students were examined not only on their knowledge of languages, church history, and theology, but on their soundness in the faith, and adhering to the truth 'against Popery, Arminianism, Prelacy, Erastianism and Independency.'
>
> "All their trials were conducted in private, and it was in private they received license to preach the Gospel. When a licentiate had accepted a call, he was ordained in private, and at a distance from the parish where he was to labour as pastor. It was recommended that, immediately after his ordination, he would retire to Scotland or some place out of the bounds of the meeting. and perform the duties of his calling 'sparingly and by degrees' before he took charge of his congregation."
> (Latimer : *History of the Irish Presbyterians.*)

In the light of these rules let us learn something of their operation, at first hand, by turning over the pages of the hitherto unpublished diary of a raw country lad, student of divinity—John Scott, Donaghadee—whose course of training was proceeding in the years 1704-6.

1704

> "Tuesday yᵉ 31st October, I went to Newton (Newtownards) to the Presbytery and heard Hugo Ramsey & Nathaniel Orr have a piece Presbyterial Exercise before them on Coll : 1 : 23. Hugo yᵉ excercise & Nathaniel the addition—Mr. Hamilton likewise spoke to them at the same time that I should come up on trials, they told him that I should be very wellcome & desired me to be present next Presbytery day that I might be examined coram."

1705

> "Tuesday 8th May, I went to Ballywalter to the Presbytery wᵗʰ Mr Hamilton, Mr. Bigger, Mr Boyd, & Hugo Ramsey & Mr Ja : Ham : Mr Hamilton memorandum when upon the road homeward told me that my name would be given up at the Synod

in order to come upon tryals : Memorandum—that same day about 7 or a quarter after it Cusin Sanders Milling died."

1705

" Tuesday 28th August I went wth Mr Hamilton to Tonnochnive (Saintfield) to the Presbytery, and was there solicited by the ministers to go under examination in order to further trials, but I not being clear for, nor willing to proceed, they laid me aside & gave me my liberty till the following Presbytery. My unwillingness to concur wth their motion was because of my unfitness for so momentous & weighty a work."

1705

" Tuesday 25th September I went wth Mr Hamilton to Tonnochnive to the Presbytery, and was again set on by the ministers to go under examination in order to further trials. I opposed it strenuously, at length old father Hutchison became crabed (crabbed) upon the account of my unwillingness & aversness to concur wth the meetings motion, however, I continued unwilling (& that God knows, only because of my unfittness for such a weighty work) at length he pleased to pass me and directed his speach to Hugo Henry who then willingly went under examination in order to further trials. And the question he posed him with was what was the work of the first day ? the answer was, tho' not answered by him : The formation of light & when they had ended wth Mr. Henry they set on me again, wch was more than ordinar, at length I resolved through God assisting I should engage and proceed, & hereupon old father Hutchison put a question to me wch was this, Did Christ take upon him our infirmities ? I answered our natural infirmities yes he did, our personal infirmities he did not, & after some more questions were proposed I was put out of the Presbytery & wth in a little called again in. The Moderator Mr. Wm. Bigger mnr of Bangor was pleased in the Presbytries name to encourage me, & to tell me that it was their mind I should go under further trials, and that they had given me a text for a homilie wch was the 119 Psalm 97 verse for the management of wch I pray for the Good Lord's assistance. I came to Ballyhigle same night."

1705

" Wensday ye 31st Sber, I delivered about 9 of the clock in ye morning a sermon or homilie before the Presbytery at Tonnochnive wch did consist of ministers as follows :—

Mr Alex Hutchison	Tonnochnive (Saintfield),
Mr Ja. Bruice	Killyleagh,
Mr Jon Gaudy	Ballywalter,
Mr Henry Hamilton	Donnoghadie,
Mr Wm. Bigger	Bangor, Moderator,
Mr Tho. Orr	Cumber,
Mr Sam Shannon	Port-ferry,
Mr Ja. Montgomery	Knock,
Mr Tho. Jackson	Downpatterick,
Mr Ja. Reid	Killinchy,
Mr Henry Livingstone	Ballynahinch,
Mr Wm. Smith	Ballie,

on the 119 Psalm 97 verse but was censured by Mr Ja. Bruice & had likewise by Mr Alex. Hutchison, but that he said he did not hear me of wch i was glad however it did pass and was accepted of as a piece of tryal ; and then had another text given me (viz) Jo^n 4 : 10.   I came home same night."

1705 " Teusday ye 27th November I went to the Presbytery to Tonnochnive and in the evening about 5 of the clock I was called to deliver my homilie on Jo^n 4 : 10 I was indeed surprized when I was called, & that because I judged it would not have been (as formerly) called for till the morning and hereby I was much confused for once I made some hesitation & stop, & was really afraid of stopping altogether, but blessed be God, I was helped to go through & after I was severely censured I came in, & it was told me, that the homilie was received as part of tryal & was desired by Mr Bigger the Moderator to attend the Presbytery for further direction.   Within some time I was called & had given me for the subject of our Exegesis, *De Sabbati Sanctificatione.*"

1706 " Teusday 5th February I went to Tonnochnive to the Presbytery & heard Mr Mairs on Pro : 8 : 32, after sermon we dined, and after diner the Presbytery was again constitute & I wth Hugo Henry was called to deliver our Exegesis but were opposed by Mr Bruce, and that because they would not have time to impunge our Theses ; and to deliver the Exegesis & not impunge the Theses will be somewhat irregular and therefore said he it is better to deferr the whole till next Presbytery and it will be of

advantage to the young men too. Mr Hamilton, Mr Orr &
Mr Bigger did oppose Mr Bruce and said that it was not im-
practicable to deliver an Exegesis on Presbytery day & impunge
the Theses the next & therefore it should be brought to a vote
whether we should deliver this Presbytery or be deferred until
next morning we being as by plurality of vote it was carried,
to deliver our Exegesis next morning."

> " Wensday 6th March I delivered before yᵉ Presbytery
> at Downpatterick an Exegesis on *De Sabbati Sanctifi-*
> 1706 *catione* and was approven and imediately had my
> Theses impunged by Mr Tho. Orr and Mr William
> Smith, wᵗʰ Mr Henry Livingstone that was about
to offer an argument but did not.   I cam wᵗʰ Mr Orr, Mr Reid
same night to Killyleagh & was there p nocte."

> " Teusday 24th September I went to the Knock to the
> Presbytry & heard Mr Ramsey deliver one piece of
> 1706 exercise about 8 of the clock at night Mr Henry &
> I were called to give an account of our skil in the
> languages & likewise we underwent the questionary
trials ; and blessed be God we were approven & got off with an
enjunction of being in readyness agˢᵗ to morrow to deliver our
popular sermons."

> " Wensday 25th September, I delivered my popular
> sermon before the presbytry, and blessed be God
> 1706 was approven of, and then was licensed to preach.
> Mr Smith Moderator & Mr Ja. Reid Clark.   I came
> home to Donnoghadee the same day with Mr Hamil-
ton & Mr James Hamilton."

The late Professor Heron, asked by the author to explain
the words ' addition ' and ' impunge,' as used by the student,
wrote :—

> " When I was a student the same phrase as that quoted (exercise
> and addition) was in use and must have been in the old Code of
> that time.   I was required to present to the Presbytery an
> ' exercise and addition.'   The ' exercise ' was an exegesis on a
> prescribed passage of Scripture, and the ' addition ' was a series
> of propositions based on the exegesis.   Nearly all the reformed
> churches had what were called the ' Prophesyings '—the
> exercises of the interpreting of Scripture.   The First Book of

Discipline of the Scottish Church has a chapter on the subject.
Basing the custom on the practice of the church of Corinth
(1 Cor. xiv. 29-32), the first speaker was required to give an
interpretation of the passage of Scripture prescribed, ' after
whom did another either confirm what the former had said, or
added what he had omitted, or did gently correct or explain
where the whole verity was not revealed to the former '—and
in case things were hid from both, liberty was given to a third.
Here, I think, we have the origin of the phrase, ' Exercise and
addition,' although, as time went on, no doubt the application
of the expressions was somewhat modified.

" The second man might ' impugn ' what the first had said.
' Impunged ' of the Diary is only another way of spelling ' im-
pugned.' "

The form of call from a congregation to a minister at
this time promised him " all dutyfull respect, encouragement
and obedience," but the ' encouragement ' in stipend was
often very small. As late as 1674, Killinchy seatholders
paid only from 1/7 to 2/8 per sitting, per annum. Stipend
was, however, supplemented, often, by a stated amount
of corn or peat, or of labour on the little farm which the
country minister had to work in order to live.

Although the Revolution put an end to the silencing of
Presbyterian ministers, it did not, by any means, end Episcopal
effort for their discouragement. In the Wodrow Collection
of Manuscripts (Fol. 51, No. 48) is a Petition of the Presbyterian Ministers and People in the North of Ireland, in William
and Mary's time, praying the Lord Lieutenant to put a stop
to the activities of bishops and their officers who were seeking
to curtail the liberties of Dissenters in various respects. The
Petition sheweth—

" That whereas His sacred Mat^{ie} & Royal Consort of ever blessed
memory from their princely clemency & pious affection to their
peaceable & loyal subjects were graciously pleased to grant y^r
Pet^{rs} full assurance of their protection in the free exercise of our
Religion which hath not been only respected since by His Mat^{ie},
but faithfully performed & continued by all in chief authority
under him in this kingdom, your Ex^{cy} also being pleas'd of late

to strengthen our hopes of its continuance, & (tho' we are not conscious to ourselves of forfeiting the favour allow'd us) we are surpris'd to find some officials in this part of the Kingdom indeavouring to deprive us of what we have so long peaceably injoy'd, as appears by their pursuing both min^{ry} & people in their courts for their non-conformity to the rites & ceremonys of the church, min^{ry} for solemnizing marriage clandestinely, as they please to call it, & making void such marriages by obliging persons so marry'd to confess publickly themselfs guilty of the damnable sin of fornication to the no small grief of yor Pet^{rs} hereby made infamous, their children uncapable of succeeding to their estates & of diverse other priveledges as being bastards ; all wch we are persuaded is done w^{t}out the knowledge or consent of the Govern^t.   Wherefore we being necessitate to fly for refuge to yor Ex^{cy} humbly beg yor patient consideration of these few things.

" 1.   Your Pet^{rs} having been a considerable body of Protest : subjects in this Kingdom now ab^t 80 years who tho' dissenting from the Establisht church in some things, yet in all revolutions continued loyal and peaceable suffering for our loyaltie, in the time of usurpation to y^t K.C. 2d observ'd it, protected yor Pet^{rs} & gave the min^{ry} a royal pension, & we can't think our late active zeal for the preservation of this kingdom can be forgot by those who found our assistance so heartily granted & usefull.

" 2.   As the Establisht Church doth so we profess marriag to be a holy ordinance of God & a hon^{ble} state by Christians religiously & publickly to be entred into with pious exhortation & prayer suitable to y^t occasion by a min^r of the Word, wherefore it hath bin & is our ordinary practise & thro' God's assistance our resolution to so do when thereto call'd, not being free in conscience to conform to what the Service Book requires in this matter whereof we are willing & ready to give our reasons when requir'd

." 3.   As no min^r of our profession hath till now of late ever been troubled on such acco^t so the civil magistrate hath never made void such marriag or deny'd yor Pet^{rs} the priveledg proper to laufull marriag.

" 4.   All official courts have hitherto granted administrations, probat of wills, &c to the widows and children of such marriages as they did to others in the like case the parish Min^r also constantly receiving his accustomed dues as if they were marry'd

by himself whereby we believe they have judg'd such marriages
laufull else we do not understand how they could demand so
much money as they have received for many years from yor
Pet^{rs}. Wherefore may it please Yo^r Ex^{cie} to consider how
grievous it may be to a great part of His Mat^{is} subjects if all
marriages not solemnized according to the rites of the Establisht
church should be declar'd void & their children thereby bastar-
dized seeing hereby not only Presbyt : Papists & Quak^{rs} must
be great suffer^{rs}, but also many of the conforming clergy & Laity
descending of parents so marry'd, of whom we are well assur'd
there be severall in this kingdom, nor can it escape yor wise
consideration hou unseasonable at this time it is to move such
debates wch can't but create animositys & disunite the affections
of Protestants, when not only the consciences of some but the
reputation & civil interest of many must be deeply ingag'd.
We hope therefore God will direct yor Ex^{cy} to put a speedy stop
to such proceedings as are not only present grievance but may
prove of evil consequence to our posterity.

And yor Pet^{rs} as in duty bound will
ever pray &c."

The Bishops, however, did not relent. If the Civil
Courts declined to compel the Dissenter to go for marriage
to the Episcopal Church, for his soul's health or their own
satisfaction, they handed him over to Satan.   Gilbert Kennedy
(Tullylish), writing to Wodrow in 1716, says (Vol. 20, No. 124) :

" Our prelates are violent where I live. Four of my flock
have been lately delivered to Satan for being married by me.
I question if they'll take as many from him these two days as
they delivered in one."

For many years yet the astonishing bitterness of prelacy
against dissent was to be evidenced by charges and accusations
of a contemptibly trivial character.   In the reign of Queen
Anne there was presented

" To the Queen's Most Excellent Majesty
        The humble representation and adress of the Lords spiritual
& temporal in Parliament assembled.
May it please y^r Majesty . . . . In many towns they (the
Dissenters) have refus'd to take apprentices that will not covenant

to goe to their meetings : and wherever they obtain'd the majority
in corporations they excluded all such as were not of their own
perswasion.''

The Presbyterian answer to this charge was, that boys
of the Established Church, apprentices to Presbyterians, took
opportunity to embezzle their employers' property and
otherwise to behave badly, while they—the employers—
were at meeting. It was necessary, therefore, to take them
to meeting for their own good. But

> " with boys of known Probity and Honesty they ask for no assur-
> ance . . . Most considerable Presbyterian traders have
> taken apprentices without Stipulation."

Another charge, pressed by the clergy, against Presbyterians, was that of exclusive dealing. Forthwith 79 conformist traders of Belfast—the oldest, nearly 100 years of
age—printed a statement (Sept. 8, 1813) that the charge was
unfounded. The accusation of exclusiveness then took
another form ; viz.—

> " That the Presbyterians confined their charity to those of their
> own body—while the conformists gave generally."

Kirkpatrick produces refuting evidence in quoting facts
about the Presbyterian collections for the poor of Lisburn
after the great fire.

> " In april 1707 two men in Belfast collected £54 in 12 hours, and
> of that £51.15.0 was contributed by Presbyterians, which sum
> was handed to the Bishop of Down and Dean Wilkins, who
> entrusted it for distribution to two church wardens and two
> elders of the Presbyterian congregation in the district."

In a later case instanced by defenders of Presbyterian
generosity (quoted by Kirkpatrick) a Presbyterian collection
of £47 for distressed people was handed to the Episcopal
minister and churchwardens.

One of the most active promoters of ill-will between
the churches was the Vicar of Belfast, Rev. W. Tisdal (1712-
1736). He it was who formulated many of the charges against

the Presbyterians. Dr. Victor Ferguson of Belfast, with knowledge of Tisdal's pernicious activities, expressed in his *Vindication of the Presbyterian Ministers in the North of Ireland* what must have been the thought of fair-minded men of the laity, Episcopalian or Presbyterian.

> " O that men would look into their own state and infirmities, and lay aside all this *Bigotry* and *Unchristian Calumny* and attempt more the Conversion of Souls by the *Gospel Rules ;* which is the far better method to unite Protestants, and make them *truly Loyal*, than by these uncharitable aspersions."

In later times, freedom from the persecutions suffered by the fathers of the seventeenth century, appears, in the early eighteenth, to have bred a certain laxity in the religious observances of the sons. The Presbyterian remained Presbyterian, but that fervour which appropriated for its expression the words of Hebrew Psalmody, and literally construed the Hebrew singer's figurative expressions into rules for daily practice, had distinctly cooled.

> " I will awake early . . . evening and morning, and at noon will I pray and cry aloud : . . . My voice shalt thou hear in the morning, O Lord."

So wrote and sang the old Hebrew, and John Mein, brother-in-law of Robert Blair, modelled his praise and prayer on such words in their literal understanding.

> " He used, summer and winter, to rise about three o'clock in the morning, and always sang some Psalm as he put on his clothes : and spent till six o'clock alone in religious exercises, and at six worshipped God with his family." (Livingstone's Characteristics.)

But carelessness came with relief from trial. An article in an old manuscript book in possession of the Presbyterian Historical Society, and belonging to this time, gives six reasons for proclaiming a Solemn Fast. Two of these are—

> " 1. The Abounding of all Sorts of prophannesse, specially pride, swearing, Drunkenness and Uncleanness, and that of all sorts.
>
> " 2. The great decay and backsliding of those who once seemed to have a work of God upon their spirits.'

Reid, a successor of the saint-like Livingstone, at Killinchy, preaching on the 6th January, 1719, while admitting that it is not because they have waxed fat in worldly things that they have become poor in the heavenly, has some hard things to say to his hearers.

> " Alas ! there is plainly a great change to the worse in the state of Religion in this congregation since the removal of your former Pastors and even since my settlement among you. Many who who were great proficients in Godliness under the ministry of those eminent servants of Christ (his predecessors) are since removed by death, and the rising generation is not likely to equal their ancestors in piety. Before, and at my coming to Killinchy, there was in it a sett of Ancient Christians in whom the precious gifts and graces of the Holy Spirit eminently dwelt ; who spent much of their time in spiritual meditation, strict self-examination, fervent prayer and heaven.y conference, and were examples of holy conversation, but most of those excellent persons have now got to the Mansions of Rest and Glory, and we do not often see their rooms filled by a succession of other godly men . . . When specially in some years past I have gone through the Parish visiting from house to house where dear saints of God some time dwelt ; and when I have viewed the pews in the Meeting House where I had formerly seen Christians, indeed, sitting . . . and have sought to have my spirit refreshed with the beneficial converse or pleasant sight of some other good men risen up in their stead, I have found but very few such. Good grapes are very thin and rare in this part of Christ's vine yard . . . Yea, how many visibly Godless Persons and Families are there in Killinchy at this day . . . Many of you are under poverty and straits as to worldly things. Your diet and other provisions and accomodations are very scanty, mean and uncomfortable. Are you, at the same time rich in Faith, rich towards God ? "

An isolated voice crying thus in the wilderness might be taken as an example of humanity's tendency to call the former days better than these ;—there is, however, abundant evidence that religious fervour in Down had cooled. One cause, and perhaps the main cause, was the introduction from Scotland of that kind of teaching and preaching to which the term ' Moderatism ' was applied. A chance use of the words ' New Light ' in speaking of non-subscribing ministers and their teaching, gave the name to a party— for a time, the dominant party—in the church that had been one in faith and doctrine in the times of persecution. When ministers began to be unsettled in expression, especially on such an important subject as the Divinity of Christ, it is not to be wondered at that an uncertain voice in the pulpit should produce, first, a bewildered, and then a divided and careless people. It would be foreign to the purpose of this book to treat this subject at length—Reid and others have told the story—but space may be found for a few extracts from manuscripts in the Wodrow Collection, being portions of letters from Irish Presbyterian ministers of Down, or adjacent territory, to correspondents in Scotland.

" Among other tokens of God's Displeasure, we may justly reckon it not the least, that a spirit of mutual jealousy and suspicion is so unaccountably spread among our brethren in the North (both ministers and people) instead of being allayed is rather spreading more and more." (Boyse, Dublin, to Principal Stirling, Dec. 13, 1720.)

. . . .

" If some on both sides do not cultivate a better temper and more moderate sentiments will certainly rend us in pieces." (Lang Loughbrickland, to Wodrow, May 23, 1721.)

. . . .

" Our case continues deplorable . . . no appearance of peace and cordial understanding. . . . Love among ministers and people is colder than ever . . . some carefully fish for matter of reproach to the grief and scandal of others." (Kennedy, Tullylish, to Wodrow, Nov. 17, 1722.)

. . . .

" We are in the sieve and Satan is helping to sift us. We are threatened, flattered, imposed upon and subtilely dealt with, . . . We are like to be run down, not by persecutors, or open enemies or strangers, but by our bosom friends." (McCracken, Lisburn, to Principal Stirling, Nov. 12, 1722.)

" It is lamentable that woeful spirit of division and animosities
that is brought in among us seems to rage." (McCracken
Lisburn, to Principal Stirling March 26, 1723.)

This " woeful spirit of division," plus difficulties connected
with maintenance of ministers, plus land troubles, worked
to the disadvantage of Presbyterian growth in the eighteenth
century. In the early part of the period, remembrance of
ancient feud was strong enough to prevent any considerable
leakage of Presbyterian membership to the Established
Church ; but, later—when the remembrance of old wrongs
had faded—the multiplication of parish churches, while Presbyterian buildings showed rare increase, and the " class influence
of Episcopacy," accounted for a considerable transference
from Dissent to Conformity.

Although the title of this and the following chapter is
" The Kirk in Down," meaning, strictly, thereby, the church
of the Scottish settlers and their descendants, and its
affecting, or being affected by, the Church, by law established,
it may be thought strange that no mention is made of Roman
Catholicism as a force of the time in the religious life of that
part of Down with which this work is chiefly concerned.
The reason is that it was practically non-existent in this
territory at the middle of the eighteenth century. O'Laverty
quotes the following figures from returns made in 1764 :—

Hamilton and Montgomery settled territory.

Population, by religious denomination.

" Donaghadee—Established Church, 100; Protestant dissenters
1,848 ; Pap sts, none.

Bangor—Established Church, 400 ; Protestant dissenters, 3,025 ;
Papists, 12.

Newtownards—Established Church, 60; Protestant dissenters
4,750 ; Papists, 50.

Comber—Established Church, 315 ; Protestant dissenters, 1,220 ;
Papists, 165."

CHAPTER VIII.

The Kirk in Down—II.

FOR the first hundred years of the establishment of the Scottish Kirk in Ireland, the session of one of its congregations constituted a court of morals for the parish in which it was situated. In that district it dealt with every violation of God's law, of which it had cognizance, and which was not one to bring the culprit within the power of the civil arm. It had a high conception of its duty and of its authority, which was claimed to be none other than that of a Court of the Kingdom of Christ on earth—none so high in rank, and none so poor and low, as to stand outside its jurisdiction. To the little whitewashed session-room of barn-like meeting-house were cited alike the Earl who had broken faith with God's people, and the illiterate maid who had fallen from virtue.

True, the Court had no power to enforce its decrees. The cited might decline to 'compeir,' in which case the obstinate were cut off the ordinances of the Church until repentant ; but so strong was the attachment of the masses to the principles of their faith, and so compelling the influence of public opinion, that cases of refusal to submit to the Church's censures were comparatively rare. Submissive, the offender was admonished in private by the session, and, if evidence of true repentance were forthcoming, was absolved from his or her offence, on complying with the order to stand on the stool of repentance, before the congregation, for times commensurate with the heinousness of the trespass.

When the first Earl of Mount-Alexander, who had been Presbyterian in his youth, and who had co-operated zealously for a time with the Scottish party in Ulster, accepted a commission from Charles II. without the knowledge of the Kirk, his rank did not protect him from denunciation by the ministers assembled in Presbytery at Carrickfergus, on the 29th June, 1649. The concluding sentences of the letter, addressed to the Earl, read :—

> " The Lord will visit your family with sudden ruin and irreparable desolation, for that you have been so grand an instrument to destroy the work of God here. We exhort your Lordship, in the name of the living God, to whom you must give an account, in haste to forsake that infamous and ungodly course you are now in, and adhere to your former professions, otherwise all the calamities that will ensue will be laid on your score. The Lord himself and all the faithfull will set themselves against you, and we will testify of your unfaithfullness to the world, so long as the Lord will give us strength."

A second letter, written on 2nd of July, concludes thus :—

> " But you have involved yourself already so far in the guilt of unfaithfullness to the cause of God and your own subscriptions, that we cannot but testify against the course you are in, and denounce judgment upon your person, family, and a.l your party, till the Lord persuade your heart to return." (Reid.)

And even when his mother—who adhered to Presbyterianism when her son joined the Episcopalian Church—sought to have her grand-daughter,—the bonnie short-lived Jean, who was born while the Earl was a prisoner in the hands of the Irish,—baptized, by Presbyterian ministers, they refused unless the Earl would acknowledge his offence and profess repentance,—which he declined to do.

The fullest record of the disciplinary proceedings of a kirk session in the neighbourhood of the Scottish settlements, is that contained in the Session Book of Carnmoney; and no better way of exhibiting the strength and weakness, wisdom and foolishness, of the old kirk Session as a court of morals, can be found than by quoting liberally from its pages—as a whole yet unpublished. It opens with the note under date

1686

"Apryle 12th. The Session considering that after their long desolation it hath pleased the Lord in his mercy to grant them again a gospel minister settled amongst them they doe ordain all the elders to make dilligent enquiry concerning scandalous persons and delinquents in their severall quarters that they may be brought to the session to give satisfaction."

A later entry indicates the care taken to prevent neglect of duty on the part of the elders.

1697

"Feb. 2. Whereas there is a necessity that every corner of the parish be seen to as to the state of every family. The Session appoints that every elder duily inform himself within his prospective bounds whether there be any neglect of family worship, or any other scandalous sin and report the same to the Session, this to be done every month that the session may take course seasonably for redressing these anormitys."

The disciplining elder was, himself, subject to a discipline by his fellows. At certain meetings the practice was observed of Privy Censures. Each member, in turn, left the room, and while absent had his conduct and carriage discussed. As these were satisfactory or otherwise in the opinion of his colleagues, he was commended or rebuked and admonished. The following entries refer to this practice :—

170½

"Feby 15. This day privy censures were observed in this Session, and every one spoken to by ye minister as cause appear'd, and exhorted all to go on cheerfully and faithfully in their Master's work."

1700

" July 24. Every elder being remov'd his carriage as
Christian and elder was considered whether suitable.
Having gone through all nothing did appear to
ye contrary they were encourag'd & exhorted to
be faithfull and humble."

1711

" Jany 28. There were a few of the session who met
for prayer—who met not were rebukt and were
exhorted to be more punctual in the observance
of so great a duty."

Even the Session Book could be ' visited,' as appears
from the entry in handwriting different from that of the
time—

1703

" Sep^tr. Mr Patrick Ada r & Mr James Cobham
visited ye Session Book of Carnmoney and it is
approven."

The form of entry introducing a new case for consideration and discipline is in these words :—

" .... reports
that there is a *fama clamosa* of..................................that
.... is
agreed that..be cited to our next session."

Sometimes one who was not an Earl, and quite a common
person, treated the call of the session with disdain, as witness
an entry on 19th October, 1698, recording that one, cited,
replied that he " would not obey any such citation." Therefore it was signified to him that, while he continued refractory,
he was not to be allowed church privileges. Continued refusal
to submit, in another case, was punished by a review of the
refractory person's conduct after sermon—and the culprit's
excommunication.

" Mr Craford dec.ar'd after sermon (having deduc'd the whole of
the carriage both with respect to Presb^y & Session) Walter
Purdy to be none of our Comunion and exhorted all from any
such practices which may terminate in so dolefull issue."

A person, quitting the neighbourhood, could not join
a church in his new parish unless certified free from scandal

by the church of the old.   The first of the following extracts
refers to the case of a man who had asked for a clearing
testimonial, but it being in the knowledge of the Session that
he had written a scandalous letter, he had to mourn before
satisfaction :—

1705
" Sep^t 7.   Not being convinced of his sin in writing
such a scandalous letter we would not certify him
free of scandal, he was required to mourn for what
he has done & after that apply to us."

1706
" Decr. 19th.   Tomas Neil reprov'd for an offence
which was pardoned—applying for a testimonial,
this was granted . . . .
with an admonition that wherever he goes that
he be tender of the credit of the Gospell."

Accused persons could clear themselves by denial of a
fault on oath, but persons so willing to testify, and believed
by the Session to be guilty, were not allowed to add perjury
to their sins.

1698
" July 18.   Tho all due diligence has bin us'd ab^t
Isabel Young the Session can't get that light whereupon warrantably to found a process in order to
suitable censure.   She was willing to purge herself
by oath, but the Session finding these things in her
carriage, viz. too much levity could not safely admit her to her
oath lest she perjure herself.   Her danger was held out to her
both from the Sin, denyall, etc.—the Session would not proceed
judicially, but appointed she be dealt with by some privately
to see if she will . . . wth guilt."   (The missing word is
illegible in original.)

1698
" Sept. 4.   Jim Bryce who had offered to declare on
oath his innocence in a charge of scandalous conduct
—the Session considered the matter and think there
are grounds for considering him guilty—therefore
the Session thinks not safe to allow him his oath for purgation."

The most serious cases to come before the Session were,
naturally, those connected with breaches of the seventh
Commandment.   Whether exactly the same procedure was
observed, in such cases, by every Session cannot be stated.

At Carnmoney, the guilty parties were called before the Session,
and after admonishment were directed to confer with the
elders of their districts. These reported to Session what
was favourable or unfavourable in the attitude of the offenders,
who were again questioned and admonished by Session, and
again referred to their elders. For a third time an appearance
was required at a meeting of Session, and, this time, on evidence
of true repentance, the offender was ordered to " stand before
the congregation," as a penitent, for a certain number of
Sundays, generally three. Not for very many years did it
come to be understood that this exhibition of offenders of
this class at the Sunday services was more productive of harm
to the young and innocent than of good to the offender.

1686

" May 15. Margaret Dury being called apeared and
confest . . . .
. . , ... declared herself . . .
for sining against God and giving offense to His
people. She is admonished and exhorted, recommended to the elder of her quarter for conference with him and
summoned to attend the next Session."

1686

" May 19. Margaret Dury being called apeared not
and is ordered to be cited to the next Session."

1686

" May 26. Margaret Dury called apeared the second
tym confessing with seeming repentance her sin
of . . . . was exhorted desyred to
repair frequently to her elder and summoned apud
area to attend the next Session."

1697

" Nov. 28. Mary Huggin . . . . having severall
times been before the Session and appearing three
Lord's days and making confession of her sin before
the congregation (according to order) is absolved."

169$^8/_9$

" Jany. 4. Izbel Young apears continues obstinate
in denyall of guilt or any tendency to it. Rob.
Barnet reports there are some circumstances such
as a woman heard them converse but there is not
that weight to be laid on such generally the Session
can't proceed any further at the time but yt the woman apear again."

1699
"Aug. 9. Eliz. Johnson having stood 3 Lord's days was absolv'd."

In endeavour to get at the truth of a matter, and to punish the guilty, the members of Session could be guilty of positive cruelty. No zeal for righteousness can justify such a course as was followed in the case of an unfortunate woman, as reported under date

1721
"April 12. Agnes Craford, a midwife in ye cong^n was desir'd if she was sent for to Mary Wilson when in childbirth that she ye s^d Agnes would lay home to ye conscience of ye s^d Wilson when in her extremity that she would declare now when she is in view of eternity how (who) is ye father of that child she is in labour of she declar'd solemly it was Edam McCrogh's.

"On last Lord's day ye s^d Agnes was sent for again had several neighbours with her viz Agnes Steall Janet Kilpatrick & others Mary McKnelie likeways to bear witness to what was to be said the s^d Agnes being very willing to find out the truth pos'd ye s^d Wilson again & again who was ye father of ye child Wilson adher'd to what she said before then Agnes told her there being something exterordainary in her labour which God in his Rightious Judgment might do if she should desembel and she did not know but she might be a grave to her child then Agnes said to the woman we will go & leave her upon which Wilson cry'd out what would you have me to say crying biterly Agnes said will you tell ye truth she reply'd if I were to be a grave to my child I have no other thing to say but Adam McCrogh is father to my child after which within a quarter of an hour she was delivered."

The Session dealt as faithfully with the difficulties of the married, composing their differences where possible, censuring and admonishing the couple or the blameworthy partner. In the case of a man who had left his wife, the Session,

"finding it a scandalous way of living, a man and wife to be asunder,"

cited them to appear at next meeting. Both being present, the man professed to be perfectly willing to live with his wife, but she would not promise to stay with him unless he promised to move into another parish, which he could not do. The woman was reproved and warned, and the man advised to seek counsel as to whether he could be legally divorced. In another case of separation, no guilt being imputed, the parties would seem to have appeared before the Session of their own accord, perhaps feeling an avowal of their fault to the church court to be necessary for peace of mind.

> " June 23. Saml. Thoborn and his wife Jenet Girvan who had impiously parted without apparent cause
> 1703 some time agone, now being convinc'd of their sin & great folly herein, desir'd access to the Session. They now appear and being rebuk'd they . . . with their great sin & seem'd humble for the great stumbling their impracticable carriage has given to others, they promis'd to be more watchfull agt these things wch occasioned animositys & so their parting, being exhorted to their duty to God and each other they were dismiss'd."

Scolding wives, as behaving in a way calculated to discredit their Christian profession, received the attention of the elders in Session. The wives of Thomas Gray and James Grainger had been calling each other names, and were required to appear before the Session with their witnesses. It was a case of storm in a teapot.

> " Mar. 20. Elizabeth Grainger said she heard Gray's wife call Grainger's wife a hypocrite and Grainger
> 1706 called Gray's wife a witch, they being remov'd the Session considered the report with the evidences, judg'd both very censurable for taking such liberty in reviling each other, they were called in, rebukt and exhorted to a more Christian deportment wch they promis'd to study and professt mutual forgiveness and future friendship."

In another case members of two families, having had some unpleasantness,

> " are to be cited to our next Session, that cause may apear of the great heat in those familys."

Appearing, the whole matter was heard,

> " and the partys exhorted to amity and peace. This exhortation,
> by God's blessing taking effect, they forgive each other and
> promise to live more Christianly."

Many cases of small slanders occupied the attentions of
the good men.

1723⁄4

> " Mar 5. Mr George Russell desir'd to lay before the
> Sess. that James McRoy told him last Lord's day
> that Tho. Dawson reported in his hearing about a
> year ago and the hearing of others that Mr Russell
> stand att the Pulpit Door collecting for the publick
> money (as he believes) he said that Tho. Dawson gave sixpence
> halfpenny to the Box and that Mr Russell slipted it in his pocket
> to Buy pins for his prowd wife for profe of which he names John
> Hurdman who are to be cited to our next Sess."

Failure to attend the Ordinances was reason for the appearance of John McKeeg before the Session.

> " Complaint being made that John McKeeg does not duly
> attend the ordinances, he was call'd, rebukt and exhorted to
> make conscience of attending Gospel ordinances he promist
> so to do so he was dismisst."

The use on the Lord's Day of any words having relation
to engagements connected with the labours of the week,
called for censure by the Session. Note in the following
case that the complaint made in February must have related
to an offence dating back to, at least, the previous harvest.

170½

> " Feb. 17. Complaint being made by John Campbell,
> one of ye elders that Alexr Mathison had profan'd
> ye Lord's day by bespeaking on yt day some who
> might help him to cut down his harvest on ye Monday
> following, Mathison to be cited to ye next Session."

1702

> " Mar. 24 Alexr. Mathison appear'd who acknow-
> ledged his sin by an unwary speaking of his harvest
> on a Sabbath evening but did not agree with any
> reapers. He was rebuk'd and exhorted to more
> circumspection which he promised to do. Upon
> enquiry the matter did not appear so ill as represented, so the
> Session did desist from any further proceeding in it."

That the Session should exercise jurisdiction in a case
of complaint about language used on the Lord's Day, it was
sufficient that such language should prove to be " unedifying
discourse." It might be entirely unrelated to week-day
business.

1708

" Jan. 1.   John Wilson of Ballhenry delated to this
Session that Wm. McNeily spent a part of the last
Lord's Day in Sam McCrery's house in unedifying
discourse and complain'd that Sam McCrery himself
abus'd the said Wilson with bitter and malicious
expressions."

1708

" Jan. 14.   Wm. McNeily was call'd and askt why he
he did so profane the Lord's Day Jenat Cook, Sam.
McCrery's wife was advanc'd a witness to prove it.
She acknowledg'd tho all was not true that was
asserted by John Wilson, yet there was not suitable
discourse for the day, worldly matter being the subject, sorrow
was profess't, being rebukt and recomended that was over.
Also Jo. Wilson and Sam : McCrery with Alex^r. Birney were
confronted. On the whole we found much heat and indecency
on all hands. They being rebukt were exhorted to study the
fear of God and mutual love wch they promist."

Until the middle of the seventeenth century, belief in
witchcraft was still strong enough to account for the bringing
of supposed offenders, not only before the Church courts,
but also into courts of Law.   Dr. Colville, an Antrim clergyman, who lent the unfortunate first Earl of Mount-Alexander
£1,000 to pay off part of the Cromwellian fine, was a very
wealthy man, and as the country population did not know
how this wealth had come to him, they concluded that he
had dealings with the Devil. The strange thing in this
connection is that a maid who had been in the Doctor's
employment, being later, in service in Scotland, and
there suspected of witchcraft, confessed that she raised
the Devil by methods she had learned from the Doctor.
Three spells were used ;—the first brought up the head of
the demon, the next his body to the waist,—and with the

third he sprang from the ground. Adair would seem to have been a believer in the power of witches and evil spirits to hurt the lives of men, judging from his account of the troubles of Mr. Shaw, here quoted from the *Narrative* (299/300).

> "Mr. James Shaw, a zealous worthy preacher, was laid by, through sickness, this strange afflicting trouble coming on his family after the death of his wife. There had been great ground of jealousy that she, in her childbed, had been wronged by sorcery of some witches in the parish. After her death, a considerable time, some spirit or spirits troubled the house by casting stones down at the chimney, appearing to the servants, and especially having got one of them, a young man, to keep appointed times and places wherein it appeared in divers shapes and spake audibly to him. The people of the parish watched the house while Mr. Shaw at this time lay sick in his bed ; and, indeed, he did not wholly recover, but within a while died, it was thought, not without the art of sorcery, though otherwise he was not only valetudinary, but broken with melancholy."

It is not surprising, then, to find the Session of Carnmoney investigating accusations of witchcraft, and dealing with supposed manifestations of evil spirits.

> "Octr. 24. After prayer agnes (surname missing) apeard before ye Sess and made complaint that
>
> 1731 Sam^{ll}. Dawson had difam'd her in calling her a witch Sam^{ll} assured that he did not call her a witch but that he had a cow that had lost her milck and upon using some means to recover it again by the Instructions of Jo^n Laird agnes came to his House in a very great haste and said that her Ears were burning out of her head."

In the next case the minister, Mr. Crawford, appears to have been as credulous as any member of the Session. He brought the matter before the Presbytery of Belfast, and by its more sensible members was warned to look for fraud.

> "June 27. Thomas and David Bell made application to this Session, shewing that their house at Monks-
>
> 1702 town is haunted with some evil spirits, this matter consdid & finding it may be probable : the Minister

proposed to the Session if two of their number might be
appointed to go thither and he himself would go when
desir'd. It was agreed that Jo : Campbell, David Ferguson,
Sam : Cay and Robt. Barnet go to that house on Thursday next,
and Alex^r Kirkpatrick wth Andrew McCormick go on the
friday, that report be made to the minister on the following
mornings of the above appointed days of what seen or heard
and accordingly proceed."

1702

" July 8. Mr. Craford reports that some of the elders
appointed to go to Monkstown were wth him and
did shew that they did hear a noise wch they supposed
more than ordinary & at such hours wherein none
in the house were moving. The Session advis'd
that the Min^r. should consult the Presb^y what further to do.
Mr. Craford told the people aggrieved that when they saw fitt
he would go over to the house which they promis'd to do."

1702

" Octr. 4. Mr. Craford reported that he consulted
members of the Presb^y at Belfast concerning David
Bell troubles at Monkestown and was advis'd that
due care be taken lest there be some fraud us'd in
the case. Bell signifys that they do not hear that
hideous noise so much as formerly. Mr Craford was not desir'd
to go thither.

Oct. 17. Noe further appears abt Monkestown."

The use of the Bible in " charming with a key " accounts
for a report under date

1703

" Aug. 1. Complaint being made that Geo : Sheldon
and Jo^n Strean had made use of the Bible in their
charming wth key and riddle for recovering what
they had lost, having been cited both appear'd at
this Session. Being convinced of their sin in so
profanely using the holy word of God profest Ignorance of the
evil of it, confesst they were rash, promis'd to have a care of
such things again, so were dismiss'd."

It is easy to belittle these old men, sitting in their whitewashed chamber, in earnest consideration of so many cases
of trivial misdemeanour, but it is well to remember their

point of view. All souls were theirs to care for—they were
the properly constituted guardians of the sheep of their
Master's fold, and it was their duty to check the very slightest
inclination to wander. We can see, perhaps that many
cases could have been better treated by an individual elder's
friendly advice, unrecorded, but that was not the conception
of faithful dealing of the Church and time ; and credit must
be given to the members of Session of these old congregations
for their strict adherence to duty as they saw it. Did a man's
conduct in all things redound to the glory of God and the
profit of himself and his fellow-worshippers ? If it did not,
then nothing that did not so redound was too trivial for the
attention of the faithful shepherds. Drunkenness, of course,
was not a trivial offence. James Russell, reported on October
24, 1690, " for being scandalously overtaken with drink on
ane fayr day," is properly cited to appear before his Session.
The last three cases here quoted are, however, of the type
which the twentieth-century mind may feel to be out of place
in the records of a body charged with spiritual oversight
of men. In a case of slander, one of the parties—
Jo : McClelland—

> " Feb. 27. said that Jo^n Wilson by his playing on the
> fidle decoy'd young people and serv^{ts} from their
> 170⅞ work. Finding there was much heat and imper-
> tinency the Session rebukt them both and exhorted
> them to a Religious conversation and mutual affec-
> tion. They both expresst sorrow for their heat & folly and
> promist to be more watchfull."

And the " making verses of a man," with which the next
extract is concerned, is hardly an offence for a Session's
consideration.

> " May 26. John Laird having formerly (formally)
> complain'd that Willm Kirk had greatly defam'd
> 1712 him by composing and singing scurrilous of him,
> Likewise W^m. Kirk complain'd that John Laird
> had also made verses of him, both of them being

cited to this Session made their appearance. Willm Kirk being
charged with that whereof Jo : Laird complain'd of absolutely
denyd that he ever compos'd or made any songs of him but
own'd that he had sung that which he heard others sing : Jo :
Laird being charg'd with his making verses on Wm Kirk
acknowledged the fact : Wm. Kirk being askt what glory wou'd
redound to God by that practice in his singing of any such songs
or Edification and reformation to Laird (tho he was guilty of
such things as therein alleg'd) or profit to himself, he own'd there
wou'd be no Glory to God nor profit anyway : he profess'd
sorrow for his so doing and promis'd to guard against any such
practice hereafter. Laird likewise profess'd sorrow for his so
doing, both being sorry for what they had done, being reproved
and exhorted they acknowledg'd their sin committed against
God and profess'd a mutual reconciliation and forgiving each
other, were dismiss'd with this express certification that who is
the first aggressor and injures the other in so far as its cognoscible
by this Sess : shall be censur'd according to known Rules."

The last case here quoted from this interesting old
church record has to do with nothing more serious than the
thoughtless ' larking ' of a few mischievous boys. As they
passed a cottage on their way home at evening, one of them
having a ' clod ' or turf in his hand, threw it at the chimney.
His aim was good, for it dropped where the boy intended it
to go. " It hath gone doon the lum " (chimney) said one,
and incontinently, they fled. Inside the cottage, at the fire,
sat a woman with a sick child on her knee. The child died
soon after, but there was no evidence whatever that death
was caused, or even hastened, by the boys' frolic. Nevertheless, on the complaint of the owner of the cottage and father
of the child, a lengthy inquisition was ordered by the Session.

" Nov. 22. Alex^r McCage complean'd to the Sess :
that some time ago some persons were so Rude as
1719   to cast turf or clods into his chimnie head about
8 or 9 o'clock at night his young child being on a
woman's knee and two of these clods hite the child
the one more gently than the other, one of these clods hurt to
y^t degree that ye child cry'd which hurt he fears might some way

be the occision of the child's death the Sess : hearing this malencoly account proposed these severall questions to him.

first how (who) they were that threw in these turf or clods he assured he was in his bed and these that threw them were without but he Laboured to inform himself from these who knew the action in some measure he named four persons David fie, Heugh Kilpatrick John & Gilbert McCrorie for proof of this he named Robert Pikin James Gorvan Jane Dukie Sam : McCrorie.

2ly whether the child was any was (ways) indisposed before it was hurt with the clode he said he did not know but it was.

3ly how long the child lived after ye supposed hurt who ansured twelve days.

4ly he was asked whither or no he went out to see how (who) they were that ofered such vilence to his hous he said he did but found none they were all away.

The Session ordered the above four persons fee and his confederate be cited to our next Sess : as also the persons named as wittness to atend the Sess : "

Evidence, at length, was taken a few days later ; some of the witnesses being only twelve years of age. The result of the investigation is missing, probably through loss of a page or pages of the book.

It must have been comforting to some of the censured of Sessions about the year 1700 to know that the ministers, Moderators of Sessions, were sometimes, themselves, the censured of a higher court. The following is taken from the Records of the General Synod of Ulster (Vol. I., p. 46), date July 1700 :—

" Overtured. First, that there were some Ministers, their wives and children are too gaudy and vain in their apparel and some too sordid, therefore that it be enacted to the several Presbyteries to reform themselves in their Faults and theirs, and study decency and gravity in their apparel and wiggs, avoid Powderings, vain Cravats, Half shirts and the like.

" Overtured 2ndly. That sumptuous dinners like feasts on Mondays after Communions be forborn in Ministers' houses and none entertained that day but their guests who lodged with them and that sumptuous prodigal dinners at Ordinations be forborn."

Much light on the conditions of life of the common folk
of a district may be gained by examination of the old Presbyterian registers of marriages and baptisms, and the records
of receipts and disbursements sometimes found with such
registers. Let it be said at once that the record-keeping in
the majority of cases is deplorably inexact. In the Book of
Dundonald, of which a page of baptismal register section
is here reproduced, the ordinary procedure noted father's
name, child's name, and date of baptism, but, as will be seen
from the reproduction, in such confused, jumbled fashion
as to make the record of little value.

> " Aug ye 8. John Drenan had a child baptized named David and
> Robert Keel had one nam'd John Agust ye 22d David Kennedy
> had a child baptiz'd nam'd James. Agust ye 22d Daniel McGee
> had a child baptiz'd nam'd Robert etc. etc."

The omission of mothers' names, fathers' trades, and
addresses, or other aids to identification, robs such a record
of much of its value ; but what is to be said of baptismal
records which omit the name of the child! as—

> " John Armour had a child baptiz'd nam'd . . . "

This congregation must have been very poor, for at many
of the services the collections are represented by such figures
as 2/-, 1/7$\frac{3}{4}$, 1/7$\frac{1}{4}$, etc., and out of these small sums are noted
frequent payments for beer for the minister supplying the
pulpit. The use of the words 'supplied by' indicates that,
for part of the period covered by the record. Dundonald was
without a settled minister. It will be noted in the extracts
here given, the minister is always styled 'Mr.,' the title 'Revd.'
not yet having been adopted by the Presbyterian Church.

1708

> " Nov. 28. Suplied by Mr Thomas Kenedy the
> generall collection sent to belfast : seven shilin &
> sixpence : pay'd to brice blair & sent for two quarts
> of beir out of ye box thrie pence."

1708

> ' Dec. 19. Suplied by Mr Kenedy and collected
> sixtine pence 3 farthings payed out for bier for
> him 3 pence."

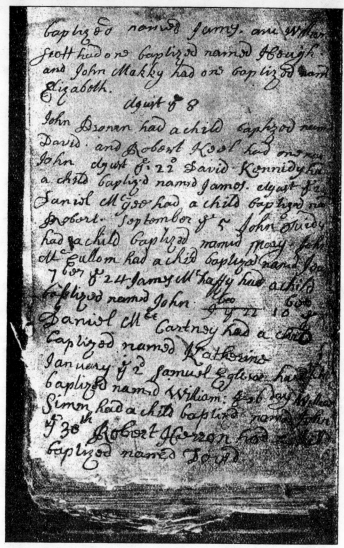

THE BOOK OF DUNDONALD. A page from the Baptismal
Register for the year 1697.

Museum of Presbyterian Historical Society, Belfast.

1708   " Dec. 26.   Suplied by Mr Wiliam Hunter and collected
        nintine pence we payed out for beir to him sixpence."

170⁸/₉   " Jany 10th.   Supplied by Mr William Hunter &
        collected seventin pence farthing whereof given out
        for beir. 6 quarte ten pence."

170⁸/₉   " Feb. 15.   Supplied by Mr James Stewart & collected
        twentie pence payed out for drinke two dayes foure
        pence."

About this date beer is regularly noted in the account after
stating amount of collection, and the quantity is sometimes
stated as ' 2 bottels,' or ' 2 quarts,' or ' on (one) quart.' In
addition to collections at services, various sums are acknowledged as received from persons appointed to ' bring in '
contributions for ' the box.' Two notes of such collections
are here given, and some typical entries of disbursements.
' Our own poore ' is a phrase frequently appearing, which
indicates that the duty of supporting the needy of the district
was recognised, but the following entries will show that
charity, beginning at home, did not rest there.

1712   " August 3.   David Kenedy brought in for yᵉ box
        eight shilin and penie half penie."

        " Septʳ 28th. John Lindsay gave in a months
        collection being nine shillings & seven pence halfe
1712   penie whereof given out to ye Scots man that was
        brocken by a law suit : by ordour of minister &
        session fyve grots. more given on Mr Stewart line
to a poore scollar going for glasgow on shilin.

To on (one) M Forbes a distresed woman robed by yᵉ french
        sixpence.

To yᵉ french scoolmaster on (one) shilin.

To David Craford a brocken man taken by yᵉ french & long in
        prison eight pence having good recomendations of his
        Losses.

To one Elizabeth Thomson who had her husband taken by yᵉ
        Turks and is yet in that miserable slavery ..   o o 9
To a distressed french Protestant   ..   ..   o 1 o

To a poor distressed man y^t had suffered shipwreck of all he
had 0 0 6

To a poor man w^t small children 0 0 4

To a Grecian priest so cald 0 1 1½

To a Scotish man in distress 0 0 6

John Thomson for his encouragement in his learning 0 2 0

To two distressed men William and Hew Montgomery
who were robbed by ye Torries and one of
them sore wounded lying . . . of
great wounds . . . ''

Names of beneficiaries among ' our own poore ' appear
with regularity, but with that irregularity in spelling which
is characteristic of the time. The ' blind lasse,' Joan or Jean
Egleson, figures at times as ' Egilshame.' Home expenses
and charities appear in such entries, as—

" A groat to mend ye locke of ye meeting-house & to a poore
Woman on peine (one penny).

To ye Smith for ane new kie and a new Spring and Staple to y^e
locke of ye meeting-house doore seven pence.

To a hollywood boy 0 0 2

For making the grave of a poor woman who died
beside us named Marion Wondrom .. 0 0 7

Given out for burying of Alexander Cowan fyve
shilin by ordour.

Given to a poor man being ane object and recomended by two of ye Session two pence.

For burying ye funline (foundling) given out of y^e
box on (one) shilin.''

Faulty as are the Dundonald entries in the Register
of Baptisms, they are much better than those appearing in
the Book of Carnmoney. Here the entries without name of
child are fairly numerous, as—

1731 " Dec 23 ——————— Dr (daughter) to Hewgh
Oiens was baptized."

At times even sex is not stated, as—

1732
"Aug. 20 ——————————— to And Muirhead was Baptized."

1733
"June 5——————————— to Joseph Cury was Baptized."

Again there are cases of recording the child's name while omitting that of the parents :

1749
"March 15, Agnes Dr (daughter) to ———————————
Octr 14, Thomas Son to ——————————— "

The Carnmoney irregularity extends to order of entries. It is evident that one of the recorders has left unfilled portions of pages, and that a successor, having a sense of the wastefulness of such proceeding, has ' made good ' by utilising the spaces for his entries, without regard to order of dates. Thus after an entry dated Nov. 6, 1727, appears one belonging to Oct. 24, 1742, and, on another page, the dates Sept. 28, 1726, June 30, 1728, and March 26, 1731-2, appear in the order here given, although elsewhere there are numerous entries of intervening dates.

When these old church records, through death of Clerks of Session, or other cause, strayed to farm-houses, the occasional blank spaces were tempting places to generations of children, on which they might write names and copy lines, to the young man ' making verses ' on his love, and to the practical farmer who, here, might enter the dates of cows calving or the particulars of a promissory note. So has it fared with the Book of Dundonald. It is a somewhat shabby little book, such as a farmer might carry in his pocket. As a church record it began its career in 1678, and appears to have been filled about the year 1711. Replaced by another, the old, probably, lay in the farm home of the Clerk of Session in charge at the time of change and was soon forgotten. It is browned with the peat smoke of more than two hundred years—the wonder is that it exists. " Command you may your mind from play

every momen of the day" has been written by one of the
holders of the old-time belief that all work and no play was
good for Jack.   What a view of pinched times is seen through
the lines of the promissory note for " one shillon and one
penny," of which a copy has been kept—

> " I promise to pay unto John Craford the Just and full some of
> one shillon and one penny St. for vellue recd the seckend Day
> of may 1764."

And here is the lover's poem of heart-outpouring which falls
away considerably after a fine opening :—

I will arise yea and I will
the City Go about
And seek hir home I Dearly love
Untill I find hir out

Tho we two Bodes have my dear
yet we have But one hart
And Ever will continue so
Untill our Lives Depart

When I do see the rainbo rise
with Collers Reed and Green
it minds me of The boney Lass
that I was with Last Night

   Turn from the consideration of Presbyterian Session
records, to that of minutes of Vestries of parish churches,
in the period under examination, and the difference to be
noted is remarkable.   Here is no concern about souls, but
much about the state of the roads.   At a vestry meeting of
the parishes of Ballywalter, Ballyhalbert, and Inishargie,
held on 6th Octr., 1706, Directors for the Highways were
appointed for a year.   Road upkeep seems to have been the
heaviest part of the vestry's charge, with care of the church
and help to the poor as minor duties.   A few entries from
these parish records are here given.

1741

" Sept. 16.   To Wᵐ Saul, Inishargie, for keeping the
slating of the roof windows coping on stone and the
Peers of the Gate of the said church in repair, to
commence from Easter next   ..   £1   0   0

1749

" For a Ladder 24 feet long and one 12 feet long
                                                £1   0   0

Entries show that a sum of about £3/3/0 was divided
among a number of poor persons—usually about 25—every
six months.

1750

" Apl. 16.   To the support of Samuel Gouidie an
Idiot £1 10   0

Sharping the Picks for two years   ..   12   5

The next entry refers to the indenturing of an apprentice
for the extraordinary term of nineteen and three-quarter
years.

1763

" April 4.   We present the sum of Two Pds for John
Davidson of Ballymullion to be given with James
Davidson an Orphant child who is to be Bound as an
Apprentis to him for the term of ninteen years &
thre quarters from the 1st Day of May next and the
Minister and church wardens with the rest of the Parishenors
then present do further agree to pay unto the said John Davidson
the sum of Twenty Shillings per Ann for two years more provided
the said Child lives so long."

1791

" Sept 6.   Resolved by the Minister church wardens
and Protestant Parishioners then and there assembled
that the sum of one penny per acre be levied off
the Inhabitants of this Parish for the repair of the
Bye Roads of this Parish."

Here follows a list of 27 persons appointed to collect and
expend the money.   The word ' object,' meaning object of
charity, familiar in the Book of Dundonald, appears in one
of these Vestry records.

" For the Suport of Robert Gleen an Object   ..   £2   0   0

From the records of Comber Parish :—

1717

" Nov 15.   At a Vestry then held in the Parish church of Comber, It was agreed, the Minister, Church wardens and Parishioners being present, that a surplice and two books of Homilies shall be bought, and that the money for the same shall be applotted and levied with the next Easter Cess.

> Patk. Hamilton, Cur^t.
>   his
> David   X   Hay
>   mark
> Sam. Adams."

" Accounts for the year.

1720

Church Cess for Year was	£10 10	0
Money spent was	£12 6	6½
The Parish is in Debt	£1 16	6½

As follows to the Sexton	6	0
To washing the linnen	2	6
To the Church Wardens fees due for the chest ..	16	0
To Kelly for stopping up the little window etc. ..	10	0
To making the Cushion	4	0

1728

" Sept 2. To the Woman that nursed the poor child	2	8½
To Pipes and Tobacco at the poor child's funeral..		10
To Andrew McBurney for maintaining ye Bastard	£2 0	0

1732

" Dec 10. (A Receipt)

This Day given to Joⁿ Gibson, Sexton, sixpence half penny for wch s^d Jon is to furnish the church bell wth cords from this time till Easter come three years as witness my hand.

>   his
> John   X   Gibson
>   mark."

1737
"April 11. Enacted—
That 5 Shill be laid on ye town of Cumber for Picks
for ye Highways."

1744
"June 25. At a vestry then held in s^d Parish Church
it was enacted by ye Minister & Ch wardens &
parishoners then present that thirty shill be laid
on said Parish for ye mentainance of Jos^h Gorley's
child & for ye defraying ye above expence one halfpenny be laid on every score of acres in s^d Parish.
                                              Annesley Bailie.

And is further enacted
yt Sam Breadly be made
Survr for st field road."

The vestry minutes of Donaghadee record levies for
upkeep of roads—in one case of 2d. per acre "and 5/5 from
every man not having land & liable to be drawn." Under
date May 8, 1798, there are notes of small sums levied
for expenses, such as Elements, Sexton's wages, washing
linen, and £1 12s. 0d.,

"to reimburse the Churchwardens & this is the last time they
ever will be repaid if they exceed the sum laid on for Incidents."

An account of procedure surely unique in burial practice,
is furnished by the records of Ballylesson. A deceased
person, brought there for interment, had "to be attended by
some person of credit to answer for the good behaviour of
deceased when alive." The declaration of the Churchwardens
at the first funeral in Ballylesson graveyard on 21st December,
1788, reads :—

"Mr Hull & Mr. Beers, the Churchwardens attended before the
corpse was put in the ground. Mr Hull said that the Churchwardens came there to the first funeral to make it publicly known
that the churchyard of Ballylesson was given by the original
owner of the land, conditionally, that the present churchwardens
had promised in the name of themselves & their successors for
ever, that the remains of no immoral person should at anytime
be admitted to lie in that Churchyard—that in future every

deceased person brought there for interment must be attended
by some person of credit to answer for the good behaviour of
deceased when alive, or a certificate from the minister by whom
such deceased person had been instructed to that effect. Mr
Beers said he was sure that what had been said by his worthy
colleague would be generally approved of, that it was in every
man's power to have his bones laid to rest in that very desirable
place by being honest. As to John Johnstone whose remains
lay before them, he said he could with truth vouch for his having
been an honest upright man, not a bigot, but rather negligent as
to formal show in respect of religious matters. It was by being a
good neighbour, a friend to the distressed & on every occasion
within his reach proving himself a worthy member of society
that he chose to show himself a Christian. Mr Beers recommended in the strongest terms he was capable of, more attention
to the burying of the dead. He said the dissenters could not
deny but that it would be decent to have at least a psalm suitable
to the occasion sung at the edge of the grave, by such means he
thought the idle attention of the by-standers might be collected,
at least for a short time, & directed to that Almighty Power
from whom we every moment receive fresh mark of his beneficent
attention, & from whose mercy & goodness we hoped for ever-
lasting life."

Messrs. Hull and Beers surely took upon themselves a
great responsibility when they promised, in the name of
themselves and their successors for ever, that the remains
of no immoral person should at any time be permitted to lie
in that churchyard.

Vestry accounts may include, as seen above, a charge
for books of Homilies; in others, unquoted, are noted payments
for New Bibles. In Presbyterian accounts may appear
disbursements for " a new Session Book," or, as at Dundonald,

" 19th Feby 1709/10 the sum of Foure shilin & foure pence to
pay ye book of Church Government,"

but in available accounts of either church, at no time is
chronicled expenditure on tune-books. For the Presbyterian
service these would be very small, with, perhaps, not more
than twelve tunes. Probably these were everywhere hand

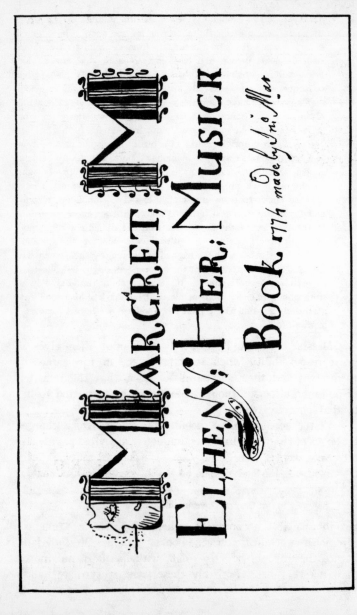

TITLE-PAGE of a manuscript Book of Tunes used in Presbyterian services : 1774.

Exuberant Art in the ornamentation of Psalm-tune titles.
From a Presbyterian Tune-book of the eighteenth century.

made copies—the work of the choir-leader. An example is the
book of Miss Margaret McIlhenny, which is here in part reproduced (p. 194). It will be seen that it is the work of a person
of exuberant artistic imagination, probably an admirer of the
young lady whose name it bears. Another of these surviving is
excellently produced, and contains the tunes French, York,
London, Elgin, Dublin, Abbey, Newton, Savoy, Martyrs,
David's, Mary's, and Brunswick, with words suitable for singing
to each at the practice classes; for such was the old Presbyterian
reverence for the sacred words of the Psalms that their use
in singing, other than for God's praise, could not be tolerated.
Hence the composition of verses in different measures for use
at choir practices. The twelve to be sung with the tunes of
the book above-mentioned are worth preserving as relics
of the old country ways.

Tune—*French*.

The first of all begins with French;
    The second measure low;
The third extendeth very high;
    The fourth doth downward go.

Tune—*York*.

The reason that this tune's called York
    I never yet could know;
They might as well have call'd it Cork,
    Carnmoney or Raphoe.

Tune—*London*.

O! London, thou art threatened sore
    By France, to pull thee down,
But Providence is thy defence,
    Thou city of renown.

Tune—*Elgin*.

In Scotland fair a river runs,
    And Elgin is its name,
And many a bonny lad and lass
    Do walk about the same.

Tune—*Dublin*.

In Ireland doth fair Dublin stand,
  The chief city therein ;
And, as is said by many men,
  The chief city for sin.

Tune—*Abbey*.

Abbey, thy walls are beaten gold,
  Thy windows crystal clear,
Thy gates are made of ivory,
  Where beauty doth appear.

Tune—*Newton*.

This Newton tune doth break my heart,
  For I can't it begin ;
Come, raise it on the middle key,
  And then you can it sing.

Tune—*Savoy*.

Beneath the Alps Savoy doth stand,
And Piedmont valley doth command ;
There the Waldenses felt the stroke
Of Papal power and Papal yoke.

Tune—*Martyrs*.

This is the tune the Martyrs sang,
  When they were going to die,
When they were to the scaffold brought
  The truth to testify.

Tune—*David's*.

King David mourned over Saul
  And over Jonathan ;
Saying. the Chief of Israel
  Lies in yon Valley slain.

Tune—*Mary's*.

Saint Mary, and the Marys all
  Together sweetly sang ;
They had no jarring in their voice
  But all appeared as one.

Tune—*Brunswick*.

O ! Brunswick but I love thee well,
Thy harmony is sweet,
Thou'rt set upon the treble clef
In common time complete.

Poor compositions perhaps, but in accord with the excellent penwork of the music in being free from ridiculous or incongruous idea which might obtrude on mind of the Sunday singer who was also a member of the practice class. Later, the singing masters or choir leaders allowed members and pupils to supply verses of their own composition, which were used if suitable in measure, and, then, particularly wretched doggerel was sung to old and solemn tunes. A lover might praise his fair, and even mention her by name, while she was free to reject him in rhyme composed by or for her, on the spot. Verses in execrable taste would hold up a member to ridicule for physical or other defect ; others, and the majority, were merely senseless aggregations of words in lines, with approximation to rhyme in the endings. The few here given have been preserved in the memories of old folk in different localities, or in the notebooks of collectors.

A saucy girl who had strait eyes
Came here our singing to despise,
She left her manners at the school
And came up here to play the fool.

Within this room I do behold
A maid of beauty bright,
And if I had ten thousand pounds
I'd shar't with her this night.

The fair one here of whom you sing,
She values not your coin,
For if ten thousand more you'd bring,
She would not with you join.

Newtown is a purty place,
　　It stands beside the sea ;
Scrabo is an ugly hill,
　　Three times one are three.

Young man, your head I do compare
　　Unto a lemon skin,
Which weather beaten is without
　　And empty is within.

No mastiff minds the yelping cur,
　　No rock the foaming wave,
No lion raises up his fur
　　When monkeys misbehave.

As I sat down to scrape the pot,
　　My love she did appear,
I drop'd the cutty in the pot
　　For to embrace my dear.

These are by no means the worst of surviving examples.
It is told of an elder that, displeased at the frivolity and
worldliness of the lines sung at a practice class, he composed
a stanza which should serve as a model for the young poets.

King David said why need I murn (mourn)
　　For Absalom my son,
For he will never come to me,
　　But I will go to him.

The quality of the verse speaks for itself, and the inaccuracy
in applying David's cry over Bathsheba's son to the story of
the loss of Absalom speaks ill for an elder's acquaintanceship
with Biblical story.　The practice of singing these absurd compositions to psalm tunes was continued into the 19th century.
An explanation of the fun and jest of the doggerel may be
found in its association with the hilarious spirit of the singing
class.　The life of the Down farmer for 150 years was of the
hardest,—the young had too few opportunities for relaxation
or amusement.　The singing class furnished an opportunity

for the young of both sexes to meet, and for innocent fun
after the practice was over.   A gentleman, only lately
deceased, who furnished some of the examples here quoted,
remembered their use, which was discontinued about seventy
years ago.   The custom, he said, was to meet for the practice
in barns, the owners of which supplied tea or other refreshment.   After the psalm-tune practice the gathering became
one for amusement, with songs, recitations, kissing games,
etc., etc.

A counteracting influence to the ' Moderatism ' already
referred to as dividing Presbyterian forces, came with the
Seceders about the middle of the eighteenth century.   The
movement they represented began, in 1732, with the secession
of four ministers of the Church of Scotland on a question of
exercise of patronage.   It grew rapidly among a people who,
with the blood and traditions of the Covenanters, turned
disgustedly from the insipidity of ' Moderate ' teaching.
Spreading to Ireland, it soon accounted for the establishment
of congregations in Down and throughout Ulster.   Its early
ministers, in contrast to the dominant section of the ministers
of the Synod of Ulster, were Evangelicals,—but Evangelicals
who appealed to reason as well as to emotion.   Great numbers
attended their services, and secession congregations sprang
into being over a wide area in the North.   In Gamble's
View of Society and Manners in the North of Ireland, published
in 1813, the writer describes the scene at an open-air service
of the early Secession years.   The " thin dapper figure "
was probably Patton of Lylehill, near Belfast.   Montgomery
speaks of him as " a little, active, sharp-eyed man."

> " They (the Seceders) have now public worship generally in
> (meeting) houses—formerly it was almost universally performed
> in the open fields . . .   I recollect being at one of these
> meetings when I was a very little boy (probably about 1750),
> it is present to my recollection as fresh as if it were only yesterday.
> I see it now as if it were before my eyes ; the bright sun and clear
> sky—the wild glen and the dark woods and foaming torrent—

the thin dapper figure—the sharp face and keen visage
of the preacher as he projected his head from the little pulpit
covered with canvas, placed on the verge of the hill ; the immense
multitude of all ages and sexes, in scarlet cloaks and grey mantles,
and blue and russet colored and heath-dyed coats—in hoods and
bonnets and mob caps and old-fashioned hats, standing, sitting
and lying around. The sermon lasted upwards of three hours.
The text was taken from the first Chapter of the Song of Solomon,
' While the King sitteth at his table, my spikenard sendeth forth
the smell thereof.' The preacher in this text, clearly perceived
a type of something pertaining to the Christian Dispensation
and emblematic of the future glory of the Church.''

The end of the century saw the decay of ' Moderatism,'
which had largely become Arianism,—while the Evangelical
Seceders had enormously increased in number. In 1788
was born at Maghera, Co. Derry, Henry Cooke, the man who,
beginning at Killileagh in Down, made it his lifework to draw
to its ancient orthodoxy the church of his fathers ;—preparing
the way for that Union of Synod of Ulster and Secession
Synod which took place in 1840.

The man of North East Down is still a Scotsman and son
of the Kirk's upbringing. To many centuries' endurance
by his ancestors of the rigour of a cold northern clime, he
owes a hardy physical frame. Three hundred years of Kirk
teaching and discipline have wrought in him for it a fitting
mentality. Sub-consciousness knows far more than the
experience of the individual. In that of the Down men are
ever sounding, to sad and ancient tunes, words of mourning
and pleading—words of waiting with patience, which generations of his ancestry have sung in voicing their appeals to
God in times of trial. In days when men run to and fro, and
knowledge is increased—new days of greater ease and freedom
—the old sounds must become fainter. Still, for generations
to come, the cry of the Hebrew, sung by Scots to the music
of sad ' Dundee,'—the later more melancholy ' Coleshill,'—
the yet later and most melancholy ' Ballerma,' will find

an echo in the breast of the Down man's descendants. To them will be emotion-stirring without their understanding why, words and sounds such as

I wait-ed for the Lord my God, And pat-ient ly did bear

At length to me He did in-cline My voi-ce and cry to hear

Of the many influences which have moulded the character of descendants of the Hamilton and Montgomery settlers, none has been more potent than that exercised by that faithful daughter of the Old Scottish Kirk—the Kirk in Down.

CHAPTER IX.

The School in Down

WHEN Hamilton and Montgomery took possession of a vast Irish territory, administered until their coming according to ancient tribal custom, they were bound to make provision for the education of the children of their settlers.

Hamilton, who had been a schoolmaster, founded and endowed a number of schools—at Bangor, Ballyhalbert, Holywood, Killileagh, Dundonald, and one at the ford of Belfast. The building of the last-mentioned was in existence at the end of the eighteenth century—as certified, in 1848, by an old woman named Jenny Boyd, to Lord Templemore's agent. She remembered seeing the school about fifty years earlier, and stated that there were large stones about, on which the children, in fair weather, used to sit. Lowry, in his notes to the Hamilton Manuscripts, calls attention to a building appearing on the Map made for Lord Claneboye by Raven in 1625, in a position corresponding exactly with that of the schoolhouse described by the old woman, and adds that there can be little doubt that this is the original school-house referred to in Lord Claneboye's will. The masters of these schools were to have five pounds sterling per year,

> "besydes such monies as they shall have from the scholars for
> their teaching."

Exactly how many schoolmasters Montgomery ' planted '
is not known, but we have a few details of what was doubtless
the principal school—that close to his own great house at
Newtownards. While his record may show self-aggrandize-
ment to have been the ruling motive of his actions, it is clear
that Montgomery, with pride in newly-attained rank, had a
desire to exhibit a grand style in his house and appointments,
and the school which was to rank as the first on his estates,
and was beside his dwelling, shared in the liberality of scale
on which the mansion of the new family was founded. The
author of the family story was, himself, a boy at Newtown
School until he went to finish his education at Leyden. The
first Viscount, he says,

> "built a great school at Newtown, endowing it, as I am credibly
> told, with twenty pounds yearly salary for a Master of Arts to
> teach Latin, Greek, and Logycks, allowing the scholars a green
> for recreation at goff, football and archery, declaring that if he
> lived some few years longer, he would convert his priory houses
> into a College for Philosophy ; and further paid small stipends
> to a master to teach Orthography and Arithmetic, and to a
> Music-master who should also be precentor to the Church, so
> that both sexes should learn all those three arts; the several
> masters of all those three schools having over and beside what
> I have mentioned, wages from every scholar under their charge."

Among the first masters of this school was John Maclellan,
an able but difficult man, who abandoned the school to become
Presbyterian minister at Kirkcudbright. Later the Newtownards Academy was presided over by John Hutchinson,
" an ingenious man . . . of universal learning."

It is probable that all the masters of these early school
foundations were Presbyterian, as were the ministers placed
in charge of the Scottish settlers by Hamilton and Montgomery. It is equally probable that, with the eviction of the

Presbyterian minister, the Presbyterian schoolmaster was
also cast out. Inoperative Acts of Henry VIII. and Elizabeth
charged each incumbent with the duty of maintaining an
English school in his parish. Although incumbents did not
or could not establish and maintain such schools, they looked
with disfavour on Presbyterian teaching ; and when, in the
seventh year of William III., the old Acts were renewed, and
the incumbents were obliged to take an oath to teach, or
cause to be taught, English schools within their vicarages or
rectories, they took measures to prevent any teaching other
than their own. Some members of the Hamilton family
had started a school of philosophy at Killileagh on Lough
Strangford, with Rev. James McAlpin as master. This
school, continued for many years, was very successful,—to
the great chagrin of the clergy of the Established Church.

The Bishop of Down (Walkington), in 1698, petitioned
the Lords Justices in Ireland to put an end to the "unreasonable libertie" enjoyed by dissenters. After enumerating the
Presbyterian ministers' offences of celebrating the Office
of Matrimony, celebrating the Sacrament of the Lord's Supper
in congregations so formidably numerous that they "preach
in the fields and continue their a great pairt of the day,"
of holding openly their sessions and provincial synods, etc.,
etc., he goes on to say that they

> "have set up at Killileath a phylosophicall school in open violation
> and contempt of the laws, by bold and unreasonable attempts,
> and the probable consequence of them if not prevented by your
> Lordship's wisdome and care, your petitioner and his clergie
> will be extreamly discuraged," etc.

But their Lordships declined to order the closing of the
school. An inquiry was held a month later at which was
summoned to appear Rev. John McBride, of Belfast, one of
the sharpest thorns in the side of northern Episcopacy.
McBride was required to explain his calling himself "minister
of Belfast" and a meeting "a provincial synod" on the title-
page of a sermon of his which had been printed. This matter

settled, he was questioned about the school at Killileagh—
whether divinity was taught in it, etc.

> " He told them noe divinity was taught there, and as to ye philos-
> ophy it was noe more y^n what was done in ye reinge of Ch. 2
> in whoes time there were two such schools y^t Mr McAlpin had
> a license. The B^p of Down and Connor asked from whom—
> he replyed from Mr. McNeale, chancelour to ye Diocess. This
> was Munday 8^{ber} 10. Mr McBride was dismissed with an advice
> to him and his brethren to cary respectibly (respectfully) towards
> ye established Church, and to them (the accusers) to them
> (the accused) to cary moderately."

McAlpin was still teaching at Killileagh in 1712, to the
great ' discuragement' of bishops and their clergy. The
intemperate Tisdal, Vicar of Belfast, whose pen was dipped
in gall when it was a matter of writing of Dissenters, in this
year issued his *Conduct of the Dissenters of Ireland with
Respect both to Church and State*, in which he sets out the great
offence which the school gave to clergy of the Establishment.

> " The Dissenters of Ireland . . . have erected a Seminary in
> the *North of Ireland* at a place called Killileah, where students
> are taught their course of Philosophy, and afterwards have been
> sent to be instructed in their Divinity Lectures by the great
> Professor, *Mr. McBride* at *Belfast :* This Notorious Fact has
> given great Offence not only to the Bishops and Clergy of this
> Kingdom and to the University of Dublin, but even to the
> *House of Commons.*"

Another school of lesser celebrity—possibly the second
school mentioned by Rev. John McBride in his examination
referred to above—was in existence at Comber in 1687. It
was taught by John Binning, stepson of Rev. James Gordon,
Presbyterian minister of Comber. This Academy was closed
during the excitement of the Revolution, and apparently
was not re-opened.

Although the authorities declined to close the few
Presbyterian Seminaries at the bidding of the bishops, all
education in the eighteenth century was, by law, placed in

the hands of the Established-Church clergy, and Parliament voted money only for support of schools under episcopal control. This state of affairs continued until the establishment of the National Schools.

The industrial exploitation of children of tender age was much favoured by the privileged class in the early years of the eighteenth century. Among the Castle Ward papers is an undated copy of a proposal made by the Honble. Sophia Hamilton of Bangor, to the Trustees for the Flaxen and Hempen Manufactures—a Board constituted by Act of Parliament in 1711. The proposal, as will be seen, makes no mention of teaching anything but spinning, and if ' constant employment ' in the document meant all-day employment, it is clear that nothing else was considered necessary for poor folk's children, and that the sentiment of the time was not in any way wounded by the idea of eight-year-olds spinning all day and every day.

" To the Honb^{le}. the Trustees for the Flaxen & Hempen Manufactures.

The Proposal of the Honb^{le} Sophia Hamilton.

I do propose to Provide a Good School house at Bangor in the County of Downe ; and a sufficient School mistress, & constantly employ in spinning Linnen yarn, a number of children not Greater than twenty nor less than twelve, between the ages of Eight and fourteen years, & furnish the said Mistress with sufficient Quantities of Flax for the Constant Employment of such number of Children as shall be instructed in such school : If the Trustees for the Linnen Manufacture will allow me the Following Encouragem^{ts}.

1st. The Benefit of the yarn spun by such Children ;

2nd. Such number of Spinning Wheels, to be Provided at their Expence (to be Distributed among such Children Gratis as Continue one whole year in the said school) as may be necessary in proportion to the number of Children in such school.

3rd. Six shillings p^r ann for each Child, to be Instructed in such School, as wages for the mistress who shall instruct them.

4th. Sixpence a week to be given to the Parent of each Child,
towards cloathing & Dieting the child she sends ;

5th. The School to be erected the 25th of March next, at which
time the Wheels are to be Given, & the allow^ce of 6s p^r
ann & 6d per week to Comence from that time.''

The industrial element entered largely into the Charter
School scheme launched with great flourish of trumpets in
1733. Two of these schools were established in Down—one
at Killough and one at Ballynahinch. Although under the
Act of William III., c. 4, there had been founded parochial or
elementary schools, and a certain number of seminaries
affording education of a higher order, the masses were not
educated—Presbyterian and Catholic poor did not take
kindly to the Church schools. Even the Archbishops and
Bishops saw that all was not well, and, with many of the
nobility and gentry, they presented to George II. a petition
praying for the formation of an incorporated Society for the
education of poor Protestants and Roman Catholics. But
before incorporation of the Society it would appear that the
mind of the projectors had changed, and that the benefits (?)
of the scheme were to be for ' popish ' children only. Allowing
contemporary voice to make its statement, here follows an
outline of the proposed work—from the pen of Primate
Boulter. The letter is addressed to the Bishop of London
and dated 5th May, 1730.

" The great numbers of papists in this kingdom, and the obstinacy
with which they adhere to their own religion, occasions our
trying what may be done with their children to bring them over
to our church ; and the good success the corporation established
in Scotland for the instruction of the ignorant and barbarous
part of that nation has met with, encourages us to hope if we were
incorporated for that purpose here, that we might likewise have
some success in our attempts to teach the children of the papists
the English tongue, and the principles of the Christian religion ;
and several gentlemen here have promised subscriptions for
maintaining schools for that purpose, if we were once formed
into a corporate body. This has set the principal nobility,

gentry, and clergy here on presenting an address to his Majesty to erect such persons as he pleases into a corporation here for that purpose, which we have sent over by the Lord Lieutenant, to be laid before his Majesty : the copy of this address I have here sent your Lordship, in which you will in some measure see the melancholy state of religion in this kingdom. And I do in my own name and that of the rest of my brethren, beg the favour of your Lordship to give it your countenance. I can assure you the papists are here so numerous that it highly concerns us in point of interest, as well as out of concern for the salvation of those poor creatures, who are our fellow subjects, to try all possible means to bring them and theirs over to the knowledge of the true religion."

The Society was formed, the King's Bounty secured, and the Archbishops, Bishops, Clergy, Nobility, and Gentry congratulated themselves on the happy future of the land where were established the Charter schools of their wise devising. An extract from Harris's *History of the County Down*, written after the Killough school had been in being for a few years, will show the development of Primate Boulter's plans, and what was expected from their working.

" A small Walk from the Town a Charter Working School is erected for the Reception and constant Imployment of 20 poor popish Children, trained up to useful labour, and carefully educated in the Principles of the Protestant Religion. It was raised at the Expence of Mr Justice Ward, who set apart 12 Acres of Land at a low Rent for the Accomodation of the Children, and added a Benefaction of £20 a Year for seven Years certain for further Encouragement. Some of the children are transplanted hither from remote Parts of the Kingdom, the better to preserve them from the Influence of their popish Relations. Their chief Imployment is in the Linen Manufacture, and a Work-house and Looms are erected here for that use. They dress and cultivate by their own Labour the Land belonging to the School. The Garden affords them all necessary Vegetables, and the Flax raised by the Sweat of this little Family is spun and wove in it for their Linen Cloathing. Some of the Boys in the Winter Evenings are employed in making Fishing Nets, a few of the more robust are fitted for the Sea, and the rest apprenticed to Protestant Farmers and Linen Weavers.

" The Design of the Charter Scheme is now so well understood by the good Effects of it in several Counties of the Kingdom, that we may soon expect to see it universally received. All Protestant Gentlemen condemn the superstitious and idolatrous Worship of the Church of Rome ; they abhor and detest her bloody and destructive Doctrines and Principles ; they eagerly wish to see their Lands tenanted, planted and improved by a Race of honest and industrious Protestants, that they and their Posterity may continue to live in Peace and Quiet, free from the danger of any future Insurrections or Rebellions ; and the Wit of Man could not suggest a more effectual or rational Scheme for making this a Protestant Nation. As penal and coercive Laws, which in their Nature are odious in respect to Religion, can have but little Influence on the Minds of People, especially the lower Sort, who have nothing to lose ; yet is it not strange that so many sit coldly down as unconcerned Spectators, and take no share in this glorious design of securing the rising Generation of Papists to the Interest of that Protestant State, which their Popish Fore-Fathers have more than once brought into very great Danger, and caused much Blood to be shed in Defence of it ? If Men of Fortune are not to be wrought on by the Motives of Charity, yet out of human Policy, the better to improve their Estates by continually training up a Race of young and laborious Protestants, sure one would think this useful and beneficent Undertaking must claim some part of their Attention. This Scheme will at the same Time employ Multitudes of poor Children, who in every Nation are certain Branches of Wealth. Charter Working Schools promoted by Gentlemen in their respective Counties, conducted by their Influence, and under their own Inspection, can never fail of answering every good End for which they were instituted."

Alas ! they failed, and failed miserably. To know why, it is only necessary to study the regulations for the working of the schools as ordered by the Archbishops, Bishops, Clergy, Nobility, and Gentry.

" 6th February.

" Object of the Society. To train the children of the Popish and other poor Natives of this Kingdom in the habits of Labour and Industry and to bring them to a true Knowledge of the Christian Religion.

1733

Arrangements for Teaching.

> The Children to be taught to read English, and such of them
> as the Local Committee shall judge fittest shall be instructed
> in Writing and Common Arithmetick but this only for two
> hours in each Day ; and to be employed during the rest
> of the School Hours in proper Work and Labour, particular
> Regard being had to the Linnen Manufacture, as the best
> ways of Raising, Preparing and Dressing Flax and Hemp,
> Spinning and Reeling Flaxen and Hempen Yarn ; also
> Knitting, Sowing (sewing), Marking of Linnen, Brewing,
> Baking, the Business of a Dairy and all such kinds of Work.

Salaries of Masters or Mistresses.

> The Salary to any Master or Mistress to be not less than
> Five Pounds *per Ann.* and not to exceed Twelve Pounds
> *per Ann* and such of them as shall acquit themselves best
> to be raised to the highest Salaries.

School Hours.

> From First of March to the First of October shall be from
> Seven in the Morning to Eleven and from One in the After-
> noon to Five ; For the other Five Months the School Hours
> shall begin at Eight in the Morning and end at Twelve and
> begin at One and end at Four in the Afternoon.

Rewards and Encouragements.

> As incentive of Diligence and Improvement the Children
> may receive Rewards such as Two shillings for paying the
> Hearth Money for their indigent parents, or a certain
> Portion of Bread to be distributed every Sunday after
> Divine Service,"

and at the discretion of the local committee a certain proportion of what was earned by the girls was divided between
the schoolmistress and the parents " for Encouragement
of Both."

" Extracts from Prayers. (In Morning Prayer).

> Teach us to be Contented with our Lot, submissive to our
> Superiors, and modest and humble towards all.

The General Thanksgiving.

> More particularly we magnify thy Name for putting it into
> the hearts of our Benefactors to set up this and other

> Nurseries of Religion and Industry in this Nation, by which
> means we . . . from a State of Sloth and Idleness
> are brought up in an active and industrious Life."

It is hardly possible, reading these prayers nearly two
hundred years after they were written, to avoid feeling anger
at the composers' smug appreciation of themselves as God-
appointed ' superiors ' of the unfortunate little ones. A
letter from John Hansard on the advantages of the schools
to the children and community, is quite in the vein of the
prayers :—

> " This will be a fit Nusrery for Servants and other Persons proper
> to fill the offices of low Life who will by this means be early
> taught to fear God and to honour and obey the King and all that
> are put in authority under him, to learn and labour truly to get
> their own Living, and to do their Duty in that State of Life
> unto which it shall please God to call them."

The Charter School child's outfit was designed on a scale
which can hardly be called sufficient—much less liberal.

" For a Boy.	A Coat, Waste-Coat, Breeches with		
	Metal Buttons and a Cap ..	7	6½
	Two Shirts and two Stocks ..	3	4
	Two pair of Stockings	1	3
	Two pair of Pumps	2	8
		£0 14	9½
For a Girl.	A Gown and Petticoat	5	6½
	Two Shifts	3	1
	Two Coifs and two Bands ..	1	9½
	Two Aprons of Blew-Checkered Linen	1	5
	A Pair of Bodice and Stomacher ..	1	5
	Two pair of Stockings	1	3
	Two pair of Pumps	2	8
		£0 17	2

For some years after the establishment of these schools,
while buildings were new and while the Bishops, Clergy,

Visitors, and Donors were active and interested, the intention of the founders may have been realised in a measure. But no great foresight was required to see what was likely to happen, and what did happen. The schools were, of necessity, boarding schools ; and it was part of the Society's policy to cut off all intercourse between the children and their friends. No substitute for the natural affection of even bad or improvident parents was to be looked for in the over-sight of masters and mistresses in receipt of from five pounds per annum. The miserable little outfits wore out quickly in the long and hard labours of field and loom—Harris's note appears to indicate that the hours of labour were exceeded, as he mentions employment of the boys in the evenings. Here and there an exceptional master may have really cared for the children, but nothing short of miracle in management and supervision could have produced desirable results from the Charter Schools. Speedily they fell into disgrace.

Howard the philanthropist, from what he heard, was induced to visit a number of these establishments in 1784 and 1787. Examined subsequently, before a Parliamentary Committee, he stated that

> " he found the children generally ill-fed, ill-clad and ill-taught, sickly, pale miserable objects, a disgrace to all society. Some of them had been six years in the schools without knowing how to read—their time being occupied in working for their masters."

Sir J. Fitzpatrick, Inspector of Prisons, visited twenty-eight Charter Schools in the years 1756-7. According to his report the children were barbarously ill-treated—

> " were puny, filthy, ill-clothed, without linen, indecent to look upon, schoolrooms dilapidated and dirty."

Matters became even worse as years went on. About the beginning of the nineteenth century the schools were visited by two clergymen of the Established Church, who reported :—

> " Children lived in hunger, nakedness, filth and ignorance. Learning and religion almost entirely neglected,—Pupils compelled

almost to slave labour at farms, looms, etc. for the benefit of
their masters.   The sullen and dogged appearance of the children
betrayed some dreadful violation of the laws of nature."

Mr. Lee (one of the two clergymen), comparing the least
miserable of them with the children of Erasmus Smith's
schools, and of the day schools of the Association for Dis-
countenancing Vice, observes :—

> " I was invariably struck with the vast superiority in health, in
> appearance, in vivacity and intelligence of the half-naked and
> one would almost suppose, half-starved children who live in
> their parents' cabins, over those maintained and instructed in
> the Charter Schools."
>
> .   .   .   .
>
> " In the Charter Schools all social and family affections are dried
> up.   The children have no vacations—they know not the feelings
> of home   .   .   .   and so are frequently stunted in body, mind
> and heart   .   .   .   the system without soundness,—every-
> where corrupt."

And the shame of the Charter School clung to the
unfortunates. Few chose to take them as apprentices, even
when tempted by large fees. To their fellow-servants they
were known as " Charter School brats." Yet the system
endured for a century,—the grants being entirely withdrawn
only in 1832—nearly fifty years after Howard's adverse
report.

With the improvement in welfare and manners, and the
weakening of Church and Kirk animosities, unattached
elementary schools multiplied in the populous parts of Down.
Few records of these are available, but it is reasonable to
assume that in character and working they resembled the
schools of Holywood parish, described in *Mason's Statistical
Account* (1819) :—

> " There are in this Parish one licensed and four other schools, all
> kept by masters who are protestants, though not of the estab-
> lished church.   The number of scholars fluctuates in winter and
> summer, but they are, generally speaking, well-attended.   The

salary for tuition is from 6s. to 4s. per quarter, according to the
classes.   These schools are attended by male and female children
promiscuously ; but there are two kept by mistresses for females
alone, one of which is supported by donations.   The books in
use are principally the Old and New Testament, and the smaller
catechism of the Church of Scotland, vulgarly called the Questions.   In some schools, by way of improvement, the Speaker,
and other books on Elocution, have been introduced, and chiefly
Murray's Reader.   When boys remain at school until they have
mastered this common course, the English translation of Tele-
machus is put into their hands ; this however rarely occurs.
The parents in general appear anxious for the education of their
children.   When they employ them at home, it is usually in
assisting them at husbandry or domestic business."

The following notes, which refer to the schools known as
Diocesan, for clothing poor children, and educating them in
the Protestant religion, are taken from *A Topographical
and Chorographical Survey of the County of Down* (1740) :—

" DOWNPATRICK.
>   A Diocese School, and An English School for forty children,
>   who are cloathed and educated in the Protestant Religion.

MOIRA.
>   Here is an English Protestant School erected at the Expence
>   of the late Sir John Rawdon and endowed with £40 per
>   Ann. during the Minority of his Son, to cloath and educate
>   twenty-four poor children in the Protestant Religion.

DROMORE.
>   The Diocese School is kept here, and near it are two acres
>   of Land set apart for an English Protestant School
>   pursuant to the Statute ; where poor children are trained
>   up in the Protestant Religion and some of them set to work :
>   Twelve of them are cloathed at the Expence of the Well-
>   disposed of the Parish."

References to schools and the teaching of children
naturally appear in any large collection of family letters,
and in those brought together for this work such appear
fairly often,—not very informative perhaps, but often amusing.

A certain Mrs. Martha Lindsay, whose spelling leaves something to be desired, writing in 1730 to the Rev. Mr. Richard
Dobbs in Trinity ' Coladge,' Dublin, says :—

> " I have two sons at Scoole in Newery with one Mr Skilbun y^e
> eldest is in hommer (Homer) I fancy he will be soon for ye
> coladge."

It is of interest to find that, as late as 1744, a little boy
of good family in Down was speaking nothing but Irish—
probably learned from his nurse.   Mrs. O'Reilly, née Barbara
Nugent, writes to her brother-in-law, Andrew Savage, of
Portaferry :—

> " Patt is very forward, I think tis very early for him to read (the
> boy was about five years old).   My little boy speaks nothing
> but Irish which I fear will prevent his being a scholar so soon."

The lady's sister, Mrs. Savage, died soon after the date of
this letter, but Mrs. O'Reilly's interest in the Savage family
did not decrease.   Two years later her brother-in-law told
her that he had taken his two boys to Dublin for their education.   Mrs. O'Reilly approves, but expounds her views on
a child's time for commencing certain studies.

> " I believe Andrew is to (too) young to be put to learn latin nor
> shd he be put to learn to dance untill hes seven years old when
> they begin earlyer the (they) never dance well."

In one of the British Museum Manuscript Collections
(Add. MSS. 21131, fol. 99, *et seq.*) there is a long and amusing
correspondence which has to do with schools and schoolmasters at Downpatrick,—a town owned by the Southwell
family.   The date is 1738.   Mr. Southwell, as patron of a
school, has instructed his agent, Trotter, for reasons which
to him seemed good, to remove a schoolmaster.   He did not
ask permission from the Dean, and the ire of the ecclesiastic
is stirred.   This correspondence, like another far more
courteous between Judge Ward and Dean Delany (chap. XI.),
shows that extreme deference to their clergy was not a
characteristic of the Protestant gentry.

" Sept. ye 2nd.   The Dean of Down (Daniel) to Mr. E.
Southwell

1738   I am much concerned that I am obliged to complain
to you of the conduct of your agent, Mr. Trotter,
who has taken upon him to stop the salary of my
Schoolmaster at Downpatrick, and displace the man without
any complaint made against him, and without saying one word
to me about it, tho' the man has been seventeen years schoolmaster of the free school of Down, and licensed by the Bishop.
The case is this—Mr Dean Pratt left by will the sum of Two
hundred pound to the Free School of Down when erected,
and Mr Dean Gore as Trustee to the said will, erected the
school seventeen years ago, and placed one Butler in y^t as
Schoolmaster who has enjoyed the salary ever since. This
is the man Mr. Trotter has displaced, and has added his
salary to the salary of your schoolmaster, and put both schools
into one. Now this is a thing which cannot be done. It is
directly against law and common justice, and would be greatly
against the advantage of your town. Dean Pratt's charity
cannot by law be alienated, or mixed and blended with yours
and it is plainly the interest of your town that it should have
four or five schools open, because one single schoolmaster would
exact what rates he pleased for teaching, and if so the people
would be obliged to remove to some other town where they can
have their children taught at easier rates, and there are children
enough for eight or ten schools. In a word, Mr. Trotter has
taken upon him to do what the Law itself cannot do, and what
neither the Bishop or the Dean would venture upon. There
is another affair I am obliged to mention to you. Mr. Trotter
has put in one Dea to be Schoolmaster of your Charity School.
The man was lately a serjant in the army, and as I hear was
turned out for some irregularity. This Mr Dea is placed as
schoolmaster without any Leave from me to teach in my Parish
and without any Licence from the Bishop, or being examined
whether he be qualified for teaching the children or no. I told
Mr. Trotter that if he sent Dea to me I would give Leave that he
should teach in my parish, and would write by him to the Bishop
that he might be licenced, but he thinks it beneath him it seems,
either him to me or to take any notice of the Bishop."

Mr. Southwell, much displeased, drafts a letter of reply, which was found among his papers.

> " Sept.   Mr. Southwell to the Dean of Down. (Draft).
> My having been a journey prevented my receiving
> 1738   the favour of yours of the 2nd till 15 Inst. by w^{ch}
> I find Mr. Trotter has incurred your Displeasure &
> I should be sorry he deserved it.

" I had indeed heard that you were of opinion that you had a right to nominate a Schoolm^r to the School wch I built & wch was endowed by me & by Dean Pratt's Legacy, but I never believed you thought Mr. Butler, y^r Schoolm^r till I rec^d y^r Letter, nor can I find by the short words in his will, how the Deans of Downe are the sole Trustees of this Charity & the sole successors to his personal Benefactions : his heirs at Law are more properly so, or the parish of which S^r, you are the Head but not the whole.   Mr. Butler is very happy to be the object of y^r authority, for I am sure he coud never deserve to be the object of y^r favour.   His Demerit to me at last Election, was the only real reason of his continuing hitherto in the school, least I might be thought to resent the ill-behaviour of a man beneath my notice.

" The next point wch I find has displeased you is the nomina-tion of a schoolm^r without y^r previous leave : I know very well Sr that the leave of the Ordinary is requisite whom I take to be the Bishop, & Mr. Dea has my orders to apply for it.   But really S^r since you are so jealous of y^r own priviledges, I must follow y^r example & be as tenacious of mine, & shall take all care that neither now or hereafter any person spiritual or temporal may have the least pretence of jurisdiction over my private charity.   Whatever homage the Law enjoins shall be strictly paid to its utmost extent.   No man can reverence the Church or the Ministry more than myself, at the same time that no one can be more cautious in preserving himself from any the least excess of that Power.

" And now let me observe S^r that these trifles . . . are beneath y^r notice & mine : our station and Education ought to give us more elevated notions of things.   In the midst of my Building & Endowmt does it become y^r character to hazard a stop to my Inclinations, or to thwart them, & if I remove a man unfit for his place, is it worth while to dispute my power, or

to advance y^r own in the Defense of him ?   You are pleased to
insinuate Mr. Dea's unfitness for the school, tho' you say you
woud write for the Bishop's License for him if he applied for it,
wch betrays more regard to y^r own authority than to the man's
Demerit.

" You are much in the right to apprehend a monopoly in
Learning, & I wish there were 4 or 5 schools at Down, but, S^r,
people will send their children where they are best taught, &
Mr. Butler will enjoy a sinecure wch he is perfectly qualified
for, while Mr. Dea has a full school."

With cooling temper came to Mr. Southwell the thought
that he should have advice before committing himself by
letter to untenable positions.   He, therefore, contents himself
with formal acknowledgment of the Dean's letter, and
promises to reply after inquiring into the matter.   Then he
consults a certain Dr. Moore, who replies from London.   The
first part of the letter deals at great length with the Dean's
rights founded on use of Funds left by a previous Dean for
school purposes.   This portion is uninteresting.

" 19th September.

1738

As to Mr. Trotter's turning out the master,—that
case stands on another bottom.   A schoolmaster
properly nominated and licensed by the Bp. tho' he
does not pretend to a Freehold thinks himself not
removeable at pleasure, but upon a misdemeanour charged and
proved legally agst him by articles exhibited in the Bishop's
Court.   This man was nominated by Gore, nobody then object-
ing against Gore's authority, and was accordingly Licensed
by the Bishop, and therefore I question whether Daniel has not
the advantage in this point especially if Pratt's benefaction has
continued on the footing Gore had first fixed it on.

" I know a case in Chancery before Ld. Macclesfield where the
Bishop of Hereford as Trustee, joined with the other Trustees
of Whitchurch school, filed a Bill against the master.   After
the answer was put in Ld. Chan : refused to hear the meritts of
ye cause & declaired the Trustees might remove a master at
pleasure without assigning any reason.   But this was thought
new & very hard.   This will hold so far good.   That Mr. Trotter
may remove y^r master tho' licensed, and possibly the Church-

wardens and Parishioners might also remove the other master
on Pratt's Foundation had he continued on that footing. Now
as to the Dean's insolent manner of demanding that your Master
shall have his approbation before he obtains a License, this is
certainly a Flight against all Law & common justice in the Dean's
phraise. The qualifications that only can possibly come under
the cognizance either of the Minister of the parish or the Ordinary
are only in respect of Religion & Morals. The method then of
proceeding in this affair is after this manner. The schoolmaster
appointed by you or by y^r order may apply to the Bishop for a
License, without any application to this haughty Dean. If
Daniel sho'd think the person so nominated not qualifyed to
instruct the children of his parish, by his being notoriously vicious
in his morals, or not orthodox in his religion, his Business is to
enter a caveat in the court that such a person may not be Licensed
till his objections are heard, which he must exhibit by articles
against him, and prove to the satisfaction of the Ordinary who
sits as Judge. If they are not proved, or the facts in their nature
not sufficient objections as to the two points, a license must be
granted, but if refused the person or you may bring an action at
law agst the Ordinary for not suffering y^r Master to do his Duty &
get his livelyhood and damages & costs will be given against the
Ordinary, and you who pay him and endow the school are the
properest and only judge who is sufficient to teach and what is
proper to be taught consistent with Religion, etc. and if this man
was sent to Daniel he co'd only examine as to his Religion.

" Upon the whole I think your best way of proceeding wo'd
be in few Words to let this haughty Daniel know that you neither
design to proceed agst Law or common justice, or to the disadvantage of the town, that you shall without delay make enquiry
into the facts, & do what is agreeable to justice. I wo'd then
have all the clauses in Pratt's will sent to you, & see which in y^e
best method according to Law to consolidate Pratt's charity
with yours. And if Pratt's will has given no power to his successors, I wo'd take care they sho'd never have any. If this is
done cooly and gently you will gain y^r advantage of a march
before Daniel, by which a knowing general often gains a victory.
And if you wish to humble this proud Fellow, their are many
ways more effectual than a dagger. A skilful angler never
strikes when the fish first begins to nibble, but after they have
given them time first to gorge the bait, they can play them about

for their diversion as they please. You may assure yourself
Daniel's pride will soon drive him much in ye wrong, I see it
by his way of working : if you go on cooly & keep y^r self in the
right, you will have him in y^r power, you will gain all your points,
and nothing can expose him more to the contempt and redicule
of the neighbourhood."

Southwell expresses his satisfaction in acknowledging
receipt of this letter from Dr. Moore, who deals with the
subject again a few days later.

" 28th Septr.

1738

I was very much gratified that my opinion in respect
to the affair of your worthy Dean was agreable to
you. If Pratt by his will has made his successors
Trustees, they will always have power to be impertinent, and will generally execute that power on every
occasion, by having ye money paid into your hands by Gore's
executors it seems to me that you have it greatly in your power
to punish the Dean for his insolence. If by the will Pratt has
not made his successors Trustees, then there is nothing more
to do but to consult Lawyers, how the Churchwardens and
Parishioners may legally and firmly unite that money to the
school you have erected. By this means you will have either
way an opportunity of punishing the Pride of this Haughty
Dean."

From the following extract it is clear that Mr. Southwell
sent his reply to the Dean through Mr. Moore's hands.

" Septr 30th.

1738

Your letter to Dean Daniel was sent to the post
the night I rec^d it. I did not mention it in my
last, as I supposed you would take that for granted.

People of little & base minds never move out of
their own low spheer : and whenever publick good, justice or
any other motive is pretended, it is only to cover some mean
private view. This you see is already found to be the case of
Daniel, who to avoid doing a private justice, clamours against
the pretended misapplication of a publick charity. I think it
well worth one's while even for the Publick good, to conquer such
people, in order to lessen their influence & power, which must
be always at last turn'd to some ill end."

Mr. Southwell's forwarded communication to the Dean was in terms more polite than those of the draft made before consultation with Dr. Moore and his agent Trotter. The letter is too long to be given in entirety. Its milder tone will be apparent from the short extracts.

1738

" 15th Octr. I have paid all due regard of y^r letter of 2^d Sept. by making the best enquiry from persons, Papers & Records, into the different articles of your charge.

" If you think fit to insist in favour of Mr. Butler, that there must be a Parish Schoolmaster distinct from my own, I have ordered Mr Trotter to deliver up the keys of the old school to the Churchwardens in Vestry, & Mr Butler is welcome to continue master of a sinecure which he is every way qualified for. As to the nomination of Mr. Dea without your previous leave, I am sensible, Sr. that the Licence of the Ordinary is requisite, & Mr Dea has my orders to apply to the Bishop for it, & to him alone ; For I cannot find that the minister of the parish has the least plea or jurisdiction over my private charity. You may indeed enter a *caveat* if my master is vitious in his morals or Heterodox in his Religion, but I presume Mr. Dea is neither, because tho' you let drop some insinuation to his prejudice, you own yourself ready to grant him your leave, provided your claim & authority is submitted to. I protest, S^r, it is with concern, I find myself obliged to enter gravely into the merits of so frivolous a cause. Give me leave to recommend it to y^r calmer reflection, whether such petty cavils and Triffles are not far beneath your notice & mine ? Whether our stations & Education ought not to inspire us with more generous notions of things."

The agent's contribution to the landlord's enlightenment is of great length. As in duty bound, Trotter takes his master's side against the Dean. The more interesting parts of his statements are found in his letter to Mr. Southwell, of

1738

" 30th Septr Dean Gore brought Butler here from the County of Fermanagh about 12 years ago or there abouts but he was then seldomer drunk and the Dean chastised him with his cane upon occasion not thinking he could displace him because of the Bishop's Licence or that the landlord would interfere, but in the

next place as to Butler I was very unwilling to complain to you
against him as I would be in any case where a man's bit of bread
is at stake, but the repeated complaints from the Townsmen,
from his very wife, and being an eye-witness myself frequently,
& finding no exhortation signified to reclaim him I told you in
the general of his immorality as I think some time in November
last that it defeated any care of mine.   You ordered him to be
dismiss'd and to employ another.   I did not know whom to
employ as 'tis a very difficult matter to get a good English
Schoolmr, and by accident I met this Mr Day and agreed for
one year which will end 16 January next, upon tryal at £12,
saying that I did believe if he answered your expectation he
would in time get more ; 'tis a little uncharitable in the Dean to
insinuate that he is a bad man ; I did hear that he had been a
serjeant, but the Officers spoke of him and his only fault that
being clerk to the Troop he fell short in his cash which might
befall an honest man.   Now I have the satisfaction in my mind
that I can say honestly I have no hatred of Butler nor esteem
for Day but acted quite indifferently for the good of the children.
Altho' I would not shew him yr letter of 10 Augt last which was
writ with a very proper contempt and most inimitably, yet he
has heard of it (I believe) for I own I did not quite lock it up,
and this must embarrass him and make him thunder out his
anathemas against so & so let him !   Some good man says that
*a Heart is never touched with so delicious & lasting a Pleasure
as that is which springs from a clear conscience and a mind fully
satisfy'd with his own actions, it makes all calm and serene within
when clouds & darkness are without,* but I arrogate too much to
claim the application.

" As to the points in Law which you mention, I cannot pretend
to judge.   I sent him word that I would take out the Licence from
the Bishop as Schoolmr in my own name, and if I wanted an
assistant or Ussher I must make the best of it.

" If a Gent. has a right to take into his Family a Tutor for
children & Domesticks, is not this school to be deemed somewhat
like it, if no day-scholars are taken ?

" I see little in our Canons relating to schools, the 98th and 99th
canons aim chiefly at Grammar Schools, but in the 90th which
alone can mean schools in general there is this parenthesis in
the Body of it (Saving to all Patrons & Founders of Schools, the
right of nomination) and in the statutes of the Kingdom I do
not find any like your English one.

" By a late act, School masters and Mistresses that are licenced
may have like remedy for recovery of their wages as servants
have in a summary way. These therefore that do not want to
recover wages need not be Licenced.

" In my mind there is little objection but this to the suffering
your Master to take the Bishop's Licence. A man maybe
Orthodox & as good Moraly as the Law requires, and by no
means a good school m^r, and if a good one cannot be found out
in one year, another may ; then the Licenced Mr. is not easily
laid aside, his crime must be exhibited in the Bishop's court &
a tedious process (as I believe) before the end can be obtained.
Now a man may say that altho' he is not a very clever fellow
'tis he is within the law. I hope this step of your good Dean's
which is only a bit of ill-tim'd pride will not vex you, or cool
your good inclination."

Thirty-three years later a letter to another Mr. Southwell
from Edward Trotter, son of the writer of the foregoing, and
occupying the position his father had held, exhibits no
improvement in the relations of lord of the soil and a later
Dean.

1771

" 23rd Feby. You have gratified to the full the unreasonable vanity of our absurd Dean, who shows
your letter with the plume of self-importance. You
will smile when I tell you that tho' I dislike this man
much, his daughter & I have settled the preliminaries
of a bargain for life ; she is not handsome, but entirely to my
taste : her Father received my proposal very graciously, but
when we came to talk of her Fortune he *hitched*, as I have heard
you call it, and I am convinced means very unhandsomely.
I am determined however that I will have the girl, tho' without
one shilling—the little I shall have will be a competence for the
extent of my own desires, & I will trust her, that she will not add
to them."

CHAPTER X.

The Common Life

MATERIALS for adequate presentment of the living conditions of the multitude in North Down during the seventeenth century are not abundant. It is safe to assume that, during the early part of that period, while the adventurers felt under obligation to the men whom they had induced to settle on new lands, and to whom they owed the success of their plantations, the relations between landlord and tenant were much more direct, intimate, and friendly than such as existed in later times. The life of the early settlers was of the hardest, their labours long and diversions few, but while they behaved reasonably well they were not troubled by fear of rack-rent or eviction—many of them were known personally to their lords who brought them from Scotland. These hard-working folk kept no diaries and wrote no letters—many could not write, and we know of their life conditions mainly from records which have to do with lettings of lands or are concerned with matters of Religion, Law, or Trade. A letting agreement dated 4th March, 1644—preserved at Portaferry House— indicates the values of various kinds of farm produce and of

field labour in the lifetime of some of the first settlers, or of
their sons.   The agreement is between Sir James Montgomery
of Rosemount, as governor of his nephew, Hugh Savage of
Portaferry, and Gilbert Dunlop and Thomas Stemson, who
are to pay the

> " ssume of ffyve pound yearly at two equall payments May day
> and hallow day yearlie together with two ffedd swyne at Easter
> yearly or twenty four shillings yearly in lieue of the s^d two swyne
> with three dosen of hennes and three dosen of capons the one
> half thereof to be in kind and if so they cannot conveniently
> get fowles to pay they are to pay in lieue thereof ffoure pence
> ster for each henn & sexpence for each capon as for the other
> halfe that they are to pay in kind if they fail in payment thereof
> they are to pay for the same as the s^d Sr James shall pay himself
> for them in county and likewise they are to pay nyne score dosen
> of eggs or in lieue thereof twenty shillings, the which henns capons
> and eggs are to be payd when they are demanded as also twentie
> four dayes shearing or fourpence ster. for each day."

The chapters on The Kirk in Down have dealt with the
religious side of the first century settlers' lives.   Assize
records show law affecting life, but here our view is limited
to life which has become subject to law's penalties.   In the
treatment of the culprit, we have, however, indication of the
temper of a time.   While William Montgomery of Manuscript
fame has painted an Arcadia in the Ards under the benign
rule of the first Viscountess of his family, the real rudeness
of those days can be seen, in part, reflected in the ordered
punishments of criminal law.   A County Down man of
Hamilton territory, tried at Carrickfergus, in May, 1615,
for theft, at Belfast, of a piece of iron, a mantle, and a chisel,
of the total value of eight shillings and eight-pence, was
sentenced to death.   At the same assizes, one who had stolen
a bridle worth five shillings was sentenced to death, and the
like penalty was paid by two men who had entered a house
with intent to commit a felony.   It is curious to find in indict-
ments for homicide of this date the mention of the value of
the weapon.   Brian O'Gribben wounded a woman, " a faithful

subject," with a " cudgill worth one halfpenny," so that she died. He is found guilty; but while the thief of a bridle suffered death, Brian, by saying that he was a clerk, claimed benefit of clergy, and the claim was admitted. According to the custom of the time he was branded in the left hand and delivered to the Ordinary. The reason for stating the value of the weapon in such cases is said to be that the instrument was forfeited to the King, and if it were not forthcoming, the township was liable for its value. The statement of worth in cases of larceny had for reason the important distinction between grand and petty larceny; the former being the case in which the value of the stolen article exceeded twelve pence, and its punishment death by hanging. Such terrible punishment for venial offences was inflicted all through the Plantation times, and, indeed, as late as the days of George IV.

In the second and troublesome half of the seventeenth century, many of the Scottish settlers took to the business of victualling the armies, buying cheaply at one place to sell at full value in another. According to the author of *A Discourse Concerning IRELAND and the Different Interests Thereof* (1697),

"Vast numbers of them (Scottish Presbyterians), men and women, followed the Army (of King William) as Victuallers, Suttlers, etc. and having plenty of Money purchased most of the vast preys which were taken by the Army in that Campaign, and drove incredible numbers of cattel into Ulster.

"The Winter following they were able to supply Dublin and the greater part of Leinster with Beef, Mutton, etc. and had still their Emissaries with the Army at the Frontier to buy up the Preys wh they took daily from the Enemy in great numbers.

"The army began no sooner to Rendezvous in the year 1691 but their old Acquaintance were up with them again, and followed the same trade until Galway and Limerick were Surrendered, at which Juncture, having more Money, and indeed understanding the *Laganeers* Trade, or Scampering better than the English, they swept away most part of the Cattle of Connaught and Munster with them. And to my certain knowledge, within two Months after, the Cows which they bought for 8 or 10 shillings

were purchased from them by the rest of the Kingdom at five
and fifty shillings, and some at Three poune a head . . .
so that several of them that used before the late War to beat
upon the Hoof after a Pony laden with Pedlar's Goods to the
Fairs and Markets, . . . are now Masters of Ships at sea
and of Warehouses crammed with Merchants Goods at Home.''

For the eighteenth century, material for reconstruction
of the common life conditions in Down is much more plentiful.
The impression made by study of very many documents, is,
that for the greater part of the century life for the farmer
and small trader in Down was very hard indeed.   The gap
between land owner and land cultivator had widened.   A
hundred years of occupation had freed the former from fear
of princely or legal interference with his lands.   What a
James or Charles had given a James or Charles might
reclaim, or might charge the gift with new burdens ; but, the
time of the Stuarts past, old occupation was held to give
inalienable right.   The landlord paying a merely nominal
rent for vast territory was now absolute owner of the lands
he held.   The forefathers of the tenants built their own
houses, cleared and drained their lands, holding these lands
often at very low rents, and with consideration of their lords.
But, after a century, old leases or agreements having expired,
improved land had to pay the landlord vastly improved
rents or its occupier might go.   True, he had the right to sell
the goodwill of his holding, a right which was the foundation of
Ulster Tenant Right Custom ; but sons and sons' sons desired
to stay on the land of their fathers and, to the landlord, through
middlemen or agents, paid rents which left them little for
growth in comfort.   Many of the poorer sort in Down lived
in constant fear of arrest of crops for non-payment of rents.
Here are extracts from letters of various land agents in different
parts of North Down, during the quarter century beginning
1725 :—

1725   " The rest of the tenants are not worth a groate except
what little graine they have and that is in a very

bad condition with them.   What shall be done with the
. . .   tenants, for there is no such thing as money ? "

1726   " What shall I do with the tenants of . . . and
about it ? for I can't get one farthing from them."

1727   " There shall be noe pains spaired that's in my power
to get in money but I never yet knew it soe hard
to be got as its at p'sent."

(A Dundalk agent to a Down owner).

1727   " The tenants have not paid any rent yet, which
occasioned my goeing yesterday among them &
pressed for money as much as I could, but could
not get any : therefore seized their corne."

1737   " Yesterday took up all the cattle and seized all the
grain.   The McElmals & Stranys are looking for
Bail . . .   The McElmals offers their sons
Bonds for the whole arrear after selling all they have
except the plow of horses & one cow, and will even
get seed from their friends to sow it with."

1738   " R—— K—— of this place was committed to
goal (gaol) of Down on Saturday last upon an execution at the suit of J———— F———— for £29
I have seized every penny worth on his concern."

(Agent, out of Down, to a Down owner).

1740   " I got into Jas. Kerby's house and turned him out and
put Patrick Fling into possession, I did not find any-
thin worth distraining, there not being in my opinion
goods value 5/- little wooden cups and trenchers
4 or 5 and all ye hopes I have to get any of the arrears
from him is by arresting him."

1742   " Money is still scarce.   All I could doe was to send
you the Inclosed bill for £60 . . .   I don't think
the scarcity of mony is so much owing to the bad
sale of Barly in Dublin as to the covetousness of
such wretches as still expected to get more than the
late high prices . . . such Tenants as hold Barly ground
and don't pay their rent well this year will never pay well."

" Pursuant to your Order, Cristy Quail distrained Jnᵒ
Chambers, & Mct Fadions, the Fitzymonses seeing

1745   they were distraining Jnᵒ Chambers they took
opportunity as I suppose thinking theirs would be
the same fate made off with their horses and I suppose
a Cow or two we got only at first one Cow & two small heifers
. . . I hear they had sheep we found none upon yᵉ premises,
their grain is very little only one part of a stack of Barley, &
two small stacks of Oats & that but bad, we have drawn the
grain to Mr. Haydolls Hayyard as to their household goods we
found none worth carrying off."

" Your Tenntˢ are very backward in paying, I find there
are a great many of them abᵗ this town, whose

1745   crops I must arrest when cut down, . . . for
I cannot get one penny from them at present, neither
is there any distress that signifies to be met with."

" Poverty of tenants Townland of Ballygrot . . .
than which I never saw so bad a corn country nor

1752   tenants more with the face of poverty as they are
constantly flitting, being only from year to year
and at will."

In the early days of the Plantation, land was let to the
settlers at a shilling per acre or less. In a hundred years
even the poorest land fetched six or seven times as much.
Agents' letters report lettings of mountain land at 5/8 per
acre, and ' strand ' at 7/- per acre. Perhaps the most striking
example of the increase in North Down rents during the
eighteenth and the early part of the nineteenth century, is
found in Mason's *Statistical Survey of Down*, published in
1819.

" To give the best idea of the rise of land in this country, the writer
has, by his permission, made enquiry into the circumstances of
the estate of Hugh Kennedy, of Cultra, Esq. with a view to
ascertain the different values which have been set upon it at
different periods. It comprises the townlands of Ballyrobert,
Ballydavy, Craig-a-vad, Ballygrainy, Ballycaltre in the parish of
Holywood, and Garrowreagh, and Ballybun, in the parish of Dundonald, amounting in all to 4,000 acres, not including the demesne.

In the year 1705 all these lands were let to tenants upon leases
of three lives and 31 years, for the sum of £297 16. 5d. In the
year 1802, they had risen to £1,850 per Annum. In 1814, the
greater number of leases having been made from the year 1741
to that of 1755, the rent roll was £5.300 per annum : and if the
whole were to be set at present in proportion to the last granted
leases, it is computed that it would give £9000 per annum and
upwards. To prove that this computation rather falls short of
the truth, we shall state the circumstances of a single farm.
Woodsides farm, 45 acres, which is neither the best nor worst
kind of land, but is nearly equi-distant from both, in 1741, let
for 2s. 6d. per acre ; but in 1809, it let for £114 2s. which is at
the rate of about £2 10. per acre."

Land in the Portaferry district earlier fetched a higher
rent than paid in the Scottish settled territory to the North.
In 1641, the Portaferry estate of 3,225 acres, was let for £738
—or, roughly averaged, 4/6 per acre. A hundred years later
the rental was £1,440,—nearly 9/- per acre.

As the wealth of landlords increased, the distance between
them and their tenants widened. This century saw erected,
in great part, those endless miles of stone walls that surround
the estates of landowners—fit figure of the barrier of new
manners and customs and ideas rising between owner and
cultivator. To the feeling of distance from the land chief
followed that resentment on account of rents considered too
high, and on account of tithe exactions which the Presbyterian Scotch paid most unwillingly. The landlords fostered
the idea that it was tithe-paying which kept the farmer
poor, in order to keep his mind off consideration of what
over-renting had to do with the matter. Primate Boulter
deals with the subject in many of his letters to the Lord
Lieutenant and others.

"Mar. 8. Indeed the gentlemen have ever since I
came hither, been putting it into the heads of their
1728   tenants, that it was not their rents, but the paying
of the tythes that made them find it hard to live
on their farms. And it is easy to see that this was
a notion that would readily take with Scotch presbyterians.

" I need not mention to your Lordship what I have been forced
to talk to several here, that if a landlord takes too great a portion
of the profits of a farm for his share by way of rent, (as the tythe
will light on tenants share) the tenant will be impoverished :
but then it is not the tythe but the increased rent that undoes
the farmer. And indeed in this country, where I fear the tenant
hardly ever has more than one third of the profits he makes of
his farm for his share, and too often but a fourth or perhaps
a fifth part, as the tenant's share is charged with the tythe, his
case is no doubt hard, but it is plain from what side the hardship
arises."

" Mar. 13. The gentlemen of this country have ever
since I came hither been talking to others, and
1728   persuading their tenants who complained of the
excessiveness of their rents, that it was not the paying
too much rent, but too much tythe that impoverished
them : and the notion soon took among Scotch presbyterians
as a great part of the Protestants in the north are, who it may
easily be supposed do not pay tythes with great chearfulness.
And I make no doubt but the landlords in England might with
great ease raise a cry amongst their tenants of the great oppression
they lie under by paying tythes.

" What the gentlemen want to be at is that they may go on
raising their rents, and that the clergy should still receive their
old payments for their tythes. But as things have happened
otherwise, and they are very angry with the clergy, without
considering that it could not happen otherwise than it has,
since if a clergyman saw a farm raised in its rent e.g. from 10
to 20 l. per ann. he might be sure his tythe was certainly worth
double what he formerly took for it. Not that I believe the
clergy have made a proportionable advancement in their composition for their tythes, to what the gentlemen have made in
their rents. And yet it is upon this rise of the value of tythes
that they would persuade the people to throw their distress."

High rents, tithes, disabilities suffered because of religion ;
bad harvests for ten years, turned the thoughts of the
settlers' descendants of the early eighteenth century to the
American colonies. In the previous century, religious
persecutions had sent some of their fathers to the western

continent, where they saw awaiting them land almost for the
cultivation, and freedom and equality. About 1720 started
a stream of emigrants for the American colonies,—a stream
gathering volume as the years rolled on. Hanna, in *The
Scotch-Irish*, says that in 1736 there were at one time in
Belfast 1,000 families waiting for opportunity to get across
the ocean.

To aggravate discontent came, at the beginning of the
second quarter of the eighteenth century, a succession of
bad harvests. An enlightening letter of Primate Boulter
to the Duke of Newcastle paints very clearly the situation
in the North, and shows that the remedy of forcible detention
was, for a time, under consideration. The letter is dated
from Dublin.

"Nov. 23. I am very sorry I am obliged to give
your Grace so melancholy an account of the state
1728   of this kingdom, as I shall in this letter, but I thought
it my duty to let his Majesty know our present
condition in the North. For we have had three bad
harvests together there, which has made oatmeal, which is their
great subsistence, much dearer than ordinary, and as our farmers
here are very poor, and obliged as soon as they have their corn,
to sell it for ready money to pay their rents, it is more in the
power of those who have a little money to engross corn here,
and make advantage of its scarceness, than in England.

" We have had for several years some agents from the colonies
in Amercia, and several masters of ships that have gone about
the country, and deluded the people with stories of great plenty
and estates to be had for going for in those parts of the world ;
and they have been the better able to seduce people, by reason
of the necessities of the poor of late.

" The people that go from hence make great complaints of
the oppressions they suffer here, not from the government, but
from their fellow subjects of one kind or another, as well as of
the dearness of provision, and say these oppressions are one
reason of their going.

" But whatever occasions their going, it is certain that above
4200 men, women and children have been shipped off from hence
for the West Indies within three years, and of these above 3100

this last summer. Of these possibly one in ten may be a man of substance, and may do well enough abroad, but the case of the rest is deplorable, the rest either hire themselves to those of substance for their passage, or contract with the masters of ships for four years servitude when they come thither, or if they make a shift to pay for their passage, will be under a necessity of selling themselves for servants for four years for their subsistence when they come there.

" The whole north is in a ferment at present, and people every day engaging one another to go next year to the West Indies. The humour has spread like a contagious distemper, and the people will hardly hear anybody that tries to cure them of their madness. The worst is that it affects only protestants, and reigns chiefly in the north which is the seat of our linen manufacture.

" This unsettled state puts almost a stop to trade, and the more so as several who were in good credit before have taken up parcels of goods on trust and disposed of them, and are gone off with the money, so that there is no trade there but for ready money.

" We have had it under our consideration how to put some stop to this growing evil : we think that by some old laws we can hinder money being carried abroad, and stop all but merchants, that have not a licence, from going out of the kingdom.

" By this post we have sent my Lord Lieutenant the representation of the gentlemen of the north, and the opinion of our lawyers what can be done by law to hinder people going abroad ; but these are matters we shall do nothing in without directions from his Majesty. But whatever can be done by law, I fear it may be dangerous forcibly to hinder a number of needy people from quitting us.

" There is one method that can do no hurt, and we hope may do good, which is keeping corn at a reasonable price till next harvest, so that dearness of bread may drive none from us. And to compass this we are subscribing for a sum of money to buy corn where it can be had the cheapest, and to sell it to loss in the north, to keep the markets down there ; and I believe we shall have good success in our subscription.

" But I fear except leave be given to prohibit by proclamation the exportation of corn from hence, we shall fail even in this project."

After reading the Lord Primate's sensible letter, it is
worth the time needed to learn how the writer of the toadying
epistle here copied, would free the landed gentry and the
clergy of the Church Established from any responsibility
for the miseries which produced the emigration movement.
The Lords Justices had asked Judges on circuit to report
on the causes of flight from the land, and Mr. Ezekiel Stewart,
of Portstewart, will place the blame on the backs which should
bear it—those of Presbyterian ministers and farmers' wives
who want husbands for their daughters. The letter is
addressed to the landowner and Judge—Michael Ward of
Castle Ward.

"March ye 25th. Beeing informed yt yr Lords
Justices have desired ye Judges in their Circuits,
to incₐ.ire into ye rasons, of the Protestants of ye
North of Ireland, transporting themselves to New
England, and other forigne Plantations, I have made
bold to offer my thoughts to yr Ldship thereon.

1729

" The raisons those unhappey people give for their goeing
are as various as their circumstances, ye Richer Part say, that
if they stay in Irland, their Children will be Slaves, and that it
is better for them to make money of their leases while they are
worth something to inable them to transport themselves and
familys to America, a pleace where they are sure of better tratement, and allthough they should meet with some hardships,
they are very well asured their posterety will be for ever happey.
The poorer sort are deluded by ye accts they have, of ye great
weages is given there, to Labouring men, their Ignorance leads
them in, not knowing ye value of their money.

" The Presbiteirin ministers have taken their shear of pains
to seduce their poor Ignorant heerers, by Bellowing from their
pulpits against ye Landlords and ye Clargey, calling them
Rackers of Rents and Scruers of Tythes, with other reflections
of this nature, which they know is pleasing to their people, at
ye same time telling them that God had appoynted a country
for them to Dwell in (nameing New England) and desires them
to depart thence, where they will be freed from the bondage of
Egipt and goe to ye land of Cannan, etc.

" There are two of these Preachers caryed this affair to such.

a length that they went themselves to New England and caryed
numbers with them, their names are Cornwell, & Taylour, ye
first minister of Clougher and ye latter minister of Astraw both
in ye County of Tyrone, but these two gentlemen not finding
their acct in ye project, returned themselves but left their
Cargoes behind, the incourigment given by these men, and ye
corruption of human nature together (makes us fond) of partners
even in afliction & missery, which prevales with numbers of these
unhappy people that goe thither to make use of all ways and
mains to seduce their freinds and acquaintance to follow them,
in order that they may be more happey, & live better, what they
insinuiat to them is to this purpose. Here ye rents are soe small
that they can hardly be called such noe Tythe mongers noe
County . . . nor Parish taxes noe serviters money, noe
Ester groats, noe Bailifs Corn, these and ye like expressions I
have red in several of their letters, at ye same time setting forth
that all men are there ipon a levell & that it is a good poor man's
country, where there are noe opressions of any kind whatsoever.

" That maney have cause to murmur & complain cannot be
denyed, some by ye opression of their Landlords (but these
Gentelmen, I will venture to say are for the most part strangers
to our country) others by Tythemongers, some by ye Country
Courts & a good number by Justices of ye Peace, but I will
venture to say that all these put together bare noe proportion
to these greivences, which are only imaginary & which people
clamour against, in order to have some Excuse for their goeing.

" I can assure your L'ship ye Women are a great cause of
many of our people leaving ye Kingdom, the accts ye masters
of ships and their confedrets bring from New England are so
very agreable to the women that they listen to them with great
atention and everybody knows that ye have often been thought
very proper ingens to worke upon, & very successfull in carying
a poynt, where they themselves expected to be gainers, by ye
bargen. The Masters of Ships as I have said before tell ye
Women that ye are much more desireable there than ye natives
of ye Country because they are much better Housewifes ; yt ye
men there use their wifes like gentelwomen, this makes ye women
that have Daughters to marry to prevail wth their Husbands
to go thither in hopes of makeing them Gentelwomen, and those
Women that have noe Daughters are in hopes of getting rid of
their Husbands and getting better ones.

" I will not presume to give my opinion which are yᵉ best
methods to prevent this evil, but will humbley submit my
thoughts thereon to you gentelmen lerned in yᵉ Laws & I thank
God it is our happeyness to be governed by soe wise a legislature
that we have not yᵉ least rason to doubte, but yᵗ yᵉ will take al
necessary care for the good of the Kingdom, & ye preservation
of his Majesty's Protestant subjects therein, I shall give your
L'ship no further trouble at this time than to assure you that
I will with great cheerfullness give my small aid & assistance
for ye service of my country. I am with all due Respect

Your Lordships

Most obliged & most faithfull

freind & Humble Servᵗ

Ezek. Stewart.

P.S. I cannot but think that the want of Industry amongst us is
ye true cause of all our misfortunes at present."

The state of the farmers grew steadily worse as the century
grew older. Poor farming, and an insufficient area under
tillage, left good harvest years with little more food than
satisfied the needs of the population ; and when bad years,
and a succession of them, came, a state of famine existed.
The years 1740-1 were years of great distress. Oatmeal,
largely the support of Down folk, was twice or thrice its
usual price ; intense and long-continued frost at the beginning
of 1740 had destroyed, in great part, the stocks of potatoes.
Writing from Killough to Judge Ward on 14th April, 1740,
the agent Lascelles says :—

" All sorts of grain is risen to so great a price that I doubt the
allowance to our Charter School will not do, of which the master
complains greatly. Oatmeal in Down last market at 18 pence
a stone, Barly at 4/6 per cwt, Meal £1.10.0 per hogshead, Butter
not to be had, Pottato at 2/· a peack. These dry easterly winds
has burn'd up any little shoe of Spring we had."

The changed purchasing power of money must be remembered in considering this extract ;—for comparison with
present prices these figures must be multiplied by varying
numbers. After the famine came disease, and thousands (in
all Ireland, it is estimated, four hundred thousand) perished.

No wonder the desire to get away from the country rose to what Primate Boulter terms ' frenzy.' For some years at this time the emigrants leaving Belfast and Derry for America were not fewer than twelve thousand annually ;—nearly all of Scottish descent and Presbyterian.

The opening of the third quarter of the century saw the tide of emigration ebb, to flow again in larger volume about the year 1771. For a clear and concise statement on the subject of eighteenth-century Ulster Emigration to America, and the causes of it, the reader is referred to Chapter XIX. of Woodburn's *Ulster Scot.*

The loss of her youngest and best to Ulster was irreparable —Down, perhaps, suffered in lesser degree than other counties, yet severely. A writer in 1777 described the country near Dundonald—which, from its proximity to active Belfast, should have been prosperous — as " black and barren." Better farming methods, and, perhaps, the growing requirements of Belfast, brought to the cultivator a degree of prosperity as the century approached its end. The farms here and along the southern shore of Belfast Lough ranged in size from ten to eighty acres, most of the land being tilled. Seaweed was largely used as manure. The Scotch plough was used, and the fixed axle spoke-wheel cart had displaced the revolving axle block-wheel car, which, at an earlier date, had displaced the wheel-less ' slipe.' At the beginning of the nineteenth century there were in the village of Holywood three employers of workmen making carts and ploughs, and their work was said to be " scarcely inferior to that imported from Glasgow." The field roller had been introduced, and, most surprising and upsetting to the conservative,—the winnowing machine. There is an amusing story found by the author in a Down manuscript, which exhibits what the old and steady thought of this innovation. An enterprising man had ordered one of the new machines, and, before its arrival, many were the discussions of its powers, and much the wonder at its ability, as alleged, to separate grain from chaff *on a calm day !*—winnowing had been done from time immemorial by wind. On a certain day there was assemblage of neighbours to see the wonder at work. Soon after starting, a part of the mechanism gave way, and the machine stopped.—whereupon a bystander clapped his hands, and declared that good luck could never attend such an invention—" taking the power out of the hand of the Lord who made the wind."

Still, in time of trouble, America—no longer a British Colony—was the land of refuge and hope. Let us see what a Down man said of it. In the year 1794 Archibald Hamilton-Rowan of Killileagh was sentenced to imprisonment for two years and a fine of £500 for offence against the Government. He escaped, and fled to America, where he remained four years before he was granted pardon and permission to return to Ireland After two years' experience here is what he wrote of the new land :—

> " It is a heaven for the poor and industrious, a hell compared to any part of Europe for any other rank of Society. The climate, the manners, the state of Society . . . . are all against idlers coming here."
>
> . . . . .
>
> " The American youth are the most ill behaved I have ever met with, not to say ill-natured and they do not improve much when they come to be men. The freedom which they assume . . . is most impertinent and insupportable."
>
> . . . .
>
> " It is not the soil or climate of Ireland that I regret but the Society. The Aristocracy of wealth here is insupportable, for it is mixed with the grossest Ignorance . . . the men, in general, are more supportable than the women."
>
> . . . .
>
> " The servants are the worst on earth."
>
> . . . .
>
> " Were I as rich as Mr. Peel (a calico printer), I would give up the whole for Society, manners and climate of Europe with a small annuity."

Of the small boroughs of the Hamilton and Montgomery territory, Newtownards seems to have been the most prosperous

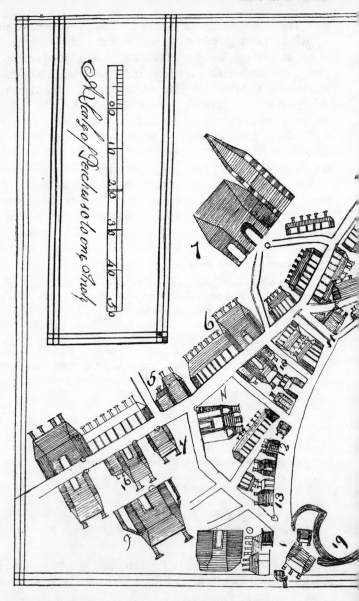

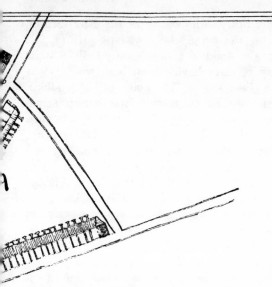

THE TOWN AND HARBOUR OF
DONAGHADEE IN 1780.

maker of this curious and interesting plan has attempted the
ssible. He has tried to show in one view both gables of a house
w of houses. Although he calls his work " An Exact Plan,"
very inexact. Unfortunately the key to the work is lost, but
of the buildings are still standing (1920). No. 1 may be taken
Custom House. No. 6, with the curious buttresses, is probably
resbyterian Meeting-house. This is not its true position, but
urveyor may have intended to indicate that it was on the road
ing off from Manor Street. No. 7, the T plan church of the
had three gables : the surveyor has had to be content to show
The spire was of wood, and was burned or otherwise destroyed
end of the 18th century. No. 9 is the fort or moat. No. 10
school, still standing on School-house Brae. No. 13 is prob-
the building now known as Arthur's Hotel. No. 16 is still
ng. No. 19 is, of course, the old harbour. The little circles
bly indicate position of wells. This plan was made by John
, for Daniel De la Cherois. Esq., in the year 1780 (see p. 246).
l in the Manor House, Donaghadee

in the eighteenth century,—the wealth of the later owners,
the Stewarts, being the cause of its welfare. In 1777 it
consisted of about five hundred houses, mostly built of stone
and slated ; sixty of these having been built within eight
years of the date given above. The house of the landlord,
Alexander Stewart, "large but not elegant," was in the principal
street opposite the market cross. The church of this time
was the old one repaired by Hugh, first Viscount Montgomery,
but the congregation was so small that the building had
been suffered to decay, and a small chapel at the eastern end
sufficed for the worshippers. At the same time the Presbyterians had three large meeting-houses. The market house
was considered extremely fine. The following description
of its principal rooms was written for the Hibernian Magazine,
a few years after erection of the building :—

> " The new market house—Over the centre arch is a most
> beautiful room, 32 feet long and 22 wide, which serves for a
> drawing room to the larger or assembly room. This room is
> most elegantly stucco'd, the walls painted a light green, and
> bordered with gold,—a large branch for 20 candles hangs from
> the ceiling,—the marble chimney piece is hardly to be equalled.
> " Over one wing of the market house is the assembly room 50
> feet by 24. The walls of this room are painted a light blue and
> bordered with gold, the ceiling is beautifully stucco'd, from it
> hang three brass branches which hold 20 candles each : the stair
> case is elegant. The steps are of white free-stone, the balustrade
> of iron gilt and the hand rail mahogany. . . . The language
> spoken here is broad Scotch hardly to be understood by strangers."

Bangor had lost the importance it had in the days of
the masterful Lord Claneboye In the time of Harris—about
the middle of the century—the custom house, towards the
erection of which King James I. had contributed, was in
ruins. Lord Claneboye's " fayre stone house " had been
replaced by " a low modern structure " of no dignity, but the
gardens were considered exceptionally fine. There was a
schoolhouse—that of the old endowed school ; the inhabitants
spun considerable quantities of linen yarn ; and to round out

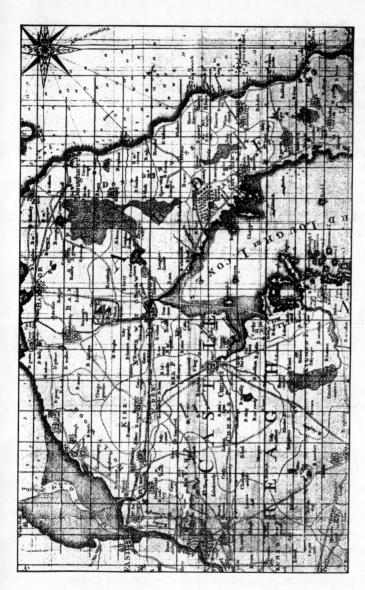

NORTH DOWN. From a late Eighteenth-century Map.   Original at Roddens, Ballywalter.

his description of the town, Harris adds that there is a slate
quarry within a mile of it, and, not far away, a bog of a
thousand acres.

In 1777 an article in the Hibernian Magazine describes
the houses of the main street as very badly built, thatched,
and few more than one storey in height. A second street,
at right angles, is of the two rather the worse built. " There
is little or no trade in the town . . .   the whole presents a
picture of poverty . . ." yet so unequal is the representation of the

> " Commons of Ireland in Parliament, that the same number of
> Burgesses are said to represent this borough as the Metropolis
> returns, but even those Burgesses are not chosen by the inhabi-
> tants of the town but by the Sovereign and twelve Burgesses—
> few of whom dwell here. . . . Adjoining the Church is the
> Parsonage house, a handsome new building, and by much the
> best house in the town : as poor as the inhabitants are, without
> doubt they are able to pay their tythes."

The importance of Comber was even less than that of
Bangor. A manuscript in the possession of the Stone family
of Barnhill states that

> " In the year 1743 when the late Mr. Stewart purchased the estate
> of Comber there was not in the Town or in the whole Extent
> of the Parish a dwelling House with a slated roof, unless the old
> house of Ballybeen had such, and that of the Glebe House w^h
> was rebuilt a year or two before that Date."

Holywood at the end of the eighteenth century was a
seaside resort for Belfast people. It was considered to be
" superior in neatness to the generality of Irish villages."

Donaghadee was the favourite port of the Down settlements. In the Manor House has been found a curious
plan made for the Lord of the Manor in the year 1780, and
reproduced on pp. 242, 243. The surveyor has attempted
the impossible in sketching elevations which show every
gable of a building. Unfortunately the key to the numbers
marked on the principal buildings has been lost. The church

appears with a spire which must have been of wood—
for it is known that in Montgomery's structure the tower in
stone was not carried above the gable against which it is
placed. For at least a hundred years before the late Daniel
De la Cherois raised the tower to its present height, it was a
bell-less stump, and all tradition of a spire had been lost.
The crescent harbour of this plan disappeared when the
Government constructed the existing pier and breakwater,
but many of the old single-storey houses shown on plan remain
and are still inhabited. For the two-hundred-year period
here considered, the traffic in goods and passengers between
Donaghadee and the Scottish shore was very considerable.
On favourable days two and a half hours sufficed for the
passage—there are records of crossings which were not
effected within three days of sailing. Passengers arriving
at the little town with intent to cross had often to take
up their abode in the village for days, while "waiting for
the wind," a necessity which made for the prosperity of
Donaghadee.

An old document in the Bodleian Library, Oxford
(Carte MSS. 62, f. 213), addressed "To our well beloved
Sir John Davies, Knight, his Maiesties Attorney Generall,
or Sir Robert Jacob, Knight, his Maiesties Solicitor," and
endorsed "Sir Hugh Montgomerie's warrant for Donaghdie,"
preserves interesting particulars of the Cross Channel service
by Donaghadee in the early years of the Scottish Plantation.
The document, dated 16th January, 1616, is worn into holes
—the missing parts are indicated by dots in the following
copy :—

"Whereas accordinge to his . . . . . . lettres bearinge
date at Beau . . . . directed a Commission to
Captain Edward Treaner Ma..cke . . . . . . Thomas
Rand, Esquires, to enquire whether the Towne & Harb. . . .
. . . . Ardes in the Countie of Downe were not the only
fittest place in the . . . . a Porte-towne & to be
a Ferry or Pastage, from whence only all menn should be transported from the Ardes aforesaid, to the Rinnes of Galloway or

Porte Patrick in Scotland & to be a certaine landinge place, for
the avoydinge of dailie disorders in conveyinge of stolen goodes
out of any of the said kingdomes att Bye Creekes of that Coast,
& bringinge in of Idle & lewd people to the hinderance of the
Plantacion of those partes ; and if they found that Donaghdy
were the fittest place for his Majesties service and that purpose
& for the good of the country.   Then to consider what nomber
of Boates would be sufficient to be kepte for the Transportacion
and what Fraught fitteinge to be allowed to every Boate, respecte
being had to the nomber and quantitie of Passengers & theire
goodes : Which said Commissioners have retourned Certificate
vnto vs, that vppon the veiw of Bangor, & other Creekes alonge
the Coast in the Ardes they finde Donaghdy to be the only fittest
place, betweene the River of Strangford & the River of Knock-
fergus for the saftie of Boates, the good ease of Passage, and the
abbilitie of the Towne for entertainemente of Passengers ; &
that the Passage cannot be supplied vnder the nomber of sixeteene Passage Boates, of eight, or Tenn Tunne apeece or there-
aboutes ; Lastly that the Fraught of each boate from Donaghady
to Port Patricke in Scotland ; which any Mann shall hyre for
himselfe, not beinge above . . . . . Horse should bee
XVs. Shillings sterling in the Somer ; and XXtie Shillings in
the Winter, and for every Boate takeinge in Common Fare ;
the Horse & Mann in the Sommer should pay 2s 6d & in the
Winter 3s.   And every Horse without a Mann in Sommer 2s
& in Winter 2s. 6d. sterling And every Mann or Woeman Pas-
senger 8d sterling thorought the whole yeare & for every Cowe,
or Oxe, js 6d in the Sommer, and in the Winter 2s And they have
also certified their Opinions touchinge diuers other perticulars
in the same Commission, for the good of the Country & his
Majesties said Service, as in the returne of the said Commission
is more att lardge expressed : Which for your better direccion
wee send you herewith, & therevppon in accomplishmente of his
Majesties Pleasure signified in the said lettres.   Wee doe hereby
will and require yow forthwith vppon sight heerof to drawe
forth a Fiant in due forme of lawe of Lettres Pattentes for the
makeinge of the said Towne & Harbor of Donaghdie the only
port & Haven within the said Barrony of the Ardes as well for
exportacion as Importacion, of all Passengers, Merchandizes,
Goodes & Cattell whatsoever & that noe other Harbor or Creeke
within the said Barrony of the Ardes bee from henceforth taken

or . . . . Harbor for the Arivall & Roade of any
Shipps, Barke . . . . with a Prohibition not to
land or Take a board any Pas. . . . . other
Creeke in the said Barrony of the Ardes but only in the . . . .
vpon payne of Forfeiture. And likewise to establish a perpetu.
. . . . betweene the said Harbor of Donaghdy,
and the Rinn . . . . Port Patricke ; And also
to incerte in the said Grant . . . . Aucthority
vnto the said Sir Hugh Montgomery his heie . . . . .
ever to seise in his Majesties name ; and to his Majesties vse,
all s. . . . . other vessells, & all Merchandizes Goods and Cattle as shal be forfeited . . . . . .
And likewise meetinge in the said Grant a Covenaunt on the
parte. . . . . . . Sir Hugh Montgomery his Heiers,
and Assignes to keepe & . . . . cause to bee
kepte, & mainteyned att the said Harbor of Donaghdy . .
supp . . .inge the said Passage or Ferry sixeteene good and
sufficient Boates . . other vessells with Menn, Anchors,
sailes, & Oares, for trannsportinge of Passengers, Merchandizes,
Goods and Cattle from the Port of Donaghdy vnto the said
Rinnes of Galloway or Port Patricke And likewise to give and
graunt full Power and aucthoritie vnto the said Sir Hugh his
heiers and Assignes to appoint one able and sufficient Clarke
to keepe a true Booke or Register to write and enter the name
and names of all Passengers comminge to, or goeinge from the
said Porte of Donaghdy, And likewise to Minister the Oath of
Allegiannce to any suspitious Person comeinge to, or goeinge
from the said Port of Donaghdy ; and likewise to booke, or
Register the parcells and quantities of all goods, and Merchandizes
and the nomber, and Markes, of all Horses, Geldings, Cowes,
Oxen, & other Cattle commeinge to, or goeinge from the said
Port ; And likewise to give & Graunt vnto the sayd Sir Hugh
Montgomery his Heiers and Assignes the said Ferry, or Passage,
betweene the said Port of Donaghdy, and the Rinnes of Galloway or Port Patericke. And likewise to give and graunt vnto the
said Sir Hugh Montgomery his Heiers and Assignes All such
Fraughts, Fares, and Fees as are beforemencioned and certified
by the said Commissioners for Fraught of the said Boates ; And
also to aucthorise the said Clarke soe appointed by the said Sir
Hugh Montgomery his Heiers or Assignes to demaund and receave
for bookeinge every Passengers name commeinge to or goeing

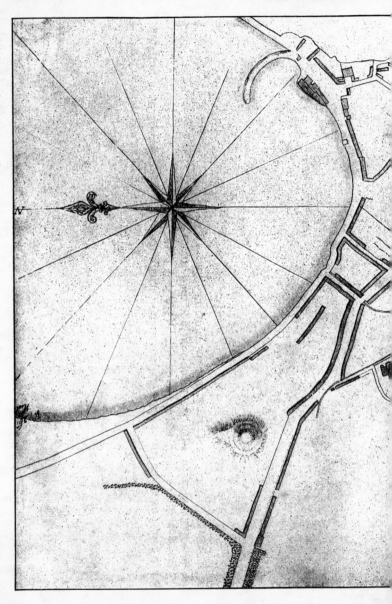

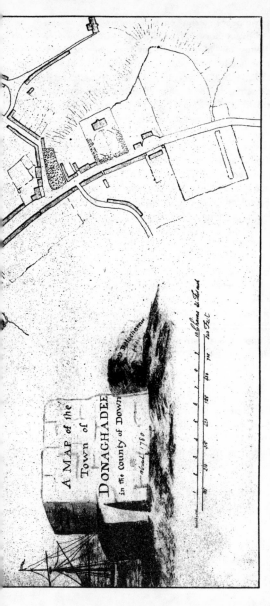

A MAP of the Town of DONAGHADEE in the county of Down

March 1780

THE TOWN AND HARBOUR OF DONAGHADEE. This plan, made for, or by, Mr. De la Cherois, and dated "about 1780," is, as survey, much more accurate than that of Dillon. It must have been made later, but not much later, than the latter. The streets connecting the Shore Road with the main or upper road are (beginning at harbour) Manor Street, New Street (then in course of reconstruction), Hunter's Lane (Union Street was not yet in existence), and, beyond the fort or mound, East Street (then called Bullock Row). On this street Dillon shows no houses : this map shows a row on ground now occupied by coastguard buildings.

Original in the Manor House, Donaghadee.

from the said Port two pence sterling curraunt monny of England
and for Bookeing of every horse, Mare, Geldinge, Oxe, Cowe, or
other Cattle one Penny like Monny, and for bookeinge of every
Packe, or Fardell of goodes one penny like monny. And also
that noe Boate takeinge in Common Fare be compelled to setto
sea vntill his Fare doe rise to 20s sterling after the rate aforesaid.
And also to incerte a Graunt of a Court to the said Sir Hugh
Montgomery his Heires & Assignes, to Hould Plea of all matters
whatsoever not exceedinge the somme of Tenn Powndes sterling
To be held before the Seneschall or Steward to bee appointed
by the said Sir Hugh his heiers or Assignes, And that the said
Seneschall soe appointed shal be a Justice of Peace within the
said County of Downe, and also bee a Clarke of the Markett
within the Towne of Donaghdy ; and also to incert therein a
Graunt vnto the said Sir Hugh Mountgomery and his Heirers
for ever accordinge to his Majesties said lettres ; One Fair to
be kepte yearely on the Tenth day of June ; (if the same bee not
Sondaie) and if it bee, on the Monday followeinge and two daies
after ; and a Weekely Markett on every Wednesday reservinge
for the same vnto his Majestie the yearely Rent of . . . per
Annum. And forasmuch as wee have beene certified by the
Commissioners aforesaid, that the Abbay of the Comb^r by reason
of the situation, if it weere well planted, & endued, with Immunni-
ties would bee of good vse to strengthen those partes : Theis
are also to require you t. . . . . . . the said Sir
Hugh Mountgomery of . . . . . . aforesaid on the
28th day of October . . . . . . Monday followeinge
and three daies after, and of a Weekely . . . . . .
Maiesty for the said Faier & Markett . . . .
& to Hould the said Faiers and Markettes . . . . . .
& Assignes for ever with all Priviledges, Immunities, and . .
. . . . . accustomed in like Graunts. And haveing thus
drawne forth the . . . . . . send the same vnto vs
fair Ingrossed in Parchmente vnder your hand to be further
passed as apperteyneth, In doeinge whereof this shal be your
Warraunt. Given att his Majesties Castle of Dublin the Xvjth
day of January 1616."

Another document in the Bodleian Library (Carte MSS.
154, f. 24) gives the names of the port staff and their salaries
for the year 1660.

" Sallaries per annum.			
	l.	s.	d.
Eliazer Hodson Collectour	.. .. 080.	oo.	oo
William Aplyn Waiter	.. .. 030.	oo.	oo
Henry Tayler waiter	.. .. 035.	oo.	oo
John wislett Tidesman	.. .. 012.	oo.	oo
Henry Davis Landwaiter	.. .. 020.	oo.	oo
Robert Brearly landwayter	.. .. 030.	oo.	oo

The Rawlinson Collection of manuscripts, also preserved
at the Bodleian, contains a Report " To the right Worshippfull
Commissioners of his Majestye's Revenue in the Kingdome of
Ireland " (MS. B510, f. 7b), which represents the state of the
port in April, 1675, as follows :—

" Port Donoghodee.

" Lyeth upon the main but 10 leagues from Portpatrick in ye
County of Galloway in Scotland, Mr. Hugh Campbale your
Collectour & dextrous man but shair's in Vessells and Trades
with Merchants.

" So likewise hath William Osmotherly your Riding-Officer
there.

" Robert Collingwood your surveyour and Waiter seems to
be sober and ingenuous.

" John Ashdowne Riding waiter at Groomsport and also
Tho. Roe Riding-Waiter at Hollywood both reputed sober &
diligent.

" I examined all Books of accompt, Files, Invoyces & out-
voyces etc. and found them all well kept.

" There is about eighteen Vessells Burden for 20 to 60 tuns
belonging to this Port.

" There is nothing of imported Excise stands out.

" There is nothing in the Warehouse for which Custome is
not paid."

At the end of the eighteenth century the cattle traffic,
through Donaghadee to Scotland, was of great importance.
It was from this port that De Latocnaye, the Frenchman,
who walked through Ireland in 1796, returned to Scotland
after his pilgrimage. He says :—

" The number of cattle taken from here to Scotland is something inconceivable. On the day I crossed there were four hundred horned cattle taken over to Scotland, and in the six weeks previous there had been transported nearly thirty thousand. The farmers are obliged to submit to the impudent impositions of the owners of the boats which take the cattle. They ask as much as twenty guineas for a crossing ; and as they hold the farmer in the hollow of their hand he is obliged to pay what they ask, and this means that the cost of transport for horned cattle is as much as one guinea per beast. It seems to me that the country authorities ought to establish a regular tariff as is done in many places. Here the distance is scarcely twenty miles.

" In two hours and a half I was carried to the opposite side of the water, saluted anew the coast of Scotland, and counted myself happy that at last I had arrived at a place where I could rest in peace."

A letter from Charles Echlin, Judge Ward's agent at Bangor, under date May 15, 1728, shows how absolute was the control of the landowner over parliamentary representation of these little boroughs. The letter is addressed to the Judge.

" I received y^r letter from Derry. I have put up a notice according to ye Act & we shall proceed to the Election of your son on thursday. I suppose by this you have an account of John Jolly's Death, which makes another vacancy in our Corporation be pleased to let me have your orders about same."

As Michael Ward was married only in 1710, his son, elected burgess, must have been a mere lad at this date. The landlord made burgesses of whom he would, and his nominees elected Members of Parliament, who were in no sense representatives of the people. The excitements of contested elections are dealt with later in this chapter.

While the buildings in towns were as bad at a late date in the eighteenth century as the quoted matter indicates, it is not to be expected that the poorer farmers were well housed. Madden, who published his *Reflections and Resolutions Proper for the Gentlemen of Ireland* in 1738, has an

indiscriminating form of assertion for all matters pertaining to Ireland, while, undoubtedly, conditions varied,
so that it is uncertain whether his description of the poorer
farmers' dwellings is correctly applied to Down. He says :—

> " They, the tenants, (I speak of the poorest and greatest part of
> them) have rather Huts than Houses, and those of our Cotters
> are built like Birds' Nests, of Dirt wrought together and a few
> sticks and some straw.
>
> " Numbers of them have no Chimney either from want of
> Wood or skill to build one, but vent the Smoak like those of the
> Hottentots."

While the general application of this to the country in Down
is doubtful, existing remains of clay houses show that it not
incorrectly describes the cottages of labourers in certain parts
of the county.

From the time of the Huguenot immigration Down took
an important part in the cultivation of flax and the manufacture of linen. Here is not space to treat the subject at
great length, yet any picture of eighteenth-century life in
Down which should omit mention of such important industry
would be defective. Mason, in his Statistical account of Down,
published in 1819, mentions the belief that the first flax-mill
in Ireland was in Holywood parish. Two of the Trustees
for Ulster, of the Board of Development of the Linen and
Hempen Manufactures in Ireland, constituted in 1711, were
Michael Ward and the Earl of Mount-Alexander, and many
of the old letters preserved at Castle Ward deal with the
efforts of the Board and of individuals to increase the cultivation of flax and hemp, and the manufacture of linen and
hemp cloth. In *Precedents and Abstracts from the Journals
of the Trustees* is found the following short sketch of the
Board's activities :—

> " They arranged for the bringing of flax and hemp seed from
> Holland, which seed they sold at under cost to farmers who
> bound themselves to sow a certain quantity. They appointed
> a number of travelling teachers or inspectors, called by them

itinerant flax or hemp men, and it was the duty of these persons to assist farmers and merchants by giving them information and advice in matters of proper land for sowing, the proper soil, the manner of cultivating the same, the qualities of good and bad seed, the best way and times of watering, weeding, and dressing the hemp or flax, as also the manner of spinning, reeling and making the same up in hanks. Other men were employed to teach the mystery or trade of weaving damask linen, the manufacture of tapes, candle wicks, canvas, cordage, etc. etc.

" Men were sent to various places in England and Scotland such as Bristol to learn all that was necessary with regard to sail-cloth, to Manchester, Liverpool, Whitehaven and other places to find what was to be learned of the various branches of linen and hemp trades at these places, other men were sent further afield to Holland, France and Flanders.

" Another branch of the Board's activity was provision of spinning-wheels, the giving of bonuses to encourage the sowing of flax and hemp seed, the establishment of spinning-schools, the establishment of looms. Inspectors were also appointed in this business to take charge of the country's reputation for linen. These men examined the linen exposed in the markets and took steps to prosecute merchants or weavers who offered material short in quantity or deficient in quality.

" They occupied themselves also in all the details of bleaching, providing model plants, and loaned or sold the tools necessary for Breaking, Swindling, and Hatchling of flax. (' Hatchling ' is hackling.)

" An example of the kind of contracts which the Board were willing to make will be found from their minutes of Saturday August 21st 1725. ' We the Committee appointed to consider the Proposals of Mr. James Hamilton Maxwell, for setting up a Bleachyard at Drumbegg, in the county of Down, and to give our opinion, how the Bleaching of this Kingdom may be improved, have met, and are of opinion, that the best method that can be taken for the improvement of the Bleaching of this Kingdom, will be, to bring over Bleachers from Holland, who have followed that business there, and are well skilled therein. We are therefore of opinion, if Mr. Maxwell will enter into Articles to make a Bleachyard and Build a Buck-house, and provide the same with the utensils mentioned in the Plan hereunto annexed, and also bring over from Holland, a Bleacher

well skilled in the Dutch Methods of bleaching, who shall bleach
after the best manner used at Harlem, and shall bring such
Cloths as he shall bleach, to as good a colour as those whitened
in Holland, and shall be under contract to stay in this Kingdom
for three years, and follow the said trade, and instruct three
apprentices in the best methods of bleaching used in Holland,
that then Mr Maxwell be allowed the sum of 40L. per annum for
three years, as wages for the said Bleacher, but we are farther
of opinion, that after the said three years, he the said Mr. Maxwell
be obliged to carry on the Bleaching Trade, after the Dutch
manner, for seven years, at his own expence, without any farther
encouragement from this Board.

" ' Your Committee is likewise of opinion, that Mr Maxwell
be obliged to send some pieces of his bleaching, every year during
the first three years to be laid before this Board.'

" Another experiment will be found noted in the Minutes of
April the 30th 1726. ' Ordered, That forty pounds weight of
Linen Yarn, of four dozen to the pound, be purchased for making
an experiment, how the said Daniel Chappell can dye Yarn in
large parcels, and at what prices the same may be afforded, and
that he be directed to dye ten pounds thereof of green colour,
ten pounds of a yellow colour, ten pounds of a purple, and ten
pounds of a red colour ; and that the said experiments be made
at Mr. Justice Coote's house.'

" In the year in which this Hall (the Linen Hall at Dublin)
was built there seems to have been spent £10,428 . 0. 5½. £5800
of this was spent in hemp and flax seed.

" It would be interesting to find the cost per barrel of hemp
and flax seed in the year 1730. This cost is detailed in the
minutes of the Board for Saturday May 6th 1732 : ' And we beg
leave further to observe, that the first-cost of one barrel of the
Flax-seed, imported in the year 1730, at Riga, was £1 6 0

The freight of that Barrel	..	..	..	0 5	0
The Insurance	..	..	..	0 2	0¼
The Post-charges	..	..	..	0 0	1
Commission	..	..	..	0 0	10
Cooperage	..	..	..	0 0	8
Total of each Barrel of Flax-seed	..	..	£1 14	7¼
Premium deducted	..	..	..	0 2	5
				£1 12	2¼

" And that the first-cost of a barrel of Hemp-seed at Riga, imported in the said year 1730, is £0 7 1

	£	s	d
Insurance	0	0	7
Freight	0	2	6
Commission	0	0	3
Total of a barrel of Hemp-seed	£0	10	5
Premium deducted	0	2	5
Total	£0	8	0

" The first-cost of one barrel of Flax-seed imported in the year

	£	s	d
1731, at Riga	£1	14	8
Freight	0	4	6
Insurance	0	2	10
Post-charges	0	0	1
Cooperage and landing	0	0	8
Commission	0	1	0
	£2	3	9
Net Premium	0	2	5
One barrel of the Seed stands the Board in ..	£2	1	4

A work of the time of the Huguenot colony, *A Discourse concerning IRELAND and the Interests thereof* (London, 1697), testifies to the eagerness with which the smaller farmers and labourers devoted their evening hours to the production of yarn.

" They are so intent upon this kind of manufacture that the very Husbandmen and their servants, when they return from their Labours abroad, such as plowing, Sowing, Fencing, etc. do imploy themselves by their Firesides in this kind of work and sit reeling of Linnen-Yarn while the Women are busy in Spinning, and by this Constancy and Diligence that Country produces great quantities of good Linnen yearly."

Hemp and hemp-seed are mentioned very frequently in the early records of the Board and in letters ; but it was found, after lengthy experiments, that soil and climate were not suitable for hemp cultivation. William Rainey, a Belfast

merchant, writing to a member of the Board in 1725, in the
interest of his friend, Robert Wilson, of Belfast, who had
contracted to sow a large area with flax and hemp-seed, says
that the flax had turned out all right, but the hemp was a
failure, and he solicits for his friend the Board's consideration of
the loss incurred. The late Mr. Isaac Ward, writing to the author,
states that it was Crommelin who recommended the sowing
of hemp-seed, and that it was abandoned about 1735 on account
of the losses due to failure of crops. In the year 1736 the
hemp-seed imported into Ireland was value for only £27 4s. 4d.,
while of undressed hemp the import value was £11,987 10s. 4d.
In the same year flax-seed to the value of £14,592 10s. 0d.
was imported, while the undressed flax coming into the
country was value for only £3,491 18s. 9d., from which it
would appear that Ireland, at that time, grew nearly all the
flax she turned into linen. In 1738, however, according to
another authority, Ireland imported seed and undressed flax
to the value of £30,000—evidently an estimate. It has
been alleged in recent times that the Board, in its encouragement, unduly favoured the North. This matter is referred
to in Mr. Ward's letter already mentioned.

> " One of the Linen Inspectors for the Dublin Linen Board was
> from near Antrim, named Robert Stephenson, who travelled
> over all Ireland, and gave a monthly report, from the different
> counties, of the progress of the Linen Manufacture. The last
> report of his I have seen was dated about 1763. . . . . .
>   " Four or five years ago I wrote a short sketch of the history
> of these Linen Bounties for the Belfast Chamber of Commerce,
> when there was some kind of Vice-regal Commission in Dublin,
> and it was alleged that Ulster had been favoured in the 18th
> century by these Linen Bounties, but Stephenson's reports
> showed that every county in Ireland had the same advantages.
>   " I believe Robt. Stephenson's son was the well-known Dr.
> S. M. Stephenson of the early part of last century, who died in
> Waring Street in 1833."

The Board built the Linen Hall at Dublin, and there had
its headquarters. There is nothing whatever in its records

to indicate any preference for the North, while Mr. Ward's statement of equal attention to the other provinces is confirmed by the following letter from Samuel Waring, of Waringstown, to Michael Ward. It belongs to the period under consideration.

> " Several persons have been with me since I left Dublin, enquiring about yᵉ Flaxseed to be disposed of, which they would gladly take on any terms yᵉ Board would propose. I must own I would rather have it propagated at present in ye other Provinces of this Kingdom, whence a better correspondence woud arise between them & this of Ulster by their furnishing us with the flax when we shall want it, and we yᵐ in return with yarn till they have Spinners of their own, wᶜʰ may be a means of keeping more of our yarn in the Kingdom, and making our Linnen trade more extensive at home than it is now."

Unfortunately, it was only in the North that the industry took root—growing more and more prosperous, and less and less indebted to Boards and their teachers as the century progressed. At first the trade, apparently, had to contend with the prejudice against linen making, as being a low occupation with which persons of education, family, or wealth did not care to be associated. Among the documents of the Crommelin family is copy of a letter, written by their ancestor Louis Crommelin, in which he refers to this feeling. He writes :—

> " To remove some prejudices that seem universally to possess the minds of the People of this Kingdom in relation to that Trade which are these—1st that the Spinners, the weavers and the Bleachers' trades are such poor abject trades all the World over & particularly in Ireland, that it is impossible for men of a free generous spirit (such as the People of this Kingdom must be allowed to be) to conform themselves thereunto. . . . They must not, however, judge . . . they have not yet learned how to make the trade great and profitable."

The prejudice must have disappeared quickly, for, in *A Topographical and Chorographical SURVEY of the County of Down* (Dublin, 1740), from which some extracts are given

below, progress of the linen manufacture is reported from
many parts of the county, and to it is attributed the improved
condition of the people in Down.

> " The Staple Commodity of this County is the Linnen Manufacture :
> a due Cultivation of which hath been of great Service. The
> Northern Commonalty already feel the Benefit of it ; being
> freed from much of that Poverty and Wretchedness, which are
> too visible among the lower sort in other Parts of the Kingdom
> where this Branch of Trade has not yet been improved to purpose.
> The County in general may be said to be populous and flourishing
> and daily increases in Wealth and Inhabitants."

Among the notes of progress in district may be quoted—

> " DOWNPATRICK. The Linnen Manufacture spreads here as
> it does in most other places of this County."

> " BANGOR. The town . . . hath little trade but spins
> considerable quantities of fine Linnen Yarn."

> " NEWTOWNARDS. It is famous for its fine diaper Linnen."

> " KILLYLEAGH. Here the Linnen Manufacture has spread to
> Advantage and the fine White thread made in it is remarkable."

> " MARALIN. Here are Linnen Weavers and Bleach Yards ;
> scarce a farmer but carries on some Branch of the Linnen
> Business."

> " WARINGSTOWN, where the Linnen Manufacture which
> shew'd itself very early, has spread so considerably that a Colony
> of Linnen Weavers have gone hence and settled at Dundalk."

A few curious items of information discovered in ransacking
old records, dealing with flax growth and linen manufacture,
may be given here.   The first is in a note from Lord Limerick
at Whitehall to Michael Ward, in Down.

> " February 2nd. I was last night at a meeting of
> several merchants, as well English as Scotch and
> 1787   Irish, who were unanimous about applying to
> Parliament for taking off the drawback on foreign
> linnen. I myself have spoke to two gentlemen of
> our house, who are the greatest proprietors in America, who
> have both assured me that they will be with us, and one of them

said he shou'd be willing to consent to an act that the Negroes
shou'd be cloath'd in nothing but the manufactures of Ireland
and Scotland."

The next, from *The Dublin Society's Weekly Observations for
the Advancement of Agriculture and Manufacture* (1756), shows,
in the case of hand-spun yarns, an extraordinary difference
in value between unmanufactured material and the finished
product.

" A stone of flax, the original price of which, before it has undergone any change from labour, is only two and six-pence, may
be drawn into threads of different finenesses gradually encreasing
in value from one penny to four pounds an ounce."

From the same source is taken the following account
of the Dutchman's method of estimating the quality of
flax-seed :—

" I proceed at present to give you my thoughts upon the nature
and properties of good flax-seed, and the time and manner of
sowing it. Nothing is plainer, than that the farmer cannot be
too nice in the choice of his seed, since the value of his crop must
chiefly depend upon its goodness. In general the shortest,
plumpest, thickest, oyliest, heaviest seed, of a bright brown
colour, is esteemed the best. The Dutch boor is very exact,
in examining these several qualities, and makes his trials in the
following manner. In order to discover thickness, he takes a
large handful, and squeeses it, until the edges appear plainly
between his finger and thumb ; for it is entirely from the edges,
he forms his judgment in that particular. To try its weight, he
throws a handful into a glass of water ; if it sinks soon, he is
sure it is heavy and good ; if otherwise, he judges it unfit for
his purpose. To examine its oyliness, he throws a quantity
into the fire, if it blaze soon, and crackle much, he thinks he may
depend upon it. After all, he sometimes sows it in a hot-bed,
and in short, leaves no method untry'd, which will ensure him
that his seed is of the best kind."

Agriculture being the principal employment of inhabitants
of Down, after notes on linen production, there is not much
to be said of trade and manufactures of the county. Mason

notes, early in the nineteenth century, as strange that Holywood parish had not a single bleachgreen, " though the
neighbourhood of Belfast, in general, abounds with them."
He adds—

> " We have a few calico and muslin looms employed by Belfast
> Manufacturers. Stocking weaving, however, seems to be a
> more favourable pursuit. The hosiers' looms in the Village,
> (Holywood) and its vicinity are at least 20 in number."

For agricultural produce Belfast was the great dis-
tributing centre. Numerous references in books, diaries,
and letters, testify to the great quantities of country produce
dealt with at Belfast. William Ramsay, the Belfast merchant,
already mentioned, writing to Judge Ward, August 30, 1725,
says :—

> " We have had thiss Month of Augt 200 tuns of butter come to
> thiss town it holds up 21/6 pr hund the ferken & 22/6 the Tubs
> to the Country."

Smuggling from the Isle of Man to various points on the
Down coast was much practised. The poet of Ardglass,
Burdy, makes known to us, in halting verse, what were the
commodities carried on the outward voyage—fruit, flour,
flax, whiskey, potatoes, and, strange to say, tea.

> " The pretty traders, with their bags of meal,
> Their fruit, and flax and whisky too for sale,
> Their flour, potatoes, and their fine bohea,
> Pass o'er in boats along the watery way,
> And thence return, almost in time to dine,
> With sugar, coffee, and the cherry wine.
> But should the cruizer, on a luckless day,
> Observe their vessel in his search for prey,
> He then pursues, it quickly flies before,
> And strives to gain Hibernia's friendly shore,
> Too oft in vain, and then with streaming eyes
> They see the cruizer snatch the lawfull prize.
> In hopes the little smack at least to save,
> Sometimes they cast into the briny wave
> Wine, sugar, coffee, rum, the precious goods,
> As far and wide they're scatter'd o'er the floods."

The movement of produce through Down was much facilitated by the well-made roads. Writing from near Downpatrick to Gloucester, in 1744, Mary Granville (Mrs. Delany) writes—

> " Tho weather is so excessively bad that I don't believe we shall be able to set out to-morrow for home as we designed ; not that we have anything to apprehend from the roads, for I never travelled such fine roads as are all over this country, but I shall be afraid of the Dean's travelling in damp weather,"

and the *Dublin Society's Observations*, already quoted, speak of the results following turnpike Acts as remarkable.

> " We shall here take notice of a late improvement among us, which is a great ease and benefit to inland commerce, that by means of our turnpike acts we have the finest roads in Europe and perfect gravel walks from one part of the kingdom to another."

The members of the Boards having charge of turnpike roads were persons of high standing in the districts they supervised. Some eighteenth-century records of a Board, regulating the business of road-making and repairing near Belfast, are now in possession of the Corporation of Belfast, and from these the information following has been taken.

The various gates were farmed—sales of the tolls for a year being made by auction. Malone turnpike tolls for 1763 were auctioned for £100 ; but the bidder, alarmed at having offered what he considered too much, drew back—and the gate for twelve months was resold at £90. Thirty-eight years later this gate was let at £390 per annum. The Board had trouble with the farmers of tolls,—defaulters were frequently committed to jail for debt, and their securities sued.

The tolls were not heavy, and the benefits conferred on agriculturists were certainly great. Nevertheless, these tried to practise economy at the Board's expense, as will be seen from a resolution of 19th April, 1764.

> " Resolved, ' That it is the oppinion of the Board that two Carrs tyed together without being Loaded shall not be deemed a Carriage but separate Carrs with horses and pay accordingly.' "

The attempts to evade tolls were ungenerous, for the
Board members gave freely of their time for the benefit of
the county, and made no profit on their charges.   Money
for new work was raised on 4% Debentures.   In 1788 the
amount of this Board's debt was £2,897 11s. 11d.

Interest at 4% required annually	115	17	10½
Interest was in arrear to the extent of ..	805	5	1
The Annual value of the tolls was	220	0	0
Deducting Interest and Salaries from tolls, there remained for repairing roads, discharging arrears of interest, etc.—only	91	2	1½

Very surprising it is to find frequent mention of
foreign coinages in eighteenth-century everyday trade
transactions in Down.   The pistole, Louis d'or, and moidore
appear with great frequency in the accounts and letters of
the county through the greater part of the eighteenth century,
and, it goes without saying, in wonderful varieties of spelling.
When that " greate desstroyer of money " Mrs. Smith, buyer
in Belfast for the Hamilton family at Bangor (see page 302),
says she received from Mrs. Hamilton ' six pistols,' she does
not mean firearms, but ' pistoles.'   A merchant's account of
1724 gives credit for " two moydors £3 0s. 0d."   In the valua-
tion of the goods and chattels of Daniel Cormier, one of the
French immigrants, deceased, there is account of cash in the
widow's hands—

" 1 Moydore	..	..	..	£1	9 10
2 Guineas	..	..	..	2	6 0
¼ Moydore	..	..	..		7 6 "

The large old gold coins were commonly spoken of as ' broad
pieces.'   When Scott, divinity student of Donaghadee, says
in his diary that he gave his sweetheart " a broad piece of gold,"
at the peat-stack, it is to one of these coins he refers.   The
allowances for light weight and charges for exchanging were
very productive of trouble or loss to the common folk.   A
lady's letter to her nephew—date 1719—will give an idea of

BELFAST LOUGH about 1775. From an old pen-and-
shows that it was customary to land passengers

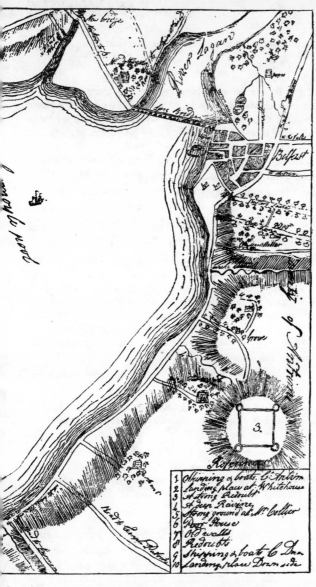

Reference.

1	Shipping of boats. Co. Antrim
2	Landing place at Whitehouse
3	A stone Redoubt
4	A deep Ravine
5	Strong ground at Mr Collier
6	Dog House
7	Old walls
8	Redoubt
9	Shipping & boats Co. Down
10	Landing place Down side

...ving in possession of Miss Tate, Belfast. This map
...o from deep water at Cultra and Whitehouse.

the complex calculations involved in the handling of such currency.

" Dear Nephew,
  I got by Mr price 20 levedores of wch there was light 2 double ones wanted 8d a piece ye other double one 4d 8 single ones wanted 6d a piece and ye ither six 4d a piece which I think is in all 7s. 8d so y^t if I count right I have got 18^lb 2s 4d," etc. etc.

The letters of the very practical Lord Primate, Boulter, abound with references to coinage difficulties, in which these French, Spanish, and Portuguese coins, and the costs of changing them, are mentioned. The few extracts here given belong to letters of the second quarter of the century. The first is of date 1736.

" A moidore, which is worth about 27s. in England, passes here for 30s. Irish, or 27s. English, and 9d. and the rest of our gold is in the main proportion to the value of the moidore. And whilst this is our case, no man in trade will carry a moidore from hence, to instance in one piece of gold, if he can get silver, when he loses 9d. by the moidore as soon as he lands at Chester ; nor will he bring from Chester 27s. English, when he can gain 9d. by bringing a moidore."

" The lowest price of changing a moidore in most parts being 8d. and often 1s. or more."

" Our want of silver here is such, that it is common to give six-pence for the change of a moidore, and to take a guinea or pistole for part of the change."

" I have nothing farther to add to my memorial on that subject, but that upon considering that in the scheme formerly proposed, foreign silver is set at the lowest price it is ever sold for in England, and that our people are afraid, if the Mexico piece of eight were set at 5s. Irish."

The scarcity of small change led to the issue by merchants in Down, as elsewhere, of copper tokens,—little roughly stamped coins of very small value intrinsically, but which, as acknowledgment of indebtedness of the issuer to the holder, were accepted generally at their face value of 1d. or 2d. as

O. SENESCHALL,
DOWNPATRICK, 1664.

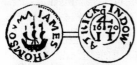

JAMES THOMSON,
DOWNPATRICK, 1670.

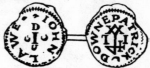

JOHN LAWE, DOWNPATRICK.
(UNDATED: 17TH CENTURY.)

JOHN GUTHRY,
DROMORE, 1663.

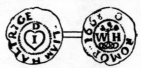

WILLIAM HALTRIGE,
DROMORE, 1668.

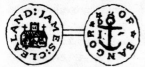

JAMES CLEALAND, BANGOR.
(UNDATED: 17TH CENTURY.)

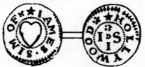

JAMES SIM, HOLYWOOD.
(UNDATED: 17TH CENTURY.)

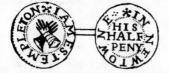

JAMES TEMPLETON, NEWTOWNARDS.
(UNDATED: 17TH CENTURY.)

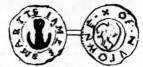

JAMES SMARTTS, NEWTOWNARDS.
(UNDATED: 17TH CENTURY.)

Co. Down Trading Tokens—17th century.
From the collection in the Public Art Gallery and Museum, Belfast.

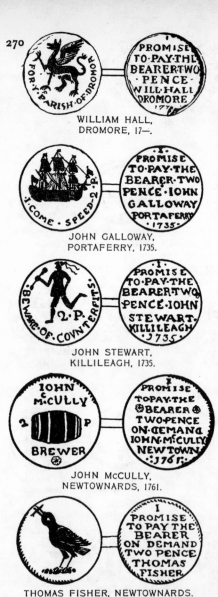

WILLIAM HALL,
DROMORE, 17—.

JOHN GALLOWAY,
PORTAFERRY, 1735.

JOHN STEWART,
KILLILEAGH, 1735.

JOHN McCULLY,
NEWTOWNARDS, 1761.

THOMAS FISHER, NEWTOWNARDS.
(UNDATED: 18TH CENTURY.)

Co. Down Trading Tokens,
18th century.

From the collection in the Public Art Gallery and Museum, Belfast.

stamped. The earliest known date from about 1650. The issue of these tokens was more than once prohibited by Proclamation, but the crying necessity for small coinage made dead letter of Proclamation, and private issues of coin continued to be made at intervals until the year 1820. Farthings were issued much later, rather as advertising media than of necessity. All token or imitation-coinage issue is now illegal. A few of the older Down issues are illustrated on this and the preceding page.

Postal service was costly and irregular before the middle of the eighteenth century. A letter from Clarendon, Lord Lieutenant, to Lord Sunderland, dated 26th February, 1685-6, outlines his proposition for a mail service.

" I am commanded by the 26th instruction, to establish a packet-boat between this kingdom and Scotland ; if I shall find it necessary for the king's service, I am humbly of opinion, that it would be very useful ; there being no way of corresponding with his majesty's ministers in that kingdom, but by way of London : whereas, if there were a packet-boat, all letters would be sooner at Edenburg from hence, than they are at London, besides, it is said, it would bring on a trade between these two kingdoms. The charge to the king for two boats will not be above fourscore pounds a year ; and for that, I am sure, I can have it undertaken. If the king please to have the tryal made for one year, if it does not answer expectation, the boats may be put down again."

Among the ancient documents at the Manor House, Donaghadee, is an account of the carrying of mails between Scotland and Donaghadee, for Duke Schomberg, from 22nd August till 30th December, 1689. It will be seen from this that in calm weather, or when the winds were contrary, the despatches were carried in yawls, rowed the whole way across.

" The Charges of the Paquetts to Scotland from Donnoghadee from the 22nd of August to the 30th December, 1689. With Insident Charges and Alsoe from Scotland to the Duke, etc.

" 1689 23rd of Aug. I Rode to Carrickfergus with a Packet Direckd to Captain Rooke & Major Generall Kirke, Cost me in Travelling Expences ..	..	oo	09	04
" 24th I Waited on his grace the Duke of Schomberg etc. to gett his graces Answer to a packet from Scotland, Charges ..	..	..	oo	08	11
" 26th I waited on his grace at Carrickfergus wth a lettr from Scotd ..	..	..	..	oo	10	08
" Sept 12th I sent an express on horseback to the Camp of Dundalk with a letter from Scotland to his grace cost me ..	..	..	..	oo	17	06
" 23rd I sent Another Express on horseback to ye Camp to his grace ..	..	..	..	oo	17	oo
" Novemr ye 2nd I sent Hugh Matland express with 3 letters to his grace att Dundalk camp..	..	oo	18	oo

" 19th I sent Jon Parke to Lisburn wth Letters from Scotld to his grace 00 04 00

" To a post for carrying Letters to & from Belfast in sd time 02 07 09

" To the Packett Boats in the said time And to Yoals & men to Rowe them Over in calm Weather & Contrary Winds when the Packett Boats cold not sayle 15 00 00

" For my Sallery for the said time according to the Allowances given by the Ld Liet & Councell of Ireland on ye like occasions 21 05 00

    42 18 02

" The Postage of all letters that went for England & Scotland was received there, What came from thence was received in Belfast, Lisburn & the camp by the respective Post masters, Soe that noe part of it came to my hands Dated this 31st of December 1689.

        Frank Allen.

from the 31st of December 1689 to the 20th of May 1690 paid by me to John park, Post & others & due to my self as Sallery by Mr. John Whalley was then post Mster-Generall & did not pay one penny of this Expence which amounts to About

          Totalls .. 15 00 00

    £57 18 02

A regular mail service between Scotland (Portpatrick) and Ireland (probably Donaghadee) was in being in 1748. The Pinkerton MSS. contain a memorandum of proposal for a post leaving Dublin on Monday at noon,—to be at Groomsport, Co. Down, on Thursday,

" where the passage shall be always ready, the wind serving to depart with the morning's tide, to be at Edinburgh by Monday, noon, following."

The proposed rates were high. A person posting a letter
in Dublin was not to be required to pay anything—the
receiver in England or Scotland was to pay ninepence per
letter, or two shillings and sixpence per ounce, if in packets.
Persons posting to Ireland were to pay in England or Scotland,
threepence per letter, and the receiver in Ireland, sixpence.
Madden, in his *Reflections and Resolutions proper for the
Gentlemen of Ireland* (1738), complains of the postal delays.

> " In wintertime especially through the carelessness of the post-
> masters, the idleness of the post-boys, bad horses, and sometimes
> even want of horses great delays occur."

His proposed remedy was the fining of the post-masters
and whipping of the post-boy, if the mail, without good cause,
should be two hours late.

Correspondents, however, took care to avoid Post Office
charges whenever and wherever it was possible to procure
a frank. A common apology for lateness of a communication
in these Down letters, is the difficulty of getting a frank.
The permission granted, somewhere about 1660, to members
of the Houses of Parliament, to pass their letters through
the post without charge, was, in the eighteenth century,
greatly abused. The postal service was made to undertake
the carriage, not of letters only, but of heavy and bulky
merchandise, without charge—simply because a member of
Parliament had signed his name on the address. Down to
1764 this was all that was needed ; in that year it was enacted
that the whole direction should be in the handwriting of the
franker. Still later, continued abuses led to an enactment
that franks should be dated, and that the letters should be
posted on the day, as dated. Other changes limited the weight
of franked letters, and the number which a member could
frank, or receive free, daily. An old collector of franks in
Down says, in an article in the *Antiquary* of January, 1880 :

> " Members supplied huge packets of franks to friends and adher-
> ents. Some sold their privilege for large sums to banking and
> business firms ; they also accepted douceurs for allowing letters

and newspapers to be directed to them although intended for
other persons ; and servants' wages were frequently paid by
franks which were subsequently sold by them to tradesmen
and others. It was computed that a banking house having one
of the firm an M.P. effected thereby a saving of upwards of
£700 per annum."

Readers of eighteenth-century Down 'histories' will,
not infrequently, meet with the phrase 'a curious gentleman.'
This does not mean that the person referred to was odd, or
unconventional, but that he was a dabbler in science, a
collector of the odd or curious in information or object ; and
very 'curious' were some of the facts of Natural History
provided for him in books of the time. The following notes
are from Harris's *History of Down* :—

A rare Zoophyte.

"South of Newcastle, you come to a place, where several
curious Subjects of the Zoophyte, or Plant-Animal Species, have
been discovered.

"In the year 1738, one of these was found on that Shore left
by the Tide. It's Body consisted wholly of a blewish Cartilage,
without a mixture of anything more dense, or that might bear
a Resemblance to Bone. It was of a roundish flat Figure, about
fifteen Inches Diameter, with some Inequalities, that seemed to
imitate Leggs. On the Edges it was about the thickness of ones
Hand ; but in the middle part thrice as much. It has no Head ;
but its Belly (as I must call it) was partly open, and discovered
a plain Representation of the Bowels ; in which nevertheless
there was no continued tube or Gut, but the whole consisted
of an Assemblage of Bladders of several sizes and Shapes, and
such, as without a closer Examination, might be taken for an
animal Abdomen laid open. In short it seemed to be something intermediate between a sensitive and vegetable Body,
or looked, as if Nature had attempted to form an Animal, and
been disappointed. Upon spreading it on a Rock, by the power
of the Weather and Sun, it all gradually dissolved into Salt
Water."

The King Fisher.

"It stands erect, and is extremely shy. It is said to build
its nest and Brood it's Eggs on the Rocks, in the very brink of

the Sea, in the calm season, about the Brumal Solstice, which
is called St. Martin's Summer ; and from this Bird, the Halcyon
Days, or a Time of Tranquility.   Some say it makes it's Nest
of the Foam of the Sea indurate, which is called by Pliny Hal-
cionium ; and that the Word Halcyon is derived from its hatching
in the Sea, Schroder affirms, that some Persons hang the Heart
of this Bird about the Neck of Children to cure the Falling
sickness."

The Chough—a bird which sets houses on fire.

" In the Neighbourhood of Killough are sometimes seen,
though not many in Number, a Species of Birds, which (as far
as appears) are Strangers to the rest of Ireland, except a few on
the Shores of Lough-Earn, in the County of Fermanagh, and
(as we are informed) some in the County of Clare.   It is the
Cornish Chough or Daw, called in Cornwall the Killigrew, by
Aristotle, Coracia, and by Pliny (who imagined it to be peculiar
to the Alps) Pyrocorax, a colore rostri igneo, from the fiery
Colour of its Beak, (as the Naturalists say) in Greek, signifying
Fire, and a Crow.   One would, however, rather chuse to give
it that Name from its Qualities, being found by the Inhabitants
of Cornwall to be an Incendiary and very thievish Bird ; for
that it often sets Houses on Fire, by carrying lighted Brands
in its Beak, and is fond of stealing Pieces of Money, as our
Common Daw is.   It is a Beautiful Bird, nothing resembling
the Irish Daw, except in its Pipe.   It is jett black, with a slender
red Beak, and red Legs, and in Size almost equals a Rook.   This
is the Bird that Bellonius calls the Graculus, and Dala affirms
that the Flesh of it outwardly applied dissolves Tumours, and
helps in scrophulous Disorders."

A Sea Monster.

" Before we close this Chapter, we cannot but take Notice
of a strange Fish lately taken on the southern Shore of Lecale,
in a Creek near Dunsport, the like whereof the oldest Fishers
declare they never saw.   It was about 20 Inches long, half of
which was taken up by the Head, which was also nine Inches
across and crooked, It had no Finns, but on each side a kind of
Leg and Foot, ending in a sort of Finny Toes, webbed, and
armed with small Nails.   The Tail was crooked, and ended also
in such a Foot, and all the Parts of it were extremely tight,
strongly connected, and unusually tendinous.   Out of the

Belly underneath (which was flat) issued two Members, exactly resembling human Hands, with four Fingers and a Thumb ; with which (we may suppose) it crept forward slowly, whilst it contracted its other Limbs, and then sprung upon it's Prey ; to dispose of which further, it was armed with several Rows of long white and sharp Teeth, fixed in strong Jaws, and with a thick Tongue, and on the Snout of it were several Horns like those on the Turbot kind. This Account was lately communicated by a worthy Clergyman, and an Icon of it furnished which we have annexed at the Bottom of the Map prefixed to this Tract, near the Place where it was taken, in regard Gesner takes no Notice of such a Fish, nor do we remember to have met the like in any Writer on the Subject of Fishes."

The close of the period under consideration shows the territory of the Scottish Settlements in occupation of an intelligent and industrious people, appearing somewhat rough in manner to the stranger, but impressing him by their independence of spirit and the appearance of comfort in their living. Earlier in the eighteenth century, alarmists saw degeneracy evidenced by the extravagances of the classes in dress and food, but the feared evil—as has been so often the case when pessimists alarm—was not progressive ; for the note in dress at the end of the century was that of plainness and comfort. A 1738 observer wrote of the well-to-do—

" Our young gentlemen are grown so immeasurably lavish in this matter (dress) that not only their rings, their watches, their canes, their swords, nay their coaches, their saddles and their horses etc. are never thought sufficiently fine or fashionable unless they send abroad for them. They must have foreign velvets to complete their dress and have so highly improved their taste for elegance herein that it is to be feared, in time they will not confine themselves only to silks for their waistcoats and linings, but they will generally use damasks and paduasoys for clothes instead of Irish broad cloths,"

and Mrs. Delany, from her home near Downpatrick, saw the working folk on the downward path. The extract following is from a letter to Mrs. Dewes.

1745

" June 21st. I am very sorry to find here and everywhere people out of character, and that wine and
tea should enter where they have no pretence to
be, and usurp the rural food of syllabub, etc. But
dairymaids wear large hoops and velvet hoods
instead of the round tight petticoat and straw hat, and there
is as much foppery introduced in the food as in the dress,—the
pure simplicity of ye country is quite lost ! "

The vast bogs of North Down furnished peat-fuel in
unlimited quantity for the larger part of the Scot's territory.
But little bog now remains, the areas exhausted of peat are
now under cultivation, and the old open hearths of the
farmhouses have given place to coal grates. Peat was never
a cheap fuel unless the bogs were tolerably near the place of
use. An early nineteenth-century note speaks of it as " more
expensive than coal," because it had to be carted a distance
of eight or ten miles.

Of diversion the hard-working folk of Down had not
much. Probably horse-racing and dancing were indulged
in to much greater extent than is now the case. Mrs. Delany,
writing to a friend in 1752, says :—

" All this neighbourhood are now in an uproar of diversions.
They began last Wednesday and are to last till Saturday,—each
day a horse-race, assembly and ball ; we did not find ourselves
inclined to enter the list. I have more pain than pleasure in
seeing any horse-race, and yesterday a poor man was thrown
down and trampled to death, such a sight would have embittered
whatever diversion the race had given. The balls are too late
for sober people and too far off ; Downpatrick is six long miles
from hence."

Mason, in his early nineteenth-century *Statistical Account*,
says, on this subject, of Holywood what is probably applicable
to the whole of North Down.

" The young people of both sexes are fond of dancing, and have
frequent meetings in the village, or in the farm-houses, where,
in imitation of their superiors, they keep up the revel from eight
or nine in the evening till day-break. Amongst their other
amusements, the game of shinny, as it is called by some, and

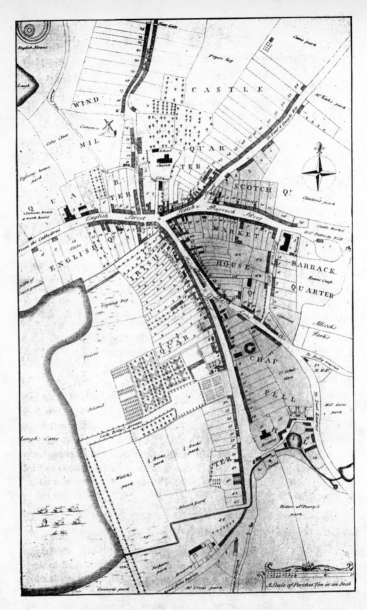

PLAN OF THE TOWN OF DOWNPATRICK IN 1729.
Original in British Museum.

common by others, is worthy of note. Common is derived from
a Celtic word ' com,' which signified ' crooked,' as it is played
with a stick bent at its lower extremity somewhat like a reaping
hook.   The ball, which is struck to and fro, in which the whole
amusement consists, is called nag, or in Irish brig.   It resembles
the game called golf in Edinburgh.   Christmas is the season
when it is most generally played.   It prevails all through Ireland,
and in the Highlands of Scotland.   Nor is it confined to any
sect, as Dissenters and Romanists seem to be equally attached
to it.

   " The trundling of eggs, as it is called, is another amusement,
which is common at Easter.   For this purpose the eggs are
boiled hard, and dyed different colours, and when they are thus
prepared, the sport consists in throwing or trundling them along
the ground, especially down a declivity, and gathering up the
broken fragments to eat them.   Formerly it was usual with the
women and children to collect in large bodies for this purpose,
though nothing can be, to all appearance, more unmeaning than
the amusement and they yet pursue it in the vicinity of Belfast.
Here it is generally confined to the younger classes.   It is a
curious circumstance, that this sport is practised only by the
presbyterians, though it is admitted that it is a very ancient
usage, and was spread over the Russian Empire and Greek Islands
long before the Reformation."

It may be that the effect of amusement—the breaking
of the monotony of the daily round—was achieved in the old
days by certain excitements which no longer affect the
country life, one of these being the contested election.   The
ballot of decision, within hours, or at most a few days, is a
tame thing compared to an eighteenth-century county election,
which proceeded with much excitement and, to certain voters,
some profit and entertainment, for many weeks.   That
indiscreet minister, the Rev. W. Steele Dickson, justifying,
in his autobiography, his action in a County Down election
contest between the Hillsborough and Stewart families, gives
us a picture of an incident in this exciting contest which
lasted thirteen weeks.   After five weeks' voting, Mr. Stewart's
prospect of election was very uncertain.   Dickson, however,

was holding voters in reserve, and a few days before the close
of the election, he brought them up in dramatic fashion.
There were, he says,

> " About 40 freeholders whom I had engaged to wait for my call
> . . . They were all wealthy farmers and remarkably well-
> mounted, and as Volunteering had given them some idea of
> order I brought them in in Indian file, and after proudly parading
> the town (Downpatrick) drew them up two deep, before Mr.
> Stewart's lodgings."

Through the county the landlord's hold on tenant farmers
usually ensured their support for his candidate—if they voted
against his candidate they were likely to suffer. In the
boroughs he had to deal with the ' potwallopers '—defined
in Sir James Stephen's *Commentaries* as " such as cook their
own diet in a fireplace of their own." Such persons, prior
to 1832, in certain boroughs, had a right to vote at parliamentary elections. Them the landlord or his candidate had
to conciliate by polite attentions or seduce with gold. In
one of the British Museum manuscript collections, there is
a letter from Edward Trotter, at Downpatrick, to his employer
Mr. Southwell, from which will be seen that the cost of in-
fluencing these voters was fairly large.

> " Downpatrick.
>
> " February 23rd   I this day had your letter of the 13th
> and can assure you of the most perfect tranquility
> 1771   and generally good disposition among the people.
> I think I might venture to engage that there will
> not be an opposition in your time . . . Our
> day of election will be the 5th or 6th March. We have not yet
> fixed the mode of entertainment for our vile potwallopers, but
> from the various methods proposed I fear it cannot be done
> under £150."

The landlord had to keep his own agent in good temper,
and stimulate his activity by judicious gifts. In the letter
above quoted Trotter acknowledges the sum of £200 for himself.

> " I cannot express what I feel from your generous kindness as to
> the £200—the one half the sum overpays my expenses ; & I

am too conscious that my services, on the occasions you mention,
were not of a farthing's value . . . I will endeavour to
deserve your goodness by an unremitting attention to your
interests while I shall live."

Dickson's allusion to improvement of his voters' carriage
by ' volunteering,' introduces this subject, an excitement of
the late eighteenth century, which can be treated here only
in very brief terms.   England, in 1778, was at war with the
American Colonies ; and France, taking advantage of her
difficulty, sent warships into British Seas, and projected
descents in Ulster.   Dickson's Narrative paints in vivid
colours a picture of the times of the Volunteers.

" During some years after this, little occupied the public mind or
employed the public tongue except volunteering and Volunteers.
. . . Our Country was considered by all as in imminent danger
and Government had declared its total inability to defend it.
In this awful emergency the desire for self preservation gave
birth to the general idea, and general resolution of arming in
self defence.   The city of Cork and the town of Belfast took the
lead—soon the country swarmed with Volunteers.   Industry
forewent a portion of its usual rest whilst idleness betook itself
to labour and profligacy became sober, that they might be enabled
by their earnings or their savings to appear in arms and in
uniform.

" Physician, surgeon, and apothecary, lawyer and attorney—
all were soldiers—even the Presbyterian ministers were so fully
inspired with the patriotism of the day that, in several places,
the rusty black was exchanged for the glowing scarlet, and the
title of ' Reverend ' for that of ' Captain.' "

One of the Presbyterian ministers of Down exchanging " the
rusty black for glowing scarlet," was the Rev. Samuel Barber,
of Rathfriland.   His corps voluntarily submitted to the
discipline of the standing army, and in their Rules, signed
in 1779, promise

" to be obeydient to our superior officers and to march and do
military duty where they command us within the County of
Down."

What a formidable force the Volunteers became when armed
and ordered by military training, is learned from figures
supplied by Rev. Alexander McCreery, of Killileagh.

> " In 1779, the year after the enrolment of the first company at
> Belfast, they numbered 42,000, and in 1782, the year of a memor-
> able demonstration at Dungannon, 100,000. Their uniforms
> were costly and beautiful."

Fifteen years after the formation of the first company,
the Government of the day became alarmed at the growing
power of the force in politics and disbanded the Volunteers.

The language of the people at the opening of the nineteenth century was still pure lowland Scotch, almost un-
intelligible to the stranger. With the coming of the railways
and spread of education, and wider circulation of newspapers
and books, the old dialect began to disappear. But even
now, in outlying districts, it survives to a surprising extent,
and very few of the old peculiarities of word have been lost.

CHAPTER XI.

Michael Ward—Landowner, Trader, Judge

In this chapter are used the letters, memoranda, and accounts of a man of Down to present a picture of his place and period. The man is Michael Ward—Landowner, Trader, Judge,—an outstanding member of his family, perhaps the most important man of the county in the first half of the eighteenth century. Through a long and strenuous life he seems to have had a Mohammedan reluctance to destroy a piece of written or printed paper, and fate has respected his feeling in this matter, for the great collection of documents he left is as complete to-day as when he died in 1760. Possibly there is not, in these kingdoms, another case of such preservation, for so long, of a life's documents—letters from wife, children, brother, friends, servants, agents, correspondents, distinguished and undistinguished, copies of letters sent, estimates of expenditure, household accounts,—every sort and kind of writings born of circumstance in the long life of a man of wealth, high position, and unbounded activities.

By the loving care of one of his descendants, about 2,000 of these have been ordered, indexed, and protected in such fashion that, barring the accident of fire, these documents should survive for centuries to come. Some of them are of the most trivial importance—papers which show the cost, in a Down household of over 200 years ago, of " A hing to adore " to have been eightpence, or that the sum of fourpence was paid for " driling a hole in ye skrue of ye nokkor." Such documents were without interest or value when they came into being, but, after more than two centuries, the triviality of their record is an attraction to us who so rarely have opportunity to touch centuries-old household life in its perishable petty detail. In using letters, or portions of them, to paint the activities of a long life and their scene, there must, of necessity, be a rapid presentation of many different subjects. The bond of union is association with an individual. A rough chronological order is observed.

Born about 1680, Michael Ward at the date of the first letter given is nearly 29 years of age. He is a barrister, and has come into his inheritance, for his father was killed in a duel in the year 1690, and the heir, Michael's elder brother, died young. Let us begin with the man in love.

" Dublin, Jany. 28, 1709-10.

" Madam,

I find 'tis impossible for me to live without you, I can enjoy nothing wth satisfaction in y^r absence, there's so great a difference between the pleasures I enjoyd in one moment's conversation with you & all the flat diversions I can invent here, y^t I can't forbear murmuring at ye obstacles y^t keep me from you ; nothing can please me till I flye to ye thoughts of you, there I find unexhaustable treasures of joys, I contemplate every one of y^r beauties, each of them possesses me wth equall pleasure & astonishment, then I compare ye beauties of y^r body to ye excellences of y^r mind and 'tis a pleasing combat between my reason & my senses which of y^m I ought most to admire in you ; when I represent you all goodness and compassion I am nothing but raptures and my enamourd soul melts into y^e softest joys of love ; but when I sett y^r vertues on y^e throne they deserve then I prostrate myself at y^r feet & y^e respect and admiration they command fill me wth no less pleasure, thus I spend y^e happy

MICHAEL WARD of Castle Ward, on the southern shore of
Strangford Lough, who married Anne Hamilton of Bangor
in 1710. An able man and one of many activities.
Appointed Judge of King's Bench in 1729.

Portrait at Castle Ward

" I compare y^e beauties of y^r body to y^e excellences of y^r mind." ANNE HAMILTON of the love-letter, daughter of James Hamilton of Bangor and grand-niece of first Lord Claneboye. Married, in 1710, Michael Ward, who was appointed Judge of King's Bench in 1729.

Portrait at Castle Ward.

minutes that otherwise would be too tedious to be endured, flattering my self that I may sometime be blessd with more sollid joys & be fully rewarded for all my past sufferings which will encrease ye pleasure by reflecting on you. Must one dear Letter be all you will give me in so long a time ! I must be an importunate as well as constant Lover for tis not in my power to cease from perpetually begging y^r favour and telling you y^t I shall for ever be

> Madam, y^r most faithful, most devoted humble serv^t
>
> M. Ward."

Addressed (on cover)

> " To
>
> > Mrs Anne Hamilton
> > att Bangor
> > near Belfast."

The lady was Miss Anne Hamilton, grand-daughter of William, brother of the first Lord Claneboye,—living at this time with her widowed mother, the Hon. Sophia Hamilton, and her sister Margaret, at Bangor. It will be remembered that in the division of the Claneboye estates following the lawsuit with Lady Clanbrassil, the Bangor property fell to James Hamilton. He married the Hon. Sophia Mordaunt, and had one son and two daughters, the elder of these being the Anne of the love-letter. The male line failed here again, for the boy died at an early age, and his sisters became co-heiresses of their father's estate.

On the authority of Mrs. Reilly, a member of the Montgomery family, it is stated that Mrs. Hamilton did not look with favour on Michael Ward's proposals for her daughter's hand. The young people, however, had their way and were married in the year of the love-letter, 1710. There were Wards of importance in Down before Michael—his father, Bernard Ward, was High Sheriff of the County in the year of the duel,—but none, before Michael, was ambitious or forceful. He appears, in many ways, to have resembled the first of the Hamiltons, Lord Claneboye, part of whose property was to pass into his hands. Like the first great settler, Michael Ward craved more and more land ; like him he was an able administrator, utilising the services of many men in the management of his many properties. His income must have been a large one after the death of his wife's mother placed the Bangor estate in his hands. Yet outgoings were great, and developments and purchases of new lands required the use of money at interest. One of his managers advising the purchase of certain lands, jointly, mentions a friend who will let them have £700 if the purchase is effected. Interest on money in his hands, at the beginning of the eighteenth century, is generally calculated at six per cent. On money borrowed from an aunt in 1705 the interest is made up in account at seven per cent.

The acquirement of his wife's share of the Bangor estates gave Ward a controlling interest in the affairs of the little borough, and, in practice, the appointment of its provost and parliamentary representatives. His duties in Dublin and interests at Castle Ward, and elsewhere, did not permit of residence in Bangor, and management of his demesne lands, and care of the " fayre stone house " built by the first Hamilton, were placed in the hands of a certain Charles Echlin, who appears to have shared, in a small way, the passion of his principal for acquiring control of lands. He is continually found making proposals that leases of lands becoming vacant should be granted to him.

In 1725, the " fayre stone house " of the early settlement is beginning to decay. It is then occupied by Gilbert Hamilton, doubtless one of the now large Hamilton connection, and, judging from a reference to Echlin in the following letter, a poor man living in the old house rent free. He wishes to make some return for the privilege by caring for his benefactor's property, and complains that he has been very scurvily treated by Echlin for his pains. The letter is dated Bangor, Jan. 25th, 1725, and is addressed to Mr. Ward. It is given here in contracted form.

" troubles him to acquaint him that there are three ashes cut in
the plantation since he was last in town.   John tells him that
' he tracked 'em to Whiny Wilson's ground ' & on Friday ' John's
servant found Wilson's son snedding a scyamore tree newly
cut ' the ' old fellow and his eldest son plowing on the Hill above,
pretty nigh him ' from wch he concluded that they are guilty
of all etc.

. . . .

" the trespasses are not so frequent as formerly tho' the swine
have plowed up the long walk & ye back walk and little Garden
adjoining the Summer house—the pett Sheep continue still—
on Friday last I drove them, 6 cows a bull and three Calves out
of the Cross Hill.

. . . .

" Saul is not yet come and the Sink continues unscour'd so
that upon the least rain The Hall and Parlour are filled with
under-water I desir'd John to speak to Mr Echlin to redress
that by taking away the Dirt.   He made no answer but Blood
& Wounds he was not to receive orders from me, that it was
pragmatical and Impertinent in me to meddle with that and he
would do it when he pleased or tho't it convenient.

. . . .

" I'me sure to have all my irregularities musterd up & blazond
abroad in the Blackest Colours, but no motive whatever you
think but lends to your service, etc."

Michael Ward has evidently too much on hand to allow of
much attention to the house of his wife's girlhood, and
Hamilton, a year later, still in occupation, paints it as deplorably out of order.   He refers to a talk with Echlin, who
doesn't know whether Mr. Ward will renew the roof or mend
it.   He (Hamilton) recommends a new roof ; he says,

" there is hardly a room dry if rain comes and y^r furniture will
suffer much more, and this too much spoyled alreddie."

In a still later letter he urges haste in undertaking the repairs,
for, he says,

" there fell a great dale of rain these 2 days . . . in some of
the rooms bucketfulls,"

which he mopped—at dinner he was obliged to retreat to his
room.

Echlin continued as Bangor agent for many years, but there are indications that his principal was gradually coming to look upon him with distrust. The agent is very ready to accuse others of bad faith, when writing to his chief.

" Hamilton (John Hamilton of Ballyvernon) has neither Honour nor Honesty, nor can he speak a word of truth."

Of another he says,

" I think he made himself a Knave to doe your cause a prejudice."

Of his zeal in his master's interest he gives evidence in two letters here copied. A boy of seventeen has cut " a small siccamore " in the park, and the landlord's agent gives a warrant to the constable to whip the boy through the town, and as if that were not severity enough, orders the culprit's father, possibly without knowledge of the lad's misdoing, " to give up his Land at alsaints next."

" Bangor Jany 30, 1729.

" Sir,

I have got certain proof that John Wilson commonly called Whinny Wilson's son a Boy about 17 years old cut a small siccamore tree in the Plantation Park ; there are three ash Poles cut out in the same place & it is very probable that he cut them, I gave a warrant to search but could not find them be pleased to send me orders how he shall be punished."

. . . .

" Bangor February 13th 1729.

" Sir,

According to your orders I have examin'd the evidence about Wilson's son, which was that Bowman John Cowdans Servt found the Boy in ye Plantation cutting ye branches of the stick after it had been cut down. I have given a warrant to ye Constable to whipp him through ye Town & have ordered the Father to give up his Land at alsaints next. I was at Cumber about ye 33th on Wednesday last but Mrs Meredith is in sich a condition that she is not fit for any Bussiness & in my oppinion she is litle better than stark madd.

I am your most Dutyfull
& most obedient Humble Servt
Cha : Echlin."

On the death of Echlin the agency was given to his son, who
proved to be even less worthy of confidence than his father
and had to be dismissed.

Michael Ward had, south of Strangford Lough, an extensive estate on which stands, on a land-locked bay, the little
town of Killough. Harris, in mentioning it (1744), speaks
of it as " now called Port St. Anne "—a name probably given
in honour of Anne Hamilton. The change cannot have been
approved by the inhabitants, for the village is now, and has
been for long, known by its ancient name, Killough. It is
a sleepy little place, with, about it, an air of having seen
better days, and the quay, with a few rusty old cannon as
mooring posts, no longer sees unladen goods which have come
direct from foreign ports. Ward, who had here the services
of his younger brother, Robert, gave much thought to the
development of this part of his property. No streams of
any magnitude flow into the bay, and the full salinity of its
waters made the village on its shore a suitable place for
salt-works, which were established and worked for many
years. Mr. William Montgomery, with James Feattus as
bookkeeper, and Mr. Robert Ward, appear to have been
responsible for its management in early years. Montgomery,
who addresses Mr. Ward as " Dear Cozen," worked apparently
under a partnership agreement. Later, a certain Francis
Lascelles managed for Mr. Ward's sole account. The letters
show that the venture was not a very profitable one, and that
continuous outlay for upkeep was called for.

" Killogh, ye 11th Jully 1724.
" Sr,
It is full time we shoud begin our Cisterin & thinks it proper
to Let you know that you may order one of ye best masons in
the country to doe it and fix ye time you intend to begin it for
we are dayly at a vast expence by the Leaking ye p'sent one.
I have been most part of this week at Lurgan Dromore Lisburn
& ye other towns thereabout, & has disposed of small parcells
of Salt for a tryall, they all in y^t country has promised us all y^e
encouragement they can provided we sell as cheap as the

merchants of Bellfast & Newry does. I meet with a man from
Newry who tould me Mr Martin had sould the last cargoe salt
sent him & intends sending for more he believes in a little time
we may get ye better of ye english trade.

> I am yr most humble & obedient servant
> > James Feattus.

(To Michael Ward, Esq)."

The next is from William Montgomery (joint owner ?) to
Michael Ward. The 'Successful' was a ship owned by the
partnership, or Mr. Ward.

" Dear Cosn

by my last letter to you I was as particular as possible in
my accounts of our Saltworks ; I now am to acquaint you that
our other pan begun to work last thursday night, and dus very
well ; I am very doubtfull were we ever so much inclin'd to
import a quantity of Rock when it came here we would not gett
it fast enough discharg'd ye Successfull wch came in Loaded with
coals near a fortnight ago is not yett half discharg'd there not
being above 4 or 5 Labourers in town has carrs & horses & they
are so perversely Lazy y^t they will work only ye times or hours
they please ; I dont know what we shall do in this affaire pray
send yr advice the Successfull has suffered very greatly this
stormy weather since she came into the harbour being loaded.
. . . . . Will Saul was here and we discourc'd him about
our Sisteren, he will not undertake to make one that may be
depended upon before ye Spring ; and then he says y^t he will
forfeit ye cost of it if it be not stanch. it would be of particular
advantage did it Lay your way to secure some substantial dealer
in salt in Dublin to take ours from us even at the curr^t price of
ye English tho ours be worth much more to all retailers ; for
after slaughter is over I'me sure our tradeing may be somewhat
sloe here and we have yett no Storehouses tu putt our salt
in. . . . .

> ye much oblidg'd affec^{te} humble servt
> > William Montgomery."

The 'Successful' appears to have belied her name. A
letter from Montgomery dated Jan. 29th, 1725-6, expresses
fears for her safety, out on " so ugly a voyage "—where to
is not stated—and speaks of need of supplies of rock (salt)

and coals. From this it is apparent that the salt produced was not entirely by evaporation of sea-water. The enterprise is not paying, but Montgomery is hopeful of retrieving all losses. He says,

> " Ye creditt of our Salt is now very well established. Drumgool proposes to agree for 300 tons a year."

Feattus has given notice to leave.

> " He is very stout about it—his circumstances would seem to be very good since he makes so light of £20 per annum."

The next letter carries bad news about the ' Successful '—

> " now very little reason to hope ye ship is safe—'tis an ugly shock for poor pockets."

A cargo of timber, arriving for the works, is of quality to make Montgomery very angry.

> " May ye 25th 1726.
>
> " Dr Cosn
>
> Yesterday morning we gott all the timber and deals ashore, the plank are pritty good but are not according to the length directed, the oak timber is so bad that in my life I never saw such rubitch John Mahood says as dus many more yt its excessive Dear at £1 : 5 per tun, a great part of it is so rotten both out and insid yt it wouldnt even be firewood and non of it ye size and length bespoak being vile crukitt dirt yt will take great Labour to work it, it is norway oak except 6 pieces ; I had it all measured rotten and all included there is 3 tuns 12 foot in it there is 26 pieces, the Knees are not bad tho they be old and has been long in some ship, and are unnecessarily large, we must make the best shift we can, but he yt you employed to buy the timber etc as well as ye fellow he bought ym from are grand chating villians ; I was very angry at Flin for takeing ym aboard I am sure you never saw ym ; their is neither trinells nor Ocome (oakum) tho both were desired to be putt into ye memorandome, but I hope we may get what may serve us in Killogh ; ye fellow yt bought ye timbers, told Flin ye cost but £3 per tun and to others he said much less, therefore pray enquire about it, they have Layn 20 years as useless timber in ye corner of some timber yeard.
>
> I am, Dr. Cosn
>
> Yr most obed : and oblidg'd humble Servt, William Montgomery."

Robert Ward, writing to his brother, at this time, is concerned about the smuggling of tobacco in the salt boats, and is puzzled how to stop it.   Smuggling, to an extraordinary extent, was going on at this time ;—a work printed in 1738 declares that farmers near the sea coasts of England cannot get labourers at harvest-time since " a guinea a day is common wages for a smuggler."

The next letters show Lascelles as manager of the works. He is also a general trader on his own account.

" Killough.

$17^{39}/_{40}$ " Feb. 7.   We soon expect our ship from Holland, and have desired the favour of Mr. Sam Hill to wait on you and Lord Killdare, beging your intrests in recomending us to supply the Board with what seed this Country may want.   We have a ship arrived from Christiansands with red double dram dails of from 11 to 14 feet long."

. . . .

1740   " April 5.   I have sent a small vessell to Whitehavn for Coles & Tobaco and if you please to have any at Castleward they shall be good & I will Deliver there at 14:6 a Tunn.

" There is 3 or 4 Cannon belonging to the Ship lost here I have the selling of them if you have a minde for them will sell at 12s per hund.   they are above a pound Ball."

These are probably the old guns now rusting on Killough quay.

The next letter is interesting as showing that exclusive dealing, under compulsion, is not a purely modern trading development.   It is from Robert Ward to his brother, and is dated from Downe (Downpatrick).

1740   " Feby 16th.   I have at last fix'd a man in Downe to sell the Killough salt, his name is Magarry reputed to be a good substance & has very good acquaintance in the country.   You cannot immagine how timerous & irresolute he was before he would positively fix tho he own's himself convinc'd that it would be much to his advantage wch shews what envious pains has been taken to prohibit the selling of it here, but if propper methods be taken I don't doubt but that they will suffer for it to wch end I hope that you will give Lascelles the strictest charge to order all y^r tenants at their perill to buy no other salt. . . . I have charg'd Magarry to set downe every pound of salt he sells wth the name and townland by wch at ye year's end we may know who doth or doth not buy."

From the next it appears that a malthouse had been erected, and that tenants were expected to use only beer brewed from malt therein produced. Lascelles writes :—

1739   " Dec. 30. They have reported that Mrs Buttler has for some time past got drink from the Brewery of Down. I have spoke to her about it, who affirms it was only when she could not get Turff to brew with, and that she paid Fisher Drymalter. They also inform of a Dragoon's wife, who lives in one of James Clark's houses, retails small beer, and that several gentlemen in Down gets their malt drink from Down."

Difficulties in connection with the working of the salt enterprise continue. On 14th January, 1743, a certain George Coulter, writing to Mr. Ward, tells of having used up all the coal and rock salt, and gives result. Lascelles, it seems, is ill, and efficient management not being available, Robert Ward, in his brother's interest, makes an effort to get the firm of Mercer & Lang to take over the works, but fears that

" the Privateer will be a clog upon carrying them on."

This privateer had been, evidently, a serious menace to coast and coasting trade for some time, for the writer adds, as a postscript,

" If we have not a few guns of 5 or 6 pounders a privateer may not only take every ship out of our harbour but beat Downe the towne of Killough."

In 1729, Michael Ward is appointed Judge of King's Bench, thereafter called My Lord, and treated with extraordinary deference. Probably to this time belongs an estimate of household and other expenditure,—an undated

document in the judge's handwriting, which gives interesting
particulars of the cost of his establishment.

" Servants wages	140	0	0
Livery & servts cloaths	32	0	0
House Rent 80 Taxes 12 Repairs Painter, Glazier, Slater, Joiner, Bricklayer 20 ..	112	0	0
Market accts Coals, Candles, Soap, Washing all small necessaries, cattle beside rent of Demesne	300	0	0
Tradesmen's Bills—Dublin	87	0	0
Wine	80	0	0
Coach & Repairs, Horses, Hay, Oats & Grass in Dublin	80	0	0
Furniture & Linnen	50	0	0
Traveling charges, freight of Goods.. ..	30	0	0
Books, Phisicians, Law charges & other casual- ties	50	0	0
Wife	100	0	0
Son & Tutor	120	0	0
Daughters allowance, Mrs etc.	90	0	0
Own Cloaths & expenses	100	0	0
Day Labourers & Country Tradesmen ..	110	0	0
	£1481	0	0

Interest of Money . . . . . .
Buildings at Castle Ward, Killough.
Insolvent Rents . . . . "

On back of the scrap of paper used are details showing how
some of the items in the account are made up. The figures
noted for salaries and servants' wages are astonishingly low ;
the like service for these days would require them to be
multiplied from six to ten times. Other items in the statement
do not represent such great variation from present values, and
the establishment may be taken as on the scale of one costing,
to-day (1920), about £6,000 per annum.

" Wages & Salaries.

Echlin	..	6	0	0
Lassells	..	10	0	0
Threlford	..	20	0	0
Gardner	..	10	0	0
Butler	..	7	0	0
2 ffootmen	..	10	0	0
Groom	..	8	0	0
Coachman	..	8	0	0
Postillion	..	4	0	0
Hellper	..	2	0	0
Stogdell	..	6	0	0
Swail	..	4	0	0
Macartan	..	0	10	0
Gardner Dublin		2	0	0
		97	10	0

Wife's maid	..	6	0	0
Daughters maid		4	0	0
Housekeeper	..	10	0	0
Cook	..	5	0	0
Kitchin girl	..	2	0	0
2 Chambermaids		7	0	0
Dairymaid	..	3	0	0
Maid in Dublin		3	0	0
Thornbury	..	0	10	0
		40	10	0

Dublin Tradesmen.

Apolsterer	..	6	0	0
Apothecary	..	10	0	0
Brewer	..	14	0	0
Grocer	..	24	0	0
China & Glasses		6	0	0
Ironmonger	..	2	0	0
Pewterer	..	8	0	0
Sadler	..	6	0	0
Smithy, house, horses	..	6	0	0
Seeds & trees	..	5	0	0
		87	0	0

Country Tradesmen.

Smith
Iron
Cooper
Masons
Lime
Brick
Sand
Pavers & Stones
Turf cutting
Mowers "

In the account the items £97 10s. od. and £40 10s. od. are taken as £140, Dublin tradesmen's accounts as here given £87, while for the fourth section separate estimates are not attempted—the sum of £110 being taken as, possibly, adequate.

Although, later, a chapter is devoted to housekeeping costs, here, fitly on the judge's estimate, may follow such intimate details of household expenditure as appear in the accounts preserved at Castle Ward. One of these belongs to the Hamilton household in days when the judge's wife was Miss Nancy, and her sister Miss Peggy, of the great house at Bangor. Their mother employed a certain Mrs. Smith, at Belfast, to buy shop goods for the household. We know nothing of this lady beyond what is disclosed by her letters and accounts, and that is that she was a quaint, humorous, elderly body, in whose probity and taste the lady of Bangor had great confidence. The selection of clothing material, and the supervision of its conversion into petticoats and other garments, have been part of her duty, and, for the young ladies, she bought shoes, gloves, mittens, ribbons, and necklaces. She reports on arrivals of muslins and chintzes, and suggests uses for them at Bangor. One can see from her writings that the labour is to her of love—she enjoys the handling of new things and the buying of them,—"yr Ladyship knowes I am A greate desstroyer of money,"—and yet she will not let the postmaster have any of it, for the reference in her postscript to the saving of fourpence is probably to be explained by supposing that she has sent her account along with her purchases by hand of the carrier.

" ffor
    the Honorbel Mrs Sophia Hamilton
            att Bangor near
                        Belfast.
    Madam
        I have sent all the thinges mentiond on ye other side only the 2 heads and Ruffels which Mr blackwood's servant could not cary ; if he had not bein so civil as to take ym thy might A bein still hear for Mrs hamilton's servant could not take aney of them ; naither was there A caryer in towne :—I shall not be Easey till I heare if these things be gote safe to bangor and I received from Mrs hamilton 6 pistols and 2 gineys ; yr Ldyshp knowes I am A greate desstroyer of money you see what A short way yt 7-17-0 is gone—there's some of ye finest Chinces cum from Corke that Ever was in ye Kingdom : and ye finest plain Musling that Ever I saw : if yr Ldyshp will bestowe A head and Ruffels on yr self of it and a suite of ye chinces on Mis Hamilton it woad do mighty well yt I could secure ye best of these things if I thought you would have ym because I believe Mr Stevenson will buye both ye musling and ye Callyco : ye paire of Chinces

will be about 17 pow_nd : there is Attlesses of 60^r pr pice—I
sent a Little Coffie becaus it was sumething cheeper y^n it was
formerly—and I knew y^r stock was but small—Mr Smith and I
wish you a mery Crissmos he presents his moste humble service
to y^r Ldyshp and allso to y^r young Ladys I heare y^e Little Master
at Winchester has A swalling on ye side of his head : all y^t
famely are cumeing to London

  I am Madam y^r Ldyshps much obligd humble serv^t

                    Mary Smith

has your Ldyship any intres in ouar newe Comisioner Mr Conely.

                December ye 20 1709.

	£	s	d
26 yds of Scarlet Stuffe at 13d pr yard	01	08	02
26 yds of Scarlet Crossband at 9½ pr yard	01	00	07
10 yds ¾ for Bordars at 8d pr yard	00	07	02
32 yds of Scarlet Crost with Silke at 13d pr yd	01	14	08
5 yds of Callyco at 3 9d pr yd	00	18	09
A wrkeing apron for Mis peggy	00	11	00
2 yards of figurd English ribbon for Mis peggy	00	03	04
a black girdle for Mis peggy	00	01	00
2 pearl necklaces	00	03	00
4 yds of English Scarlet Ribbon at 18d pr yd	00	06	00
A swite of blew Ribbon and box	00	06	06
6 pair of gloves for Mis hamilton	00	02	00
A black gaws hood	00	03	09
A black and white handkerchff	00	06	06
6 setts of wyers	00	02	06
A white gaus hood	00	03	09
A necklace for Mis hamilton	00	02	00
1 yd ¾ of Musling at 8 6 pr yd for Mis peggy	00	14	10
13 yds of Edgeing at 15d pr yd	00	15	04
6 pair of gloves and Miteins for Mis peggy	00	04	02
A gaus handkerchiff for Mis Nancy	00	03	06
A kowl for Mis Nancy	00	01	06
2 yds of green ribbon for Mis Nancy	00	02	04
6 pairs of gloves and Miteins for Mis Nancy	00	04	10
1 yd ¾ Musling for Mis Nancy	00	14	10
12 yds of Edgeing at 12d pr yard	00	12	00
A black Stomacher	00	07	00
12 pow_nd of Reasons 12b Corrans 12b of priuens	00	17	03
1 pair of black showes with black lace	00	05	06

1 pair plain showes	..	00 03 06
3 boxes 3 shellings A sacke and brown paper	..	00 02 03
Mrs Selby's note for makeing 3 Shutes ..	..	01 01 06
for reed Sarge to border ye Scarlet pettycoat	..	00 02 04
1 pownd ½ coffie at 4/6 pr pownd ..	..	00 06 09
Mrs Weldon's ould note	..	00 06 03
Mrs Weldon's note for ye 2 Swites mead now	..	00 08 00
Mrs Lisles note for 8 yds of black silke at 5/6	..	02 04 00
Mrs Rivets note for makeing a black apron	..	00 02 10

                                            18   7   8

its hard times and money scearce and 4d is better saved then given for A wraper over this—so I hope y^r Ldyshp will pardon me—Mrs Bankes presents her moste humble service to yr Ldyshp —thers a show (shoe) of Mis hamiltons sent up but no derections about it—I will send all ye notes when I have got money to pay y^m ; I will send ye heads by ye first opertunity there's no Choyce of stripe musling in towne which mead me buye what I have done forye young Ladys its a sorte that ye Ladys heare admire very much becaus thy can gete no better."

An error of calculation and one of addition are here as in original.

Twenty-one years later Mrs. Smith is buying for Miss Nancy, now wife of Judge Ward, and for her children.

" 1730 January ye 20 bought for the honble Judg Ward.

table lining and toweling as per bill apers	..	02 02 8
A yard and quarter of Lutestring for Mis Ward ..		00 3 7
2 dosen of Wast coat buttons for Madam Ward ..		00 1 0
for bringing A caske of Cheese from ye Shipe	..	00 1 0
A dosen of fring for Mis Ward ..	..	00 7 0
A pair of stockeins for the young Ladys	..	00 19 0
Sent to CastleWard 6 dry Ling ..	..	00 12 0
porteradg at severall times	..	00 00 3
blue silk to face a gown for Mis Ward ..	..	00 3 6
A comb for master Ward	..	00 0 10
A Letter from Mis Ward	..	00 0 4

                                         £04 11 2
    Recd 2 gineys 02 6 0
    1 Moie de or 01 10 0

A certain Anne Carter made shirts and neckcloths for Michael Ward, before his marriage ; costs are as per her account.

" 11 shirts maide	..	..	..	..	1 7 6	
11 shirts wiesht (washed)	..	..	..	0 3 8	
¼ & ½ of muslin at 18s yd	..	..	..	0 6 9	
¼ & ½ att 14s yd	..	..	..	..	0 5 3	
3 quarter ½ & nale att 16s yd	..	..	..	0 15 0	
6 neckcloths att 5s 3d each	..	..	..	01 10 6	
2 neckcloths att 6 9	..	..	..	0 13 6	
					5 2 2	
1 Ell of Holland	..	..	..	..	0 6 6	
					5 8 8	
					0 1 0	
					5 9 8	

Recd from Mr Mich : Ward ye sume of five pounds nine shill in full of ye Bill & all accts Witness my hand ye 28th of Mar : 1706 Anne Carter."

The error in calculation of cost of 6 neckcloths is in original.

The following item, from a locksmith's account, looks like expense in making brave the house for the bride's home-coming. It is dated in the year of the marriage.

" for Clening one Set of polleshed fire Shovels, tounges and proker with Chimbly hookes .. ..   s. d   1 2

In another account, Mary Nix makes the charge—

" For piecing and mending ye Kitching Procker ..   1 0

Tailor's charges are extremely low. Three shillings and six-pence for making a blue coat for Mrs. Ward, cannot have helped her tailor far on the way to wealth.

" 1716   John Holmes Taylor
July ye 16

To meaking yr ladey a blew bige coate	..	0 3 6
,, a velvet cape		0 5 0
,, 1 Dosson and 9 of Gould Coate buttons for ye bige Coate at 10s pr Dosn.		0 17 6
,, 6 Gould brest buttons		0 1 6

Mr. Ward's tailor was equally moderate—witness the account of Thos. Higginbotham. These accounts are without addresses.

"1723 Feby   Mich^l Ward Esqr.   Dr.

To makeing 2 big coates	..	..	..	0	6	0
To 4 Doz^n of buttons	..	..	..	0	2	8
To thread mohair Canvis & staying	..	..	0	1	8
To makeing 3 Frockes	..	..	..	0	9	0
To 4½ Doz^n of Coate buttons	..	..	..	0	2	7½
To 2 Doz^n of Smale buttons	..	..	..	0	0	4
To Silk & Twist	..	..	..	..	0	1	6
To buck^m canvis & thread	..	..	..	0	4	0
To Wading & Staying	..	..	..	0	1	0

£1   8   9¼

Rec^d the contents of this bill in full Feb 28th 1723

Thos Higginbotham."

The account of Magnus Price & Co., of Belfast, for a hogshead of claret, sent by sea, amounts to £16.

"Invoice

      Belfast 10th March 1732

      By order of Dr Prince

We send you pr the Lamb Skooner, Henry Tuckness, Ma^r one hhd of Claret at 16^{lb} (£) wch run 23 Dozen & 5 bottles which is packed up in two casks with Directions upon them for you we hope it will please you we are

            Your most obed & h^{ble} Serv^{ts}

                Magnus Price & Co."

The judge, careful and practical as he was, was affected by the South Sea venture mania, so far as to send his cousin, Mr. John Hamilton, "at his house in Castle Yard, Holborn, London," £1,000,

"to lay out for me in the South Sea . . . doe you manage it for me as you like, I'll be satisfied tho you lose."

He is offered by Mr. Arthur Dobbs, of Castle Dobbs, a share, or shares, in a venture to find the N.W. passage. Dobbs appears to have been the moving spirit of the undertaking;

he outlines his plans, estimates costs, and forecasts profit
in an interesting letter, dated March 31, 1744.

" I have been long silent upon account of your going circuit, but
as I Hope you will be Returned to Dublin by the time this can
reach you, I cant Refrain letting you know how my Affair stands
here. The French war is like to disconcert all my scheme with
the Admiralty for the season As I foresaw this I Petitioned the
King in counsel for two ships or sloops to go the voyage or in
case that could not be granted at this Time to grant such reward
as He thought Proper to Incourage private undertakers to find
the Passage. This the Council have referred directly to the
Admiralty to save time without Referring it to a Committee of
Council. The report is not made yet tho' my Lord Winchelsea
promises me not to Delay it but lets me know the Purport of it
which will be that the discovery will be very Beneficial and that
they apprehend there is a great Probability of finding it, but
that having so great occasion for ships upon so many different
services they have no vessels to spare ; but almost all concur
that it ought to be set about as soon as Possible to prevent others
from anticipating our discovery, and therefore I am advised
to apply to Parliament for a bill to give £10,000 to any who shall
find the Passage, which I believe I shall do next week, and then
I shall Prepare ships and take in adventurers with me upon the
voyage. I propose taking in 15 or 16 so as to divide it into 16ths,
so that the expense of fitting out a ship of about 150 tons and a
small sloop of 30 or 40 tons with 40 or 50 men betwixt them, with
some Trading goods, may come to about £2,000 or £2,400 which
will be about £130 to £150 a share ; I make no doubt to get enough
in Town to joyne me, but I shall be glad to know if you or any
other of my friends in Ireland will be Adventurers with me in it,
because I would reserve some shares until I can have your answer
which if it go on must be soon. If the Discovery be made we
propose giving Double Pay to the men, which will come to about
£360 more, and a proper Proportion to the Officers who conduct
the whole of betwixt 3 and £4,000 so that the Proprietors may
have £6,000 for their share of the premium and what may
occasionally be made of the Trade upon the Passage."

The investment appears to have been made in the name of
the judge's son, Bernard ; for, a few years later, the latter

received a communication from the Secretary to the Committee of the expedition, announcing its failure, and outlining proposals for obtaining from the Government a trading charter by which it was hoped the losses might be recovered, etc., etc.

Arthur Dobbs' letters to the judge are numerous and voluminous. He had been appointed Engineer and Surveyor General for Ireland by Sir Robert Walpole, and in the following communication he discourses on the probability of finding coal and lead on the shores of Belfast Lough. The letter is dated from Castle Dobbs, November the 28th, 1725.

" I went next morning to view the Mill Glen and Site above Craford's burn and am convinced that there is no Coall there, but rather simptoms of Lead it is all a slaty Rock with Spar and stands generally on an Edge under which I never suppose any Coall. I went afterwards along the shoar to Hollywood to view the freestone there which just crops out at the sea mark and Dips to the sea, it lys also too steep, and if any be there I take it to be more into the Country, and if there be any at Scrabo which is still my opinion, and they tell me they are now come to another bed of slate which I take to be another symptom for in those beds in the freestone, the Coall generally lys I imagine in that sandy country from Newton to Belfast, which I take to be only the Rotten top of that freestone, there may be a probability of some. Att Belfast they tell me that Seymor came to a small vein of Coall at Lambegg, in boring and that he is now sinking upon it."

A belief that there had been a coal mine in the hills above Holywood was current in the neighbourhood early in the nineteenth century—probably due to imperfect memories of borings and examinations of the date of the letter above.

Dobbs had evidently a liking for Colonial and trading ventures. The next note reveals him as member of the Ohio Company. How strange reads the expression of reliance on the Germans to protect us from the French in America ! It is dated from Castle Dobbs.

1750

> "March 28th. I have an account from London that our Ohio Company of which I am a member goes on Briskly. We have sent away £2000 in goods to Trade with the Indians and the King has given us £ . . . to give in presents to them. The French governors have sent threatening Letters to our several Governors not to come near their Limits which they extend far enough, but as we have 10,000 Germans gone this year to Philadelphia alone besides what are gone to other Colonies and 3 or 4000 more from Britain and Ireland I shall laugh at their Threats."

The next sees Arthur Dobbs himself Colonial Governor. He was appointed Governor of North Carolina in 1753. The extract is taken from a letter dated from New Bern.

> "My son is upon the brink of wedlock with a pretty girl of 14 . . . She has a great many plantations and above 100 negroes. The articles are signed and nothing wanting but the wedding cloathes from Virginia where my man is gone to buy them, and is every day expected so that his coming with me will turn out well, as he will have the best Rank and Fortune in the Province."

The next, and last letter of Arthur Dobbs to be quoted here, is dated from New Bern, October 31st, 1756, and is of extraordinary character. He gives, in outline, the plan of a work just completed, which is

> "to show the grand drama of Providence from the Creation and lapse of Angels to the consumation of all things."

The letter begins with a reference to the natural history of the province, a subject on which he intends to write when he has materials collected, and proceeds—

> "But the favourite subject I had in view is now brought to a conclusion (so) that I have nothing now but to look it over when it goes to the press, if it please God that I have to go to England or Ireland ; it is not very metaphysical, but an attempt to show the grand drama of Providence from the Creation and lapse of Angels to the consumation of all things, supported from the Books of the Law and the prophets and the Gospels, epistles and prophecies in the new Testament, in which I have shewn double,

and sometimes triple meanings carried on throughout. The whole which may be unlocked by the proper names and numbers recorded by Moses and the Prophets, and other prophetic symbols, and have paraphrased and made extracts from Moses and the prophets of the Old Testament and elders, which are all supported by the Revelation of S. John, and are all consistent with each other, and have given several explanations to all the old prophets not touched upon as yet as I have seen by others as also an entire paraphrase of the Revelations of St. John according to the ground plan of Doctor H More which I think I have altered and expressed so as to be evident to every Impartial reader, in which I have made out a pre-existent state and prior lapse before the Mosaic creation, the dormant state of the soul from death to the Ressurection, the Resurrection of our identical Bodies in *stamina vitæ* a double millnery state of Peace and Purity in this Earth and on the Earth renewed to us—primitive Paradise, a first and second Resurrection and first and 2nd Judgment, first of the Saints, and 2nd of the reprobate souls and Angels, the universal redemption of men and angels by a Double Redemption of Christ who is Lord of the whole Creation, first of the elect human souls admitted into his Kingdom he taking upon him the seed of Abraham and not the nature of angels to accomplish this first Redemption and then compleating the Redemption of all lapsed Beings after adequate Infernal punishments when they shall be allowed a future state of Repentance and submission when all corruption is purified by fire, when his whole Creation which was placed under his dominion and couldn't well voluntarily submit to him, when he shall destroy Death and Hell and deliver up his Mediatorial Kingdom to God the Father, when he shall be all in all his Creatures and there will be nothing void in nature. This is the scope of my Book which I think is fully supported from Scripture and is the ground work of my Faith in Christ. Whether I am faulty or not time will show, but still the further I consider it, it appears more evident to me and agreeable to all the Divine Attributes and the whole tenor of the Scriptures."

Dobbs was the author of several books—*An Essay on the Trade and Improvement of Ireland* (1729), *An Account of the Countries adjoining Hudson's Bay*, and others. It is unlikely that the extraordinary work outlined in the letter to Judge Ward was ever printed.   No copy exists at Castle Dobbs.

What may have been the charm of the eighteen-year-old Anne Hamilton is not discoverable in her letters as a wife. The romance of them begins and ends with the " My dear Life " of the addressing and the " Your own " of the subscription. The earlier letters are unpunctuated and without mention of place or date.

> " My dᵣ Life
>
> I desire yᵘ will send 15 Double drams for I can't get bog fir for yᵉ windows send yᵉ garden seeds as soon as possible for tis full late term ends yᵉ week so hope yᵘ think of comeing home next let me know when Con F comes to yᵉ country make tom buy 1 Coffee roster yᵉ Dean is heare I am in hast
>
> Yᵣ own A Ward."
>
> . . . .
>
> " I delay'd answering my Dr Life till Jeby had been at Caricknab he was there yesterday there is marl but tis 8 feet before ye come to it he says tis ye best he ever saw we go on pretty well with ye cannal ye church window will be don to morrow since I have been . . . uber I hope in return yu will give me ye pleasure of leting me know when I may hope to see yu I think yu ware very lazy yu did not write to me last post I am
>
> Yr own
>
> A Ward.
>
> " I hope yᵘ will send yᵉ rales for yᵉ church pray send me as soon as possible half a pound of carraway comfits if Robins wife has not left town send them by her."

And now she who was wooed by such burning words has daughters, and for the hand of the younger, suitors are competing. There is a half-yearly cash account, in the young lady's handwriting, among the Castle Ward papers. The penmanship is beautifully fine and regular : if character is to be inferred from it, Miss Sophia was primmest of prim damsels.

> " Recᵈ from my Papa in yᵉ Country Aug yᵉ 24th .. 2 11 6
> from my mama Septemr yᵉ 2nd 1 3 0
> more in yᵉ country 0 11 6

from my mama in Dublin Novemr ye 6th			..	3 0 0
from my papa Novemr 2nd	..	..	..	2 19 4
for a lace head	..	..	..	21 0 0
for a suit of cloaths	..	..	..	7 4 0
for ye embroiderer	..	..	..	4 17 0
from my papa Decemr ye 6th	..	..	..	4 14 8
more Feb ye 27th	..	..	..	0 5 9
more March ye 12th	..	..	..	3 0 0
from my papa for 20 yds of Lutestring	..		..	3 0 0

in all   ..   54 6 9

Sophia Ward, March the 20th, 1733.

Recd from my papa March ye 22d to pay Mrs Tibby's bill—

19 shilings."

The large proportion of the young lady's income absorbed by
the ' lace head ' may astonish the reader. ' Heads ' were
high cushions which ladies of Queen Anne's time, and later,
put under their hair to give it that erect, unnatural form,
which contemporary portraits have made familiar to their
descendants. There is a tradition in the Bangor family that
a certain Lady Clanwilliam, whose portrait hangs at Castle
Ward, wore one such erection for months at a time, and when,
at length, it was dismantled, a nest of young mice was discovered inside. A writer in *The Dublin Society's Weekly
Observations* (1756) calculated

" that twenty poor families who never taste flesh meat, might be
comfortably supplied for a whole year with as much beef and
butter as has been exported to purchase a head dress for a lady."

With the Judge's approval, a Mr. William Stewart had
proposed to Miss Sophia, and had been accepted. The lady,
however, drew back, as will be seen by the following letter
(undated) addressed by Stewart to the Judge :—

" Sr,

I take this method of leting you know that this morning
Mis Ward told me she desired to be relaced from her promise,
her behavior at first sight has the appearance of inconsistency
but I must declare to you and to all the world that she has always

acted in a manner perfectly agreeable to that good nature and
good sense which I always thought her mistress of, for which I
did & always will, Love her & esteem her until this day I scarce
know how much I loved her. I hope you will excuse my not
waiting on you be assured that it is not from want of respect
it would be most ungratefull in me not to take every opportunity
of acknowledging how much I am obliged to you for the good
opinion you have of me as appears not only from y^r words but
y^r actions. I once hoped to show my gratitude by being a
dutiful son but in whatever station of life I am in I shal have
pleasure in leting you know how much I am

> Your obliged & very Humble Servt

> Wm. Stewart.

Friday."

The Judge is evidently sorry to have this news—he
thinks that the young lady has acted precipitately, and, as
a draft of a letter preserved shows, he suggests that Stewart
should write such a letter to him as will enable him to
learn what are the girl's reasons for asking release ; and
possibly to influence her in again changing her mind.

(Undated.)

" D^r S^r,

On ye Discourse y^u had wth me at Derry & to make good
my promise to y^u at y^t time I desired my wife to talk severall
times to my Daughter & yesterday & to-day spoke to her myself,
I own I can't find a satisfactory reason why she altered her
intention in one day's time. Therefore if y^u enclose to me
such a letter as y^u think proper 1 will myself deliver it & y^u
shall either have a more favourable answer or a better reason
for ye contrary then I at present know. I believe you will
concurr in opinion wth me y^t nobody should know one word of
w^t passeth between you & Dr Sr Yrs."

Stewart's reply is characterised by manliness and good sense.
It reveals the fact that Mrs. Ward did not like him, and he
assumes, with reason, that Miss Ward has been influenced
by her mother.

" Killymoon, May 15, 1741.

" Dʳ Sʳ,

Last night I had the favour of yʳ letter which I believe lay some days at my house when I was abroad the kind offer you make I take as a most remarkable instance of yʳ friendship to me but to obtain happiness in a marry'd state I look upon a free choice in both partys to be so absolutely necessary that I would avoid everything that has the least appearance of an infringement upon that liberty. I have reason to believe that you have already recommended me to Mis Ward in as strong a manner as I could expect and much more than I deserve. Her inclination to comply with everything that you recommend to her made her act in a manner that was wrong interpreted by those who had neither the honour of her acquaintance nor the pleasure of her conversation.

" Her reasons for refusing to marry me were delivered with so much good sense & and they proceeded from so amiable a principle that altho there is scarce any room left to believe that she will alter her resolution yet I must love & esteem her and I would not despair absolutely of her changing were I not convinced that Mrs Ward by a dislike she showed to me fixt her in her resolution. I must confess sincerely that I think it in vain to trouble Mis Ward until I am sure of an intire approbation from both her parents.

" If I have mistaken Mrs Ward's behaviour to me & that altho she may dislike some things in me yet if she thinks it is in my power to make her daughter happy I will order my affairs so as to spend some months either in England or Dublin with yʳ family. If in that time I can make myself more agreeable to Mis Ward I shal think myself the happiest man in the world. The friendship you are pleased to honour me with will give me an opportunity of conversing with Mis Ward without occasioning the impertinent talk of the world so much as it did formerly. I am Sʳ your Much obliged & very Humbˡ Servant.

                                       Wm. Stewart."

Probably Mrs. Ward's objection to Stewart's suit was due, not so much to dislike of him, as to preference for another. Within a few months, Mr. Cromwell Price is found submitting his rent-roll for the Judge's consideration in connection with a proposal of marriage to Miss Ward. The suit did not prosper.

Apparently the Judge is annoyed by reports that he (the Judge)
had peevishly vetoed the marriage, after getting the settlement offers. He blames a certain gentleman for starting
these reports, and writes to him with some heat, receiving
a reply which apparently clears the accused. Price's retiring
letter is addressed to Mrs. Ward.

" May the 16th, 1741.

" Madam,

 I had the honour of yrs which I can't help letting you know
gives me a great uneasiness, but since I had the approbation of
you, Mr Justice Ward & Coz. Bernard it in some measure wips-
off the sting of so flatt a deniall, the favours. I greatly am
indebted to you and particularly my Coz. who is now in England,
for whome I have a most sincere love for now noething shall
deface it. I have been often told marriage goes by destiny soe
I know my fate, I wish Mis Ward a great deal of Hapyness when
ever she makes her choice, I beg you will make my complyments-
to Mr Justice Ward & Mis Ward.

    I am, Madam,

   Y^r Most obed^t & Most Hum^{ble} Servt

       Crom^{ll} Price.

this day my daughters
& I sett out for the
goat whea."

The " sting of so flatt a deniall " indicates that Miss Ward
acted according to her own feelings, seeing that Mrs. Ward
favoured the suit, and the Judge had an open mind. Probably
the fact disclosed by the short postscript, that the would-be
bridegroom was a widower with daughters, had something
to do with the young lady's decision. She married Mr. Arthur
Upton.

 Pass from the young lady's love affairs to those of her
brother. The youth had seen at Scarborough the Lady
Anne Bligh, the young widow of Robert Hawkins McGill,
of Gill Hall, Co. Down, had fallen in love with her, and not
being able to procure an introduction, had invoked his father's
assistance. The lady was reputed wealthy, and the Judge
took much trouble to bring about a match. His draft or

copy letters show that he sought aid of a friend, brother-in-law of the lady, in furthering the matter. The Judge on his drafts of letters does not indicate names of intended recipients.

"Dublin, Jany 26, 1744.

"Sr,

The distinguish'd & good character of your sister-in-law Lady Anne Bligh makes me zealously desire an alliance between her and my son. As she is I believe a stranger to him I must beg the favour of your advice and directions for proceeding in the most proper and respectfull maner and w^n y^u come next to town introduce me to your Lady and her Aunt and let me know to direct to Lord Darnley to give me some title to this. It is necessary I should inform you that I have an estate in the County of Down equal to what Lady Anne Macgill accepted of and if the fortunes are alike will settle an equal jointure and provision for children, if less, then in proportion. Over and above this I shall have what will be a very sufficient encouragement for my son's continuing the good son he hath hitherto been Your answer acquainting me with the time you propose to be in Dublin will very much oblige, Sr."

Probably as the result of this approach he is advised to address his proposals to the lady's brother, Lord Darnley, for there follows draft of a letter to this nobleman. The name is, as usual, wanting from the copy. It is headed "to Lord———." The Judge has learned that the lady has £9,500 in hard money, which her brother would probably make up to £10,000 if his sister married to his liking; also that the lady has many chances of inheritances as members of her family die. With this knowledge he composes his letter. He begins by speaking of his son Bernard's desire to make his Lordship's sister his wife, and makes a proposition to his Lordship, as head of the family.

"In consideration of ye portion ye world sayth y^r L^{dp} intends her of £10,000 Im willing to settle on them & their issue male lands of inheritance in ye county of Downe in ye Kingdom of Ireland value £2500 per an (excepting my wife's Jointure) one moiety for their present maintenance & ye other at my Death, subject to ye s^d Jointure which is £800 per ann."

The negotiations were successful, and Bernard Ward married the Lady Anne, who had one daughter by her first marriage, Theodosia McGill, to whom her stepfather became greatly attached. The marriage was productive of more wealth than happiness to Bernard Ward, for, according to the statement of a member of the family, " as time went on they were not by any means a harmonious couple," and in the end, after becoming mother to seven children, the lady left husband and children and withdrew to Bath, where she spent the last fifteen years of her life.

Tithe-paying was a burning question in eighteenth-century Presbyterian Down. The form in which the Church claimed it varied very much. Robert Ward writes to his brother, December 20th, 1735 :—

> " I am desired by old John Chamber to acquaint you that Mr Daniell (the Dean) told him that if he would not pay him every tenth spade of potatoes, he would put him in Court. In the Deanery, a penny has been the modus for a garden, wch is constantly paid by those who have no other garden but potatoes, and those not enclos'd but set in the field."

The Judge has much correspondence with another Dean of Down (Delany) on this subject. The Dean has claimed from weavers—tenants of the Ward estate—a payment of one shilling per annum as ' trade-money.' The matter is brought to the Judge's notice by a letter from Charles Brett, solicitor and agent for the Judge.

> " S^r,
>
> I give you the trouble of this letter to lay before you a State of the case of certain of your Tenants (among others) who are in the Bp's Court for Substraction of Ec^{ll} dues at the Suit of the Dean of Down, the demand upon whome is a Shilling for tread money as weavers one or two of your Ten^{ts} appear'd & alledged that they ought not to pay as trades men because they wrought to their Father's house not constantly, but in a bad day or when the business of their farm which was their principal calling would permit them. This Plea was deem'd frivilous & evasive and they are admonish'd to attend at next Court (May 7th) &

take Copys of Libells then to be exhibited agt them. As the
defence of such a Suit will be attended wth insupportable expence
to these people I submit it to you S^r whether if they be not supported, it would not be better to pay the tax than engage in such
a Suit, wch in all probability a Spiritual court will decree ag^t
them, & wch if it should, an expence of three or four pounds will
be the consequence. I for my part am greatly distressed about
the affair because I shall have a much larger share of the infamy
of those Vexatious Suits than the profits arising from them will
make me attonement for. I have stated the case to you as well
as I am capable, & coud wish that your time woud permit you
to signifie your opinion to the Coll^n how the people shall conduct
themselves.

I am

S^r your ever dutyfull & obed^t
servant,

Charles Brett.

Castle Ward April 14th, 1746."

Thereupon the Judge writes to the Dean, protesting against
his action. The Judge's support of his tenants' refusal to
pay trade money, as learned from the Dean's letters, is based
mainly on the poverty of the weavers—they cannot afford
the payment ; to which the Dean replies (in effect) that he
does not believe it.

" to my certain knowledge, every sober industrious man, among
my common Labourers, can, upon occasion, lay up six pence a
week, for many weeks together, to answer any emergency for
extraordinary demand : and as for such of them, as find some
difficulty in saving such a sum, on such occasions, it is not because
their own, or the necessities of their family demand it, but because
they cannot spare it from ye Ale house & I am fully satisfied,
that the case will be the same to ye bulk of trades men, if this
small spur to industry, & check upon drunkeness be taken off
every penny that is taken out of their Pastors pocket, will go
to ye whisky, or ale house."

The Judge has questioned the legality of the claim, and has,
apparently, conceded the Church's right to tithes from the
land occupier, to which the Dean, in answer—

" My right to trade money, you are pleased to say you have a very
low opinion of ; and I, for my part, am able to form no opinion
of what the Law of the Land has determined in that point, but
thus much I think is clear from the Law of reason ; that the
support of true religion is the principal support of Peace, and
virtue in every Society is indispensibly obliged, to contribute
to that support, true religion, cannot, (in my humble opinion)
be effectually supported in any society without a proper Provision
for the publick Worship of God and how a man who occupies a
piece of Leather, or a piece of Linnen, can, in the nature and
reason of things, be more exempted from contributing any
proportion of the fruits of his industry to that purpose, than he
who occupies a piece of Land, I own, is to me utterly incompre-
hensible. . . . Some people may perhaps think it a good
plea for their salvation at ye last day, that they did all in their
power to relieve a Set of honest and industrious trades men from
the grievous oppression of contributing almost one entire farthing
a week, out of ye profits of a good trade, to ye support of God's
publick Worship upon Earth ; I earnestly beseech God, that
my poor and humble pleas for pardon before his footstool, may
be of a very different kind."

To the Judge's plea for abandonment of the claim, the Dean
replies by a reference to the known practice of landlords.

" To you, who are known to be a good Landlord, I am sure I may
without offence urge another reason ; it is a known case, in many
instances, that whatever is taken away from ye income of the
Parson, is added to his Landlord ; whatever lessens ye Tythe,
not relieves ye holder, but increases ye rent."

These brief extracts from a very lengthy correspondence
(taken out of order of date), show that the good Dean was
quite able to hold his own in a tussle with a Judge. Neither
gentleman takes off the gloves, nor hits below the belt. The
Judge is profuse in expressions of friendship, and the Dean
says some very nice things in response. But on a question
of Church's right he will not give way. He makes what must
be allowed to be a very fair and reasonable offer—

" let ye points in dispute be tried, in one instance only ; conditionally that all ye rest shall abide by ye Judgement of ye court in

that one, let yᵉ person be one of your tenants ; you are Landlord
I am Pastor, I trust in God we both Love justice, & desire only
to have yᵉ point in dispute brought to a speedy & fair determina-
tion ; let yᵉ same person be appointed to take yᵉ defence who
was chosen by yᵉ Linnen board for that purpose ; do you bear
yᵉ one half of yᵉ expense of taking yᵉ defence, & i, (who am less
able and less obliged) will bear yᵉ other ; so shall peace be
established in a speedy & Xtian manner,"

and concludes with an awful warning to the Judge :—

"I have already I fear, wearied you upon this subject, but as
your conduct in this affair hath grieved me to yᵉ heart, give me
leave to conclude in yᵉ character of a Pastor, who is bound in
conscience to admonish his people in what he thinks virtuous,
Pious, and praise worthy. I am in my 62nd year I have neither
vanity, nor avarice, nor ambition to gratifye in yᵉ prosecution
of this suit, and I sacrifice to it what I love and honour above
everything under heaven, next to a good conscience—Peace.
Can you then justly suspect me of any motives but those of what
I deem indispensible Duty to God, for yᵉ support of his true
religion in the world. I am leaving yᵉ kingdome in a few days,
if not hours, & may possibly never find any other occasion of
discharging yᵉ Duty I owe you. I beseech you then by yᵉ
mercies of God & by yᵉ hopes of your own Eternal Salvation to
admit some doubt of your own conduct for a few moments, &
to examine your conscience with that attention that will enable
you to answer for it at yᵉ last day, whether you will then be able
& clearly to Justifie yourself upon this head at yᵉ great Tribunal.
I condemn you not, I judge you not, God forbid I shou'd : but
this I beg leave to tell you, & I beg leave to tell you it, as I
sincerely intend it, without offence, in singleness of heart & as
I shall answer to God for it, that I wou'd not allow myself in
any conduct wᶜʰ a wise and good man could charge with so much
as a tendency to deprive yᵉ clergy of any of their just rights, for
yᵉ inheritance of this whole earth possibly I may err in yᵉ other
extream ; for indeed I am in yᵉ utmost terror of those Judgements
denounced by God against yᵉ withholding of Tythes and offerings.
'Will a man rob God (saith yᵉ Prophet Malachi Chap : 3. v : 8,
9, 10, 11) Yet ye have robbed me : but ye say wherein have we
robbed thee ? in Tythes & offerings ye are cursed with a curse
for yᵉ have robbed me, even this whole nation bring yᵉ *All* yᵉ

Tythes into yᵉ store house, that there may be meat in my house, and prove me now herewith says yᵉ Lord of Hosts; if I will not open to you the windows of heaven, & pour yᵉ out a Blessing, that there shall not be room enoʰ to receive it, & I will rebuke yᵉ devourer for your sakes, and shall not destroy yᵉ fruits of your ground, neither shall yᵉ Vine cast her fruits before yᵉ time in yᵉ field saith the Lord of Hosts.'

" Whether this hath been our case for some years past, & whether yᵉ *devourer* hath not been remarkably let loose upon us, Judge you. God of his infinite mercy, direct, & guard, and guide you in this affair, & deliver you, and yᵉ nation from every curse, & calamity denounced in yᵉ text now cited, & every other this, Sʳ, is yᵉ most earnest & fervent prayer of yʳ most faithful humᵇˡᵉ Serᵗ Pat Delany."

In the hard times of the eighteenth century some of the minor gentry of the county went under—among them the Bretts of Ballynewport, in Lecale. Charles Brett, acting as solicitor and agent for Mr. Ward, remains, but his brother, Mr. Bernard Brett, after a hard struggle, abandons his all to his creditors and flees to the Isle of Man. This departure is announced to the Judge in the following letter from his agent at Killough—Francis Lascelles :—

" Killough, Octoʳ 30th, 1731.
" My Lord,

Last Thursday night Mr Bernard Brett left home I believe in order for Isle of Man or Egland when to return I can't heare. I arrested all the goods in his house & has an Inventory of them. Mr Parkinson Junr. has takn an action out of this Court for £8.14.0 against his Body or goods after you are payed your arrears of rent there are several others waiting to see if any surplus for them be pleased to give your orders in this case I don't believe the whole will amount much over the arrears."

With a later letter Lascelles encloses the inventory above referred to. He thinks that the valuers, " old Mrs Feattus and her husband," have put too high a value on some things, but " Mrs. Brett would not let them value them less." The inventory is of interest in showing the furnishings of an eighteenth-century house.

" Inventory of Mr Bernard Brett's goods.

		£ s d
One Grate in Kitchen & Jacke	£2	0 0
18 pewterplates	0	17 0
6 pewter dishes	0	13 0
2 pair brass Candlesticks	0	6 6
A washing tup & 2 canns	0	3 0
4 Wooden bowls	0	2 6
2 small Coolers	0	3 6
3 Spits & pair of tripets	0	3 6
1 Warming pan	—	
1 frying pan		2 0
A settle bed & bed close		10 0
3 silver spoons	—	
1 large table		5 0
2 barrels	—	
1 rack manger		5 0
2 Iron pots	—	
1 brass Skillet	—	
1 toopaun	—	
1 Crook & pothooks	—	
in several rooms		
1 Chest of Drawers	1	3 0
A looking glass		10 0
A fether bed bedstead & blankets	3	10 0
4 chairs		5 5
8 cain chairs	1	16 0
a bigg chair		10 0
1 Oak table		4 6
1 Tea table		10 0
1 room grate & Irons	1	3 0
2 pictures	3	0 0
Hangins of Arrowse (Arras)	2	10 0
1 bedstead Curtains & blankets	2	10 0
1 Chime quilt	1	8 0
1 Callico quilt	—	
1 large looking glass		14 0
2 trunks	—	
1 do lesser	—	
1 chair	—	
6 dressing boxes	—	
2 pair of window curtains		10 0

6 pairs of sheets ..	..	..	..	2	10	0
18 towels ..	..	..	..		10	10
2 diaper table cloths	..	..	..		18	0
7 Huckstable cloths	..	..	..	1	0	0
6 Napkins ..	..	..	..		4	0
Bedstead & Curtains	..	..	..	2	10	0

Lascelles explains that the blanks are against items which are to be valued according to weight, or are things claimed by a Captain Johnston. Considering the standing of the Bretts, the action of the Ward agent may seem to be very unfeeling, but a letter from the Isle of Man exile, dated seven years later, represents the Judge in a much more favourable light— Brett, indeed, acknowledges that to him he has been indebted for his main support. Probably, after seven years' assistance, My Lord, and his friend Lord Limerick, thought it right that Mr. Brett should fend for himself and family—they have asked him to return to Ireland, and have proposed employment. Very pathetic indeed is the old gentleman's reply ; but it is easy to see that, having lived for seven years in tolerable ease, after a hard struggle to make ends meet, he has no mind to begin a new life at the age of sixty-seven.

" My Good L^d,

It is now more than time for me to acknowledge y^r constant and repeated favours to me without which I must freely owne I cou'd not subsisst, for tho I must owne with great gratitude that I have rec^d particuler favours from many friends, yet my main support has been from you, which I am never to be sufficiently thankfull for nor can I make any other return but my dayly and fervent prayers to God for the well-being of you and your dear family ; I had a hint given to me that y^r Lords^P was of opinion I ought to go over, my inclinations are good if I knew where to go ; I had a letter with a p^{e}sent from my good Ld Limerick last July, wherein he told me that he had recommended me to one of the Commissioners, but desired me not to mention it to anyone till he cou'd find what effect it would have, but I never heard more of it since.

" But when I consider I am now 67 years old, it wou'd not be easy to get an Imploym^t in the Revenue, that I cou'd be capable of executing, nor cou'd I refuse anything that were offered me without rejecting the endeavours of that Noble Ld to serve me, which is a shocking consideration ; and considering the great troubles I have undergone, I canot be supposed to live long, and to involve myselfe a new in the affairs of the world Just at the close of my days, when in all probabillity I shall not have long to prepare for an endless duration is a thing that often perplexes my thoughts, indeed if I cou'd hope for any thing by which I cou'd hope to make my poor children the better, I shou'd think it my indisspencible duty both to God and them, to spend my old carcass to the last thread, and to ease my friends of the burthen of my support, tis true I have lived here seven years by a providence thats next to a miracle, and tho very often without clothes to cover my nakedness and but a goats Hare Wigg to cover my head, I can without vanity and with some comfort say, that I have the universal esteem of every one, and more especialy our worthy Governour who has disstinguished me from all strangers in this Isle, and has obliged me to dyne with him every Sunday since ever he came over, he is a man of great humanity, sobriety and worth and tis a great trouble to me that I have no friend of disstinction that knows him, that cou'd take notice of his civillity to me, I have now tired yʳ LordsP and will only ad that I am to yʳ LordsP and family

> My Dr Ld
> a most obedient and most
> affectᵗ humble Serᵗ
> > Ber. Brett.

Castletowne
Apr. 26th, 1738."

The Scottish rebellion of 1745, and the initial successes of the Pretender, caused great excitement in Down. Companies of Militia were formed, drilled, and armed, in a manner which will provoke a smile on the modern face. The Pretender's forces were expected to land at Carrickfergus, with intention to defeat any loyalist forces opposed to them, and, this done, to receive vast accessions to their ranks from disaffected Irish. The first letter on the subject is from Charles Brett, addressed to Judge Ward.

" Bangor, Jany 4th, 1745.

" Sir,

As I had no business of consequence to trouble you with
since I came home, I have neglected writing to you & have been
diverted from it these three weeks past till I could give you a
distinct answer how we are circumstanced here wth our Militia.
Some time after the alarm of the Rebells being in this bay, Capt
Blackw^d issued his order to the people to attend him in order to
be disciplined, and above four score I believe, of as good men as
any in the county attended him the first day tho' some of them
refused to inlist under him, I believe with too much contempt to
wch he very tamely submitted. He had a Serg^t for a fortnight
to instruct them to whom he gave seven & sixpence & then
dissmissed him and told the men that if they were not perfect
enough in their exercise they must be at the expence of the man
themselves for the time to come. He had sent for a Barrel of
Ale and intended giving them a dinner, but as the woman could
not afford them under sixpence a piece she having no profit
upon the Liquor & he offering four pence. The dinner was
postponed & the ale remanded home. The munday before X^t
mass twenty men of the corporation of Bangor went to his house
& presented him with a remonstrance setting forth that as there
was no place in the County where a Company of good men was
more necessary for the defence of it, so there was no place that
could more easily raise them, or was more willing & Loyal, and
that they could not but greive that when they went into any of
the neighbouring towns, they were obliged to either submit
themselves to the scoffs of the people or quarreling & beg'd
that he would continue to have them instructed or accept of the
expence he had already been at of wch they made him a Tender
and they would according to their ability hire a man among
them they beg'd him also to be assured that what they were
doing was from that zeal wth which they saw every one animated
and not from any resentm^t for his having shewn them no Act
of Courtesie whatever. He has been spoke to by a great many
people & by me so often, that I believe he imagins me the author
of the paper tho' I never saw it till the night before he rec^d it.
The man who wrote it is a Son of George Calvin's who told me
that they intended petitioning for another Capt but I diverted
them from that by what means I could & he is resining the Care
of them tho' I think with a worse grace than in the first instance

I hear that Mrs Ward & my Capt are at Lord Ikerrin's I do not know whether she had left town before she rec^d my Letter in wch there was a Bill of fifty pounds we are in a Melancholy condition here, famine is begining to Stare at us. Wheat is nine shillings the hundred & I much doubt whether there be as much sound Oats in the parish as will sow it, a great part of the Harvest not being gather'd till late in October. I hope you keep free from Colds.

I am,

Sr Your ever obed^t Servt

Charles Brett."

The valour and loyalty of some of the King's soldiers are suspect to correspondents of the Judge. The following is from his brother, Robert Ward:—

" Lisboy, Feby 10th, 1745.

" Dear Brother,

Mr. Gillot is to be in towne to-morrow to perfect the Bond wth the Subshff^e.

" I am sorry that a Comiss^n for a 2nd Lieut is not to be had I'm told Mr Hill Willson & Mr Knox have got it, nor can I see any reason why it should be refused to any it was at ye request of my Lieu^t y^t I ask'd it, who tho' he is a man dilligent in business & loves mony very well yet he has been at great expence & has neglected his business out of zeal for King George, & has largely contributed to form a Company who for good discipline & zeal for our happy constitution are second to none in the Kingdom, & his reason for desiring it was y^t he might for the future have more time to spend on his private affairs. As matters have turned out there doth not seem to be any great occasion for an extraordinary zeal. But if the hand of God had not visably appeared in our deliverance by daunting the Courage of the Rebells I fear that we should now have been in but an indifferent situation for I will not suppose that our Army made a Bargain with the Rebells to run away with a proviso that they would not pursue it is then demonstration to me that 2 Regiments who only made a common stand, Beat & daunted their whole Army. And that if the Rebells had but half ye Courage they were generally supposed to have they might with ease have cut these two Regiments in pieces & then have taken or destroyed all the rest of our Army. But now that our Brave Duke has put himself at the head of our Army, they will certainly fight under him for they love him dearly, so y^t I cannot believe that the Rebells will dare to stand hin unless promoted by dispair. Our late seeming defeat has doubtless raised ye Spirits of ye Papists here. One instance of wch Ile give y^u by a fellow I sent yesterday to goal for drinking ye pretenders health. The examinrs say our Guard took up Shean McMullan a farmer in Carricknab & one Murtogh Sheil suspected to be a young priest about 3 a clock yesterday morning and brought them into an ale house in downe, they had no sooner come in but McMullan called for a quart & drank to ye Landlord (who is one of my Company) the Chevaliers health upon wch ye Landlord snatched ye quart out of his hand & threw ye liquor in his face secured him and sent for more of the guard to carry him safe to the Watchhouse, as soon as they aim'd McMullan call'd for more liquor but they told him that they had allready heard of what he had done & warn'd him not to doe it again notwithstanding he fill'd a glass & said here is the Chevaliers health & I wish that the right may get his right upon wch they carry'd him away & delivered him in charge to him they call'd ye Captn of the Guard. McMullan then said that they had comitted him for Treason but that he would drink it over & over again in spight of all present and that if he was hang'd for it 500 of them should hang along with him. Sheil being a stranger they examined who he was & finding him to be of ye Ballykinler breed some of whom pretend to be protestants they asked if he was a papist he answered he was & said that tho' he had deny'd his King he would not deny his religion for which they carry'd him to the Guard house & as he was going he told them that he could get 6 men out of Ballykinler who would beat 50 of them when McMullan first drank the Chevaliers health Sheil abused him & gave him some strokes tho' gently so y^t I took bail for Sheil but comitted McMullan who pleaded that he was drunk as he really was it was against my grain to Bail Sheil because I really suspect him to be a priest & that he was going about upon a villainous interest. If I have done wrong to Bail him please to let me know it & Ile endeavour to get him taken.

I am Dr Brother,

Most Aff^{ly} y^{rs}

Robert Ward."

The next, from the Judge's son, is addressed to Castle
Ward, and makes the charge of cowardice, or worse, against
Hamilton's dragoons with the loyalist forces. The writer's
position at time of writing is not stated.

"Saturday Sepr 27 1745

" Dear Sir,

On the 21 Ins^t a Battle was fought about 7 miles from
Edenborough, our forces consisted of 3 Regiments of foot & 2
of Dragoons the Rebells killed 400 & took 1000 prisoners. Coll.
Gardiner is in the number of the killed, Sr John Cope, Lord
Lowdon and some other officers esceped to Prestonpans & went
on Board a small Man of War which lay there, it is imagined
that the small remainder of our Army fled to Berwick 54 Officers
prisoners, 150 Carts of Baggage,—Cannon 2 Mortars & the
military Chest of £2000. Hamilton's Dragoons behaved ill,
never fired, helped to break our Men & several of them are said
before or after the engagement to have joined the Rebells. The
Pretender has demanded of the town of Edenborough 6000 pair
of Shoes, 200 Targets 6000 Flasks for carrying water, 100 tents
to contain Six men each, & 1000 horses all to be ready as on
monday last. The Rebells were 6000, & we 3000, they are
encamped at Pinkey house about 4 miles East of Edenburgh
this is the sum of this days Scotch news, which I fear may be
depended upon.

I am Dr Sir,

Y^r most oblig^d

B. Ward."

Bernard Ward to his father :—

" Dear Sir,

I was in such a hurry when I wrote to you last post, & so
much affected with the thoughts that any part of the Kings
forces should be beaten by a parcel of Banditti, for I can give
no better name to the whole nation, that I could only give you
the heads of the bad news which the Scotch packets of that day
brought, I have now enclosed a Copy of a letter from a person
in Scotland to Mr Ross a considerable Merch^t of this town the
Copy of which I sent by last post to Lord Molesworth ; our
Scotch packet of this day brings no news, but a Whitehaven
ship which arrived last night says that Cope in his retreat to

Berwick met 6000 English forces with which he marched back,— attack'd the Rebells, & after a bloody & an obstinate battle entirely routed them, this news, considering how it comes to us, is not I fear to be depended upon nor in truth do I see what there is to prevent the Rebells from marching directly to England, where as well as upon the road, their small success, will probably induce most of the indigent dissafected to joyn them, tho' I think nothing gives a more contemptible notion of the rabble with which the pretender is attended, than the first article of his demand upon the City of Edenburgh, I mean the shoes, but should these bare footed beggars get into any of the rich towns of England what havock they will make, plunder undoubtedly is their chief aim, which pretty plainly appears by their indiscriminately laying the whole Country under contribution, & tho' I am credibly informed that a person of the name of Stewart who at a Council endeavoured to disswade the pretender from doing so unpopular a thing as laying the Country under contribution, was that night murder'd, without any enquirey being made after the murderer.

" I own I am surprised that no orders have come from the Government about the Militia, we have a notion that raising them without such an order wou'd involve the active persons in the guilt of High treason, how that matter is, I cant pretend to say, Lord Hillsborough wrote for dirrections but has, as yet got none, the Adress is in a good forwardness I this day sent it to Belfast to be signed by the Several Gentlemen of Down who live there & to-morrow it will be sent you thro' the Ards, dispatch it to all your neighbours as soon as you can from you it is to go to Mr Ross & I find it is expected to be ready for my Lord to carry to Dublin with him, I understand he sets out on friday next. Lord Barrington with whome I spent yesterday at Beavoir says he cannot entertain the least suspicion of the Provost of Edenburghs being a Traitor, he is personally acquainted with him, & tho' he was always in the opposition yet he has the caracter of a Staunch Whig.

I am Dear Sir,

Y^r ever obliged

& most faithful

Ber. Ward.

Monday ye 30th Septr 1745."

There were not wanting those of the Established Church, at this time, who tried to use the rebellion to discredit Dissent, alleging that the northern Scots were disloyal and ready to join forces with the rebels, if these should land in Antrim or Down. It is said that an Antrim clergyman rode, post haste, to Dublin, to warn the Lord Lieutenant against placing any trust in the loyalty of dissenters. He was very coldly received. Lord Limerick, a member of the Hamilton family of Tollymore, expresses an opinion, very different, in the subjoined letter, which he addressed to the Judge.

" I take the liberty of sending you the copy of a very strange letter, the contents of which—communicated to the Government. I thought it very proper you should be acquainted with it as Mr Upton has so considerable a property & interest in the County of Antrim, &, as I verily believe it to be a partial and unfair representation of the temper of the Dissenters there. I think I can see the drift of this foolish artifice is to exclude the Dissenters from having any share of arms from the government. As I should dread the consequences of such a proceeding not only in that County, but all over Ireland, I hope that the true friends of our Constitution will join in laying things in a true light before the Government.—have already writ to Mr Secretary Liddell on this occasion, & propose going to Dublin to morrow for a few days, when I shall speak my sentiments very freely to my Lord Lieutenant on this subject. Oppression, they say, will make wise men mad & I don't know but false suspicions may make honest men traitors ; it is an experiment i shall never desire to try. I beg you will not shew the copy I send you but will make such use of the contents of it as you think fit. I beg my compliments to your Lady, and am

Dear S^r
your most obedient &
affectionate humble serv^t
Limerick

Dundalk, Oct. 6th 1745."

We have not a copy of the Judge's reply, but, from its acknowledgment, it is clear that he was entirely in agreement with the view of Lord Limerick, who writes :—

" Dublin, Oct. 10th 1745.

" Sr

    I have received the favour of yours, which has confirmed
me in the opinion I always had of the fidelity of the Dissenters
to his Majesty. I have talked with my Lord Lieutenant on the
subject of the letter, & found it unnecessary to say much to him
on the occasion for I found him as fully convinced of the loyalty
of the Dissenters of the North of Ireland as you or I can be. I
think however they have a right to have justice done them on
the Authors of these vile aspersions, & that the nation is concern'd
in seeing it done. . . ."

From the following letter from William Macartney to the
Judge, it is clear that the Government were culpably negligent
in organising the available forces of the threatened counties,
for defence.

" Dear Sir,

    We have certain Advices by many different Ways that the
Pretender's Son & Rebels in Scotland finding it vain to attempt
meeting our forces, have seized all the Ships & Boats on the Coast
of Scotland, & are determined to land at Carrickfergus, of this we
advertised the Government by Saturday Nights post, & of
farther Accounts last Night by Express. I send you this Express
that we may have instantly a General Meeting of the Gentlemen
that what force there is of Men may be collected together upon
the shortest warning, for which purpose we have sent out Boats
to take Notice of the Coast and to raise the Alarm by fires upon
the high Grounds, when our Enemies appear we hope every
Body will light fires on their highest Grounds to alarm their
neighbours, & that the Protestants in each Parish will immediately collect themselves at a proper Rendezvouz & leaving a
fifth or a sixth part of them to take care of the Habitations, come
directly to Belfast & Carrickfergus, not only with Guns & Swords,
but pitch Forks, Saythes, Flails & every other kind of Weapon,
for if we do not make a proper Stand here, but suffer them to
get into the South, they will be joined by their friends & we
may expect the fate of 1641 which fate could never have gone a
fortieth part so far, if they had not been gulled by the apprehen-
sions which the Papists gave them that they were only to have
their Lands first, next only to kill the English not the Scotch,

& so divide, distract & delay us, but I hope it will be far otherwise
now, & that they will find in us one Boast, one Mind, one Soul,
to undertake & speedily execute every thing that may be for
our Liberty & our Country against Massacre & Slavery.

> I am, Dear Sir,
>
> Yours etc. in haste,
>
> Wm. Macartney.

Belfast Oct 28, 1745."

The next is from Robert Ward to his brother, the Judge, who
has succeeded in getting from the Government a grant of
condemned or cast arms.

> " Lisboy, Novr 10th 1745.

" Dear Bro^r

I am fav^d with y^{rs} of 14th Ins^t and as my Sister being on
her journey as far as Downe was put back upon inform^n that
the Roads were unpassable for a Coach I sent it to her we are
glad to find our danger not so imminent as we were made to
fear if the like happens again I hope we shall be better prepared
to receive them for most Gentlem^n seem to be now industrious
to get their men well disciplined. There appeared a brave
Spirit in the common people after they were told that ye Enemy
were expected to land every hower And they seem to have such
an abhorrence to ye Pretender & popery that I am confident a
little prudent management would make ye Militia of this Country
very usefull. I am glad to hear that you are like to get some
Cast Arms for I am entitled to a good share of them, I have 70
men exceedingly well disciplined and the half of them are yet
without Arms nor are they able to buy any for as all my men are
Inhabitants of Downe I was forced to take such as I could get
Mr Trotter & Mr Price having taken as many of the towne people
as they could get & they have got at least 15 from me who are
able to furnish themselves with Arms, we have now thank God
nothing to fear at present but least Gen^{ll} Wade should despise
the Rebells too much and attack them before his whole force
comes up, if when the Belfast post comes in there be any news
worth telling y^u Ile write to you again.

> I am Dr Bro^r
>
> Most Aff^{ly} Y^{rs}
>
> Robert Ward."

With the defeat of the Pretender's forces at Culloden the danger
passed, but, had the initial successes of the rebel forces been
followed by others, and the proposed landing in Ireland been
effected, only the bravery of the Antrim and Down men,
plus discarded muskets, and their own " pitch Forks, Saythes,
Flails & every other kind of Weapon," would have saved
them from disaster—for Government did nothing.

The following letter, found among the Castle Ward papers,
and, presumably, addressed to the Judge's son, shows that
1760 found the counties still without adequate means of
defence against landings of enemy forces. The French have
taken Carrickfergus.

(Place of writing not indicated).

" Sir,

At a meeting of severall Field Officers yesterday in Down,
it was requested I shou'd go to Belfast & get the best Intelligence possible, which is, that one ship from 36 to 40 one from 22
to 24 & the third of sixteen guns Landed men to the number of
One thousand some say 1500, the Castle of Carrick was Given
up at Ten on Thursday night, the Garrison consisted of 200 men,
they had but six rounds each & before they surrendered threw
stones at the French. Col. Jennings, or My Lord——— a Captain, I forget his name is Wounded, it was not known in Bellfast
at seven last night which of them it were. A french officer with
a native of Carrick came in a boat to Bellfast yesterday morning
Demanded thirty Barrells of Brandy & other provisions to the
same amount Gave but two hours to Consider, if not comply'd
with they would burn Carrick, Comply'd with & sent up in two
sloops. Captain Gordon a veter^n Commanded a Detachm^t
of the Strodes & Militia to the amount of four hun^d went out in
order to give battle to the French who are Intrench'd and wou'd
not stir, there were Detachm^{ts} from severall Regim^{ts} of this
County in Bellfast to the amount of 800, & I do believe by the
time y^r Regm^t & others arrive which will be this Day they will
be two Thousand, & I hope & belive that to morrow we will
drive them out of their Intrenchm^{ts} which will certainly be the
Day of Action if ever any happens. We are badly armed I dare
not find fault with people in power, but if I survive & behave

like an officer of yours, I hope you will use your Power & Interest
to serve him that wou'd Die in his Countrys & your cause

             I am Sir, your most faithfull
                  & obed^t serv^t
                                                Robt Patterson.

Saturday morning 10 o'clock 23 Feby 1760.

Just Going to March from Down pardon the Incorrectness of
this haveing Rode yesterday in 5 hours' back & forward for the
above Intelligence from Down to Bellfast in as Dreadfull a Day
as ever fell, farewell! My Dearest Colonel."

The deference shown to a Judge may, sometimes, turn
his head ; and if he is large owner of lands as well as judge,
with all the power over the lives of men which ownership of
land in the eighteenth century conveyed, then it is almost
certain that, at times, he may think of himself more highly
than he ought to think, and will need a reducing medicine.
This is certain to be provided, where or when required, in
every life,—and Judge Ward knew what it was to have the
remedy administered. Clewlow's letters to him from Bangor,
informing him of Mr. Blackwood's attitude, and commending
the policy of absenting from a meeting of his tenantry, will
be remembered. The Judge's letters to the person he suspected of vilifying him at the time of the proposed marriage
of his daughter to Mr. Price, indicate that he knew of some
who loved him not, and his brother's little note, here copied,
shows that even in his favoured Killough were some who bore
him ill-will.

                          " Downe, February 16, 1740.
                                (Downpatrick)

" I was much mortified to hear from Mr Lascelles that ye new wall
   of ye quay next potatos was in danger of falling & it vexes me
   the more because I am sure it will give great pleasure to some
   scrubs here."

What Alexander Carleton, Esq., Barrister-at-Law, thought
of Judge Ward's temper and his control of it, is learned
from a Memorial which he, the Barrister, addressed to His

Excellency, the Lord High Chancellor of Ireland. It is endorsed " 4th December, 1740."

At the Monaghan Assizes one, Skinner, owner of a bleach yard, made a claim for damages for robbery, to be recovered from the County, and Carleton appeared to oppose the claim—as he says " by desire of some Persons of Note in the County " and for himself, in his quality of Freeholder, Leaseholder, and Inhabitant of the County. His complaint to the Lord Chancellor is thus stated :—

> " Your Memst after ye Petitioner's Councel had stated ye Facts ; rose up on behalf of ye Country & objected that ye s^d Petition was not within ye Act, tho' the Facts were true ; to which Mr Justice Ward with some Heat & Passion ordered the Memst to sit down & said he would go into Evidence to which your Memst submitted. That the first Witness that appeared on ye Table pretended that he could not speak English, upon which an Interpreter was sworn, & the Witness likewise.
>
> " That this Memst was informed ye Witness spoke very good English & pray'd ye Court that ye Interpreter might ask him upon Oath if he did not speak and understand English ; thereupon Mr Justice Ward with great Warmth asked your Memst Did he Disturb ye Court ; Who fee'd your memst, called your Memst a most Insolent Fellow ; said to your Memst sit down Sirrah, & without any Provocation on your Memorialist's part ordered ye Sheriff to take your Memst into Custody ; & upon the Sheriff's not doing the same that Instant, ordered ye Clerk of ye Crown to fine ye Sheriff an hundred Pounds ; upon which ye Sheriff sent ye Under Sheriff to take your Memst to ye Common Goal, which was accordingly done ; & your Memst was kept there near 3 Hours & in ye Sheriff's Custody for 2 Nights & a Day."

This letter-life of a Down magnate began with his impassioned love-letter to the young Anne Hamilton of Bangor, and may end fitly with letters by her hand. She has learned to date her letters, but still fails to indicate where they have been written, and, except for an occasional dash, she has no care for punctuation. Internal evidences, in the two communications following, show that they were written from Dublin to the Judge at Castle Ward.

" My Dear
        the Dr thinks Nick (her grandson) better I have not got the
Barrack money—yesterday being St Patrick's Day there was the
greatest Mob ever was known here they got a cart painted black
with the speaker in his gown and large wig in it a paper on his
breast was wrote in large letters he betray'd the city in 1749
they follow'd the cart saying he must die was carring him to the
gallows and when they had Hang'd him designed to take Sr
Arthur Gore and put him in the speaker's chair in the house of
Commons they was forst to have all the Army to disperse them
the Ld Mayor was in great danger—I am sure what ever you do
in my walk I shall like
                                I am,
                                        Your own A Ward
        March 18 1756 "   .   .   .   .   .   .

" My Dear
        it gives me vast pleasure to find you are in so good spirits
and are so well this excessive cold weather pray God continue it—
I don't find there is any time fixed for my son's leaving town
why did not you kill the Veal etc they will be good for nothing
if kept too long and sure nobody deserves them better than
yourself have you good malt Liquor this is the time for Brewing
Ale and small Beer for summer if not allready done I have seen
Ld Carrick often as he say'd nothing to me it was to nice a subject
for me to touch on he is now at Clontarf goes soon to Bristole.
        " I have not got the Barrack money yet nor don't know when
I shall I am
                                Your own
                                                A Ward
        March 27, 1756."

When the next letter was written the lady was a widow.
There is not, in the great mass of preserved correspondence,
a line to indicate that the Judge and his wife were ever other
than the best of friends.   Yet one may wonder, reading the
lady's letters, so free from trace of the romantic or senti-
mental, whether he who wrote that flaming declaration to
eighteen-year-old Anne Hamilton, ever missed the note of
softness in that girl, made wife.   Her letter following, addressed to her agent, Henry Waring, at Bangor, is that of a

person who will not brook interference with her rights—it is hardly the letter of one very considerate or compassionate. If Mr. Blackwood won't attend to his duty to the church, " why is he chose Church Warden."

She *must* have her rents—

> " The May rent at Novr & the Novr at May—they that can't do yt must not think of staying on ye land."

Imperious old lady !

> " Sr,
>
>   Yours of the 28 I recd yesterday I coud have wished what repairs the church wanted had been done before this bad weather if Mr Blackwood wont attend why is he chose Church Warden I earnestly desire that the church may not be neglected I shoud be glad to know if you had finished the dividing of the town Parkes—I am much surprised to hear you have not recd the Novr Chieft-Rents which are due the 20th if they dont pay why dont you distrain I insist on your doing it immediately I did not forget the letter of attorney I have it ready for Ld Carrick to sign when he comes to town—I desire that you will write Mr Halliday that I am much displeas'd with you for not send me his May rent what I told you I now repeat agen I expect the May rent at Novr & the Novr at May—they that can't do yt must not think of staying on ye land.
>
> I am yr Humble Sert
>
> A. Ward."

And a letter from the lively Theodosia Crosbie (née Bligh), to a sister, contains a paragraph which serves to show that Mrs. Ward could be ' difficult.' The young lady is a visitor to her sister, wife of Bernard Ward, at Castle Ward, whose mother-in-law, the Judge's wife, has been absent, presumably in England. Thus Theodosia to her husband, September 25th, 1749 :—

> " Madam Ward is at last arrived (in Ireland) there was a letter from her yesterday she has not fixed a time for coming here as she is to stay to bring servants etc so that, perhaps, she may not come till we are gone, at least I am in hopes of it as I believe we are much better without her."

CHAPTER XII.

The Diarists

As an aid to the seeing of our forefathers as they saw themselves, the private diary of their time and place is of the highest value. The letter is good, but it is of a day, often of a subject, and exhibits the writer as he wishes to appear to one person ; while the diary is often of years, may be of a thousand subjects, and the self-revelation of the writer, even when his mind has harboured the thought of others seeing his notes, is generally far greater than he suspects.

The century of Evelyn and Pepys was the century of diarists. As a fashion in dress, showing first in rich material on My Lady, is adopted by rank after rank until, in cotton, it appears on the kitchenmaid, so the private daily record, at first the fashion of the few and great, saw its use spread through wider and lower circles in the eighteenth century, and before abandonment (as fashion) came in the early nineteenth, quite commonplace folk made, daily, quite commonplace remarks in note-books, for no other reason than that it was a proper thing for gentility to do.

Of the thousands of daily-made records of personal experience, the product of the seventeenth century, few, doubtless, had the value of the writings to which we owe such lively pictures of the Stuart times. Yet even the baldest of such records, escaping destruction, becomes interesting and valuable with the passing of years ; for its writer has, inevitably, put into it something of the life of his time, which the contemporary historian rejected as valueless, and which, because of its perishable character, is only in the rarely-preserved diary available for the chronicler of later times. If only we had diaries enough we could spare the historian better than the diary writer. The former paints an impressionist picture,—often untrue,—of people in mass ; the latter furnishes us with a perfectly accurate miniature of an individual. And even the most individual of these miniatures has enough background to show something of the friends and surroundings of the pictured one. The diary of Lady Elizabeth Mordaunt, from which extracts are here given, is concerned not with daily event, but with her soul's health ; yet in it, past the face of a tender-hearted gracious lady, we can see a cross of her life—the Lady Peter, and some features of the dearly-loved, yet wayward and ' passionat ' husband, who neglects his prayers when he has been kept up after his accustomed bed-time.

Diaries of the old time are of two kinds—the one, like that of Lady Mordaunt, a record of painful introspection, a mirror in which the flesh is asked to look daily and be ashamed ; the other noting, generally, daily event,—its writer dealing only with questions of conduct, feeling, and duty to God at set times, such as birthdays and days of the New Year. Writers of both sorts see the need for their daily remembrancer in the tendency of poor human nature to let days, months, years, slip by,—the one without growth in grace,—the other without adequate effort to attain material success. Both recognise the obligation of the daily entry, and both, being human, find faithful dealing with themselves

too hard a task for every day.   Hence the sops to conscience
on the days of failure, such as the Donaghadee divinity
student's repetition of " I was domi p.diem," and Lady
Roden's dates satisfied by a " same as yesterday."

Discovered diaries of old Down are not numerous.   Of
those here presented, two were not written in Down, or not
all there written, but their inclusion in the study is to be
justified by the writers' connections with, and interest in,
the county, during the period with which this work is concerned.

Elizabeth Carey was daughter of Thomas, second son of
Robert, Earl of Monmouth.   She married John, Viscount
Mordaunt, and became intimately connected with Down by
the marriage of two of her daughters.   Anne became the wife
of James Hamilton of Tollymore, and Sophia married his
namesake and cousin, James Hamilton of Bangor.

The diary begins in 1656.   It is a record of the soul's
conflict with evil and aspirations after good.   The day's
entries divide into two parts,—confession of weakness or
sin, and thanksgiving for mercies.   A prefatory statement
indicates the purpose of the record.

1656

" A Medetation of the Strictnes we aught to observe
thru the holle Corse of our Life, being not only to
account for our thoughts words and actions but
for the very appearanse of Guilt."

" The Medetation of the appearanse of Guilt.

That sence we must uppon no termes sufer any action to pase
without so strickt exsamination of which we may give an account
as wel of the apperanc as of the intention of theme   .   .   . etc."

There is a most pathetic entry under date June 2nd, 1658,
by which the loving wife records her husband's escape from
death at the hands of the Republicans.   For his activities
in the interest of Charles I., and share in Lord Holland's
attempt to rescue that Monarch, Mordaunt was put on trial,
with but small chance of a decision in his favour.   Mrs. Reilly,

in her *Historical Anecdotes*, states that some of the judges were bribed by Mordaunt's wife. Her own statement in the diary is as follows:—

1658

" June ye 2. In the yere of our Lorde 1658, on the first of June, my deare Husband was tryed for his Life by a Corte, calede the Highe Corte of Justis, and on the secont day of June, was cleerd, by one voys (voice) only. 19 condemning of him and 20 saving of him and the twenty had not prevented but by God's emedeate Hand, by striking one of the Corte with an illness which forced him to goe out, in whous absens, the vots (votes) wer geven, and recorded, so that his returne no way preiudis'd Mr Mordaunt, tho in his thoughts he resolued it (Prid was the person) Many outher meracolus blesings wer shod in his preservation, for which blesed

Be God

He was the first exsampule that pleded not gilty that was cleerd be for the Cortes."

Another special entry is that headed

" A prayer of thanksgeving For my Deare Husbands safe returne Home when he went out with the Duck of Yarck to see (Duke of York to sea)

Wensday Decem ye 7
1664."

The words of this thanksgiving are taken from the Psalms. She does not forget to pray for husband and children,—for one of these she prays even before its birth.

" Now that I draw neare the time of my travill . . . Lord grant my child Life and opertunety of babtisme, and Lord preserve it from all deformety what soever, give it a cumly body and understanding soule and thy Grace from the Cradell to the Grave, and Howsoever thou Shall⊤ dispos of me, either for Life or deathe, sanctephi that to my deare Husband and grant that by it he may become derer and nerer unto thee . . "

From the ordinary entries, for which the day of the week is given without indication of month or date, a few extracts are here given,—some of them from the side of confessions, some from the notes of praise and thanks.

Side of confession made, and pardon asked.

" Sunday (1st entry for 1657)

" to aske pardon for ofended by disputing with my Husband and
then by geving him a trubel having bin wedded to my owne
opinion and not yelding . . . by not spending this thy
Sabeth day so well as I aught to dow, but was drowsy at the
evening sermon."

" Sunday.

" to ask pardon . . by not spending this thy Sabath day so
well as I aught to, but was drowsy at the evening sermon."

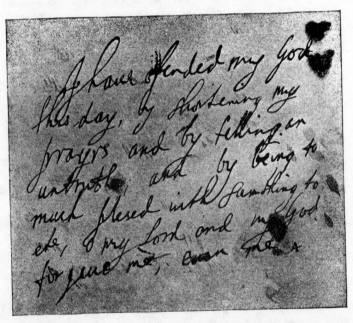

The writing of Elizabeth, Viscountess Mordaunt.

" I have ofended my God this day, by shortening my prayrs and by
telling an untruthe ; and by being to much plesed with sumthing to
ete, O my Lord and my God forgeue me, even me."

"Munday.

"To repent of having spent this day in Veseting. I fear I may have ofended with my tung. I am shure I have by not saying my prayrse this afternoone and by making other Pepels indiscretion my devertion."

"Tusday.

"To aske pardon for I have sayd one or to things that were not exactly true."

"Sunday.

". . . that I tould a thing to one that might insence her aganst another, which was ill tho the thing wer true."

"tusday.

"I have ofended by sufering my illness to slaken my devotion and by spending mor of my time in reding a foulish play than was spent in thy servis."

"thursday.

"O Lorde forgeue my having ometed this day's account."

"Munday.

"O my God forgeue me, this days ofences, and thos of my hole Life; I have ofended by being to sensabel of Lady P. ingerys, and by having sayd to many things to her disaduantag. O Lord send my deare Husband save to me agane and forgeue, my knone and secret Sins, I feare I tould a Lye this day."

"Saterday.

"forgeue Lord my keping up my husband till his slepyine mayd him neglect his prayrs and my neglecting them to often my selfe, and the pryd I exprest today by being angery at my Lady P. not staying for me, and all outher my ofences bouth of this day and all past . . ."

From the side of praise and thanksgiving.

"tusday.

"I bles my God for geuing me patient to ber with my Husband when he is in his passionat Humers. Lorde breke him of them, or if thou hast desined them for a scurdg for me geu me grace to reseue them as may best ples thee."

" tusday.

" praysed be my euer-mercyfull God for all his mercys this day
bestoed, for my Lady peter being kinder than she uses to be,
and for my deare Husband's helthe and hapynes and his Kindnes
to me, and for the countenanc of mine."

" Sunday.

" Blesed ever Blesed be my Lorde for all his blesings unto me, and
for the desire I have to serve him tho my performanc be very
very weke, but Lord increse my sele."

" Saterday.

" to returne thanks for the gret mercy that nether me not my
husband nor any that belongs to me hath reseued any priudice
this day, and that I have bin abel to ete mete without being very
ill after it, and for all outher thy unspekeabel mercys I prays
thy Holy name."

Surely never was conscience more tender than that of Lady
Elizabeth.

It is a far cry from these heart-breathings to the notes
of a Donaghadee divinity student, in love with the minister's
daughter. He is John Scott, son of Captain Matthew Scott,
mariner, of Donaghadee, and appears to have been reported
by the Down Presbytery to the General Synod of Ulster,
at its meeting in June, 1707, as having been licensed to
preach the Gospel. Jean Hamilton, the ' domina ' so frequently mentioned, was daughter of Rev. Henry Hamilton, of
Donaghadee.

1704

" Fraiday 15th December I was att home and in
company wth my father who was same day under
Physick, when Hugh Campbell wth Wm. Pinkstane
came to my father wth his Bill of Cost : presented it,
& after some time, he was provoked, tho' no cause
was given, to give my father a blow, whereupon I gott up, gott
him in my arms & desired him to be sober, and att length gott
him pulled from my father and then interposing betwixt them
quite him, he made towards my father the second time, I again
interveans & desires him to give me the blow & not meddle with
father, & so I gives him a blow wth my fist on the face he was

afterward pretty sober, only told me he would give me a blow another time, and promising the same elswhere namely Pinkstan's in the audience of Capt. Montgomery, Jo^n Mc Cormick of Newry & Arch Milling he was indeed as good as his word, for same night Fraiday 15th he came in Street door & chamber door being open ; & as he entered the room door he drew his oak cudgel, wth this expression, were you not a base villan to beat me so in the morning & so let drive att me, but ever blessed be my God, who at all times safeguards his own, destined one of the beams of the house to receive it from me, & when it was over, namely, the blow, I clapt in to him & gott hold on him and att length gott him under me, and so beat him wth my fists untill I was allmost weary, and at last I gott him putt out of the house, & while att the door & chamber window he threatened to put me from preaching & to burn the house upon us."

1705   " Fraiday 16th March I was domi p diem only in the evening went down to Mr Hamilton's where I was for some space of time wth the mistris."

1705   " Wensday 14th March I was att no sermon the Sabbath before Mr Hamilton had given intimation that there would be no weak days sermon because of the sowing."

1705   " Teusday 17th April I went to Belfast and bought a hatt price 5s : 10d and two yards & 3 quarters of broad-cloath at 5 as I judge it may be, because it was not paid then p yeard. I returned same night."

1705   " Wensday 15th August I heard Mr Hamilton on Jon 4:2 & was domi p diem. Memorandum that same day I went to Tho : Wrights who was going to my father to Dublin & gave him the Key of my father's chest & at my return I overheard Janet Barkley cursing Jon Blair whom I reproved but the wase she was at length I was a little out of humour through her & she was pleased to declare throughout the town that I abused her when God knows it was the glory of God & the good of her poor soul that I designed by the reproof by me reached her, but I fear poor woman she is given up of God."

An example of the student's sops to conscience, during a week of failures to make the daily entry, is here given.

1706

" Munday 21st January I was domi p diem.
Teusday 22nd, I was domi p diem.
Wensday 23rd, I was domi p diem.
Thursday 24th, I was domi p diem.
Fraieday 25th, I was domi p diem.
Saturday 26th, I was domi p diem."

The next refers to a communion service, which, of nine
tables succeeding each other, and with a ministerial address
at each, must have been of extraordinary length.

1706

" Sabbath 26th May I heard Mr Jackson lecture on
Psa 27 4 verse and Mr Shannon the action sermon
on Isai:53:10 last clause. There were 9 tables 1
served by Mr Shannon 4 by Mr Jackson & 4 by Mr
Smith. Mr Smith preached in the afternoon on
Ezra 8·22 last clause. But his power and his wrath is against
all them that forsake him. Glory to God that my eyes beheld
such a sweet comfortable & desirable day."

1706

" Saturday 8th June, I slept till near 4 in the afternoon,* about 5 it was noised through the town that
the Meeting house was on fire, as soon as I got my
shooses on my feet & my coat on my back, I ran as
fast thither as possibly I could and found true what
was noised, but blessed be God it was soon quenched, so that it
did not much harm, the occasion of it was Jamie allen the coll^rs
son his firing a musquet at a bird that was upon the house, and
the weather being dry & the forrage of the gun carring to the
thatch set it on fire by him not designed I am persuaded."

* He had been riding from Antrim all night before.

The next is interesting, as fixing the time required for
the journey between Belfast and Donaghadee.

1706

" Teusday 11th June I went to Belfast wth Mr Hamilton his wife & daughter who went thither to the
school, Mrs Alice Crymble Ja: Kennedy & Tho:
Lench were likewise in company ; we left Belfast
about 8 at night and came home about 1 in morning."

1706

" Munday 20th September I was in Donoghadee it
being a fair day. I was some time with Mr Ja.
Hamilton in Ja. Kennedy's & Ja. Hay's, God pardon

the sin of mispending time, precious time. Memorandum Mr
James Hamilton sent with Mitchel to Ed^r for a perriwig about
five & twenty or thirty shillings price. Mitchel was to return
within 6 weeks."

1706

"Sabbath 3rd November I was in Donnoghadee and
did lecture on Psa 17 & preach on Gal.2:20 both
forenoon & after. Mr Hamilton was at Lisburn wth
Mr M^{tt} Cracken who same day had his communion
ever blessed be my good God, for what strength,
furniture & sufficiency I had communicated to me from him,
throughout the whole day both forenoon and after."

1706

"Sabbath 10th November I was in Donnoghadee and
heard Mr Hamilton p diem on Gal:3:1 lecture and
Col.1.17 for sermon. Memorandum that same day
the boat wch Lady Land went off in upon
Saturday the 9 day was again put back with a
contrary wind, and was put in a little below the meeting house
and staved to pieces : but all the passengers were safed & wonderfully preserved."

1707

"Teusday 15th April I went to Belfast and bought
as much black cloath 8 shil p yeard as made me a
coat viz. 2 yeards and ½ & ½ quarter black cloath
from Tho Lyle I also bought as much serge dinnim
as was for bretches. I also bought a hat price being
6 Shill. ster. Memorandum that I heard at that time Mr David
Thome preach in Belfast meeting-house on these words work
out your salvation wth fear & trembling. I came to Donnoghadee
same night."

1707

"Teusday 26th August I was domi p diem only after
dinner I was in Mr Hamilton's where I had occasion
of seeing a letter from Mr Abigail Young to Mr John
Moor signifying more than ordinary intimacy and
familiarity betwixt them. Yea that they were in
love and affection mutually engaged aye captivated."

About this time his own love entries commence—a few
here are copied. He guards against possible exposure of his
thoughts to others, by making the notes in Latin, but, word

and form failing him often, he supplies the missing parts in English, with ridiculous effect. The Latin, at the best, is not good, and requires a sense translation.

ORIGINAL.	SENSE TRANSLATION.
1707. " Saturday the first day of 9ber I was in D.dee about eleven of the clock I went to Mr Hamiltons & meet wth Doâ Janâ in ostio quam alloquatus (? allocutus) eram & promisit me circa horam noctis sextam circa templum obviam ire cui, mentem, circa eodem tempore, revelatam feci & mihi promisit in mei consolationem, se velle de eâ re de quâ cum illa loquebar desiderare (? cogitare) : circa duas horas eram cum illâ prope templum domum separavimus."	1707. Saturday 1st November I was in Donaghadee about eleven o'clock. I went to Mr. Hamilton's and met in the entrance Mrs. Jean, to whom I had spoken and she promised to meet me about 6 o'clock near the church. At that time I disclosed to her what was in my mind, and to console me she said that she would think over the matter about which I had spoken. I was with her about two hours and we separated near the church.
1707. " Munday 3rd November I was in D.dee and in the evening went down to Mr Hamilton's & habui solum modo verbum cum Doâ I went wth Mr Henry Hamilton Mr Hamilton Mrs Jean & some others home with Mr James Hamilton & Lady to their lodging in William McMechen's and again accompanied Mr Hamilton & wife wth Mrs Jean praecipue home wth whom I supped."	1707. Monday November 3rd I was in Donaghadee and in the evening went down to Mr. Hamilton's. I had only a word with Doâ. I went with Mr. Henry Hamilton, Mr. Hamilton, Mrs. Jean (the Domina or Doâ) and some others home with Mr. James Hamilton and lady to their lodging in William McMechan's and again accompanied Mr. Hamilton and wife with, especially, Mrs. Jean, home and supped with them.

1707

" Teusday 4th November I was in D.dee p diem only in the evening went to Mr. James Hamilton's lodging where I meet wth Doâ I went home wth her to her pater's and from thence came straight home."

" Fraiday 7th November I was in D.dee and in the afternoon went out with Mrs Jean Hamilton Mr

I 7O7   James Hamilton & his wife to Killachyes we returned home same night ; and I at my return went down to Mr Hamilton's went in and meet Doâ in armatorio, where about the space of an hour I was wth her and had indeed a desirable time tho' still very nice."

' Armatorio ' may be a mistake for ' armario '—cupboard, which Scott may have thought could be used in the sense of ' small room,' or perhaps ' tool-house.'

ORIGINAL.	SENSE TRANSLATION.
1707. " Nov. Munday 10th I was in D.dee p diem & in the evening went down to Mr Hamilton's & meet Dôâ in armatorio; where I was with her p spatium 6 vel 7 horarum & pater & mater were in Belfastum."	1707. Nov. Monday 10th I was in Donaghadee during the day and in the evening went down to Mr. Hamilton's and met Dôâ in the small room, where I was with her for six or seven hours— father and mother in Belfast.

" Wensday 12th November I was in D.dee and did preach on Rom : 8:1:1 dinned in Mr Hamilton's

I 7O7   I was in the evening in Mr Hamilton's, and took occasion to signify to Mrs Hamilton quam maximum amorem (how very great love) I had for Dôâ Janâ ejus filiâ she told me she would not be my foe but rather my friend, for wch I returned her many thanks. I was for some time at the Turf stack same night cum Dôâ."

" Thursday 13th November I was domi p. diem and in the evening went down to Mr Hamilton's & meet

I 7O7   Doa in armatorio where I was illa cum circitur duas horas : (intended for ' cum illa circiter duas horas '= was with her about two hours) I supped in Mr Hamiltons. I gave Marrion Hamilton a handkerchief & Gloves."

" Fraiday 14th November I was in D.dee p diem & in the evening went down and meet wth Doa in ostio

I 7O7   we were in the guest chamber from 6 to ½ 9 Mrs Hamilton came and called Mrs Jean and so we were necessitate to part. I came straight home."

1707

" Saturday 15th November I was in cubiculo p diem and in the evening went down towards Mr Hamiltons but did not see Donâ & again I went and did not see illam ; I came home and about 9 of the clock I went down and meet wth Dōa I was illa cum circitur semi horam et illae dedi Gloves. (I was with her about half an hour and gave her gloves)."

1707

" Wensday 19th November I was at sermon & heard Mr Hamilton on Isai:55:2 In the evening I was about 2 hours wth Dōâ from whome I had the following encouragement (for Wednesday the 19 of 9ber I expected a reply to what I had some time before proposed to her : wch was that if she did not alter she would accept of and in due time reward my service ; but if she altered then she was to be free."

1707

" Fraiday 21st November I was domi p diem only in the evening went down to Mr Hamilton's there supped wth Mr Bigger after supper I met wth Dōâ at the haystack and stood about a quarter of an hour with her, and at the same time presented her with a broad piece of gold, of wch wth much pressing she did accept."

The " broad piece of gold " was one of the foreign gold coins current in Down at this time.   See page 265.

1707

" Wednesday 26th November I was in D.dee and going to sermon went to Mr Hamilton and was told by Marion Hamilton that Dōâ was gone to Mr Moor's of the Roddins, whereupon I returned home and went not to sermon, but took horse and went straight to Mr Moor's, but found her not there, wch was to me most disquieting I came from there straight to Mr Wallace's where I found her & had only two words wth her and returned home to D.dee so burdened wth concernedness for her absenting her father's house that I thought I should never have got to D.dee, when I came to D.dee I went down to Mrs Hamilton & entreated that she would tomorrow send for Mrs Jane she told me seeing me so much concerned that she would."

"Teusday 2nd December I was resolved to have gone
to the presbytry but it proving a bad day I stay^d

1707 at home; I went down before daylight to Mr
Hamilton's and was cum Dôâ in the guest chamber
from 7 of the clock till near 9. I was wth her from
half eleven till ½ three in the afternoon : in the evening I just
saw her she being bussied making a furbelow'd skerf in order
to go to Mrs Mair's Dorothy Hamilton's burial. I gave, memorandum, to Isabel a handkerchief and pair of gloves."

"Fraiday 5th December I was in Donnoghadee and
in the evening went down to Mr Hamilton's, and was

1707 with Dôâ in her closet from 6 to 10 of the clock. I
did same night present her wth a little bottle ; she
was pleased by her carriage towards me to evidence
more concernedness for me and love to me than ever formerly."

"Munday 8th December I was in D.dee & domi p
diem only in the evening I went down to Mr Hamil-

1707 ton's and was told that Mrs Hamilton and Mrs Jean
were gone to Crebuy I sate for some time wth the
children & came home much disconsolate that I
was not favoured wth a sight of Doâ."

"Thursday 18th December I was domi p diem only
in the evening went down to Mr Hamilton's and was

1707 with Dôa in the guest chamber from 6 to 8 of the
clock, she told me that her father same day after
breakfast was speaking to her and telling her that
he would not further her to keep me any longer company ;
because my father had never taken occasion to make known to
him what was betwixt her and me, wch same night occasioned
much indisposition to me, for about the space of an hour I was
very bad and thought I should have fallen by ; Mrs Hamilton
came in and told me that Mr Hamilton was not in the least
disatisfied with me, but he thought my father might have spoken
to him."

"Munday 22nd December I was domi p diem, only
in the evening I went down to Mr Hamilton's and

1707 was with Doa in the guest chamber from six of the
clock to nine, my father did same night to Mr
Hamilton make known the respect I had for his

daughter Mrs Jean ; and his reply to him was that he would give
me his daughter to wife, rather yea and sooner than to many
wth 400 p annum wherewith my father was mightily taken ;
and indeed no wonder for it was much more than he was expecting
and looking for from him."

1708

" Sabbath 14th March I was in D.dee and in the
morning was taken wth a pain in my head wch did
obleidge me to keep my room, about ten I went to
bed, resolving to sweat for it, the wch I did vehem-
ently till 8 at night. Memorandum that same day
about 1 in the afternoon my father was seized wth the gravel
and continued most violent to 6 of the clock Munday's night about
7 of the clock at night Mr McCracken Mr Hamilton Mrs Hamilton
& my Dear Mrs Jean came to see my father who then was much
tormented Dōa came to the back of the bed to me where I had
occasion to see and speak wth her and had from her 3 oscula
(three kisses) wch were at that time to me very refreshing."

The entries of like character continue for four months
longer—the last being that for Tuesday, 20th July, 1708.
Here all record of Scott ends.   As far as is known he was not
called to charge of any congregation, and the lady of his
attentions did not marry him.   Five years later she became
the second wife of Rev. Robert Gordon, of Rathfriland.
His first wife was Margaret Hamilton, who, on her deathbed,
requested Gordon to marry her cousin, Jean, which he did.
Fifteen years later he married his third wife, Esther Scott,
sister of Jean's student lover.

Gordon, called " greeting Gordon," because his feelings
in the pulpit often moved him to tears, has also left a diary,
or, more properly, a family record.   He was Presbyterian
minister of Rathfriland, that little town perched on a hill
in the middle of a plain, across which shows grandly the great
rampart of Southern Down, the Mountains of Mourne.   A
much-married man, his diary is entirely concerned with the
world of himself, his wives, and his extremely numerous
children.   The births of twenty-five are noted with great
exactitude as to day of week and hour.   From the manner of

the record, it would appear that some of the infants came into the world with labels bearing their names attached.

1725   " Jany 30. My dear wife was delivered of a son called Hamilton."

1744   " Jany 20. My dear wife was mercifully delivered of a daughter called Isabell."

Thirteen of the children died very young. The monotony of the record of births, baptisms, and deaths, is broken, at parts, by little remarks about the children.

1731   " June 21st. (Of Mabel). ' She is a very hopeful child. O that God may give her grace.' "

1733   " Jany 9th. (Of Matthew). ' He seems to be a child of a brave spirit. O that he may be in a capacity and have holy courage . . . ' "

If the child had not developed special character at the time of writing, the good man contented himself with the pious wish—

" May God preserve him (or her) for his Glory."

On the death of his second wife (Jean Hamilton, the Domina of Scott's diary) he writes :—

" On the Thursday following being the 8th of 7ber (1726) my heart my life my brightest and best of wives departed this life at 12 at night. She was a godly woman, most exemplary to me and her children for true piety. She died, much lamented & the 10th of 7ber 1726 was buried in the Reverend Mr Alex^r Gordon's grave in the churchyard of Ballyroney. This great loss I fear will never be made up for now I must say I never knew her fellow in all respects. We were marryd I bless God thirteen years except twenty days and O that I may have grace to follow her footsteps and may her children imitate her in her pious ways."

He is much impressed by an escape from death while attempting to drink milk and beer mixed.

" Memorandum. That on the 30th day of May 1710, I met with a very mercifull dispensation of God's providence for having that day been at J. Henderson's burial, and after I was a considerable time at home, my wife, my father and mother, and Capn Ja. Stewart of Newry being at supper about 9 of the clock in the afternoon and I being desirous to drink milk and beer mixed together readily got it and the very first mouthful of it almost choaked me so that I was not able to speak wch soon caused the terrors of death to cease (seize) upon me and I believe I had instantly dyed had not my father given me a drink out of his own hand very quickly. Now I promise to be for God and to bless Him while I live for this amongst many other of his favours wch God help me faithfully to perform expecting God's assistance for performance of this my vow I'll subscribe myself his servant

Robt Gordon."

Out of this self-centred story comes the knowledge that children were baptized at an age much earlier than is customary at present. Several of the entries record the baptism on day of birth,—some on the day following. Others were baptized at two or three days of age, and, let it be noted, at least one of the one-day-olds went for name to the meeting-house, while another babe made appearance in that building at three days of age. Also, it is of interest to note that, coming home from his studies in Edinburgh in 1707, Gordon, starting on 9th October, reached Glasgow on the 11th, and leaving Glasgow on the 9th of November, he landed at Carrickfergus on the 20th day of same month.

A crowded diary of a crowded life is that of Rev. John Kennedy, Presbyterian minister of Benburb, whose grandfather was brother of Rev. Gilbert Kennedy, of Dundonald. We read his name and place and date,—read, perhaps, a speech delivered by him at a meeting of Synod,—and we have a vision of a decently clad pastor, at home in a more or less comfortable manse, his life not very unlike that of a country minister of the present time. The diary shows a man in the saddle for great part of the day, and sometimes far into the night,—in fair or foul weather travelling far, baptizing, marrying, catechising, visiting the sick and dying, attending markets, buying cattle, and, it would appear, slaughtering them.

With his own hands he puts on laths to carry the thatch on the roof of his new meeting-house, and cuts the scraws (sods), to be laid on the laths as foundation for thatch. He quarries, carts manure, plants hedges, sows, reaps,—his life is half that of pastor, half of farm labourer. On first page of the diary he notes that for seven years he had lectured on the Psalms.

" Lectured 1st throu yᵉ psalms for 7 yrs now since on Job now begin Job 29 cap 7ʳ 15 1723 prov. next."

1724 " Monday 1st June. I preached on 1 pet 5. 17 passed ye time of ye Journey in fear cam home."

1724 " Saturday 12 September. thatched ye corn & crown'd ye hay rick."

" Monday 28 payd tom hodge bletchg got a pistoll before & now a guinea & 11 pence 17 pence pr score for thirty one score allowd more 2 sh stipend for May 1724, thatchd hay cok."

1724 " Thursday 1 October. Was at home till afternoon bought 12 bushels of barly from Jo Wilson at 12 sh."

1724 " Wednesday 14 October was in Ardmagh at Synod, Mynoch & Arch. behaved very foolishly."

1724 " Sabbath 1 November at home prov 1 psall 65. 4."

" Monday 2 went to Charlemont fair bought a beef from —moor at 1.9.6 she provd well was litle but had 3 stone bought two candle sticks at 6sh came yᵗ night killd 2 beefs yᵗ night."

" Wednesday 4 yᵉ boys went to Newry took hides."

" Thursday 5 boys came home I was at home."

" Sabbath 8 prv 1 psal 65. 4."

" Monday 9 I was at home will set blackthorns on farm March."

" Friday 17 I went to see James Kennedy's family & Nath hays wife. Went to Dungannon fair bought sarge for Jennat a coat for Rob."

1724 " Monday 7 December Exam at yᵉ Meetg house."

" Tuesday 8 Exam at Jo Clarks."

" Thursday 10 went to Stewartstown yᵗ night got a letter from Mr McClave concerning Ricky took down 6 of Gilbᵗˢ books sold one of yᵐ to Kate Connell at 15 pence."

" Saturday 12 at home taylors here all this week."

$172^4/_5$ " Saturday 2 January. Went to Newtown Sabbath 3 preached at Newtown lectur'd 2 pet 2 begin Song 2.7."

1725 " 6 Aprill. Brave dry season."

" May 1 A very gloomy day of wind and rain."

" July 18 A brave pleasant week."

" August 19 at home, my hay flooded."

" August 20 came here in ye morning I led some hay came on rain."

" Monday 23 August a terrible rain all night & till 4 o'clock this day, a terrible flood."

" Friday 27 August a gt rain Judgment like was at home."

1725 " Tuesday 14 Sept. at home at hay all day."

" Wednesday 15 at quarry at Drumslugh two horses there."

" Thursday 16 Went to meeting house, brave weather these 2 weeks (blessd be God)."

" Monday 27 put in ye hay a brave day."

" Thursday will came home after^n went all ye way got no herrings."

" Friday at home brave day."

1725 " Wednesday 6 October I went to Minterburn Mr Cochran was there a very wet day my wife was taken ill after I went away & I was sent for I came hom in haste she was somthing easd was ill that night."

" Sat. ye doctor came here afternoon afoot, stayd till tuesday morning brave day."

" Sabbath 10 Doctor & I went afoot to meetg Prov 11 latter part ps 31. 24."

" Monday 11. at home a brave day put in corn John Wilsons and mine all by barnpark."

" Wensday 12 put in all at hom this day the doctor went away in a gt pet this morning bec (because) I could not get stayg w^t him the night before & this morng I went to Englishtown abt ye time he was away befor I cam back."

1725 " Saturday Novr 27. at home reckoned w^t James Armstrang for a pair of boots to self & shoes & to tom y^t to make a pair to peg & let & 3 to Jam : & will & haf soals to peg oliphar in all 5sh & 6 pence 4 of it for stipend 1s & 6 for a bible in part I went to baptize Jo : Wylys child."

1725 "December 31. visited Wid. Blakely old Will : hodge his wife
bad w^t a bruise y^e chimney falling on her. A child of 2
year old standg at her knee & was untouched, & heaps of
clay all round it. gt care of providence a wonder of mercy
this hapned Monday night last children all abt y^e fire &
none burnt."

172^5/$_6$ "1 January. O to begin ye year in ye fear of Gd O for
a new years gift of grace to me & mine, renew cov^t w^t
Gd fr me & mine, engage wt God for ane loving service. I
am now. (Here he has made a ' 4 ' and then erased it).
O to number day & years aright & to pass time in fear.
Meditaon on a view of ye . . . opinions of men som
are overvalued som are overlessen'd all men appear in disguise in som degree how much need to be wary in Judgg how
tru Gd sees otherwys then man sees, a very gloomy cold
rain."

" Wednesday 19 January, exam'd at Jam : Stirlgs."

" Thursday 20 visited And : & Wid trimble married Dick
Tinsly & Agnes paton went to Jo: McGees baptized Will :
Campbells child went hom y^t night."

172^5/$_6$ " Friday 4 March was at home sowed pasneps."

" Friday 11 clean'd some seed corn."

" Saturday 12 I laid quicks w^t tom McCulloch."

" Sabbath 20 prov 16.20 Rom 9.2 baptiz'd a child to Jos Car
who stood for irregular marriage 2 more."

" Thursday 24 went to anabridge married a man & maid of Mrs
Moors saw Will Craig he died y^t day married Rich : Donald-
sons sister saw tom Adams son & stepson in fever, dav
blakelys mother died this morng called there went to Dung :
(Dungannon) saw old John Stirlg by ye way Jo & Dan
bought 20 score near I rec^d Xmas quarter of Rd went to
Stewartstown y^t-night."

1726 " Wednesday 7 September bought 15 pd soap 4 ounce of
blew."

" Friday 9 at home very ill."

" Saturday 10 at home bad still shoemaker here this 3 days."

" Monday 12. was at b.w. town got a moydor from Marg^t
McNear."

" Friday 14 October led out dirt from meadow ditch."

1726 " Saturday 22 at home bad day Sent billy to portadown for hops
6 lb & candles a dozen pepper h: a pd Logwood a pd I owed
4 sh for h.a.qrtr sop a qrtr pd of blue 1s 4d I sent 2 moydors
at 2 pence light each & a guinea to pay McCulloch 3 pd for
36 doz ribs for meetg house."

1726 " Sabbath 23 October prov 22 1—6 Luke 9.23 baptiz'd a
child to George Aiken cry'd on Tom Miller's daughter."

" Monday 24 at meetg house a meetg ap^{ted} none bt 2 or 3
there, brew'd."

" Tuesday 25 at home set boxwood & cherrys &c."

" Saturday 29 at home set more boxwood & some straw-
berries, put out dung."

" Tuesday Nov 1 I went to Charlemont fair bought a cow from
Ned Moor for 2 pd 6s gave him a moydor in hand."

" Sabbath 13 November prov 22 24—end prov 15. 24 pulpit
out I stood in own seat a cold day."

" Saturday 19 at home went a while to meeting house, ye little
couple reard 2^d gavel up window high." (Couple = roof
principal, Gavil = gable).

" Monday was at meeting house lattg."

" Wednesday 23 Scraws some cut came on rain I married Rob.
Rids daughter went to tom hodges baptized his 1st grand-
child came home late."

" Friday 25 went to meeting house latted all day 2^d gavil
finished."

" Friday 2 December was at meeting house latted it out &
scraw'd it all but one bay."

" Saturday 10 December gt frost & som snow I went to Market-
hill was 6 oclock had hard going very cold & icy a mercy I
was safe."

172$^6/_7$" Sabbath 1st January prov 24 12—24 heb 2.3. was in
new house a new years gift of $\bar{g}$ra comftable begin ye year
in fear of Gd."

" Monday 30 got ye shingles sent to meetg house a very
gloomy day—pd McCulloch a moydor of y^m."

" Friday 3 February gave Mr Cochran a gold cob & moydor
each want 2 pence."

" Monday 27 at house did out first gutter."

" Tuesday 28 at house begun ye 2nd gutt^r did 16 rows of it."

172⁶/₇ " Monday 27 March set potatoes."

" Wednesday 29 This day was buried Nicholas buchanan aged 109 years."

" April we set potatoes."

" Saturday—sow'd flax."

" Wednesday 12 at meetg house put up ye glasse in ye west window."

" Monday 8th May Dongannon fair—bought 2 cows at 2.11.8."

" Wednesday June 7 met abt seats at meetghouse did little good and saw pride & folly."

1727 " Thursday 28 September came home. a sore rain."

" Thursday 5 October I went to meetg house with Richardson & Lawther—went to Dungannon with them   We all drank a botle of bruntin wᵗ Mr Cumin."

" Wednesday 1 November went to Charlemont fair wᵗ 2 cows & colt sold none came home sold cow to Jo. Wilson at 31s 6d."

1728 " 1 April very melancholy wet season   this long time & continues."

" 28 April always wet rainy weather most of March & Aprile Judgment like weather."

1728 " Saturday 4 May. at home. A heavy rain & thunder a very wet season still Judgment like Gᵈ speaks wrath yᵉ ground terrible wet yᵉ potatoes rotten in yᵉ ground wᵗ constant rain barly can't be sow'd ye gᵈ is so wet."

1729 " Thursday 3 April 6 eldest children all down in measles."

" Friday 4 children bad & peg olipher in measles."

" Tuesday 8 I came home even'g got physick for children."

" Monday 14 children took physick."

" Tuesday 15 At Ardmagh, got physick agn for children."

" Wednesday 16 at home sow'd some barly & pasneps & turneps, children took physick."

1730 " Friday 11th July.   went to seek Dan McLean, he is gone with my 2 guineas."

1730 " November Wednesday 11 this morning br Stevensons litle child Sara died early Jealous overlayg." (' Jealous ' is the Scotch ' jalouse,' suspect,—imagine.)

" Went to Ardmagh wᵗʰ Jeremy, got him of (off) the oath of churchwarden."

The diary of Anne, Countess Dowager of Roden (1797-1802), is of interest rather as study of mentality, than as picture of life conditions. The notes written to placate conscience in the matter of the vow of daily record are very numerous and very trivial.

> " I spent the day as usual."
> " I think I was at prayers."
> " I walked a good deal in the morning."
> " The weather was still rainy but not windy. Spent the day as usual."
> " The same as usual."
> " I can't recollect."

Each of these is a complete entry for a day, and there are very many like them. Her Ladyship is, however, aware of the futility of such entries.

> " These foolish little notes of the occurrences of each day are no further use than as they help my memory ; but it is my reflections upon my own conduct that are to be of use to me, and the consideration of how I fulfil the duties of each day, and how unworthy I am of the hourly mercies I receive. Let me endeavour to consider the situation I am placed in, and to consider the duties arising from it ; and my earnest prayer is, that every day it shall please God to add to my life I may advance in holiness and virtue."

Some of the notes are, in character, very like those of Lady Mordaunt, of whom, indeed, Lady Roden was a descendant.

> 1799 " 28th February. The same. This day I have indeed much to lament for the faults of my own temper ; nobody, I believe, can feel them so severely as I do, nor can I think any mortification I can meet with too great."

> 1799 " 20th April. The neglect of retrospection has done me no good, neither have I advanced as I heartily wish in conquering those feelings which I am very conscious of ; nothing can enable me to do that but, with the help of God a firm determination to contradict all those propensities."

1799 " 29th April. I feel most truly how strong a check I want upon those feels of peevishness which are usually ascribed to age, when all relating to this world has decreased in its value as it must in the course of a long life."

1799 " May 11. With my usual irresolution I have neglected this examination of my conduct for many days. The events during this space of time relating to myself, have been only John and Margaret's leaving town, and Sophia and Mr Arbuckle coming to us. I then thought to leave town this week (written on a visit to Dublin) till the certainty of the French fleet being out rendered it prudent to wait for the event."

1799 " 28th June. I have resumed this account of my time to be more exact in the consideration of my own ways, and sad are many reflections I have to make upon myself that I have endeavoured to bear affliction and yet sink under vexation and am conquered by it."

When the entries are not of this introspective character, and are not conscience sops, they are concerned only with weather, and trivialities of movement or visits. Even from these entries, however, there are little interesting points to be noted by those who are familiar with the localities mentioned. At Annadale, the diarist speaks of " going to Belfast." If her Ladyship could revisit the scene, she would be surprised to find Annadale in Belfast. Visits of ' Mr Rider ' to wind the clocks, are noted. Rider's name is still to be seen on clocks made in the last quarter of the eighteenth century. Even the very numerous notes of unseasonable weather may be of value in confuting grandmothers who insist that, in their days of childhood, the summers were uniformly warm and sunny,—the winters, cold and frosty.

But when Lady Roden has an important and engrossing subject she is worth reading, and the diary story of her flight to Scotland in the Rebellion days of 1789, is as illuminative of the time as anything that has been written. It is used as ending to the last chapter of this volume.

CHAPTER XIII.

The Letter Writers

WE have, in the earlier part of this work, an example of the diplomatic letter in that of the Earl of Abercorn, addressed to John Murray, but intended for King James I. (p. 41), stuffed with flattery of the prince for whose reading it was concocted, and carrying a meaning which is not that appearing on the surface. In some of Hamilton's letters to Secretary of State, Cecil (Hamilton Manuscripts, pp. 8-9), we have examples of another type,—the intentionally obscure in parts, indirect in approach, with thought wrapped in an overpadded garment of word as though the clear exhibition of its form were an indecency. The writer of a letter of this type was always asking, or preparing to ask, for something, from a great—perhaps the greatest—person of the realm. He does not know whether his communication shall be received well or ill ; and if ill-pleasure is expressed by the great person, it is an advantage that the letter shall be worded in such manner as to allow the writer to declare that the meaning was quite other than that of the prince's understanding. Throughout this work are numerous specimens of plain, matter-of-fact letters, which convey, without embellishment, to the receiver information which it is necessary or desirable he should have. But when we speak of Letter Writing, or the Art of Letter

Writing, what is meant are relatives' letters of gossip,
affection or duty, or the news letters of friends or dependents,
wherein matters of the utmost unimportance are handled
more or less smartly,—in brief, letters of which the purpose
is to give pleasure to the receivers, or to satisfy a not very
strong sense of duty in the senders ; and it is with these,
mainly, that this chapter is concerned.

A noticeable feature of old Down letters is the extraordinary formality of address observed in the case of near relatives,
when these are of Scottish descent.   It has been noted already
(p. 75) that young Claneboye addresses his mother as ' Your
Ladyship' five times in a very short letter.   Bernard Ward
addresses his father as ' Dr Sir ' and signs ' I am Dear Sir,
Yr ever oblig'd & most faithfull Ber. Ward,' or ' I am Dr Sr
yr most oblig'd.'   Letters from Thomas Montgomery to his
father, Earl of Mount-Alexander, are addressed ' My Lord,'
and signed ' I am, My Lord, your dutifull and obedient Son.'
Judge Ward's aunt, writing to her nephew, signs ' Yr truely
Afftt Aunt & humble Servant.'   Arthur Dobbs, addressing
the Judge as ' Cozen,' signs ' Yr most obligd & obedt Humble
Servt,' and even the Judge's sister adds ' & humble servant '
after ' your Affectionate Sister.'   Andrew Nugent, of Portaferry, writing in June, 1738, to Andrew Savage, who, a month
earlier, had become his son-in-law—and the letter is a very
friendly one—begins his communication by ' Dear Sir,' and
signs ' I am, dear Sir, your most humble servant & affect
Father.'

The deference to rank, and the ceremony of the time, are
well exhibited in the absurdly obsequious letter of Lawrence
Steele, who invites his brother-in-law, the Judge, to stop at
his house on his way north on circuit.

" Rathbride 6th June, 1735.

" Sir,

The repeated favours you placed on me wn last in town
obliges me to return you my thankfull acknowledgements for
them, and since you were pleased wthout any reluctancy to

give me one of ye best of women, I shall never be unmindfull
of ye obligation you have Lay^d me under : therefore I cant
avoid putting you in mind of y^{or} only sister whose happiness
you have at heart expects & earnestly desires ye favour of y^{or}
company here before you goe to ye North it will be but five
hours riding out of ye way for this place is almost as near Drogheda as Dublin. I would urge it in the strongest manner if I
could claim any Interest in your friendship however as I am
related to you by y^{or} Kind condescension I hope you believe
since I doe assure you, y^{or} Company will be very acceptable
& not anyone will receive a heartier welcome, your complyance
herein will greatly oblige

Sir Y^{or} Affect. Bror

& obliged Humble Servt

Law. Steele."

An equally absurd letter of another type is the fulsome
epistle of the Rev. Vere Essex Lonergan, curate of Down, to
Mrs. Ward ; having, ostensibly, no raison d'être other than
to beg the lady to grant him a favour, which is—that she will
believe him to be what he signs himself. Mrs. Ward's acumen
was doubtless sufficient to detect in the lines a lively sense of
favours to come.

" I need not now, Madam, take up your time in informing you what
obligations I am under to Y^r Family ; I perswade myself,
Madam, that you have known me as long as you have known any
one person now living ; and tis impossible you shoud have that
knowlege of me wthout at ye same time seeing ye long, & un-
interrupted course of favours wch I was for ever receiving from
y^r Blessed Parents. I have ye comfort, perhaps tis ye vanity
of my heart, to believe that were y^r ever worthy Father now in
being that he would not be ashamd of me, nor repent of what
he did for me nor can I recollect that among the many clergymen
to whom he gave bread, he ever was grossly mistaken in any one
instance.

" Happy it is for us of ye Inferior clergy as we are calld that
there are such a number of worthy persons now in ye world as
Lay Patrons. The Church's bread is now made as much y^e
private property of our Bishops, as their Coaches, their armd
chairs or Damask nightgowns, their sons and daughters, Heirs

and Heiresses apparent, nephews, and nieces presumptive
to ye revenues of ye Church.   I pray God prosper ye Lay Patrons
say I still.   I humbly entreate you, Madam, to grant me one
favour wch I hope I never shall forget wch is that you woud
please to believe that I am and ever shall be to you & yours
> wth utmost sincerity Respect & Gratitude
> a most Faithful & Devoted Servant,
> > > Vere Essex Lonergan."

With this formality of address in letters there went often
a startling freedom in use of words.   When a spade is to be
mentioned there is no trouble taken to find a boudoir name for
it ; words now considered unprintable are freely used.   Thomas
Montgomery, at home at Comber, writing to his wife in Dublin
on business of law, tells how, as he came out of church, he
received on his bare head a little attention from a passing
bird.   He takes it as a good omen,—" it gives me," he says,
" great hopes that this day will prove a lucky one for us."
Here the incident is mentioned only to record that the verb
describing the bird's action would only be heard to-day in a
mining camp.   Even that charming young lady, the delightful
Theodosia Bligh, permits herself the use of language which,
to-day, would be considered strong from the mouth of a
Lancashire mill-lass.   And the staid Robert Ward, writing
to his brother about the arrest of a supposed rebel, quotes a
word which no publisher of to-day would print.

We gain an insight into the characteristics of a community
by reading letters to, as well as by, its members.   The world
outlook of Down in two centuries was part of the life of Down,
and, therefore, some of the letters admitted to this chapter
are those of non-natives or non-residents.   First place must
be given to a letter of Oliver Goldsmith,—here printed for the
first time.   The Rev. Guy Stone, member of an old Gloucester
family settled in Down, and still, happily, represented at
Barnhill, Comber, lived with his parents at Newtownards.
Presented to the living of Ballymahon, Co. Longford, in 1754,
he stayed there long enough to fall in love with Margaret

Bryanton—' Peggy ' of Goldsmith's letter,—whom he married
and brought to Down. He served the cures of Holywood
and Newtownards for a few years,—and, afterwards, until
his death in 1779, that of Comber. The Bryantons were
friends to Goldsmith—the letter is addressed to the lady's
brother.

"Edinburgh, Sept. 26th, 1723.

"My dear Bob,

How many good excuses (and you know I was ever good at
an excuse) might I call up to vindicate my past shamefull silence,
I might tell you how I wrote a long letter at my first coming
hither, and seem vastly angry at not receiving an answer, or I
might alledge that business (with that you know I was always
pestered) had never given me time to finger a pen, but I suppress
these and twenty more equally plausable and as easily invented,
since they might all be attended with the slight inconvenience
of being known to be lies. But I speak truth, an hereditary
indolence (I have it from my Mother's side) has hitherto prevented my writing to you, and still prevents my writing at least
twentyfive letters more due to my friends in Ireland. No
turnspit Dog gets up into his wheel with more reluctance than I
sit down to write, yet no Dog ever loved the roast meat he turns
better than I do him I now address. What shall I say now I am
entered ? Shall I tire you with a description of this unfruitfull
country where I must describe their hills all brown with heath,
or their Vallies scarce able to feed a Rabbit ? Man alone seems
to be the only creature that has arrived to the natural size in
this poor soil,—every part of the country presents the same
dismal landskape—no grove or Brooks lend their musick to the
stranger or make the inhabitants forget their poverty. Yet with
all these disadvantages to call him down to humility a Scotsman
is one of the proudest things alive—the poor have pride ever
ready to relieve them if mankind should happen to despise them.
They are masters of their own admiration and that they can
plentifully bestow on themselves. From their pride and poverty
(as I take it) results one advantage this country enjoys—namely
the gentlemen are much better bred than amongst us. No such
character here as our fox hunters, and they have expressed great
surprise when I informed them that some men in Ireland of
£1000 a year spend their whole lives in running after a Hare—

drinking to be drunk &c &c. If such a being equipt in his hunting
dress came among a circle of Scots gentry they would behold
him with the same astonishment that a country man woud
King Willm on horseback. The men here have high cheek bones,
are lean and swarthy,—fond of action, dancing in particular.
Now I have mentioned dancing I must say something of their
Balls which are very frequent. When a stranger enters the
dancing hall he sees one side taken up with the Ladies who sit
dismaly in a groupe by themselves. At the other end stands
their pensive partners that are to be—but no more intercourse
between the sexes than there is between two countries at War.
The Ladies, indeed, may ogle and the Gentlemen sigh, but an
embargo is laid on any closer commerce. At length, to interrupt
hostilities, the lady-directress or intendant, or what you will,
pitches on a gentleman & lady to walk a minuet which they
perform with a solemnety that approaches despondance. After
five or six couples have thus walked the gauntlet all stand up
to country dances, each gentleman furnished with a partner from
the aforesaid Lady Directress, so they dance much, say nothing,
& thus concludes our Assembly. I told a Scots gentleman that
silence resembled the antient procession of the Roman Matrons
in honour of Ceres, & the Scots gentleman (and faith I believe he
was right) told me that I was a very great pedant, for my pains.
Now to the ladies, and to show that I love Scotland and everything that belongs to so charming a country, I insist upon it,
and will give him leave to break my head who denies it, that the
Scots Ladys are 10000 times finer and Handsomer than the Irish.
To be sure now I see your Sisters Betty and Peggy angry and
surprised at my partiality,—but tell them flatly that I don't
value them or their fine skins, or eyes or good sense, or a potatoe,
for I say it and will maintain it. And as a convincing proof (I
am in a very great passion) of what I have said the Scots Ladys
say it themselves. But to be serious, where will you find a
language so pretty become a Lady's mouth as the Broad Scotch—
the women here speak it in its highest purity. For instance,
teach one of the young Ladys to pronounce ' Whoar will I gang '
—with a becoming wideness of mouth & I'll lay my life they
wound every hearer.

" We have no such character here as a Coquet but alas how
many envious prudes—some days ago I walked into my Lord
Kilcoobreys (don't be surprised) My Lord is but a glover, when

the Dutchess of Hamilton, that fair who sacrafised her beauty
to ambition, & her inward peace to a title & gilt equipage, passed
by in her superb chariot, her battered husband or more properly
the guardian of her charms, sat by her side, straight envy began
in the shape of no less than 3 Ladys who sat with me, to find
faults in her faultless form, for my part says the first, I think
that I allways thought that the Dutchess has too much Red in
her complexion. Madam I am of your opinion says the 2 &
I think her grace has a polish cast too much on the delicate order
— & let me tell you adds the 3 lady whose mouth was puckered
up to the size of an Issue—that the Dutchess has fine lips, but
she wants a mouth, at this every Lady drew up her own mouth
as if she was going to pronounce the letter D—but how ill my
Bob does it become me to ridicule women with whom I have
scarce any corraspondance—there are tis certain handsome
women here & and it is also as certain they have handsome men
to keep them company—an ugly & a poor man is society only
for himself & such society the world lets me enjoy in great
abundance—fortune has given you circumstances, & nature a
person to look charming in the eyes of the fair world nor do I
envy my Dr Bob, such Blessings, while I may sitt down and laugh
at the world and at myself the most rediculus object in it,—
but I begin to grow splenetic & perhaps the fitt may continue
till I read an answer to this. I know you cant have much news
from Ballymahon, but such as it is let me have it—everything
you write will be agreeable and entertaining to me, has George
Conway put up a sign—or John Tinchly left of drinking drams
or Toni Allen got a new wig—but I leave it to your choice what
to write. While

Oliver Goldsmith

lives know you have a friend.
Give my sincerest regards, not compliments, do you mind—to
your agreeable family—and give my service to my Mother if
you see her for as you express it in Ireland I have a sneaking
kindness for her still.

direct to me Student in Physick Edinburgh.

Robt Bryanton Esqre
Ballymahon."

That liberty of criticism already mentioned as characteristic of letters from the Protestant gentry of Down to their

clergy, finds an example in the letter of Mr. Patrick Savage, of Portaferry, to his Rector (McNeal), the Chancellor of Down. The letter is dated June 8, 1708.

" Rev Sr

Yr of 27th instant I have wherein you say that you understand by some discourse I had of you with Mr ffulerton you believed I was not satisfied with you truly I began noe discourse of you but it was Mr ffulerton began something of you & said he was sorry there should be any difference betweene us, whereupon I told him that the very last conversing you & I had was in your owne house before your lady after we had walked a considerable time in the fields and as I thought had discussed sufficiently for once of my damn & withall of the new ditch opposite to the gleabe & as it seemed to me I thought we parted as friendly as ever we did before how I gave you occasion for offence since that I know not but it seems come which it will give you freedome of railing & exposing of me & of my reputation to all manner of persons both gentle & simple & not only these but to most of all the pittifull fellows that goes by your gate complaining that I am a cruel man and a greate oppressor & that I robb you of your freehold which you likewise confirm yourself by yr letter. I hope you are not ignorant of a dam being there before ever any of your familie came to this Kingdome & if my familie gave the church that gleabe I hope it will not hinder me of keeping a dam there still you are pleased to write that I have drowned eight pounds worth of your gleabe & that there is as much under my water as you have uncovered, at which I believe all men that heare it will admire . . . I remember how often you found fault with considerable of your hearers & particularly with myself when we came from church on Sunday that we should dispose of any worldly and temporal matters on the Lords day but dedicate the remaining part of that day to devotion & reminding of what was presented to us which was very well done, but I find you doe not practice that yourself for that most of your discourse to Dr Lofty & the rest of your guests was of my cruelty & oppression in drounding your ground and showing them how far the water overflowed."

The use of the word 'admire' in this letter may appear strange. There is, however, evidence of its use in conversation and correspondence of the time, to express the coupled ideas of surprise and censure. In this sense it appears in the following letter from young James Hamilton, descendant of a brother of the Lord Claneboye, to his brother Patrick, ' at Mrs. Wilkinson's in Belfast, Ireland.' The letter is dated from London, January 25th, 1702. The ' Mr. Hamilton ' is his uncle, of Bangor,—' hot press ' is, of course, an active press-gang.

" Dr Brother,

Feal not to goe to Mr Hamilton and tell him I admir he never answered none of mine. I thought I should not have troubled him in heast only for the matter of five or six pounds which Cosin Matthew hath passed his word for Cloaths to me but now an Inbargu being Laid upon Shipin here and a hot press following I am forced to confine myself indoors or ey be Lyable to apress the former of which I have chose But can not long continue without the supply of money which I hope Mr Hamilton will not Let me Want unless He designs to Ruin me which I am satisfied will be no advantage to him : this with duty to Ant and Mr Hamilton and Lady and Love to Sister and Cosins and all friends is all from your affectionate Brother

James Hamilton.

Cosin Mathew gives his duty to his mother and Love to brother sisters & cosins hath been verry ill But he is pritty well recovered But he is in as great scearcity as I am Cosin Will : I hope is near Virginia by this pray give my service to Alexander Porter and Jean : and Likewise to John Clark : feal not to answer this pr first post."

Patrick, himself, at college in Dublin a few years later, has the same pressing need of money, and writes to his uncle at Bangor :—

" Dublin, August ye 10th, 1706.

" Hon^d Sir,

After so long impatiently waiting I find to my sorrow that all my hopes are baulk^t but necessity presses me again to desire that you will send up this quarter's allowance by the next post, there are few in the colledge that don't clear their quarters notes before the first month be ended, which now is past, and

besides I am plagued out of my life by some people that I owe
money to, and I cant hardly get them put of from post to post,
always expecting that you will send it up to me, Sr I hope you
will consider this and by the post answer your humble servant

Patk Hamilton.

My duty to your Lady and love to my sister."

In another letter he tells his uncle—

" I have not a shoe upon my foot to stir abroad in, and severall
other little odd things I want att present which I can by no means
gett till you send me up some money."

This impecunious young gentleman became, in time, Rector
of Killileagh.

Those who have studied the literature of eighteenth-
century elections will remember a feature of the wretched
doggerel produced for or against a candidate, to have been
references to names by initials and terminal letters, having
between them dashes of lengths relative to the number of
letters in the fully-written name. Sometimes the disguise
was made thinner by the insertion, between initial and terminal, of one or two intervening letters. In the scurrilous
verse printed at election times there may have been reason
for the practice in the real or fancied immunity from punishment for libel which it gave, but for the use of the method in
private correspondence it is difficult to account. The example
here following is from an unsigned letter dated March 22nd,
1756, addressed to Bernard Ward.

" Jokes apart, if there were 70 at the meeting I w^d have some hopes,
as witht Doubt many of the opposite Party, Particularly the
great William Br——low & the little Billy Ri——ds—n will
be greatly shagreened to see that scoundrel J—n G——le who
was formerly Merry Andrew to Clark the Mountabank, gett
200 a year Pension & their great abilities & services Slighted."

When Lady Anne Bligh became the wife of Bernard
Ward, she had already a lover—of her own sex—as vehement
in declaration of love, and as exacting in response, as man

could be. She is the Letty Bushe of the Mary Granville
(Mrs. Delany) letters,—" the ingenious and agreeable Letty,"—
and the fervour of her admiration, and the acknowledgment
it claimed, must have been somewhat embarrassing to the
Lady Anne. There are fifty-eight of her letters preserved
at Castle Ward. They are full of the gossip of the day—
not infrequently the wit is strained and the sentiment forced—
but, always, they breathe out a passionate love for the lady
to whom they were addressed. Even when she has seen the
object of her love daily, she writes of her affection. Indeed,
from the letter first quoted it would appear that she had
seen her love on the day on which this was written. The
following extracts are all from letters to Lady Anne :—

" A great deal of love in a capricious mind makes a whimsical
medley. My sentiments this night tho such as should please ye
person who caused them are of a sort not to be put on paper or
trusted out of my breast. You looked very well & so mighty
gay, neither of these circumstances should give me disturbance
nor do I say they did. You believe me I hope when I seem
indifferent upon such occasions, nothing but my Heart Belyes
me. In good nature one wishes their friends entertained but
if one considers right, this is a kind of mixed wish for who with
any nicety of affection would desire to be entirely forgot, left
ill and alone and neither regretted or thought of for several
hours, and if one carries regrets of a masquerade it is impossible
to act in a chearfull character. This shows how often we are
at war with ourselves & how many contrarities are formed in
our minds. You were in the right to lay down in the morning
when I wanted to have done with you, since you design by your
air in the evening to demonstrate your carelessness of me. Oh !
to be able to shake off affection as one does sleep & resume
freedom as well as get spirits and wakefulness.

" My own Jewel & ever dear Patsy, I am grown reasonable
again. I hope you do not understand one thing I have said for
to be sure I am raving on paper and know not what I would be
at. The only sense of all I have ever wrote or can say to you
is I value your friendship & I wish to preserve it, and tho I
flourish sometimes and run off from the main matter I desire

a reasonable quiet degree of it such as Mrs Allen & Mrs Grey have
for each other for aught I know, or the woman who fries pancakes
on the bridge feels for her friend who foots stockings at the opposite corner. All beyond this is vanity and vexation of spirit.
When I am with you, though I have a thousand matters to speak
of I am tongue-tied and mind-bound. No sooner are you gone
than my thoughts flow, and I should give a good deal for an
opportunity of chatting with you. My own odditys amaze
me,—What must they appear to you? One consideration I
hope reconciles you to them, there breaks through all a very
true regard for you, & tho it may not show itself in the form you
like best, since you are sure you have it correct, but do not
utterly give me up. New vagaries, far away wedding, sups of
brandy, puckers, faddle, feck, and what not ? Ah me, what a
flutter you are in and why should you not ? One would imagine
I expected the calm Bray temper to last for ever. As my
genious is for landskip rather than history I paint with some
delight. A still evening, a warm horizon, a green bank on the
river side the sweet prospect of an arch of Bagdad Bridge, cattle
grazing, women scouring vessels at the waterside, and John
airing his master's horses on the lawn before us. These are
poor objects compared to Belles and Beaux in graceful attitudes
dancing sprightly measures, pleased with themselves and emu-
lating who shall conquer most. Fie-fie, mine is a low taste.
You are born for a Palace I for a cottage, content to dwell with
me there and I shall not envy lofty turrets and gilded roofs.
Come nigh my own Petsy I hope you are this minute very chearfull and much pleased."

    .   .   .   .   .

" Tuesday 18th February 1739.
Past eleven
My own dear Pet and Jewel I am very impatient to know if
you have escaped cold—yesterday's expedition has encreased
mine terribly. You must not mind my airs in the green,—I will
not suffer you to have a moment's doubt of me—you may be
certain I can never love anything better than you ; I think not
so well."

    .   .   .   .   .

" If I dine at the Bp of Corkes I will call to see you, or if you
had a mind to Rattle about—no, you go to the Play—where I
wish you all diversion possible, I read since I began this the

advertisement of your Picture, & believe if it be redeemable you will get it. That day I don't see you is very gloomy and my Spirits much oppress'd—you are sunshine and cordial to me, but my own Jewel & dear are there not many Dismal days reserved for me when it wont be in my power to converse with you ? I won't think of it. Adieu, yours ever faithfully."

While reading the letters of Letty Bushe, one cannot help thinking that if letter writing in the eighteenth century was an art, it was also, sometimes, a disease. The following specimen of her light and airy manners is taken from a letter of five closely-written quarto pages, averaging four hundred words to the page:—

" To my thinking, Lady Bourk is the most agreeable of the whole litter of Agars. She is a good-humoured merry, lollopy soft woman, with a very obscene face & a twisty cum twasty with her eyes that the men understand very well. If you had never seen her you must at first sight know her by this picture to which add an out with her back & belly & a sinking in her breast & stomach, which tho' not a genteel carriage for an English lady, yet has a marvelous & surprising effect upon all beholders."

This letter ends with a farewell—for a matter of hours or days.

" My own sweet Jewel & Petsy farewell—Health & pleasure dance around you, the smiles & loves attend you, & all the prettyest equipage a Poet's brain cou'd form wait on your steps—in all your ways & at all times reckon on the sincere wishes of Yours affecly."

The most entertaining specimens of lively letter writing in the Castle Ward collection, are found in the letters of the Lady Theodosia Bligh, sister of the Lady Anne who married Bernard Ward. This sprightly young lady is met, first, in letters to her eldest sister, Mary, whom she calls Bug,—then in letters to Lady Anne at Castle Ward, and, after 1746, when she married William Crosbie, to her husband. This gentleman was eldest son to Sir Maurice Crosbie, of Ardfert Abbey, Co. Kerry, afterwards created Baron Brandon. In succession to his father he became second Lord Brandon, and was

created Viscount Crosbie in 1771, and further promoted to
the Earldom of Glandore in 1776. The lively Theodosia
was therefore, successively,

> Lady Theodosia Bligh (youngest daughter of John
>   Bligh, first Earl Darnley),
> Lady Theodosia Crosbie,
> Lady Brandon,
> Viscountess Crosbie, and
> Countess of Glandore.

The first letter here copied is addressed to her sister,
Lady Anne. The writer has been disappointed in not receiving expected letters from her sisters.

" For God's sake have you taken an oath never to have anything
more to say to me, it is now six weeks since I writ to you and the
post before that to Bug, but never a word from either of you
since. Bug I allow to be Lasy, there is some excuse for it, but
your not writing prevokes me beyond anything. If one was to
judge of you by your letters I shoud have thought by your last
you were indifferent to London and its gayitiess but I supose
there was no diversions then or at least not to your taste, but
that damned confounded maskerade has set you stark staring
mad. I realy was so unreasonable as to expect a discription of
it & how you liked it, but that was I must own great presumption
to expect a court Lady to remember her dirty Irish kindred, but
tho you are not disposed to write yourself I shoud even be glad
you woud make us (use) of the parson's advice to Mrs Gore for
realy your character depends much upon it. People here make a
great wonder that in five packets (mail boats) at a time I shoud
not hear from you but that is nothing to two months. Even
Miss Harman, your second self, is in great fury with you. Sometimes I am such a fool as to tell lyes about it for I realy am
ashamed to expose you to strangers. Certainly I am mightily
good natured but I cant answer How long it will last. Sooner
or later truth and then all Ireland will rise and tear you to peices.
I wish the wind was not easterly then perhaps I woud not think
of you so much but the prevoking people are continualy babling
packets in my ears & the wind blowing full in my face as I set
at the scrutore makes me so cross that I am fit to keep company
with nobody but Mr Spencer. Poor Charles Lambert is dead,

the town say for love of bell Curtis, but that's not part of my
creed tho its very much the fashion to run mad for love. A
Clerk to Councelor Smith saw a Lady coming out of church and
was Smitten that he never left the churchyard since but walks
continualy night and day for this month past. I dont hear of
any weddings but Lord Thomond and Nancy cuffe who is at
present in great vogue. She has many admirers, Lord oxman-
town dances with her constantly at the assemblys & miss hand-
cock says makes violent love to her. They were to have gone
out of town a month ago, but the two lords went to their father
and begged a reprieve for they coud not live without em (? her).
One of em must have her to be sure but it is not resolved which.
Molly, tho she is not handsome does not want admirers, I make
a match between her & Major hill's son & then I think they are
both disposed of very handsomely. Kitty that's married to
hayly had a hundred p^d laid out on wedding cloaths. I am
afraid the young man will pay for his fancy, for my aunt cuffe
says the father will never see him nor give him a farthing that
he can hinder him of but I presume there is something settled
or they would both be in a bad way. She behaves to Mrs cuffe
much better since she was married.

   " There is great alteracions going to be in our family, alick
& Mathew has had a boxing hour for which Mathew and his
wife are to be discharged in a day or two. Dont you think that
one of the wonders of the age that Miss kitty should part with
Mathew but alick has sworn he won't live in the house with him
and she considers that a good coachman woud be a greater loss
to her than any servant. She has tryed in vain to reconcile
em but is forced at last to part with her dear friend Mathew, to
her great grief I assure you. So much for family afairs. I must
now give you an acount of your Lovers. Munny enquires very
much about you whether you are Lady Anne Bligh still—I
generaly give him a short answer that I know nothing about you.
My jack has gone back to his old mistress Miss Deamor, I cannot
say he seems to pine much after you but perhaps he puts on that
careless air before me on purpose that I may give you an acount
of it. Love to Sweet William & Bug who I hope continues very
well. After all d^r Nancy I hope you won't be morriss (?) at
what I have said but let me hear from you soon, for you know
in your conscience I have great reason to be in a passion. I
know you will say that I am very pert to my elders but tis the

nature of the beast and therefore you must excuse it. I wish
you all many happy new years & am my dr^st nancy your affect
sister, a little huffed

Theo Bligh."

To her eldest sister, Bug (Mary), she writes from a
country house, July 28th, 1746 :—

" I would have writ you a second letter before I received yours
if it had not been for an old rusty grunting bishop who has been
here this fortnight and plagues me out of my life he is such a
formal piece. One wd think a man wd be no trouble to one, but
he is as bad to me as any Mrs. . . . . whatever, for he is
so feeble he can't walk abroad with the men & so is left upon our
hands the whole day long and a heavy load he is, God knows.
I believe I shall never endure the sight of a black gown again,
for there is such a regiment here of em every day, dancing
attendance after him that it quite kills me."

The letter next following, addressed to " My Dear Bug,"
gives an amusing account of a dinner in her and her husband's
honour, when, as a bride, she was on her way to pay a first
visit to her husband's parents at Ardfert Abbey, Co. Kerry.

" Out of Limerick we were met by a strange comical woman and
man, who, it seems, is my lord's wine merchant, and press'd
violently to come in and dine with em, which they excus'd first,
but the good woman cried they must, for she had potatoes for
the countess.

" Well, by much ado, they were persuaded, and so we went to
unload the coach, and returned back in chairs . . . At
dinner I was plac'd, convenient, between the mother & daughter,
and then Dean Swift's ' Tatler ' came strongly into my mind
for every minute it was ' Mama, Lady Bligh has no stomach,'
and then my plate was heaped up. It's no lye, I assure you,
when I tell you that I had six great slices of mutton on my plate,
besides roots, and ten quarts (?) of butter. I stuff'd to humour
them . . but all the while 'ate nothing.' I must do the good
woman the justice to say she was very considerate, for after the
cloth was taken away, she whispered us both that she was afraid
we were too straight-lac'd and begg'd us we would let her loose
our stays, which was really no more than necessary after all that

cramming. And to the Countess it was ' please your Countess-
ship & will your Countess-ship eat a bit of this.' When I
attempted to refuse (which I did not think of doing until I was
dead sick) she cried to me ' Indeed Lady Bligh, you must,—
your spouse must press you to eat this little bit ' and then she
would turn to him & say ' Persuade Lady Bligh to eat for she
is quite starv'd.'

" This is but a very small sketch of the oddness of the feast,
were I to tell you all it would take up twelve sheets of note paper.
Then the tea was call'd, & their valet de chambre, who was the
very image of Parnell, brought in the cups, wrapt up very nicely
in a dish-clout that had been wiping the dripping-pan, I am very
sure, the minute before, but it was in vain to say nay, for I knew
till I dropp'd down I sh^d never be left alone. Then there was
a pewter teapot but I believe it was designed for silver and a
pewter dish for bread and butter—the first layer, and over that,
three dozen (for I counted 'em) of saffron-cakes, made in the
town, wch indeed was the best thing we had that day, but I cd
hardly eat 'em, I was so stuff'd before ; but I got through with
it and was more distress'd that I c^d not laugh than at anything
in the world ; when she went to her closet and brought me some
very good cherry-brandy, & that went down too, and indeed I
thought it very comfortable."

The next letter is dated from Castle Ward, where the
lady, now three years married, is on visit to her sister. It is
addressed to her husband.

" Castle Ward

" My dearest Life,   Oct ye 5th, 1749.

I got your letter yesterday. Remember that I think I
have as much reason to be in a fuss as others but I am mild and
gentle My heart, I have nothing to tell you but the old story
that I love you and longs very much to see you. The day is not
fixed for our leaving this yet, when it is you shall know. It
cannot be further off than the end of next week. Mrs Montgomery
is brought to bed of a daughter and had like to have kicked up
her heels. You must know lovely that we have just done dinner
and I declare I think I am a little concerned with the strong beer.
They are calling for the letters so can say no more but that I
am my comfort's own

Most affectionately   T. Crosbie.

Nancy's & the squire's love to you. Mine is at yr disposal. My
Love, upon reading over this letter, I fear you will think it
skittish therefore, my heart I must tell you the reason I couldn't
write in the morning.   I was entic'd to walk, & so I didn't come
home till the bell rang for dinner, and that's the whole truth
my precious, so don't put on a lightning face.   You doesn't
care for me."

The next, a year later, is also addressed to her husband.

" Gillhall, September 3.
(no year—probably 1750)

" Long looked for is come at last, my love's letter a Saterday, and
this day is an extraordinary honour, but, to speak seriously of
ye matter, Jewel, how could you think of being a whole fortnight
without writing ?   I must say your excuse on ye road was a
very lame one, for surely though it didn't answer directly to the
minute, you might have left it behind you, to have been forwarded when the post went out if you thought much about it,
but I presume your attention was wholly taken up with your fair
traveller.   No sort of notice of your not writing the night before
you left though you got a letter from me the day before it, one
might have thought would have been a pleasre to you, but—
I suppose as you generally pretend great ignorance about post
days you didn't imagine that it left Dublin of a thursday and
Lord Kingsborough's champaigne confirmed it.   Well so much
for the scolding but indeed, my heart, you deserve ten times more
for them ugly ways.   Many a heartache I had during that fortnight, nay it was 2 days more, and I think the least satisfaction
I can have is to abuse in gentle terms.   Squire Tighe and his
beloved left this at seven this morning, they were ready to go
yesterday but the day prov'd bad. Squire Ward went to the
assizes (that the whole world is pestered with at this present)
last fryday and returns to-morrow.   The Masserenes are here
still, My Lord came a thursday from attending the old dons at
Carrickfergus and there is an end of 'em I hope for some time.
Now, Lovey, that I am a little composed and calm, I think
proper to tell you that ye sight of your letter saterday was beyond
expressing interesting to me, to find that you got safe and well
and had such good company, for I think, Diamond, I dos care
for you a little bit.   We are to go this evening to visit Lady

Hampton and Mrs Marford who is there so I must go.   Adieu
my Lamb, and be assured I am your own pig,

Most affectionately

Theo Crosbie.

My duty to Sir Maurice and Lady, love to Mary. I hope you
don't expose my letters to the house, if you do, it's a very ugly
way let me tell you, Nancy's love to you (you don't love me at
at all, at all)."

One can overlook the petulant opening of the first letter
of this little selection, in view of the winsome character in
the later extracts.   Surely the husband of this sprightly and
lovable person had not heart, often, to turn to her the ' lightning face.'

CHAPTER XIV.

Writing, Spelling, and Pronunciation of the Literate in Old Down

A WRITER, contributing to the Ulster Journal of Archæology an article on an old Presbyterian Session Book, expresses astonishment that the record should contain a note of three men's partnership in a goat. The mis-read entry has no connection with goat-keeping. Correctly read it states :

" John Riges is wilinge to take heugh gemble and Steven Whytt to be partners in his seat (pew)."

The contributor had forgotten, or was ignorant of, the fact that, along with changes in spelling and sound of words which have taken place during the two centuries we are considering, or since the end of the second of them, there have been made, also, changes in the form of script letters. These changes have been sufficiently numerous to give to documents of the seventeenth and early eighteenth centuries, for eyes accustomed only to modern forms, the appearance of

writings in a foreign language. In the case above-cited, the
old Session-clerk has used the long S and the loop E of his
time, thus—

ʄoat

which, to the modern eye, certainly looks like ' goat.'

*It is ordered that none within this congre-
gation shall sell or make away their seats
without the consent of the session which
is to be signified to them the next Lords
Day.*

Fac-simile of
entry in the
Session Book
of Carnmoney.

" It is ordered that none within this congregation shall sell or make away their seats
without the consent of the session which
is to be signified to them the next Lord's
Day."

The letters anciently very different, in script, from
modern forms are c e k p r s v . Some of these were written
in various ways ; at times a letter may appear in two ways
in one word, and the difficulty of the unpractised in decipher-
ing documents in which these old forms are used, is, of course,
greatly increased by the astonishing freedom from rule or
standard in spelling, even in writings of the educated. The
letters which differ from those of the Italian or modern script,
and which appear frequently in Ulster documents of the
period 1600-1725, are exhibited on next page, alone and in
combination.

In script, also, as in printed characters of the time, ' j ' is
represented by ' i ' and ' v ' very frequently by ' u.'

How very strange an appearance words most familiar
may present when these old forms of script have been used,
will be seen from the following examples, all exactly copied
from documents used for this work.

T	C (capital)		
𝑒	c	*obiḋonco*	evidence
𝑒	c	*pofitḃo*	positive
𝑎	e	*donyos*	denyes (**denies**)
𝑒	e (final)	*womoḃo*	remove
𝑙𝑒	k	*Horíulos*	Hercules
𝑦	p	*voign.*	reign
𝑦	p	*rhuxsh*	church
𝑤	r	*boix*	beir (**beer**)
𝑥	r	*fyḃoʒ*	fyve (**five**)
𝑜	r	*bofydoḃ*	besydes (**besides**)
𝑔	s	*Yoofol*	peopel (**people**)
𝛾	s (final)	*rowwḃed*	received
𝜷	v	*thofo*	these

To the reader's difficulties of different letter-form are to
be added those of long-disused conventions of contraction,
prefix and terminal. A few of these, taken from the old
documents found at Portaferry House (see p. 91), are here
given.

n final, as in *mad.* man

nt   „   *mol*   ment

nts   „   *molz*   ments

pro   as in *providentiall*   providential

That spelling was still largely phonetic and unstandard-
ised until nearly the end of our two-centuries period, is evident
from the unmodernised letters so largely quoted in this volume.
Even after the multiplication of books had resulted in settled
forms of spelling for printed matter,—extreme variability of
spelling characterised the letter-writing of the wealthy classes,
supposedly cultured.

The seventeenth and eighteenth century pronunciation
of many words differed very much from the modern.   Evidence
of this is of three kinds : (1) the rhymes of old verse, (2) present
day pronunciation of Irish peasants, descendants of those
who learned English as a foreign tongue in the time of Elizabeth
and the Stuarts, and (3) the treatment of vowels, single or in
diphthongs, as interchangeable in writings of the period
considered.

A long dissertation on the changes in vocalisation of
diphthongs, and the shiftings of accent, which have taken
place in many words of our language during the last century

and a half, would be out of place here : yet, if we are to know
our ancestors of Down as they lived, a short treatment of the
subject is necessary. From many letters in this book we have
seen how they wrote ; we have yet to hear them speak.

Briefly, then, let it be stated that nearly all the words
containing *ea*, to which we give the sound *ee*, were, by
them, pronounced as if the diphthong had the sound we attach
to *ā*, *ai*, or *ay*. Sea, speak, cheat, please, release,—were by
them pronounced say, spake, chate, plaise, relace. The
evidence from rhyme is, by itself, convincing. Pope's couplet,
oft-quoted in this connection,

> " Here thou, great Anna, whom three realms obey,
> Dost sometimes counsel take and sometimes tea,"

is, of course, standing alone, no more evidential of the *tay*
sound of *tea* than it is of an *obee* sound of *obey*. But all poets
and versifiers between 1600 and 1800 rhymed *ea*, in nearly all
the words containing it, to *ā*, *ai*, *ay*, or *ey*. Drayton rhymed
seas with *raise ;* Cowper rhymed *sea* and *way*. Croker, in
the poem *Doneraile Litany*, rhymed *Doneraile* with *seal, veal,
weal, peal, meal, steal, reveal, congeal ;* and to come to low
quality, Burdy, the Down versifier at the end of the eighteenth
century, rhymed *meal* with *Sale*, and *bohea* with *way*.

Another old-time pronunciation, differing from modern
and evidenced by rhyme, is the *ā*, *ai*, or *ay* sound of *ei* in such
words as *receive, conceive, perceive*, which were pronounced
by our forefathers as *re-save, con-save, per-save*. It has been
pointed out that Tate and Brady's version of the Psalms offers
no fewer than 47 examples of *ei* rhyming to *ā*.

> " The plots are fruitless which my foe
> Unjustly did *conceive* ;
> The pit he digg'd for me has prov'd
> His own untimely *grave*."

Pope's verse offers evidence that *stood* was pronounced
as *stud* and *would* as *wud*. Hume (*Essays on Down and Antrim*)
finds, also, in verse, proof that the cultivated gave to *e* in

The writing of James Hamilton, first Lord Claneboye, while yet of Trinity College, Dublin.
It exhibits many of the forms of early Elizabethan script illustrated in this chapter.

certain words the sound of *i* (short), and that even the very
vulgar *divil* and *yit* are but examples of persistence of the old-
time pronunciation of cultured folk.

When the vowel *e* and the diphthong *ea* were followed by
two consonants, the first of these being *r*, they took the sound
of *a* in *far*, and are frequently represented by this letter in old
writings. Thos. Montgomery, writing to his father, Lord
Mount-Alexander, at Comber (May 3, 1729), says,

> " Molly gives you her duty and *sarvice* to Jenny " ;

and Lord John Hay, writing to Major Agnew, in Holland
(February 13, 1704), speaks of a concocted story of a plot to
buy

> " arms and ammunition to *sarve* the french interest."

Pope rhymes *reserve* with *starve*.

> " But still the great have Kindness in *reserve*,
> He helped to bury whom he helped to starve."

An example of *ea* represented by *a*, as in *far*, will be
found in Harrison's *Description of Britain and England*, in
the account of a thanksgiving for delivery from the peril of
the Spanish Armada.

> " the Queene her selfe, & her nobility came to St Paules Churche
> in London November the 19, where, after she had *hard* the Divine
> service, & in her owne person geuen solemne thankes to God
> in the hering of soche as were present, she *hard* the sermon at
> the Crosse preached by the bishop of Sarum."

It may be objected to the conclusion here drawn that the
a of *sarve* and *sarvice* and of *starve* in Pope's couplet, may have
been pronounced as *ā*. This brings us to (2) the evidence
furnished by the pronunciation of the Irish peasant, descendant of men who learned English in the time of Elizabeth
and the Stuarts. He speaks of *vartue* and *sarvice*, *narves*
and *narvousness*. He " *arns* his bread," and when he gives
his boy a cuff on the ear for misdeeds, he says, " that's *to larn*
ye," illustrating in the phrase a persistence of word use, as
well as of letter sound, by his employment of the verb *to learn*

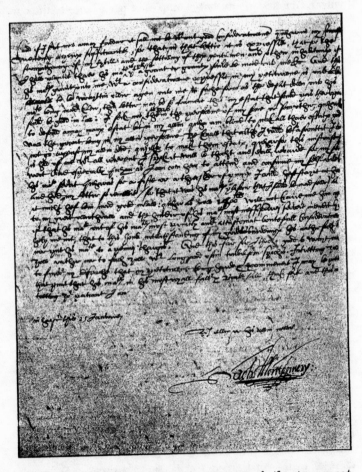

The writing of Hugh Montgomery, one of the two great
planters of N.E. Down. Created Viscount Montgomery of
the Great Ards, 3rd May, 1622. Died May, 1636.

Original in the Advocates' Library, Edinburgh.

in the sense of *to teach* : now an inaccuracy, but perfectly
correct English in the days when, in his ancestor, he learned
to speak that language.   All the words in which the diphthong
ea has suffered sound-change since the end of the eighteenth
century are by him pronounced in the old manner.   *Sea* is
say, *tea* is *tay* ; *wheat*, *treat*, *heat*, *meat*, *neat*, etc., in his sounding
of them will rhyme with *late*.   *Leaves* he sounds as *laves*,
stream as *strame*.   To the *e* of *complete* he gives the old sound,
saying *complate*.   He retains the Elizabethan and Stuart *ei*
in such words as *receive*, *conceive*, pronouncing them *re-save*,
con-save.

Observe that there is here no case of racial inability, or
disinclination, to produce certain sounds.   Who can say
believe can say *conceive*.   When our forefathers pronounced
the latter *con-save*, they pronounced the former as we do
to-day, and the Irish peasant, following the usage of the time
when his fathers were taught English, while he says *con-save*,
gives correctly the old (and modern) sound to *believe*.   Nearly
all the vulgarisms of the Irishman are preserved specimens of
old-time correct—even classical—English.   And this statement may be made even when it is question, not of vowel
sound, but of word sense (as in the instance *to learn* for *to
teach*), the use of noun as verb, or the placing of accent.   The
Irishman says *to loss* for *to lose* ;— *contrary*, as he pronounces
it, is *contrairy*.   In *The Fulfilling of Scripture* (1681), the hard
s or *ss* is represented by *sse*, as in *crosse*, *lesse*, *expresse*, &c.,
and, in it, occurs the phrase

" content *to losse* a son every day."

Milton's accenting of *contrary* was, as is the Irishman's—
contrairy.

" Fame, if not double-fac'd, is double-mouth'd,
And with *contrary* blast proclaims most deeds."
Samson Agonistes.

In (3) the interchangeability of letters $\bar{a}$, *ai*, and *ea*, in the
writings of educated persons of the eighteenth century, and

The changing script. Conveyance from John Stevenson of Ballywoolly and his son Hans to John Hutchison of Ballygrot; date 1693. The loop e, and the e of modern form, appear at times in one word.

Original in the Muniment Room at Clandeboye House.

in the books of their time, there is abundance of proof that
their *ea* was sounded *ā, ai,* or *ay*.   The sound of the diphthong
ai has not changed ; old rhymes and Irish peasant agree in
evidencing *fair, pair, chair,* &c., to have had, in seventeenth
and eighteenth centuries, the sound they have to-day.   If,
then, in writings of cultured, and in printed books, we find
an indiscriminate use of *ā, ai,* and *ea,* it follows that, at the
time used, all had same sound value.   Many examples will
be found in letters of Down people, quoted in this book.   A
very few may be noted.

ā for *ea.*

Ezekiel Stewart, writing to Judge Ward, spells *treatment,
tratement* ; and *reason, rason.*   William Stewart, suitor for the
hand of the Judge's daughter, writes that the young lady

> " asked to be *relaced* from her promise."

The account of the attempt of Blair of Bangor, and his fellow-
ministers and friends, to reach New England, contains the
sentence :

> " their vessel . . . was like a riddle with so many *lakes.*"

ai for *ea.*

Mrs. Ward, the Judge's wife, writes of

> " dram dails for the church."

The term was obscure until, in another letter of the time,
mention was found of Drammen deals,—*deals* shipped from
Drammen, Norway.   Ezekiel Stewart, above-mentioned,
writes ' *mains* ' for ' *means.*'

ea for *ā.*

Dean Delany, writing of dues claimed by the clergy from
artisans, uses the term ' *tread*-money '—which is ' *trade*-
money,' and the Ezekiel Stewart already quoted, writes
' *pleace,*' ' *weages,*' ' *sheur,*' for *place, wages,* and *share.*   A
longer consideration of the subject on these lines might be

considered tedious, and these notes must terminate here, leaving unsettled many interesting questions. Did Lady Mordaunt, of the tender conscience, reading over her note, " I Feare I tould a Lye this day," pronounce ' *tould* ' as ' *told*,' or did she say ' *towl'd* ' (*ow* as in *cow*) as do the present day vulgar ?

What has been said will prepare for hearing the old Down folk speak. Let us imagine ourselves present while the young Anne Hamilton of Bangor reads to her mother. The time is about 1708. The voice of the girl who captured the heart of the clever and good-looking young Michael Ward was, we may be sure, refined and melodious. Be it remembered that the word-sound we find so different from what our modern ear expects, had, for the young damsel and her listener, no vulgar associations. It is, of course, only by association that a sound is vulgar. *Leaves*, pronounced ' *laves* ' is vulgar, but there is nothing displeasing to the cultured ear in the same sound heard in

" Her lovely limbs the naiad *laves*."

Let us hear what Anne read, set out in modern spelling.

" The mother was seated by her daughter on the balcony.

" ' I'm weak and weary,' said the girl, throwing back her head ; ' I have done with life.'

" A footstep sounded near, and a servant appeared, carrying a tea tray with china cups and saucers.

" ' Take some tea, my dear,' said the mother, but the girl shook her head wearily. The mistress poured out the tea, saying, ' You can't refuse tea from these lovely lilac and gold cups,— the merchant says Queen Anne has not better.' Then, to divert her daughter, she began to tell of her visit to Erinah. ' I thought little of the place and its keeping,' she said ; ' the aspect of the room I was in was extremely bad. There was a stream close by the end of the house, and it was choked with rubbish, and heaps of manure laid down beside it. And as for what the future of your cousin and his wife will be, I don't know. Tom concerns himself mighty little with preserving the property ; the lease is nearly out, and it is no use speaking to him, for it only makes him do the contrary.

" The girl listened, and made uneasy movements, but uttered never a word. Indeed, she had not heard what her mother said. Her thoughts were of the man who had deceived and deserted her within a week of her wedding, and who was away now across the sea to marry another. The elder woman divined her daughter's thought.

" ' Forget him, dear,' she said ; ' don't answer his letter,—I wouldn't please him by that much. Listen to reason, my sweet one ; 'tis no fault of yours that he left you basely. Oblige me by putting all thought of him from your breast. If I write to him—and I have a mind to do it—I'll read him a sermon for his deceit and ill-treatment of the best girl in the county.' "

Hear now what Anne read, the words which have changed in sound being set out phonetically to represent her pronunciation. Shifted accents are also indicated.

" The mother was sated by her daughter on the balcóny.

" ' I'm wake and wary,' said the girl, throwing back her hade ; ' I have done with life.'

" A futstep sounded nare, and a sarvant appaired, carrying a tay tray with chayney coops and saucers.

" ' Take some tay, my dare,' said the mother, but the girl shook her hade warily. The mistress poured out the tay, saying, ' You can't refuse tay from these lovely layloc and goold coops,—the marchant says Queen Anne hasn't better.' Then, to divart her daughter, she began to tell of her visit to Erinah. ' I thought little of the place and its keeping,' she said ; ' the aspect of the room was extramely bad. There was a strame close by the end of the house, and it was choked with rubbish, and hapes of mánure, laid down beside it. And as for what the future of your cousin and his wife will be, I don't know. Tom consarns himself mighty little with presarving the property ; the lace is narely out, and it is no use spaking to him, for it only makes him do the contrairy.'

" The girl listened, and made unaisy movements, but uttered niver a word. Indeed, she had not hard what her mother said. Her thoughts were of the man who had desaved and desarted her within a week of her wedding, and who was away now across the say to marry another. The elder woman diveened her daughter's thoughts. ' Forgit him, dare,' she said ; ' don't answer his letter—I wouldn't plaise him by that mooch. Listen to rason, my swate one ; 'tis no fawt of yours that he left you basely. Obleege me by putting all thought of him from your braist. If I write to him—and I have a mind to do it—I'll rade him a sarmon for his desate and ill-tratement of the best girl in the county.' "

This little essay deals only with the English of the literate in Down—the speech of men who had travelled, and of their children educated in England or by tutors at home. It is not concerned with peculiarities of the Scottish tongue which persist, and are too well-known from books and the speech of living people to need account. Still, in the remoter parts of farming Down, by the elder and untravelled folk, is spoken the language of the men who came from the lowlands of Scotland at Hamilton and Montgomery's call, three hundred years ago.

CHAPTER XV.

The Reading of
Our Ancients

ON a certain day in 1696 or 1697—writing in 1712, he will not charge his memory more exactly—the Reverend W. Tisdal, Vicar of Belfast, and most contentious parson, was asked for his opinion of ' Mr.' Milton's works. After seeing them all, he told his querist what he thought of them. He tells his story thus :—

" I further certifie, That about the same time (1696 or 1697) the Right Honourable the Earl of Donnegal, meeting me in the street of Belfast ask'd me if I had seen all Mr Milton's Works. I answered His Lordship that I had seen some but not all ; His Lordship said he had them bound up in one Folio Volume and would send it to me to read, which he did. And sometime after, meeting His Lordship he was pleased to ask my Opinion of it. I told His Lordship that Milton still stuck to his King-Deposing and King-Killing Doctrine, that I hoped his Lordship wou'd not spend his time so ill as to read so dangerous a Book. That I plainly perceived one of the Methods taken by Anti-monarchical men to debauch the young Nobility and Gentry of the Kingdom, was to Print, Publish and industriously disperse those Sorts of Books among them ; upon which his Lordship told me with a smile that Mr McBride (the Dissenting Teacher at Belfast) had sent him that Book, and he doubted not but that other Gentlemen in the Country had received the like Present."

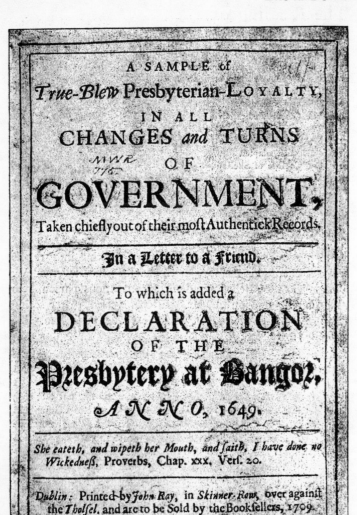

THE DISPUTATIOUS PAMPHLET: Specimen Title.

The answer is enlightening as to the attitude of the time
and place to Literature. Milton had been dead, then, about
twenty years ; the works were " *all* Mr. Milton's Works," yet
the " Reverend Divine," as he calls himself on the title-page
of the pamphlet from which this extract is made, had not eye
for a single line in the great volume which contained the whole
of Milton's poetry, beyond the political writings.

It may seem a bold thing to attempt, within the limits
of a short chapter, to indicate the character and extent of
Down folks' reading, over such a long period as two hundred
years. Nevertheless, while any classification of the books
must be very rough, it is possible, from the material yet very
plentiful in old houses, to make a fairly true presentation of
the literature of the place and time.

Let it be premised that the rough classification here
attempted excludes the works of English authors which
country gentlemen of moderate culture bought to fill their
library shelves. Taking Down reading as a whole, the concern
of the literate of all ranks, the books of the period range
themselves under four heads, and the order here adopted
agrees to a considerable extent with the chronology of production and use.

1. Books of Religion and Theology.
2. Disputatious Pamphlets.
3. Books of Statistics, Economics, etc.
4. Books of literary interest, of travel, &c.

1. The period following the Hamilton and Montgomery
settlements was one of great religious activity. The early
ministers of the Scots were capable, laborious, and self-
sacrificing, and the books they, and their successors for a
century, countenanced, were the standard religious or con-
troversial works of their time, such as an Irish traveller, as
late as 1813, found in an inn,—" mouldy and half torn in a
chest."

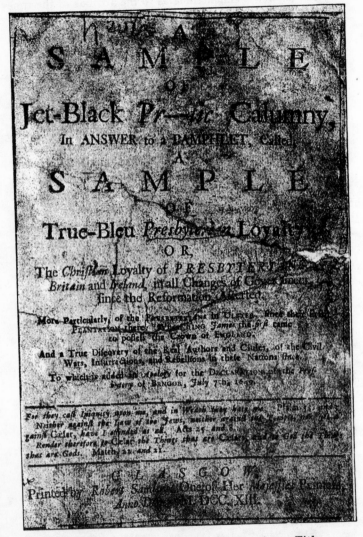

THE DISPUTATIOUS PAMPHLET: Specimen Title.

" Boston's Fourfold State."
" Boston's Sermons."
" Cloud of Witnesses."
" The Hind let loose."
" Marrow of Divinity."

2. For nearly the whole of the hundred years between
1650 and 1750, the pamphlet which may be called ' Disputatious' held the field as literature.   It was very often an abusive
document, having, as it seemed, a procreative power ; for
no sooner did one appear with a provocative title-page, which
was also a contents-bill of the work, than there was born
A Reply to, etc., and this, in turn, was responsible for bringing
to life *Remarks on a Reply to*, etc.   The supposed disloyalty
of dissenters was frequently the subject of the pamphleteer.
It was a maxim of clergymen of the Tisdal type, that the nonconformist never could be loyal, and, always on the outlook
for instances to prove dissent disloyal, they kept the subject
well before the powers and conforming public.   Tisdal
produces (1709) *A Sample of True-Blew Presbyterian-Loyalty,*
and McBride, Presbyterian minister, hits back with
A Sample of Jet-Black Pr . . . tic Calumny.   The pamphlet
was very often *A True Account* — written to give a
partisan statement of sayings or happenings in Ireland.
A True Account produced one which called it lying, or professed to give an account still truer.   Rev. George Walker,
Governor of Derry in Siege time, published in 1689 *A True
Account of the Siege of Londonderry*.   One Mackenzie, Chaplain
to a regiment in Derry at the time of the Siege, then prints
*A Narrative of the Siege of Londonderry or the late Memorable
Transactions of that City, Faithfully Represented To Rectify
the Mistakes and supply the Ommissions of Mr. Walker's
Account*.   Walker replies in *A Vindication of the True Account
of the Siege of Derry in Ireland*.   Forthwith appears *An Apology
for the Failures charged on the Reverend George Walker's Printed
Account of the late Siege of Derry*, which is followed by *Reflections on a Paper pretending to be An Apology for the Failures*

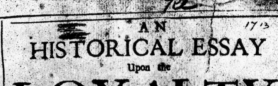

AN
HISTORICAL ESSAY
Upon the
LOYALTY
Of
PRESBYTERIANS

In *Great-Britain* and *Ireland* from the
Reformation to this Prefent Year 1713.

WHEREIN

Their fteady Adherence to the *Proteftant Intereft*, our happy *Civil Con-
ftitution*, the *Succeffion* of *Proteftant Princes*, the juft *Prerogatives* of
the *CROWN*, and the *Liberties* of the *People* is demonftrated
from Public *Records*, the beft Approv'd *Hiftories*, the Confeffion of
their *Adverfaries*, and divers Valuable *Original Papers* well attefted,
and never before Publifhed. And an *ANSWER* given to the
Calumnies of their Accufers, and particularly to two late Pamphlets viz. 1. *A Sample of true Blue Presbyterian Loyalty &c*. 2. *The
Conduct of the Diffenters in Ireland &c*.

In Three Parts.

With a *PREFATORY ADDRESS* to all her Majefty's Proteftant
Subjects, of all Perfuafions, in *Great-Britain* and *Ireland*, againft the
Pretender, on behalf of the *PROTESTANT* Religion, the *QUEEN*,
the Houfe of *HANOVER*, and our *LIBERTIES*.

Printed in the Year MDCCXIII.

THE DISPUTATIOUS PAMPHLET : Specimen Title.

charg'd on Mr. Walker's Account of the Siege of Londonderry
1689,—and so the wordy battle went on, and there is nothing
on the tops of chests of drawers in old houses of farmers to
show that the people had anything on which to cultivate mind
other than their religious and devotional books, and these
acres of acrid dispute.

3. During the last two decades of the seventeenth century, and the first half of the eighteenth, were produced many
books of Statistics of Irish production or consumption,
containing suggestions for industrial and agricultural development, etc. It is consistent with the plan of this work to allow
a characteristic specimen to speak for itself, and here *The*
Interest of Ireland in its Trade and Wealth Stated (1682),
by Richard Lawrence, speaks. In considering the subject
of Ireland's welfare, he deals with

> " Cost of vices per head,
>   Impediments to prosperity,
>   and
>   Expedients or Remedies,"

and, dealing with the first of these subjects, he assumes a
number addicted to each vice, assessing Ireland's loss at per
head in fashion as here exhibited.

> " Gaming including
>   peasantly and
>   Mechanick
>   gamesters at
>   Cards, Dice
>   Shovelboard
>   Bowling alleys
>   and Ninepins
>   say 10,000 persons
>   obstructing the
>   Wealth of the country
>   to the extent of, per ann. £52,000
>
> " Prophane Swearing,
>   costs
>   the country, per ann. £20,000

THE NEW

ASSOCIATION.

Of those Called,

MODERATE CHURCH-MEN,

WITH THE

MODERN WHIGS & FANATICKS,

TO

Under-mine and Blow-up the Present Constitution in CHURCH and STATE.

Occasion'd by a late

PAMPHLET,

Entitul'd, The

Danger of Priestcraft:

With a RECITAL of the OLD SNUGG
SOLEMN LEAGUE and COVENANT.

AND

A SUPPLEMENT, on Occasion of the New
Scotch Presbyterian Covenant.

TOGETHER,

With an APPENDIX, containing Two Clauses of a Parliament Ordnance for the Establishment of the DIRECTORY. With the Opinions of some of the most Eminent *Dissenters*
themselves concerning *Toleration:* And the Comfortable Fruits of being Exempted from PE-
NAL LAWS and STATUTES.

By a True-Church-Man.

DUBLIN: Printed by *Daniel Thompson* in
Cole's Ally, Castle-street, 1714.

THE DISPUTATIOUS PAMPHLET: Specimen Title.

" Drunkenness.
3 Winebibbers
to each Parish at £10
per Winebibber per ann.
2500 parishes £75,000

" Aletopers, 5 to a
parish at £4 ea per ann. £50,000

" Second set of Aletopers
or Fuddlicups, generally
Artists or Husbandmen
at £2 each per ann. £25,000

" Tapsters and Drawers
who might be
employed in profitable
Arts cost the
country per ann. £4,000

" Loss through bad
work of the Sots, per ann. £20,000

His calculations are made for all the vices.

One of the impediments to the prosperity of Ireland is
" fulness of bread."

> " The third Impediment is the great plenty of provisions, for ful-
> ness of bread is the cause of abundance of Idleness in Ireland
> as well as in Sodom."

Another ' impediment ' is extravagance in dress.   He quotes
with approval Dr. Hall, Bishop of Eton—

> " Oh God, how is the world changed with us since britches of Fig-
> leaves and Coats of Skin !   The Earth yields Gold, Silver, rich
> Stones, the Sea, Pearls the air Feathers, the Field his Stalks,
> the sheep her Fleece, the Worm her Web, and all too little for
> one back,"

and follows with his own remarks :—

> " Wives (of Yeomen or ordinary Tradesmen) wear not only Silk
> Gowns but oft-times two or three silk Petticoats appear as they
> walk one under another, which is intolerable expence upon the
> country.
> " Even Carmen's and Porters' Wives wear Silk hoods and Scarves
> —consuming the Wealth of the Kingdom."

Author calculates that this consumption of foreign silk
manufacture "damnifies the Kingdom £67,500 per ann."
Still another 'impediment' is the purchasing of foreign
manufactured goods. To remove this impediment he has an
'expedient.'

> "And for removing this Trade ruining, Nation Scandalizing evil,
> I would propose that no Merchant or Retayler should recover
> in any of the King's Courts any Debt contracted for foreign
> Manufactures but that it should be admitted a sufficient Bar
> against Judgment if the Debtor could prove that the Debt were
> contracted for Goods manufactured out of Ireland."

Another 'expedient' is the taxing of the single life.

> "The second Expedient is to procure Laws against single Life,
> enjoyning all English Protestants to marry, the Males before the
> age of 25 and Females before the age of 22 or from that time to
> pay a yearly penalty by Statute . . not exceeding the eighth
> part of their visible Incomes."

It goes without saying that not all the books in the third
section of our classification were so foolish as this; still, the
quantity of crude, ill-digested material placed on printed page
for Ireland's benefit was surprisingly large.

4. The books of this class were mostly published at the
expense of a patron or by subscription. As a specimen of the
former, take *A Dialogue concerning Things of Importance to
Ireland*, published in 1751, with its fulsome dedication.

> "To His Grace, George Lord Arch-Bishop of Armagh, Primate of
> All Ireland and one of the Lords Justices of the Kingdom,—
> this Dialogue is most humbly Dedicated.
>
> May it please your Grace
> The following Dialogue is perhaps the most imperfect that could
> be offered, yet it is offered in order to be made perfect. Fruits
> cannot ripen without the sun, and a Shade; the one to give
> Life, the other Protection; Nor can a Writer perfect anything
> for the Public without a Patron to invigorate and to screen.
> Your Grace is so eminently and commodiously placed to answer
> both these purposes, in that Tract of Ireland, which yields you
> both Wealth and Honour that it would be the greatest negligence

to pass you by. Your Grace having moved thro' different
stages of Preferment now gladdens our County as Arch-Bishop,
and our Kingdom as Lord Justice. Your station, almost the
highest, may seem to raise you above Praise, yet it exposes you
to Requests.

" Power and Wealth have no meaning, but in the useful
Exertion of one and Distribution of the other."

After considerably more of the same stuff, he signs—

" The whole is submitted to Your Grace by the Author who
desires to subscribe himself in the humblest manner—

" Your Grace's Most dutiful and most respectful Servant
Richard Barton, B.D.
Lurgan, in the County of Ardmagh, January 1, 1750/1."

The persons in this Dialogue are—

Gorgias	..	..	a Farmer.
Odontes	..	..	a Traveller.
Othonius	..	..	a Linen-Draper.
Philedones	..	..	a Man of Pleasure.
Hierophantes ⎱		..	Clerical persons of different
Cenophotus ⎰		..	Persuasions.

The bulk of the talking to enlighten Odontes is done by
Hierophantes and Cenophotus. Gorgias and Othonius are
allowed to supply Odontes with information about farming
and the linen trade of the country. Odontes is introduced
by Othonius, and the flatulent discourse proceeds.

Hierophantes. " Every Gentleman is welcome to me whom
Othonius introduces. Gorgias, Philedones, Cenophotus and I
were just sitting down to a frugal meal and if you will partake
with us you will do us a favour. Pray sit down. Has Odontes
been at any time heretofore in this part of the Kingdom ? "

Cenophotus. " There is nothing so agreeable to the human Mind
as the giving of information ; and there is no man that is not
capable of conveying it to another in some Respect, but the
disposition in many to flatter, the Aversion in most People to
hear Truth, the Jealousy of Inhabitants of different Countries
towards each other, and even those of the same country towards
their neighbours, have made Politeness to consist in an artful
Method of Prate, without giving or receiving Knowledge at all."

Hierophantes here takes up his parable, and continues in the same stilted strain for a time. Then Odontes expresses his pleasure thus :—

" Whatever my Sentiments are, I hope I shall betray nothing in this company that shall be in the least disagreeable ; and I am so far from having conceived an injurious Opinion of this country or anything in it ; that I think I never in my Life rode with more pleasure than I have done this morning : The public Ways are so excellent, the Houses so neat, the Inhabitants so numerous : All Objects so charming ; Rivers, Lakes, Bleach Yards, Churches, Towns and Plantations situated in such Manner as to give immense Delight. These Scenes are more pleasing to me than the present Foppery of Superstition, for Ruins of former Magnificence which remind one of Gothic Barbarism ; too frequently seen in other Countries."

Hierophantes. "Since the first Impressions, Odontes, are so favourable to us, I believe we shall not find much difficulty in making your Residence in this Country agreeable to you ; for you have as yet only peeped into it. But when you shall become acquainted with our Manufactures the Opulence arising from thence to some, and the Comforts to all, even to those of the Kingdom who are not immediately concerned in them, your Pleasure will be improved to Admiration, that so small a Part of a large Island can be so great a Part of the Wealth and Stability of the Whole : Odontes you may see without rising from your Seat, that great Lake (Lough Neagh) which contains a Hundred Thousand Acres of Water : I hope in less than half a Century that immense Basin of Water shall be incompassed with Bleach Yards and Towns."

Odontes. "You have exceedingly raised my curiosity and a hundred questions are struggling for Utterance."

Hierophantes. "Be so kind as to defer your Questions till we have dined ; I ask Pardon for intermixing so much Discourse so unreasonably with our Food. Odontes, shall I help you to another Cut of Salmon ? "

Odontes. " I have dined plentifully and delicately, and never ate better Fish : It is the first Time in my Life that I have seen a whole Salmon roasted The Form of serving it up makes me imagine it was drest so, I think it an excellent Manner. Pray

from whence is this Fish, and what might it cost ? A Fish of
that kind could not be purchased in London under Two
Guineas."

Hierophantes. " It was a present from my Neighbour Gorgias
who can answer best."

Gorgias. " I took that, with some more, this morning in a Bay
of that Lake which you see. The Price of this Kind of Fish,
is at different times with us from three Pence to a Penny Halfpenny a Pound."

Of the rubbish presented as literature, and published
by subscription, it is difficult to make selection. The subjects
are generally unimportant things or unimportant persons,
treated by writers of very great importance—in their own
estimation. The manner in which these writers intrude
themselves, their learning and literary skill, into the story
of their subject is noteworthy. One of these books, which
will repay reading for the amusement its style provides, is,
The Exemplary Life and Character of James Bonnell, Esq.,
late Accomptant General of Ireland . . . , by an Archdeacon of Armagh, William Hamilton, A.M. (1707). Mr.
Bonnell was a prodigy of piety. His own account of it, in
early youth, is thus given :—

" From the Beginning of my Life (says he) I had a great Sense of
Piety. Lord ! My Corruptions I had from Nature, I brought
them with me into the World ; this was thy Grace, thy Gift,
thy undeserv'd Favour. I remember the great Delight I took
in Reading Books of Devotion at Ten Years Old, and said then
to my Mother, If we were as Holy as David how Happy shou'd
we be ? At Eleven Years Old, I us'd to get up from my Bed-
fellows on Sunday Mornings, to say the Prayers for that Day,
out of the Practice of Piety, (which was sent to me as a Token
from a Friend, and which I was pleas'd with, as an Invaluable
Present)."

If only our Gentry could be blessed with Bonnells, there
would be, in the opinion of the Archdeacon, a great change
for the better.

" Were the generality of our Gentry, Bless'd with Instructors of
Mr. Bonnell's Temper and Piety ; his Gravity, Prudence, and
Holy Life ; with those who are acquainted (as he was) with the
Methods of Gentile Conversation ; can Dive into a young
Gentleman's Genius, and rightly form his Mind ; we shou'd
soon see a happy Change in their Principles and Lives."

Grown to man's estate, and married, Mr. Bonnell did not fall
short of the promise of his youth in respect of pious observance.

" For the first thing he did in the Morning, was repeating Psalms
proper for it, as the Sixty Third, the latter part of the Seventy
Third, and Others : And all his Dressing and Washing time he
repeated the 103. 116. and 145th Psalms. In this part of his
Devotions, it was his Desire that his Wife shou'd bear her part :
And when they were over, he at large offer'd up his own private
Prayers in his Closet. The Evening he consecrated to God, as
well as the Morning. His first Exercise (as soon as he cou'd
get free from Company) was repeating the Magnificat, and some
other Hymns of Praise, his Wife in these still joining with him.
Then he usually retir'd into his Closet and with great exactness
examined the state of his soul ; and by Reading and Meditation,
put himself into a right Temper for Prayer ; which was then
perform'd in the fullest and devoutest manner. And he concluded the day, in the same manner that he began it ; repeating
the Fourth and other Psalms, while he undress'd. And when
ready to step into Bed, he kneel'd down and offer'd up a short
Prayer, and then lay down in Peace. This was his Practice so
constantly, that neither the Coldness of the Weather, nor any
Bodily Indisposition or Weariness, made him neglect it."

Mr. Bonnell's duties as Accountant-General were not so
arduous as to prevent the committing of his Meditations to
paper on a fairly extensive scale, as witness the many volumes
of which his biographer speaks.

" And now that I have nam'd his Private Papers, which are so
often referr'd to in the Life ; I must acquaint the Reader, that
Mr Bonnell for many Years together, almost every Day, put down
some devout Thoughts in Writing ; and has left behind him
many Volumes of Meditations and Prayers on every Duty of
Religion ; On the Difficulties and on the Comforts of it ; On
every Virtue and every Sin ; On the Weakness and Wickedness

of Man ; On the Mercy and Goodness of God ; On all the
Mysteries of our Faith, and the wonderful Methods of Divine
Providence to Redeem and Save us ; On Death and Judgment ;
The Pains of Hell, and Joys of Heaven.   These Papers show the
constant Frame and Temper of his Mind ; the Warmth and
Sincerity of his devotions ; what was the greatest Biass of his
thoughts, and how he employed his Retirements.   They contain
his Secret Complaints, Resolutions and desires : with proper
Motives, and earnest Prayers, to confirm him in his duty.   And
all these being Writ only for his own Private use, design'd for no
Eye besides, but that of Heaven ; I cou'd not but conclude, that
they give us the truest view of his Piety, and are the best
Vouchers I cou'd produce for the truth of his Character."

The reader will, doubtless, wish for a specimen of Mr.
Bonnell's Secret Complaints, Resolutions, etc.

" Passions of the Mind are like a Running Gout ; It is the
same Morbific Matter, that shews it self, sometimes in the Knee,
then in the Elbow ; That causes Giddiness in the Head, Sickness
in the Stomach, and Cholicks in the Bowels : It is the same
Morbific manner in the Soul, (Irregular Passions and Unmorti-
fy'd Affections) that shews it self, sometimes in Love, sometimes
in Aversion ; then in Envy then in Ambition ; sometimes it is
Love of Esteem, sometimes of Beauty ; sometimes of Riches and
Grandure, and abundance of like Variety.   Seldom above one
of these is Predominant at a time, and then the Party is free from
others ; and all commonly is as the Bodily Temper varies.
These come and go by fits unaccountably ; but while the Root
of the matter Lives in our Hearts, we are still under the Power
of the Disease ; which we nourish by things that are Pleasing ;
as we do the Gout, or Scurvy, by Meats that please our Palate.
We seldom contract or encrease these Distempers, by eating
of Rhubarb or Aloes ; but by high Sauses and delicious Meats."

. . . . . .

" The last vice, which Religion has to dispossess and Conquer,
is Pride.   Job felt all the Blows of Heaven, with an unwounded
Soul ; and the reason is because the Stroakes of Heaven drive
us to humble our selves before God, dethrone Pride, and calm
the Soul.   But the Perpetual Grateings of an ill natur'd insulting
Man, whom you must every day see, and yet with dread and
boyling of Heart ; this stirs up our natural Choler, foments and

> awakens Pride, and renders our Misery insupportable, 'Tis the
> Boiling of Cholerick Humours in our Body, with which our Soul
> is so tenderly touch'd, and so nearly sympathizes ; that is the
> Sting of all Affliction, and this is Pride."

Equally fatuous, in a different manner, is a book published
by subscription in 1803—three years beyond our period, but
the product of its debased conception of literature. The
author, who styles himself ' Esqr.' on the title-page, lived near
Ballynahinch, and his book was printed and published at
Downpatrick.

HETEROGENEA
or
MEDLEY.

FOR THE BENEFIT OF THE POOR.

———

By John Moore Johnston Esqr.

———

He that hath pity upon the Poor, lendeth unto the Lord ;
and what he layeth out, it shall be paid him again.

———

The humane and gen'rous approve the plan,
Pleasing to God, and good for needy man.

In an introduction of great length, Mr. Johnston explains
the reason for publishing his book, and exhibits his views on
such matters as the prevalence of vice, the abounding of
luxury, the duty of the rich to the poor, the evils of absenteeism,
and many other subjects. One can almost hear him pat
himself for his generosity and righteousness of sentiment.
A few extracts from the introduction will give a touch of his
quality.

> " I intended to have left in my last will ten Pounds to the poor
> for each of the parishes of Lisburn, Ballenderry and Magharadroll,
> but on second thought judged it more judicious to apply that
> summ to their benefit in my lifetime ; and by publishing a Book
> by subscription in order to raise a larger sum, to purchase
> houses or lands for ever, would be more eligible and beneficial ;

the profits to be paid annually to them ; the Minister, Churchwardens, &c.   Trustees or a Committee to conduct the business.
Every one I have spoken to on the subject approves of the
plan. . . .

" All the opulent inhabitants of the different Parishes are
as impulsively called upon as I am, to assist and complete this
charitable undertaking.   Arise then ye great ones of the country,
and help forward the designs of divine providence : true charity
ever dwells with an elevated soul, which takes in all mankind,
sincerely wishing that all who are in error may be reformed ;
in short, true charity detests nothing but sin and vice, and
despises nothing but contracted illiberal notions. . . .

" Piety in the heart will appear in the life.   True religion has
its fruits, no fruit in the Life is a proof that there is no religion
in the heart, for as the cause produces the effects, so the effects
argue and prove the existence of the cause.   Most of the articles
in the following pages are original, what are borrowed are taken
from the best moral writers, Drs. Johnson, Goldsmith, &c. some
of them have appeared in the Hibernian Magazine, Dublin
Evening Post and Belfast Newsletter. . . . .
Every man who reads is in some measure a critic, and may point
out faults and errors in every well-written book ; but it by no
means follows, that he is able to write anything comparable to
the work, which he is capable of censuring.   There are faults
and errors, even in some of the writings of that great critic, and
scholar, Dr. Johnson.

" How often do we all in moments when our natural beneficence predominates, feel a fervent desire to contribute to the
comfort of the miserable, and philanthropic ardour, to promote
the universal happiness of mankind !   How naturally do we
participate the joys and sorrows of those around us !   From
that exquisite sympathy implanted in man by the divine being !
Let us cherish those generous propensities by the alleviation of
human misery, and the steady practice of that justice and charity,
which will in the end exalt our ' self-love, to social, to divine.'
It is the duty of an author to ameliorate the morals of society,
but errors disseminated by his seductive eloquence may deprave
thousands of intelligent beings, under this impression a good
man will consecrate the energies of his mind to virtue, convinced
that it is always a writer's duty to make the world better, if he
possibly can."

After some very fine writing about the superiority of
sunshine in the breast to the fantastic joys of effeminacy and
profligacy . . . great minds shining like lights rising
out of darkness . . . cherishing the good propensities
of the human heart, etc., etc., he expresses regret that he has
not been able to present his subscribers with a work more
deserving their attention, . . . but, notwithstanding his
failure to excite admiration or give superior entertainment,
he has pleasure in reflecting that none of his articles contains
anything injurious to virtue.

He then propounds a scheme for the improvement of
Society,—the evil-minded man is to be starved out, the good
is to have money lent to him.

" I beg leave to present the following hints to the reader's consideration ; should they contribute to convince those who have
it in their power, to bring about an improvement of society,
I shall think that I have not lived in vain ; as a useless speck
in the creation.

" Suppose a meeting of the principal inhabitants of every
parish, in this Kingdom be convened, and resolutions entered
into, that for the advancement of virtue, religion and honest
industry, they will endeavour by their voice, their purse, their
influence and example to promote good morals, loyalty, &c. &c.
That this association will employ such tradesmen, labourers or
servants, only, as shall produce a certificate of their honesty,
sobriety, &c. signed by one or more members. Suppose a fund
should be raised by subscription, a treasurer and committee
appointed, to lend out small sums of money, to industrious good
men of all denominations. I think it may be presumed, that such
or similar institutions, would in a few years contribute more to
reform the manners of this licentious and dissipated age, than
all our charity-balls, card assemblies, houses of correction, jails,
&c."

What might be done by the absentee landlord if he would
come home for good and live within his means, is now discussed,
with much heavy moralising.

" I have mentioned in some of the following essays the dissipation
of the present times. The great degree of luxury to which this

country has arrived within some years, is dreadful to think of.
Times was, when those articles of indulgence, which now every
one aims at the possession of, were enjoyed only by the Lord or
Baron of a district.   Men were then happy and prided themselves
on their submission and loyalty.   If I might presume to dictate,
I would venture to say, that a man of landed property, is never
so respectable as when resident on his estate ;   when improving
his lands and enriching his tenants, when his beneficence may be
read in the looks of the poor.   Honest unadorned freedom is
preferable to studied and fashionable deceit.   The country
Squire lives upon his estate, spends his fortune among his tenants
and his neighbours, pays his bills regularly and enables every
one round him to live comfortably and happily ;   while the fine
Gentleman visits his Domain perhaps but once in the summer
stays there as little as he can help, neglects his grounds, and
leaves his poor tenants at the mercy of perhaps a selfish proud
cormorant of an agent.   .   .   .   Retrenching our expences
when we have lived too fast, is a proof of religion and good sence,
declares an abhorence of our follies, and resolution to be in future
free.   It is very mean and degrading, to make a figure at the
expence of others.   Villains of every denomination have done
it, an honest man would despise the thought, if he finds himself
involved, will pursue the earliest and readiest means to discharge
his debts, and set himself at liberty.   He who has fewest wants,
and is most able to live within himself, is not only the happiest
but the richest man, tho' he may not be a Peer, he is a Lord of
the creation, and may look down with contempt and pity, on
the tinselled sycophant parting with a ducal coronet."

After this parting with the "tinselled sycophant" the
lengthy Introduction draws to a close.   The final words make
it clear that Mr. Johnston does not depend much on the efforts
or influence of the clergy in schemes for the renovation of
Society.

"Should any of the Clergy or others, think these lines, or any in
the following pages too keen or severe, I beg leave to inform
such, that the ideas and some of the words are from the late
Revd. Philip Skelton, Revd. Charles Churchill, Revd. John
Fletcher and Mr. Pope, and should the cap not fit, they are not
obliged to put it on.

> " I know there are many Clergymen and Teachers of all
> denominations, who are exemplary in their lives, conduct and
> doctrine, but fear the majority, as Biam says are wicked, however
> my disposition would tend rather to give praise was it consistent
> with truth, than censure half mankind, but every man who
> speaks or writes, should adhere strictly and literally to truth
> alone "

In very dignified fashion the author reproves " a few
Persons of rank and fortune " who failed to range themselves
on the side of righteousness by subscribing for his book.

> " A few Persons of rank and fortune declined to Subscribe.   I
> shall leave them to their own serious contemplation, when they
> have time to reflect.   I fear too many live in dissipation, vicious
> pleasures, and make a God of this World.   'Tis hoped that the
> charitable and well disposed, who have not Subscribed, will
> now purchase."

It is, indeed, a medley of subjects that fills the Johnston
work.   Some of the articles may contain information about
life conditions of the time in village and country, but the author
can never for long abstain from discourse about the beauty
of goodness, and the methods by which it is to be attained.
A little picture of life and land near the centre of the county
is found in what follows.

> " I have observed that the inhabitants of this part of the County,
> in many respects do not cultivate their land in a beneficial
> manner, they in general pursue the old beaten track or mode of
> their ancestors, in not ploughing sufficiently deep, the conse-
> quence is, that in a dry season, the ground is parched up, and the
> crop not productive.   In answer to which they say, should they
> plough deeper it throughs up too much of the cold tilth, but
> surely the frost in winter, and sun in summer, would meliorate
> it, and next year produce a double crop.   The people in general
> are neither neat nor clean in their habitations, which causes
> fevers, &c. as no living creature can ever enjoy health, or be fit
> for the purposes which God and nature destined him, if in his
> habitation, he does not enjoy cleanliness, and a dry bed.   Were
> the peasantry encouraged by small premiums, to whiten their

houses with lime, to keep dung and stagnated water from their
doors, it would tend to prevent fevers and other disorders. . .

" There is a reading club in Ballynahinch. The club elect
annually by ballot, a Treasurer, Secretary and Librarian ; they
have a great number of valuable books ; the Encyclopedia
Britannica, &c. &c. I have heard much talk about this club ;
but it is as harmless as any public school ; which I know being
a member myself ; but Government are suspicious of clubs,
and no doubt, from the temper and licentiousness of the times,
there is cause. I know there are some republicans in it, who are
tainted with French principles ; I have lately experienced the
dreadful effects of those principles myself. A number of armed
men came to my house at one o'clock at night, broke my windows
and demanded my arms ; I should have fired out at them, but
my wife prevented me, and made the girl give two Guns, two
Pistols and a Sword, through a window to them. Now I ask
all honest loyal men who fear God, and wish their country well,
if there was any liberty in this conduct, (we all know the terrible
consequences that followed, which nearly destroyed the Country.
Many of these men were afterwards hung and transported).

. . . . . .

" The inhabitants of this parish in general, are tolerably well
clad at Church, Meeting, Mass and Fairs, (at the latter the young
women are decked out, equal to ladies of the first rank). They
are regular in their attendance on the public worship of God on
Sundays ; they are not addicted to excessive drinking, nor are
they guilty of common swearing ; tillage and the linnen manufacture, &c. keep them in constant employment ; and a busy
laborious life prevents many excesses. As there is firing in
abundance in this Country, every man sits down to a good fire
of turf at night, and enjoys with comfort, the fruits of his honest
industry."

He has an eye for the beautiful in prospect, and, as is
his manner, will not fail to ' improve ' an occasion.

" From this hill of Ballymullan (my own estate) one can see the
spires of eleven parish Churches, viz. Waringstown, Maralin,
Moira, Hillsborough, Magheragall, Lisburn, Derriaghy, Lambeg,
Drumbo, Newtonbreda, and Belfast. Here is also a full view
of the beautiful range of Mountains, called Devish, Collin, the
white Mountain, Castle-robin, Plover-plain, &c. which are in

general a body of white lime-stone, the surface smooth and always green. The whole is so beautifully sublime, that I may say, a flood of Glory bursts upon our view ; and intoxicates the soul with rapture. But soon will these transitory scenes, the baseless fabrick of a vision or cloud pass away, if we do not honour God, and his righteous laws obey : if we do, shall enjoy more sublime raptures for ever."

From 1764 to 1780 he was in the office of Lord Hertford, under William Higginson, Esqr. As he recalls to memory the traits of this model agent, he drops into poetry.

" had Mr Higginson's judicious, liberal and disinterested conduct been afterwards followed by his successor, there would not have been any contested elections, which distracted and so much confused the town, as the whole tenantry looked upon him as a father, and all adored him.

> A man he was, to all the Country dear,
> And only had, three hundred pounds a year ;
> His like again I ne'er perhaps shall see,
> His greatest fault was much generosity."

It may be allowed to Johnston that his geological ideas are entirely original. He foresees a bad time in store for the counties round Lough Neagh should the bowels of the earth become too full.

" I shall suppose Lough Neagh to be the navel of Ireland, and all the rivers that flow into it, sink down into the bowels of the earth, through this navel which is reasonable to suppose (the lake contains about one hundred thousand acres) as there is no visible appearance that this great body of water is, or can be conveyed to the Sea. Now should the bowels of the earth beneath at any time be filled too full, it must gush up and deluge all the low lands in the counties of Antrim, Armagh, Tyrone, Derry, &c. should this happen suddenly the inhabitants would be all swallowed up ; should it flow gradually they might get up to the tops of the hills and mountains and save themselves. But where get food, they must live on air like the Camelion ; the expected Millenium would then have certainly taken place as to them. This idea I think should alarm the noblemen and gentlemen concerned."

Perhaps the reader has had enough of the medley prose,
and will be willing to follow the author into the domain of
verse. He takes Goldsmith's *Deserted Village*, changes
Auburn to Lisburn, lifts the charms of the original *en bloc*,
and composes ills to suit the locality.

" These were thy charms—but all these charms are fled.
Time was, ere temperance had fled the realm,
Ere luxury sat gutling at the helm,
Ere vanity had so far conquer'd sense,
To make us all wild rivals in expence,
To make ev'ry coxcomb dress against his brother ;
And make one fool strive to outvye another ;
Ere each weak mind was with externals caught,
And dissipation held the place of thought :
Ere gambling Lords in vice so far were gone
To cog the die, and bid the son look on ;
Time was, that men had conscience, that they made
Scruples to owe what never could be paid.
(Our times, more polish'd wear a diff'rent face ;
Debts are an honour ; payment a disgrace),
We better bred, and than our sires more wise,
Such paltry narrowness of Soul dispise,
To virtue ev'ry mean pretence disclaim,
Lay bare our crimes, and glory in our shame.
A time there was, ere Ireland's griefs began,
When every acre of ground maintain'd its man ;
For him light labour, spread her wholesome store,
Just gave what life requir'd, but gave no more.
His best companions, innocence and health.
And his best riches, ignorance of wealth."

But, " as with doubtful pensive steps " he ranges, he has
a more pleasing vision. He sees

" .   .   . Religion in her native charms
Dispersing blessing with indulgent arms,"

and hope for the reformation of the ill-doer springs in his
bosom. Even the ' sycophant,' whom his soul hates, **may**
amend. He will hope to see—

> " Loose wits, made wise, a public good become,
> The sons of Pride an humble mein assume,
> The proffligates in morals grow severe,
> Defrauders just, and Sycophants sincere."

Mr. Johnston is so pleased with his first incursion into poetic fields that he essays a second. Again he takes *The Deserted Village*, again Lisburn is the loveliest village of the plain, again Auburn's former charms are appropriated. But when the poet turns from past to present, he finds, not a decayed, but a richer, happier place and people ; and this without a word to suggest that he had ever heard of such a thing as consistency. The title of the *second* poem is *An Encreased in Contrast to Dr. Goldsmith's Deserted Village.*

> " These were thy charms, now all these charms encreas'd,
> Sweet smiling village, lovliest of the lawn.
> Thy sports much greater, nor thy charms withdrawn.
> Amidst thy bow'rs, just the man's hand is seen,
> And cultivation gladdens all the scene,
> Not one master only holds the whole domain,
> But all Portmore produces golden grain,
> Now thy rich waving corn reflects the day,
> Nor choak'd with sedges, its waters clear'd away,
> Along the glades, no solitary guest,
> No hollow sounding bittern, guards its nest ;
> Fell'd are many stately oak and other trees,
> Scarcely one left, to quiver in the breeze,
> And great encouragement from the landlord's hands,
> He grants leases, farmers improve their lands.
> Princes or lord may flourish, or may fade,
> A breath can make them, as a breath has made,
> But a bold yeomanry, their country's pride,
> Who are industrious, can never be destroyed.
> Now every rood of land, its man maintains,
> And health and plenty cheer our country swains,
> They had what life requir'd, but now much more,
> From their own labour, can have copious store.
> Near yonder groves, 'midst improved lands,
> The Revd. Thomas Higginson's mansion stands,
> A man is he to all the country dear,

And passing rich on fifty pounds a year,
Remote from towns, he runs his Godly race,
Nor ere has chang'd, nor wishes to change his place.
Beside yon lofty fence that skirts the way,
With blooming white thorns profitably gay,
There in his noisy mansion skill'd to rule,
The village master, taught his little school ;
A man severe he was, and stern to view,
I knew him well, and ev'ry truant knew ;
His honour'd name was Zacharia Day,
Who many a glass of whiskey swept away.

      . . . .

Times are better ; riches flow amain,
Lands are improv'd, farmers have double gain,
All discerning men, now must truly note,
Vast improvements, since honest Goldsmith wrote,
Scenes all transporting, set my soul on fire,
And fields and meads, their wonted thoughts inspire,
Each fruitful hedge, inviting themes supplies,
In ev'ry field, harmonious numbers rise,
Here the rich wheat, dispos'd in even rows,
A pleasing view ! on genial ridges grows ;
Its cluster'd heads, on lofty spires ascend ;
And frequent with delightful wavings bend,
There, lower, Barley shoots a tender blade,
And spreads the level plains with verdant shade ;
The wreathing flax extends its bloomy pride,
And flow'ry borders smile on either side.
Potatoe fields in sloping rows to view,
With rich flow'rs of various scents and hue,
Our fertile lands, with milk and honey flow,
And peace and plenty, cheer us all below,
Loyalty fix'd on Ireland's fruitful shore,
A stranger long, but stranger now no more,
Now peace with healing virtue in her wings,
Bids discord cease ! hence every blessing springs,
Thou God above, from whom all blessings flow,
Change the bad hearts of mankind here below,
Make them to know what tends to lasting peace,
Their nature change, ere they shall change their place.
Rejoice then ye people, and on ev'ry tongue,

In strains of gratitude, be praises hung ;
Praises for peace, so great, so good a thing,
Shall Hardwicke reign, and shall not Ireland sing.

. . . .

Brookhill, thou gay enchanting seat,
Thy delightful house, and all improvements great,
Where num'rous birds, their gaudy plumes display,
That dance and flutter, on the trembling spray,
Here vast bodies of limestone, white as snow,
The hills contain, around, above, below.
Still as I pass, fresh objects of delight,
Adorn the way, and pleasing to the sight.
Fair spires and fruitful fields, in train arise,
With mingling grace, to feast the trav'ler's eyes,
Sweet Lisburn's stately buildings, all in view,
Flourishing Belfast, and Hillsborough too.
See ! how the fertile meads lie smiling round,
With fragrant greens, and flow'ry beauties crown'd,
Enamell'd hills, high trees in shady rows,
A finish'd landskip near the town disclose.
A town with pleasure, and with wealth supply'd,
By limpid Lagan's navigable tide.
Yet more than this, superior to the rest,
With sweet society, 'tis highly blest.
Its kind inhabitants, with winning art,
Attract the soul and captivate the heart.
Whose converse, easy, affable, refin'd,
Can both improve and entertain the mind.
Whatever can administer delight,
To glad the ear, or gratify the sight.
And make the hours of life pass smiling round,
O happy Lisburn ! may in thee be found,
There could I pass the dear remains of life,
Remov'd from care, from envy and from strife.
Rejoice Killultagh, and on every tongue,
In strains of gratitude, be praises hung,
Praises, which from the honest heart must spring,
Shall Hertford rule, and shall not Lisburn sing.

. . . .

Lo ! Castlereagh, shines conspicuous in debate,
Curbs lawless pow'r, and prop'd a falling state,

Gave us firm union, its pow'rs combin'd ;
Its benefits prov'd, to ev'ry honest mind,
Of politics and trade, so much master,
And tho' a youth, equal to great Foster,
Sav'd from surrounding foes, his native soil,
And bade union, peace, and freedom smile.
Already shelter'd, by his fostering hand,
The arts revive, and plenty chears the land ;
Gay industry again her toil resumes,
Fair science lifts her head, and genius blooms,
By sad experience, now each Irishman can tell,
With union only, can peace and safety dwell.
'Tis the foundation, on which will stand,
The strength and glory, of a pow'rful land.
May bright Castlereagh live one hundred years,
And rise to greatest height among their peers."

As his reader is, doubtless, amazed at such association
of literary skill with business ability as is presented by Mr.
Johnston, he will inform him as to the acquirement of the
one, and state his methods for conservation of the other.

" I had the use of the late Earl of Moira's library, containing
thirty thousand volumes—Books in all languages, history,
antiquities, arts and sciences, for sixteen years, which equaled
college education ; as when I had leisure I employed myself
in reading all kinds of books."

. . . .

" Some people have observed to me, that they wondered how I
could transact so much business without an assistant, as agent,
receiver, and Seneschal for David Ker and Matthew Forde,
Esqrs. I answer that I generally sup about eight o'clock, take
a draught of porter, beer, or a glass or two of wine, but never
exceed, unless I have company ; my head is clear, and have good
health, (I never had any sickness but the small-pox thank God).
I generally rise about four o'clock in the morning, when I have
Letters or other writing to perform, and write until breakfast,
when much can be done in that space of time, I go to bed about
ten, and have got a good sound sleep before others have thoughts
of going to bed, by this conduct I am enabled to transact much
business, with ease, pleasure, and a tranquil mind."

A characteristic specimen of Down writing and reading
of this debased period is *The Life of the late Rev. Philip Skelton*,
with some curious anecdotes, by Samuel Burdy, A.B., published 1792. The author was curate of Ardglass. He explains
that he had intended to publish at the price of half-a-crown,
but the cost of travelling to collect material, and the unexpected
rise in cost, both of paper and printing, make it necessary for
him to charge 3/9½ per volume. Ostensibly the author writes
of his subject as if the latter were a person of distinction ;
patently he is writing to display his learning, and to make a
little money out of the stories of a somewhat coarse-minded
and, generally, abominably rude clergyman. Burdy makes
much use of the Latin tag.

> " He that gains the prize of literature has passed through a previous
> course of discipline while a boy. Didicit prius extimuitque
> magistrum."
>
> . . . . . .
>
> " The rich may slumber away their time, as they usually do, but
> the calls of nature often rouse the poor, and force them to their
> studies. Hunger is a most powerful spur to genius. Magister
> artis ingeniique largitor venter."
>
> . . . . . .
>
> " Yet he was possessed, I think, with an unreasonable dread of the
> presbyterians ; for he imagined they would have taken his
> living from him before he died, one of them, he said, who was a
> volunteer, told him so. But his apprehensions, we may suppose,
> were partly the effects of old age. Senectus falsâ formidine
> ludit."
>
> . . . . . .
>
> " But a cold phlegmatic reader is not so easily pleased as a hearer
> who is warmed and captivated by the voice, gesticulations and
> countenance of the extempore preacher. Adde vultum habi-
> tumque hominis."

Skelton had written a number of books, which, with
disastrous results to his reputation, are noticed by his
biographer. Of *The Necessity for Tillage and Granaries*,

published in 1741, in the form of a letter to a Member of
Parliament, it is stated :—

> " This letter proves his knowledge in agriculture, and contains
> many excellent precepts, which, if put in practice, would help
> to civilize the South of Ireland, that is sunk in idleness and sloth,
> and ready on every occasion to burst forth into acts of violence
> and disorder. Its style is remarkably perspicuous, though
> somewhat tinctured with vulgarity, which might possibly be
> owing to the nature of the subject it treats of. It has, however,
> been remarked by some judges of agriculture, that many of
> his calculations in favour of the farmer will not hold good in
> practice."

All the books noticed receive treatment on lines somewhat
similar. With a pretence of admiration for the writer, the
faults of his work are unmercifully exposed.

> " Their meaning is often too dark ; the things to which they
> allude are not shown with sufficient clearness."
>
>   . . . . . .
>
> " The style is also somewhat coarse ; words are usually multiplied,
> and arguments drawn out beyond their proper bounds. The
> author, in his attempts at wit, frequently fails ; he is merry
> himself, but the reader unhappy cannot join with him in the joke."
>
>   . . . . . .
>
> " His attempts at wit are certainly laudable, as employed in a
> good cause, but they are not so successful as I could wish."
>
>   . . . . . .
>
> " It consists of a variety of short observations, some of which, if
> written in an easy style, would be agreeable."
>
>   . . . . . .
>
> " To this are added *Some Thoughts on Common Sense*, in which
> there are some attempts at wit not always successful ; for his
> wit, though excellent in company, seemed to evaporate when
> communicated to paper. The rest of this column consists of
> thirteen hymns with a poetic introduction to them, and a Latin
> poem, which appear rather calculated to enliven his own piety
> in private than to excite devotion in others."

Having damned his subject's reputation in literature by
such comments on his writings, what compensatory picture

of a country clergyman's life has Burdy to offer? Only such as is formed by a long series of anecdotes of character like to the following :—

" He went once in vacation on a visit to Mourne, and showed there at a public meeting many feats of activity ; running up turf-stacks, like a cat, without stopping till he came to the top, which amazed everyone present. When he saw them surprised at his agility, he challenged any of them to play long-bullets with him. They then produced, after some hesitation, a thin poor looking body, who, they said, would play with him. Skelton viewed his puny antagonist with contempt. He looked down on him, as Goliath did on David. ' Is it you,' he said, ' that's to play with me ? ' ' Yes,' the man replied. ' Well, well,' he said, ' we'll soon settle this matter.' Skelton then took the bullet, and made a huge throw, quite confident of success. The little fellow then, in his turn, took the bullet, and threw it about twice as far as Skelton, who stood in amaze, as he imagined he could beat him easily. He declared he heard the bullet whizzing past him, as if it had been shot out of a cannon ; he threw it with such force. Thus was he vanquished by the puny body he despised. People are not always to be judged by appearance ; hence too much confidence is often foiled."

. . . . . .

" He also went as often as convenient to see Mr Pringle . . . where he spent his time very pleasantly. On his first coming there he had a curious adventure which deserves to be related. Mr Pringle's father, who was then alive, being very old and dot-ing, was unfit to manage his house, which was left to the direction of his son, who in fact was master of all. Consequently, he had a right to ask what company he thought proper. This gentle-man invited Mr Skelton to dine with him, and Archdeacon East, who had lately come to the parish, telling them his father was doting, and not to be offended at anything he said. When he introduced the Archdeacon to his father he said, ' Father this is Archdeacon East the clergyman of the parish, who has come to dine with us to-day.' ' Ay, ay,' observed the old man, ' come East, come West, come North, come South, you all come here to fill your bellies.' When dinner was brought in the old man refused to sit at the table with them, but took his seat in an adjoining room with the door quite open, where he watched

them to see how much they would eat. Mr Pringle placed
Skelton just opposite the door, desiring him to eat voraciously,
and take large mouthfuls. Accordingly he began to devour
up the dinner, as if he were starving, stuffing his mouth with
huge lumps of meat and bread. The old man staring at him for
a while, at last cried to his son, ' Johnny, Johnny, see that
fellow, he'll eat you up.' Skelton then shouted out aloud to the
servant, ' Give me a tumbler of wine,' whispering to him to put
some water in it. ' Ah, ah ! ' the old man cried, ' a whole
tumbler of wine ; Johnny don't give it to him.''

. . . . .

" His strict and rigid economy enabled him to give much away.
His curate, who lodged many years in the same house with him,
told me, he often saw him sitting up in his bed in the morning
mending his breeches. He had a trashbag, as they call it, in
which he kept needles, thread, and such like articles, to put a
few stitches, if necessary, in his clothes.''

. . . . .

" He then took lodgings with one Carshore, a low farmer in the
village . . . His situation here was even more incon-
venient than at Plunket's. He had indeed wretched lodgings.
The floor of the room was not only earthen, but also so uneven,
that he was forced to get a table with two long and two short
feet to fit it. He also found it necessary to buy a pair of tweezers,
to pick the dirt out of the keal (kail-broth) which they served
up to dinner.''

. . . . .

" He was fond of a good horse, and generally had the best saddle
horses that could be got, though he was remarkably awkward
on horseback. For he turned out his toes, and took no hold with
his knees, but balanced himself in the stirrups, like a man on
slack-wire ; so that when the horse began to trot, he jogged up
and down like a taylor.''

. . . . .

" Returning once from Lisburn with his hat tied over his face he
met with his tithe-farmer near Enniskillen, and lifting up the
brim of his hat, he saw him, and said, ' Is this you George Irwin ? '
' Yes,' replied George. ' Can you give me a guinea ? ' ' I can.'
' Can you give me a shilling ? ' ' I can.' ' O then,' said he,' I'm
as rich as a Jew, I'm as rich as a Jew.' ''

" Having a few of his parishioners with him one evening at his
lodgings, he happened to fall asleep ; and then, while one of
them blowed his nose very violently with his handkerchief,
another one pluckt the handkerchief smartly, so as to make the
noise very shrill. This instantly wakened Mr Skelton, who
said, ' What, you're blowing a trumpet in my room to insult
me,' and then starting up, he said he would beat them, and
turned them out of the room. However, he received them
again into favour, on their humbly begging to be reconciled to
him, for they did not wish to fall out with him, his company was
so agreeable."

. . . . . .

" I heard of a curious answer an old woman of Pettigo made him,
when he was just going to marry her to a young man. ' What's
the reason,' he said to her, ' you're doing this ? 'tis for your
penny of money he marries you, sure he hates you, for you're
both old and ugly.' ' Dont despise,' she replied, ' the Lord's
handiwork '; meaning herself."

. . . . . .

" When any of his poor relations came to see him, he told them
freely they wanted to get something from him."

But Skelton was rude to superiors as well as inferiors.
When the Bishop of Clogher promoted him to the living of
Fintona, Co. Tyrone, in 1766, Skelton visited His Lordship
to thank him for his promotion, and finished his expression
of gratitude by saying, " But, my Lord, you are only a puppet
in the hands of God Almighty." The Bishop was big-hearted
enough to overlook the rudeness of such an uncalled-for
remark, and, sometime after, paid Skelton a visit at Fintona,
arriving on Sunday morning. As he entered the room, the
Bishop took off his hat, but Skelton, who had put his on to
go to church, remained covered. Not every Bishop was so
forgiving. Another to whom he spoke without due respect
declined ever after to admit him to his presence.

After narration of a great deal more of like character the
thought enters the head of the author that perhaps his readers
may, from it all, form a low opinion of the subject of the

biography, and to the expression of the fear follows a lame
reason for appearance of the chronicle.

> " It may be remarked, that all this tends to degrade the person
> whose life I write ; but in my opinion it only shows, that he had
> his own peculiarities, to which great characters are in general
> more subject than ordinary men."

Burdy roughly carpentered much wooden verse (*Ardglass,
or the Ruined Castles*, Dublin, 1802), and such part of it as he
enriched by classic ornament, looks better than it deserves.
Witness :

> " Or view AENEAS, or sweet MARO'S page,
> The pious captain of the heroic age,
> On his broad shoulders bear his aged sire,
> Thro' hostile weapons, and thro' flames of fire,
> Place him far distant in a safe retreat,
> With young IULUS, fav'rite child of fate,
> Thro' stormy seas, and various perils tost,
> Attain at length AUSONIA'S happy coast,
> Subdue bold TURNUS in a single fray,
> And gain LAVINIA, and the Latin sway."

But when it was not possible to apply the decoration to
any great extent, as, for example, in his *Excursion to the Isle
of Man*, the sloppiness of material and workmanship is displayed.   He is at Ardglass,

> " In Down's fair county, on its eastern shore,
> Where o'er the rocks the foaming surges roar,"

and there his observant eye lights on some travelling tinkers
and their belongings.

> " The tinkers too, for Mona's Isle design'd,
> Frequent the town, and wait the fav'ring wind ;
> There have I seen them with their wives and lasses,
> Their smiling babies, and their little asses."

A puff of wind on the way helps him to a little bit of classic
allusion—

> " Tho' vex'd by EURUS, and his surly band,"

regrettably insufficient to dignify the mass of the Excursion.
He raises his eyes :

> " Then various birds with wonder we survey
> Attend the pilgrims on their watery way ;
> Of these the gull and gannet are the chief,
> Who eat them up as glutton would roast beef.
> The gull, like diver, rides the wave secure,
> As huntsman rides the courser o'er the moor."

The attended pilgrims, which are eaten up, are the herrings.
Alas ! these pilgrims are food for more than gull and ·gannet.

> " Herring's the food for Mona's greedy sons,
> Who eat them up as fast as butter'd buns,
> As lions eat up kids, the bones and marrow,
> Or hungry hawks devour the little sparrow."

From herring the thoughts of the poet turn, naturally, to
other abounding useful fish ; of which a reasonably complete
list is supplied.

> " But on our shore the useful fish abound,
> Both those that swim, and those that skim the ground,
> The speckled mackerel, and the gurnet red,
> The haddock firm, and cod with wondrous head,
> The gentle whiting, and delicious sole,
> Ta'en by a net extended on a pole,
> The flowk, the ray, the plaise, the bret so nice
> And charming turbot of enormous price,
> With lobsters, crabs, and others small and great,
> In verse or prose too tedious to relate."

—and so, perhaps, may be any more of Mr. Burdy's beauties
of verse.

The verse conventions of the time are well displayed
in *Flora's Banquet*, by J. Tisdall, published by subscription
in Belfast in 1782. This is a collection of poems, songs,
sonnets, etc., mostly in praise of the fair. Where the ladies
are real flesh and blood they bear their baptismal names, and
sometimes, by a very common convention of the time, by

initial and final letters and a rhyme, the surname is disclosed,
as in one of the three examples which follow.

" On Lagan's pleasant banks I saw
      The sweetest maid on earth,
My frozen heart began to thaw
      And gave sweet passion birth.
'Twas in the fragrant month of June,
      Just driving by the shore,
Ah gra mugh-chree, mugh choline ogue,
      Ma *Dolly* ma sthore.

When first I saw My Dolly move
      Her looks struck such command,
I thought it was the Queen of Love
      Had rose from Lagan's strand.
Such awe-inspiring elegance
      I ne'er beheld before,
Ah gra mugh-chree, mugh choline ogue,
      Ma *Dolly* ma sthore."

SONG,
addressed to a Young Lady of Belfast,
(last two stanzas).

IV.

" Her face was form'd by Beauty's Queen,
      Apollo wit bestow'd.
The graces fram'd their sister's mien,
      Her heart by Dian glow'd.

V.

When this was done they call'd on Jove
      To name the fair—but Pallas
Proclaim'd sweet Grace the Queen of Love,
      And call'd the charmer W . . . . . e " (Wallace).

SONG,
inscribed to Miss . . . . . of The Grove,
(last two stanzas).

IV.

" Was I possess'd of India's store,
      Or (poet-like) confounded poor,
      I'd feast—or beg from door to door
            Contented so I'd Julia.

v.

Thrice happy youth, immortal Jove,
Whom you would crown with Julia's love,
A foretaste of the joys above,
        Is lovely Julia L . . . s " (Lewis).

Where the ladies are of the imagination, their names, as
is proper in verse of this kind, are Clarinda, Delia, Mira,
Amanda, and Celia. The men are Damon, Lycas, Strephon,
and Corydon. The country of their loves is furnished with
all the ' properties ' required by pastoral verse—tree-topp'd
hills, smiling meads, purling streams, cooling shades, limpid
springs, sweet retreats. Here " op'ning flow'rs their sweets
exhale,"—" feather'd warblers fill the grove,"—here sounds
" the rustick pipe." Here, too, alas, is " love's fest'ring arrow"
in a bleeding breast. The shepherd, for love of Laura, will
say good-bye to his fellows.

" Then shepherds I'll bid you adieu,
    No more my complainings shall tease,
The pity I meet with from you
    But hightens my hopeless disease.
To the bosom of some gloomy grove
    Alone I'll in silence retire
(The last sad resource of true love),
    And blessing fair Laura, expire."

Or he will go to the war, for Polly, and be killed.

" And if pre-doom'd to press an hostile plain
'Midst gasping crowds the earliest victim slain,
More than his own thy pangs shall wound his mind
Who leaves his Polly and his peace behind."

Or, for Amanda's peace, he will consent to be extinguished.

" O stay, my muse, nor bear the plaintive tale,
    Lest it disturb Amanda's tender breast.
O let my sharpest suff'rings still prevail
    Or let me die, so she be ever blest."

Or, for an unnamed love, he will die at the end of the last verse.

> " O spare my reason, fond illusion,
>   Nor thus with fancied raptures move ;
>   My sorrows all are near conclusion ;
>   O spare my reason, tyrant Love !
>   Then triumph o'er thy tortur'd slave,
>   I soon shall triumph—in the Grave ! "

The pastoral and classic conventions lingered long in local verse. As late as 1833 a Down versifier, Henry Graham, of Downpatrick, published a book of verse, nearly the whole edition being absorbed by the country round Strangford Lough. The book takes its title, *The Abbey*, from the longest poem. This composition begins with matters which date very far back,—before Creation, indeed.

> " Ere time was measur'd by the sun,
>   Long ere the radiant orb had run
>   His first majestic motion round,
>
>   .   .   .   .   .
>
>   The Omnipotent devis'd the plan
>   Of *Nature's* being and of *Man*."

Eden appears and disappears. Across the stage the poet hurries the great of history—nations or individuals—until Patrick comes to Down. The pagan wilts under his preaching, and Ireland becomes the Isle of Saints, but not for long. Forty-six pages after Patrick come the Danes, and the pagan wins, until

> ".   .   . the aged Borhume
>   Rose to set Hibernia free."

Then event follows event (the poet moralising all the time) until, after one hundred and eighty-two pages, comes the Judgment Day with its dread scenes, and Downpatrick comes to an end.

> " Angels arrest each starry pole,
>   Suns, systems, worlds, disorder'd roll,
>   Their seas, skies, mountains, disappear,
>   And heaven begins the ' eternal year.'

> Old Chaos claims his ancient reign,
> And Nature's ruin proves our gain,
> Then Dunum and our Abbey's fame,
> Which nine times mock'd devouring flame,
> Shall end her being and her name."

The miscellaneous pieces exhibit all the exuberances of
the pastoral style. Birds are " the feather'd choirs " which
" glad the sweet embow'ring grove " with " their lively notes
harmonious." There are sounds of woe in the air, and the
poet asks :—

> " . . . does the sympathising crowd inhale
> The soft contagion of some love-lorn swain,
> Whose agonizing sighs now load the gale ? "

He takes his walks abroad, in the late afternoon, and strange
things happen. The woodland allows a song to fall, and
Philomels, ' resigning ' their mellow notes, prolong the strains.

> " Now the ev'ning rays declining,
>   Gently fall the Woodland Song ;
> Mild their mellow notes resigning,
>   Philomels the strains prolong."

On the same day, earlier, the bees were busy.

> " Hear the buzz of bees, now humming,
>   Sipping nectar as they stray,
> In the bells, mellifluous, bumming,
>   Bear th' ambrosial sweets away."

But the author is not always rejoicing with the birds
and lambs, by purling streams. He has a *flair* for the tragic
and melancholy, and writes elegies and mournful tales of
accident. He has, however, a fair idea of what comfort
means, and for himself, in *The Wish*, calls for

> " A rural cottage snug and neat,
>   Where honeysuckles creep along ;
>
>   .   .   .   .   .
>
> A velvet lawn my cot before,
>   Where playful children may resort ;
> A little court around my door,
>   Where they with cheerful glee may sport ;

With a few acres fruitful ground,
  Where two domestic cows may feed ;
And gentle sheep may graze around,
  Protected by a neighing steed."

Here, " with chosen books and faithful friend," he thinks his
Muse and flute might lend their charms " to make more sweet
the vernal hour."

Towards the end of the eighteenth century, Ireland, as
a field for adventurous travellers, was discovered. From
association with the books published by the brave explorers,
must be removed the solid works of the practical Arthur
Young, and the lively unconventional record of the walking
Frenchman, de Latocnaye. With these exceptions the late
eighteenth-century travel books of Ireland are unmitigated
trash. Pompous and pretentious as is the *Journal of a Tour
in Ireland* by Sir Richard Colt Hoare, Bart., or banal as is
the *Tour in Ireland in* 1775 by Richard Twiss, F.R.S., they
are worth a scanning, if only to show what our forefathers
were willing to pay for and read. Hoare's preface opens with
bombast.

> " The spirit and even the power of *foreign* travel is now checked ;
> we can no longer trace on the spot, those classical scenes des-
> cribed to us by the Ancient Poets and Historians, and which
> in our younger days of study, we even *read* with enthusiasm ;
> we can no longer in safety ascend the steps of the CAPITOL,
> wander peacefully along the luxuriant shores of BAIAE or
> MISENUM ; even the frozen regions of MONT BLANC are inter-
> dicted to us by the ferocious decrees of a CORSICAN DESPOT."

These great men, in visiting Ireland at the opening of the
nineteenth century, took for themselves as much credit for
bold emprise as they might, in the fifteenth, who went to
Samarkand.

Twiss's Tour is, perhaps, the most wretched piece of
descriptive writing ever printed to the loss of trusting subscribers. Where the small book is not wholesale quotation,
it is generally bald and uninteresting and useless statistics—

how many thousands of boys were born in a certain hospital
in Dublin, in eighteen years ; how many girls, how many
the births of twins,—how many earls, viscounts, and barons
Ireland owns,—how many windows are in Trinity College,—
how many arches has Essex Bridge,—how high rises the tide
in the Liffey, etc., etc. The town of Belfast is disposed of in
three and a half lines, and, true to his ideas of the value of
numbers and measurements, Twiss tells in his three and a
half lines that the town has a bridge of 21 arches. Newry
has even shorter notice ; all that he can say for it is, " I found
nothing to observe there but two shabby bridges."

But in the barren desert of useless, uninforming statistics
are a few cases of personal expression, and observation of
character and custom.

" What little the men can obtain by labour, or the women by their
spinning, is shortly consumed in whisky, which is a spirituous
liquid resembling gin. Shoes or stockings are seldom worn by
these people who seem to form a distinct race from the rest of
mankind."

. . . . . .

" It might be better perhaps if the lower classes of people throughout Europe were neither taught to read nor write, excepting
those few who discover evident marks of genius ; those acquisi-
tions only creating new wants and exciting new desires, which
they will seldom be able to gratify, and consequently rendering
them less happy than otherwise they might be."

. . . . . .

" As to the customs of the Irish gentry I know of only three. The
first is, that they have constantly boiled eggs for breakfast with
their tea. The second is the universal use of potatoes which
form the standing dish at every meal ; these are eaten by way
of bread,—even the ladies indelicately placing them on the table
cloth. The third is that of forging frankes."

. . . . . .

" As to the natural history of the Irish species, they are only
remarkable for the thickness of their legs, especially those of the
Plebeian females."

The inept, when very inept, can be very amusing.

CHAPTER XVI.

Hospitality and Housekeeping

HOUSEKEEPING notes for the very early years of our two-century period are not available. Of the easily perishable details of old-time costs of food, dress, service, and furniture, in Down households, the greater number quoted in this book have been discovered among the papers at Castle Ward. These, dating from the end of the seventeenth century till the middle of the eighteenth, relate to expenditure there and at the old house of the Hamiltons at Bangor ; and it has been deemed best that they should appear in the picture of Michael Ward and his surroundings (Chapter XI.). A much fuller, but later, statement of housekeeping costs, is found by travelling with a Down lady a few miles beyond North Down boundary to Castle Upton, where Sophia, Judge Ward's daughter, began her married life as wife of Arthur Upton ; and it may be taken that the South Antrim accounts represent costs and conditions obtaining in the neighbouring parts of Down.

Mrs. Clotworthy Upton, later Lady Templeton, on the creation of her husband, Baron, in 1776, sister-in-law of Arthur Upton above-mentioned, was Woman of the

Bedchamber to Queen Charlotte from 1772 till 1778, and her household accounts, most accurately kept, and apparently in her own handwriting, exhibit income as well as expenditure. The salary attached to her position was £285 per annum, payable quarterly, and from each payment the Treasurer, Mr. Stone, appears to have deducted, for himself, one shilling in the pound. The perquisites of a Woman of the Bedchamber realised quite considerable sums. In her notes for the years 1772-3 Mrs. Upton shows receipts on account of sales of the Queen's cast-off garments.

"Recd. for a Gold & Silver stuff Gown & Petticoat
with Trimming left on £36 15   0

For a Suit of Point lace, viz. Lappets, Ruffles Ruff
and Tucker 31 10   0

For a full suit Fine Bruselles Lace   50   0   0

Recd. of Mrs Gray for 3 pair of the Queen's stays   2 14   0

For 1 doz. p^{rs} dirty Gloves   3   0

Two p^r old Slippers 3/-   6   0

Mrs. Upton's servants at London or Tunbridge were paid at much higher rates than ruled at home. The following items belong to the English establishment. It will be noted that the footmen are always 'James,'—the real name follows in brackets.

1772 " Apl. 20.   Servants' Wages &c.

For a fortnight's lodging for the Cook
when she had the Itch   5   0

Allow'd her for her Board that fortnight   12   0

Nov. 18.   Pd. James (John) Small his year's
wages due September 22 last   3   0   0

For finding his green Plush and Leather
Breeches & Boots as by agreement ..   2 12   6

Given him for wearing his old cloaths to
save ye new ones   10   6

Dec. 8.   P^d M. Noah, Housekeeper her year's
wages & for Tea &c. 12 12   0

1778 " Oct 21. To James (Giles) Wilson one year's
            wages due yesterday 14 0 0
            To finding his 2 pr. Livery Breeches &
            Boots 2 12 6

     Nov. 28. Susan Peach a year's wages due
            yesterday including Tea & Sugar   ..   10 0 0

     Nov. 28. Alice Wilson, Cook, her year's wages   10 10 0

     Dec. 11. Sarah Damant Housemaid, a year's
            wages due ye 9th 7 0 0
            Given her above her wages 7 0

Miscellaneous expenses of the English accounts are—

1772 " Sept 5. To Lucy, a bill for 25 yards Tabbynet
            she bought me at Dublin 6 6 11
            1½ oz. Cotton thread for Garters   ..   3 0
            2 Pots Miss Keck's Pomatum 2 0
            1 pr Tanned Leather Gloves 2 2

     Oct 28. To Mrs Fry, Mantua maker for put-
            ting new sleeves &c to a Jesuitte   ..   3 6

     Nov. 12. Given Sukey for working me a black
            catgut Hood 5 0
            2lbs of Bohea Tea 1 2 0
            ¼lb Soutchong Tea 3 0
            1 pr. Green Gloves, Kid. 2 0
            1lb best & 3lb Common hair powder   ..   2 5½

1774 " Aug 6. 1 pr black leather Pumps 5 0
            6 pr White French Kid Gloves..   ..   18 6
            1,000 Middling Pins and do Short Whites   1 6
            1 pr Tabby Stays 2 5 0
            A Catgut to make a cap   7
            Pd for an umbrella bought at a shop in
            Cornhill 14 0
            1 Secondhand Pinchbeck Watch 1 18 6
            To John for a Flambeau Frame   ..   1 0
            2 doz. Flambeaux and Oil 3 0 5
            E. Bilks bill for two half Ream of Writing
            Paper 14 0

On the receipt side an entry appears which shows that
Mrs. Upton did not allow a careless laundress to go unpunished.

1772 " July. Rec^d. of ye Washerwoman at Tunb.
for a night shift she lost 6 0

At home the payments are accurately classified for comparison of expenditure under each head year by year. The
headings are—

> " Bread and Flour
> Groceries, Eggs, Cheese, &c. &c.
> Cellar
> Poultry and game
> Fish
> Butchers' meat
> Sundries for the House
> Apothecary and poor and sundries
> Servants' wages
> Servants' livery and clothes
> Apparel for ourselves and children."

Extracts from a few of these classified accounts are here
given. The dates are, after Lady Templeton's return from
London, mostly in the period 1779-81.

" Groceries, &c.

Brown Sugar per stone	..	..	10	3
China Oranges ,, doz.	..	..	2	2
Coffee ,, lb.	..	..	1	10
Green tea ,, ,,	..	..	11	4½
Lemons ,, doz.	..	..	1	6
Lump Sugar ,, lb.	..	..	1	1
Currants ,, ,,	..	..		9
Raisins ,, ,,	..	..		7
Carraway Seeds,, ,,	..	..		8
Watchlights ,, ,,	..	..	3	0
Wax Candles ,, ,,	..	..	3	3
Best Soap ,, stone	..	..	6	5

Vinegar appears very often in this section, and the use
of tea seems to have been general.

" Cellar.

Rum per gallon	..	..	..	5	o
Brandy ,,	..	..	..	6	8
Malt (in large quantity at per ' bowle ')			1	9	o
Hops per lb	..	..	..	1	8

One entry for 1 gal. rum has a note explaining that it was
" for labourers in ye drains." Rum figures rather largely in
the accounts, sometimes to the extent of three gallons in one
month.

" Poultry and Game.

1 Pullet & 2 Chickens	..	..		10	
A pair of rabbits	..	..	..	6	
6 Chickens @ 2d (others at 2½ and 3d)	..	1	0	
4 ducks at 4d	..	..	..	1	4
2 Turkeys ..	..	..	..	2	4
1 Setter Dog	..	..	..	1 14	1½
3 Geese ..	..	..	..	3	3
Powder & Shot	..	..	..	9	

" Fish.

1 Salmon 21lb. @ 2d lb.	..	..	3	6
1 ,, 13 ,, @ 2¼d ,,	..	..	2	5
1 hundred oysters	..	..	..	1	0

" Butchers' Meat.

1 Sheep 59lb @ 2¼d per lb.	..	..	11	1
6 score and 2lb pork @ 2¼ per lb	..	1	5	5
1 quarter beef 78lb @ 2½d per lb	..	16	3
A hind quarter of Mutton 12½ lb @ 2d per				
lb	..	..	..	..	2	1

" Apothecary, Poor, and Sundries.

Poor Jan 3/3. Feb 16/9½
     Apl. 2/8¼ May 14/2¼
     June 2/8½ July 7/3

Mr Cormick's bill for Medicines for 1778	4	13	11
Mr Hamilton—painter for my picture	..	6 16	6
A ream gilt paper	..	..	..	10	0

To Margaret Bryson, for spinning 16lb. Wool @ 5d	6	8
To Jane Owen for spinning 24lb Wool ..	10	0
„ Spinning 10 hanks Linen Yarn @ 4d ..	3	4
The Rat Catcher as p^r receipt in book ..	11	4½
A p^r Scales for weighing Gold	13	0
Caroline's first tooth	1 2	9
Subscription to a book for curing the bite of a dog	1 2	9
2 Foreign letters	10	0

Nothing appears in the record to explain why Caroline's first tooth cost so much.

" Servants' Wages.

The Gardener p^r y^r	10	0	0
Kitty	6	8	6
Biddy	4	11	0
Nancy housemaid	4	0	0
Given to her extraordinary		2	8½
William Meikle	6	8	6
Kitchen maid	3	0	0
Nancy Housemaid (see above)	5	0	0

" Apparel for ourselves and children.

1779	A black bonnet	14	1
	A Chintz gown	4 11	0
	A striped English chintz night gown ..	1 13	7
	A yard knotted tabby for shoes ..	7	0½
	Bill for riding hat	1 16	3½
	Clothiers' bill for my Lord's coat ..	3 0	8
	bill for my Lord's wig	1 15	2½
	a pr shoes	5	5
	11lb hair powder, box and carriage from Dublin	8	2½
	Galt Smith's bill for my Lord's black coat	3 5	8
1780	200 black pins	1	1
	8¾ yrds linen for shifts @ 2/8	1 3	4

Although at this period the use of tea was very general, and special payments appear in the servants' accounts of the

Templetown household, as " Allowance for Tea," there are
indications in Down documents of not much earlier date, that
tea drinking was, as indulgence, classed with the dram habit.
Charles Brett, writing to Judge Ward from Bangor, in 1747,
anent a proposal of one, Cawdon, to take land, says :—

" . . . Thom. Cawdon's Sons are not yet returned and I am
affraid whatever proposal they make I shall think very ill of it,
if the Glasgo Brother be not the Principal, the other is a very
idle spark & hath marry^d a Scotch gentlewoman too proud to
work ; She a drinker of tea & he of drams & Ale."

A few interesting notes of careful housekeeping are found
among the letters of Mrs. Savage, of Portaferry, addressed
to her husband. They all betray anxiety about expenses,
and fear that her husband may waste money in unnecessary
purchases. The date of one is 1738, others are undated,
but all may be taken as belonging to the second quarter of
the eighteenth century.

1738 " Dec. 5. I am much obliged for the shoes you sent me
but I must beg my dearest wont buy me anything more but what
I sent for you will want to lay out your money now another way."

. . . .

(undated). " I would not have you buy me any nightgown for
if I was to lay out money I would much rather lay it out on
moveables. I dont desire it either way."

Was it a green damask nightgown that Mr. Savage had
proposed to buy for his wife ? The letter of Rev. Vere
Lonergan to Mrs. Ward (p. 368) speaks of the bishops' nightgowns of green damask, and, alone, this might be taken as
imaginative writing—the cleric's conception of the height of
luxury. But in one of his letters to his son, Bernard, Judge
Ward gives information apparently asked for,

" eight yards of green damask makes my nightgown."

from which it appears that, about this time, the nightgowns
of the mighty and of good society were of green damask.

Other letters of Mrs. Savage to her husband, at Dublin, betray the same fear that he will spend money unnecessarily.

" if you come on Wednesday stage let me know it by Tuesday that I may send your horses to Kinnegad to meet you. You wrote me that the (they) wrote from Portaferry for a great many things by the cooks orders dont buy them. You will order Hugh Mullin to buy at Mr Kennedy's one pound of capers one pound of samphire & two pound of salt peter & a crock of anchovies which is all you will want so dont buy any more for if people was to buy everything that servants desire they would be very extravagant and soon run out their fortunes."

. . . .

" Dont hire any cook for I think you had better have let alone the gardener till you had got one from Scotland. . . . bring me half a dozen of Duble glazedfinger gloves & a dozen of chainey oranges."

Very complete accounts of servants' wages in Down near the end of the eighteenth century are found in the household books of a later Mrs. Savage, of Portaferry House. Her accounts from 1781 to 1797 show wages paid to

" Maids (duties unstated)			3 0 0 to	3	8	3 per ann
Ladies' maids ..	..		4 11 0 to	8	0	0 per ann
House Maids ..	..		4 0 0 to	5	0	0 per ann
Kitchen maid	..	..	..	..	3	0 0
Charge of Fowl	..	..	..	..	3	0 0
Man Cook ..	..	..	..	..	12	0 0
Butler ..	..	..	..	..	13	13 0
Footman ..	..	..	..	..	9	2 0
Postilion, ' to keep him self in shirts, shoes and						
stockings ..	..	..	..	..	3	8 3
Coachman ..	..	..	..	..	11	7 6
2nd Postilion ' to keep him self in Boots, Britches and						
Linen ' ..	..	..	..	..	5	13 9
Groom ..	..	..	..	..	8	0 0
Helper ..	..	..	..	..	6	5 0
Cowkeeper ..	..	..	..	..	3	0 0

The practice at Portaferry seems to have been to pay instalments of wages, as employees may have required, with

complete settlements on parting—the employers acting as
bankers for their servants. Another of our grandmothers'
fictions—the general reliability of domestics of old time and
their long service—is exploded by Mrs. Savage's private
notes made in her wages book when she has made up the
accounts of discharged or discharging servants. Some of
her maids were all that could be desired,—Mary McDonnell
and Nancy Beard were each eighteen years in Portaferry
House, and the notes against their names are alike—" Good
servant, sober, steady, honest, quiet "—but the terms of service
are, in general, as short as in modern times, and the lady's
criticisms are often unfavourable.

> " Elizabeth Keley (2 years) discharged by her own desire. She
> is sober, Honest, Quiet but not a very good housemaid.
>
> " Mary Walker (1 year)—own desire. She is a very good Servant
> and very honest. Neither sober nor quiet. I willingly part
> with her."

In six months Mary Walker was re-engaged, and this
time she remained for one and a half years, but the parting
remark is not improved :

> " a very good servant, she drinks and is very bad tempered in
> that situation."

Other comments on parting maids are—

> " She is by no means a good servant, very negligent of everything
> in her charge. Honest and Quiet."
>
> " She is a good servant when she pleases. She is neither sober
> nor quiet. I believe honest."
>
> " She is sober honest and quiet. Lazy and unwilling to assist
> in the house."
>
> " She is sober honest, Dirty, Disorderly and pert."

The earlier Mrs. Savage's mention of the gardener introduces the subject of garden expenses. These began to be of
magnitude in the eighteenth century, when it became the
fashion to lay out grounds on an extensive scale, and to form

collections of rare and curious plants.   A survey of Down
(date about 1740) speaks of Castle Ward as

> " the seat of the Honourable Mr Justice Ward, where handsome
> improvements in Parks, Gardens, Canals, & Decoy, and Great
> Plantation are already made and more designed."

Sir William Petty notes the great improvement in gardening in Ireland, representing this in figures between the years
1650 and 1675 as an advance from one to four.   Garden lovers
will be interested in the notes following, all relating to Down
gardening.

A gardener to his employer :—

> 1703 (old style) " Feb 8.   the Low Borders is planted with Cristle
> Gooseberrys and black Gooseberrys and the best white Cor^t."
>
> (currant.)

The same gardener sends to his master in Dublin

> " A list of whatt Seed the as waning (there is wanting)
>> Caritt seed half a pound
>> pasnips 6 ounces
>> Leeks 2 ounce
>> redish 4 ounce
>> Turnups 4 ounce
>> Cabich Leattis half an ounce
>> Selitia halfe an ounce
>> Long Cowcumber halfe an ounce
>> Short Cowcumber halfe an ounce
>> Indifi halfe an ounce
>> Cardis halfe an ounce
>> time halfe an ounce
>> sweet margoram halfe an ounce
>> Isope halfe an ounce
>> Moss Millon seed halfe an ounce
>> Dill halfe an ounce
>> Union seed 3 quarters of a pound
>> Clearie seed halfe an ounce
>> Savoy seed an ounce
>> White Beet 2 ounces
>> Indian hotspur pea 2 quartes
>> Windzor Bean 2 Quarts
>> Dutch Sparrowgrass seed 2 ounce
>> Silver fir Ever green Oak Ekorns and bey Berrys what you
>> plese."

Hans Montgomery, of Springvale (now Ballywalter),
asks a friend to order for him some fruit trees, saying :

"I know you'll neither forgett your own Garden nor y^r friends."

He has made his selection, as below, from a catalogue, but
asks his friend to alter the order as he may think fit.

" Paradise Aples		Dwarfe Pears	
Golden Pipine	4	Portugal	4
Golden Russet	4	,, Royal	2
Non Parell	4	Orange Bergamy	2
Jerusalem	2	,, Bouch	2
French Reinnet	2	Swan's Egg	2
White Calwell	2		—
	—		12 "
	18		

Judge Ward was an enthusiastic planter, untiring in his
search for seeds of trees new to Down. Among his papers
there is a letter, date 1725, from a friend in London who has
been trying to get for him seeds of the Cedar of Lebanon.

"There is no such thing as the seed or the Cones of the Cedar of
Lebanon to be had. The tree you mention in the Phisick Garden
at Chelsey, did last year for the first time bear one single cone,
so you may be sure none of the seed contained in it is to be
procured by me."

This correspondent advises, in the same letter, despatch of
certain trees bought for the Judge's account. Other Castle
Ward accounts of this time show payments for fir seed.
Arthur Dobbs sends his friend five quarts of acorns, and Mr.
Montgomery, of Newgrove, is gathering for him a store of
acorns and chestnuts.

1728 "Sept. 17. I told you in Dublin that I had a good quantity
of Barreys Achornes (acorns) and Irish Chasnutts—I have them
preserving in Mould y^r gardner sent a man afutt for some, and
gott what he could well carrey, therefore I have some more if
you please to send for them by the first oppertunety, there was
much peans taken in gethering them and I have them verey safe
in a firken—& conclude Y^r moste obedient very Hum^{ble} servant
Her. M^tGomerie."

The Judge's gardener sends, by the steward, a note of requirements which indicate extensive planting.

> " John Coudin is hear making ready the Ground for the Nurseries
> and has all the Holes read to plant he thinks it best to get 1000
> firrs from Hillsbourah Lekewise a 100 Crabstocks to Graft on and
> half a hundred pear Stocks, and if yo^w plese Let him know where
> to plant the Silver firrs, if yo^w think fitt he thinks proper to
> plant one row of them in the place of the Scotch firrs in the
> Decoy."

Nearly thirty years later, when Arthur Dobbs is Governor
of North Carolina, he is still thinking of his friend's garden
and grounds at Castle Ward, and sends the Judge seeds.

> " I am endeavouring to get all the seeds I can, and herein Inclose
> to you some of the seed of a sensitive briar which grows upon
> our bleak hills. Touch of a whip will make a whole bush close
> up, so that I hope it will grow upon your rocky hills."

How did they fare for food in old Down ? The answer
is, for the smaller farmers who followed Hamilton and Montgomery, at least as well, in normal years, as in Scotland. The
harvests were good for some years after the settlements, and
always afterwards, excepting in the famine years, food of a
rough plain sort was plentiful and cheap. For the travelling
beggar an unwritten poor-law provided, with certainty, a
handful of meal—even from stores not large. Mainly the
people lived, in the eighteenth century, on milk, potatoes,
and oatmeal in the form of bread and porridge. A griddle
bread made of potatoes and meal was much used. Round
the coast, fish supplied the place of meat in dietary—in the
Holywood district great quantities of mussels from the yet
unpolluted banks were consumed. The better class of farmers
cured bacon, and made cheese for consumption by their own
families. Arthur Young's note here given applies to a wider
area than that of the Down settlements.

> " Their food for three quarters of the year chiefly potatoes and
> milk, and the other quarter Oatmeal ; in the Winter they have

> herrings. They have all a belly full of food whatever it is, as they told me themselves ; and their children eat potatoes all day long, even those of a year old will be roasting them."

Strange to say, the opinion was largely held in England that the potato was unwholesome. Young combats assertions to this effect by pointing to the strength and vigour of the men, the good looks of the women, and the numbers and health of the children in rural Ireland.

An astonishing cheapness of provisions in normal years is characteristic of the Down territory all through the two-century period. The different purchasing power of money must be remembered ; but, this allowed for, prices were yet very low. When Duke Schomberg landed at Bangor and Groomsport in 1689, his ships brought for the Army an ample food supply ; but, according to a letter preserved in the Muniment Room at Clandeboye, he found food in Down so cheap and plentiful that he sent back to England a great part of the beef, cheese, and beer his ships had carried. As the letter, which was addressed to James Hamilton of Bangor, in London at the time, states :

> " They found provision very plentifull, a sheep for two shillings, a good cow for 16 or twenty shillings, butter at two pence the pound, and that there never was a better appearance of a Good Crop of corn."

A hundred years later (1778) the prices in North Down for meat of various kinds were still very low. The following are taken from a manuscript in a farm-house :—

" Butter	..	..	..	5¾d. lb
Mutton	..	..	..	2¾d ,,
Beef	..	..	..	2¼d ,,
Pork	..	..	..	2¼d ,,
A fat Turkey	..	..		10d ,,
A ,, Goose	..	..		8½d ,,
A Chicken	..	..		2½d ,,

Fish was extremely cheap. From the diary of that indiscreet minister of the Presbyterian Church, the Rev. Wm. Steel

Dickson, who was arrested for supposed complicity in the rebellion of 1798, we learn how little value was placed in Scotland on fish as food, and the Scots in Down doubtless esteemed it as little as did their friends of the Mother Country. Dickson, with other suspects, was carried in captivity of an easy kind to Scotland. He tells us—

> 1799 " Oct. 5. We had nice fresh Herrings for some days past, in addition to our other fare. The price to-day, as we are told, is two pence per Hundred,"

and a later entry gives the price ruling for cod. The rates on the Down Coast were probably no higher.

> " Complaining to the contractor that fish was not appearing on the table,—she, the contractor, a Mrs. McGregor, said that fish was so plentiful and so cheap that only common soldiers used them and she feared offering it would be regarded as an insult. The largest cod were delivered by the fishermen at 2/- per dozen."

The outstanding feature of the hospitable table in Down, during the eighteenth century, was profusion, due in part, doubtless, to the cheapness of food, but, also, in great measure to old Scottish traditions of entertainment. The accounts are available for a supper at a funeral in Scotland in 1724, and the following shows what was the caterer's conception of requirement for thirty-four invited :—

> " Besides soup and fish and some other unconsidered trifles, there was beef and mutton, roast and boiled, roast lamb, two large turkeys, four ' goss's ' (geese) a dozen of ducks, and the same number of capons, eighteen hens, besides an indefinite number of chickens and rabbits, two large pigeon pies, two dishes of ' minsht pays ' (mince pies), two dishes of tarts, hams and ' tungs ' (number unspecified), apricots, peaches, apples, pears and cheese."

The letters of Mrs. Delany are often records of food provision and consumption. Writing from Mount Panther, near Downpatrick, to her sister, on 28th July, 1750, and describing her new house, she tells that, in the garden, there are

" excellent gooseberries, currants, and potatoes—with fine salmon,
lobster, trout, crabs, every day at the door. Monday evening
went to Dundrum a mile off, a pleasant nest of cabins by the
sea-side, where may be had kitchen chairs, French white wine,
vinegar, Hungary water, and capers ; mugs and pigs, of which
we bought some. The French white wine is five pence per
bottle—we have not yet tasted it."

In a dateless fragment of a letter addressed to the same person
she sets out her table arrangements. .The quantity and
combination of viands for an ordinary dinner given by the
wife of a Dean are extremely curious. She speaks of the dishes
as being set out on one long table.

" *First course.*	*Second course.*
Turkeys endove	Partridge
Boyled neck of mutton	Sweetbreads
Greens &c	Collared pig
Soup	Creamed apple tart
Plum pudding	Crabs
Roast Loin of veal	Fricassee of eggs
Venison pasty	Pigeons

No dessert to be had."

A simple Sunday dinner of one course, for a table of twelve,
between morning and afternoon church services, is described
in a letter of 8th August, 1758.

" Sunday, we went to Downpatrick ; D. D. preached as well as
ever I heard him. We had a dinner, as usual, for as many as
filled a table for twelve people. Our dinner was a boiled leg of
mutton, a sirloin of roast beef, six boiled chickens, bacon and
greens ; apple pies, a dish of potatoes—all set on at once ; time
between church and church does not allow for two courses ;
tea after we came home, and talking over our company was
refreshing to us."

In the same month the lady gave a little dance. Tea
was served between seven and ten, when the dancers sat down
to a cold supper.

1758 " Aug. 21. Tea from seven to ten ; it was made in the
hall and Smith presided. When any of the dancers had a mind

to rest themselves they sat in the little parlour, and tea was
brought to them. They began at six and ended at ten : then
went to a cold supper in the drawing-room made of 7 dishes down
the middle of cold meats, and plates of all sorts of fruit and
sweet things that could be had here, in the middle jellies : in
all 21 dishes and plates. The table held twenty people ; the
rest had a table of their own in the little parlour, but all the
dancers were together, and I at the head to take care of them :
everybody seemed pleased, which gave pleasure to D. D. and
myself."

In another of her letters she tells her correspondent,—
not writing of her own table,—

" We had much (too much I might add) of food."

That mediocre rhymster, the Rev. Samuel Burdy, of Ardglass, in his poem *The Transformation*, tells us how the tables
were laden at a dinner of the Down Hunt at Downpatrick
in 1796. Had his account preceded the extracts from Mrs.
Delany's letters the reader might have been inclined to make
abatement for poetic license. But, while Burdy's theme
is ignoble, and his rhyme at times appalling, there is no
ground for accusing him of untruthfulness—the verse is plain
reporting.

" Brown and White Soup handed round
First took in the distant ground,
These removed from head and foot
Turbot at the head was put.
Dainty fish of costly price,
Lobster sauce to make it nice.
At the foot was smoking sirloin
That would glutton tempt to purloin,
As I've seen at borough feast
When each voter prov'd a beast.
Sides were deck'd with ham and chickens
Where you'd find some pleasant pickings ;
Gurnets too, with tongue and turkey,
Fit to please them e'en if murky.
Turkey boil'd, with sauce of celery
That would dine a Judge at Hilary ;

T'other corners chickens roasted,
Potatoes bak'd and also toasted.
Turbot taken from the head,
Turkey roast was plac'd instead.
From head to foot in order stood
Of their kind both rare and good,
Jelly, minc'd pies and plumb-pudding,
Each to stuff like gun with wadding.
In the middle, too, was sallad,
Health to serve and please the palate.
On side table round of beef
Was, of dishes, there the chief,
Also there was leg of mutton,
Both prepar'd for solid cutting,
First with cabbage well was garnish'd
T'other, too, with turnips furnished,
Sugar, pepper, salt and mustard,
Butter melted, capers, custard.
And such articles at table
String of rhymes could take like cable.

· · · · ·

Long they eat, and without ceasing,
As the dinner was so pleasing.

· · · · ·

When the first course was completed,
And keen appetite was sated,
It remov'd, now comes the second,
Dishes nice, but eas'ly reckon'd.
At the head was good roast hare,
Foot was decked with lobsters rare.

· · · · ·

At sides and near to head and foot
Tarts of different sorts were put,
Th'almonds, sweetmeats, too, and celery,
Merit praise and without raillery.

· · · · ·

It remov'd were I expert
Soon would I describe dessert.
Apples, cakes at head and foot,
Walnuts at the sides were put,

Raisins, cheese and charming chestnuts,
By nice judges deem'd the best nuts.
In the middle had their station
And of dinner made completion."

Liquors were provided on a scale as lavish as that of the
solids.

The roughness of presentation, as well as the over abundance, of food, impressed the visitor accustomed to English
ways.   Gamble, in his *View of Society and Manners in the
North of Ireland*, notes that

> " The middle class in the North of Ireland live in a kind of rough
> abundance which bears no resemblance to poverty—what is
> often wasted or given away in charity would be nearly sufficient
> to support an English family of the same rank of life."

To Gamble, the display on table of legs, ribs, shoulders, was
positively indecent.

> " The second class of Irish gentry still retain the ancient mode of
> eating their food.   They have little else than plain dishes as they
> are termed—that is, great joints of meat, ribs and sirloins,
> shoulders and legs which while retaining their ancient forms
> instantly remind us of the animal to which they belonged.   This
> I think must be ever painful in proportion as men cease to be
> savages."

CHAPTER XVII.

Ills of the Flesh and the Curing of them

THE extraordinary remedies for ailing humanity, as these are recorded in the diary of Rev. Robert Landess, of Robroyston, Scotland (1670), were of kin with some of very ancient date—as old, indeed, as the days of Marcus Aurelius. Although ' probatum est ' is written after some of them, it is probable that cures following the use of mixtures so offensive to sight and mind, were faith cures,—for proof of curative effect of so many unsavoury ingredients in combination was, of course, impossible. But, in an unscientific age, the uninquiring mind accepted these old remedies in the belief that the more complex the mixture, and the more repulsive its constituents, the greater must be its curative power. The following examples of ' physical receipts ' of the Landess Diary, are taken from *The Scottish Historical Review*, Vol. XIII., No. 51. All three are cures for the gout or cramp.

> " Take a fat Dogge, and kill him, and take out his Guts, and Bowels, and Gall, but keepe in the Heart, and Lungs, and Liver, then fill the body full of Frogges, and black Snailes, and sowe him up strongly, and rost him on a Spit, as long as he will drop

one drop, then put the Liquor in a cleare Vessell, and put thereto
a pint of Oyle of Bay, and blacke Soape one ounce, and temper
them together, and anoint the grieved Part therewith.

. . . . .

" Take an old fat Cat and flea her, and draw forth her guttes,
and bray the Cat, and put her altogether in a fat Gander's belly,
and put thereto halfe a pound of Pepper, Mistard-seede, and
Parsly seede, of each foure ounces, Worme-wood and Garlicke
a good quantity. Bole armoniack sixe penny-waight, then rost
it, and the greace that droppeth from the same, keepe it, and
annoynt the Patient withal, and by the grace of God the ache
will goe away, for being throughly anoynted therewith, it presently helpeth him.

. . . . .

" Take a fatt young whelp, scale him like a pige, take out ye gutts
at ye side thereof Then take Netles and stamp them with 2
unces of Brimston with 4 yoks of eggs and 4 unces of Turpentine,
Incorporate all togither and put it in the whelps bellie, so sowd
up that nothing of this composition come out, Then Rost the
whelp at a soft fire, keep the Dropings that comes from him and
anoint the grived place therwith : and in the mean time Rub
the paind place softlie befor you anoint it."

One of these, it will be noted, requires the containing
animal to be aged. The colour of the beast providing the
remedy was also a matter for consideration, as is evidenced
by a remedy for the falling sickness in which a dog, tied up
for fourteen days, and fed on bones, was required to be a white
dog.

Much less objectionable, and possibly more efficacious,
were the remedies of vegetable origin—the home-made decoc-
tions of hyssop, spurge, betony, fennel, garlic, colewort, and
other plants. Some of these may have been remedial : a
true instinct, in times of hoary antiquity, may have directed
the ailing animal, man, to leaves, roots, seeds, or bark, really
alterative. But, always, the belief appears to have obtained
that the virtue of the remedy could be increased by the addition of animal matter. And so, for dimness in the eyes, the
juice of fennel roots, boiled with honey and put into a box

of brass, was to have woman's milk added to it before using.
If the remedy were for outward application, the added animal
matter was sometimes of very objectionable character. At
times the power of charm was used to fortify the virtue of the
medicine ; sometimes was applied the cure sympathetic,
as when, for removing warts, a snail was rubbed on them and
then stuck on the thorn of a gooseberry bush, the warts dis-
appearing as the snail decayed. These were the common
folks' treatment of minor ailments, or of cases, serious enough,
of the nature of which the old women prescribers of Down were
ignorant.

In a class, higher in education, and with greater opportunities for procuring medical aid than had the lonely ignorant
farmer, alleviations of bodily troubles by bleeding and blistering were for long in favour. When John Wesley was in Down
and its borders, in 1773, he gave all his spare time to helping
poor patients, and found, as he says, blisters applied " for
anything or nothing." On a later visit the fashion had
changed.

> " Now the grand fashionable medicine for twenty diseases, (who
> would imagine it ?) is mercury sublimate ! Why is it not an
> halter or pistol ? They would cure a little more speedily."

Bleeding and blistering went often together. Such
violent twins, set to work by ignorant hands, must have
brought the patient often near the gates of death. Mrs.
O'Reilly, sister-in-law of Mrs. Savage, of Portaferry, wrote
(September 17, 1743) of

> " Uncle Delvin (who) was extremely ill last April & despaired of
> in London, In a fever he had a hundred ounces of blood drawn
> & was blistered quite down his back. I thank God he has
> recovered."

She adds that he complains much of want of strength.
No wonder !

Everybody who had an ailment, and who could afford
to pay for the operation, resorted to blood-letting. In simple

cases the cost was not great.   Among entries in Mrs. Upton's
accounts are such as

"Given Mr Egan for bleeding me—2/6,"

and a mother would send for a surgeon to come to the house,
and bleed a child, as a matter of ordinary procedure, on a par
with an administration of rhubarb powder.

These centuries were the times of 'humours' and
'vapours'—corruption of the 'humours' or 'liquors' is an
idea commonly expressed.   A curious quasi-scientific explanation of the ills following Adam's transgression is found in the
report of a lecture by Dr. Burnet, at London, as sent by
Rev. Andrew Gray, Presbyterian minister of the North, to
Mr. Wodrow, Glasgow.   The original, preserved among the
Wodrow Manuscripts, is dated February 22, 1724-5.

> "I heard Dr Burnet's last discourse at Boyle's lecture.   He re-
> sumed what had been the subject of his former discourses for
> the present year.   He has had this lecture now for two years
> and in the course he endeavours to prove that, setting aside
> extrinsic arguments drawn from testimony from the very nature
> of things the account that the Scripture gives is true ; and in
> his last he was justifying the history of the fall and the corruption
> that was consequent upon it.   He supposed that the reason why
> God did prohibit the eating of the tree of knowledge to our first
> parents was that the fruit of this tree was of pernicious nature
> unto the human body, and so Adam by eating of it had a disorder
> through his whole body, and the liquors were all put into a
> fermentation so that it became unfit for the serving the purposes
> of the soul, and that due subordination of the appetites of the
> body unto the dictates of reason was taken away ;   This Doctor
> Burnet is a man that has a very good character especially with
> some of our dissenting ministers."

When such a discourse represents the science of learned
men (not physicians), one need not wonder at the vagaries
of treatment to which the human body was subjected by the
entirely ignorant.   The 'humours' got out of control even
with the highest of rank—Judge Ward suffers from their

disorder.   On February 8, 1741, his brother, writing to him,
says :—

> " I am very much concerned to hear that the humour is again
> return'd to y^r neck, the rubbing of the wig will always keep that
> place tender & of consequence incline the hum^{rs} to flow that way,
> and at this time of life our juices are become more acrimonious
> than formerly."

He wishes that the Judge had gone to Bath—he had, himself,
gone, and stayed but for a little time, thinking that he did
not receive any benefit.

> " Yet for more than a year afterwards I found my stomach very
> much eased from those corroding humours that used to give me
> such violent cholicks."

Courses of "steel and spaw waters" at Bath, and elsewhere,
were much in favour with the wealthy of Down through the
eighteenth century.   The letters of Mrs. Hamilton of Tollymore, some of which are quoted, later, in this chapter, contain
frequent references to the use of the waters.   A milder fresh
air and rest cure was fashionable on the slopes of Mourne above
Tollymore, and was known as the " goats' whey cure."   A
mid-century survey of Down mentions this cure on the hills,
in the following words :—

> " These mountains of late have been noted for Goats' Whey,
> prescribed by Physicians for Scorbutick and Nephritick Ail-
> ments, and Disorders of the Lungs.   In the Months of April,
> May and June, they are much frequented by the Gentry of both
> sexes ; many of whom have found Relief, the Shrubs and Medi-
> cinal Herbs affording the fittest Nourishment to those Animals."

The freedom of this composition allows the reader to settle
for himself whether the last two words shall apply to the
goats furnishing milk for the whey, or to the " Gentry of both
sexes."

The fantastic cure had its vogue in the old time as well
as in later.   Letty Bushe, lover and lively correspondent of
Lady Anne Bligh, undergoing a course of treatment, writes
to Castle Ward :—

" Am I not to be pitied who leave my warm Bed at seven o'clock
to swallow three pills and three pints of cold, cold water."

The theoretic value of external use of " cold, cold water," was
not justified by the result of its application in a case recorded
in an old manuscript preserved at Barnhill, Comber.

" Rev. Dr. Stewart of Ballintoy married a Miss Vesey of the family
of Bishop Vesey. After having been married twenty years a
son was born to them, and being solicitous to strengthen the
Constitution of this only child of their old age they had it bathed
in a large vessel of cold water for several mornings. Mrs.
Stewart, the widow of Mr Ezekiel Stewart of Fort Stewart, being
at Ballintoy, undertook the office of bathing the child, and having
dipped the child two or three times in the Water without sufficient
Intermission for the child to recover his breath, he was wrapped
up in a blanket to be conveyed to the Nursery. When the
blanket was opened he was found dead, to the Astonishment &
Grief of the family."

How terrible was the scourge of smallpox in the old days
is learned from the very frequent references to the disease
which Down manuscripts contain. There were many deaths
of infants in the family of that much-married man, Rev. Robert
Gordon, of Rathfriland, and smallpox is noted in his diary
as the cause of some. The Rev. Philip Skelton, subject of
the absurd biography by Burdy, noted, in one of his writings,
that, at a time he indicates, seven children, on an average,
died of smallpox every day in the small town of Lisburn.

In 1725 Judge Ward's young son was sick with the
disease, and the Judge's aunt writes to convey her experience
that good nursing is of more value to a patient than the
handling of doctors.

" were (we are) well through ye small pox for I hear it is very rife
in town. I know not how it happens, but we find here y^t more
dies under ye Docto^{rs} hands y^n w^n wth (than when with) a good
nurs keeper. All bro. West's children y^t had never any advice
but our own good tendance have come safe through & not much
markt. I wish y^r son were as well through."

The following very curious bit of spelling, undated, belongs
to this time, and evidently accompanied an old-wife preventive
of marking. The letter is addressed to the Judge and is
signed " Your affectnat . . . andhumbill servant L
Lowth."

> " I lately reseved a leter from cusen fortescue whare in she tells
> me she tougt to se you in abam (? a balm) and as iam vere shour
> it would give her greate pane to have her child so marked ihave
> sent the inclosed and bedg as you regard her, that you will
> emedetly put it on and . . . before her."

" The Honourable Sir Hans Sloan, Bt., M.D., *President*
of the *Royal Society* and *Royal College of Physicians, London ;*
first *Physician* to His Majesty, *Member* of the *Imperial
Academy of Science at Petersburgh,* of the *Royal Academys* of
Sciences at *Paris, Madrid, Berlin ; Fellow of the Royal College
of Physicians* at *Edenburgh,* and *Doctor* of *Physick* of the
University of *Dublin,*" as he is addressed in the Dedication,
in his honour, of a mid-century work, was a man of the
County of Down, having been born at Killileagh in 1660.
He studied Medicine at Paris and Montpelier, and, in
1683, graduated at the University of Orange, in a land far
away in climate, scenery, sentiment, and manners from the
little village of his youth round My Lord Claneboye's keep,
by the waters of Strangford. He was a man of high honour
and great ability in his profession, a botanist, and maker of
the collection—vast for a private individual—which, on his
death, became the nucleus of what we now call the British
Museum.

The gentry of Down were proud to claim acquaintance
with such a man, and many of those who were able to visit
London made him their medical adviser. Perhaps there is
no better way of showing Down's early eighteenth-century
view of maladies and the curing of them than by adhering,
here as elsewhere, to the plan of the book, and allowing a
lady of the time to tell the doctor, in our hearing, of her own
and her family's troubles. The poor lady suffers much in

her own person and in her children. She is Mrs. Hamilton of Tollymore, in South Down, sister of Mrs. Hamilton of Bangor, in the north, and aunt of Anne of the love-letter. She is writing to Sir Hans Sloan. The first letter is dated from Bath.

1708

"Nov. 6. Before we begin to drink the waters I must desir your directions (here follow some very intimate particulars of her married daughter's illness) . . . may she bath, how much water must she drink, what dyet must she keep ? Since my son recovered of his feavours and drunk nothing but Bath water he has had his health much beter than he ust to have it ; you will let me know what quantity of water he may drink, and my two youngest Daughters. My daughter Cary who was a very Rickity sickly girle is recoverd of that Distemper but is often troubled with a swelling in her nose and stopedg in her breathing. Cosin Sloan will discrib it to you ; the Rickets lay all in her head and made her forhead shoot out which makes me apprehend there is some obstruction still in her head, wou'd pumping her head doe her good ? As to myself I am prety well but often troubled with a pain between my back & my right side with a squemishniss in my stomack. My mother and several of our family being troubled with the ston and gravel makes me fear 'tis some disorder in my kidneys : befor I conclud I must desire you to imploy some of your acquaintance to look out for a French Valet for my Boy to dress and wait upon him at table and never to let him be out of his sight, but when he is with me or at scholl and to (speak) nothing but French to him ; he reads and understands it very well, knowing you to have a great acquaintance and to be much esteem'd by the . . .nch occasions my giving you this trouble which I hope you will excuse from Sᵣ

Your humble servantᵗ

A. Hamilton.

My service to your Lady.

For Doctor Sloan at his House in great Rusel street near Southampton Square, London."

The interest in the quest for a French valet for the weakly boy is great enough to warrant retention of this portion of Mrs. Hamilton's letter in this chapter. Dr. Sloan did

MRS. (ANNE) HAMILTON of Tollymore, daughter of
the Hon. Elizabeth Mordaunt, sister of Mrs. (Sophia)
Hamilton of Bangor, in Down. Writer of the letters
to Sir Hans Sloan, which are quoted in this chapter.
Portrait at Tollymore.

"I think I was at prayers,"—a day's entry from
the diary of ANNE, COUNTESS OF RODEN, of Tollymore, Co. Down, daughter of James, first Earl
of Clanbrassil (second creation). The story of a
flight from Belfast in the days of the rebellion of
1798, with which this book closes, is from the
diary of this lady.   Portrait at Tollymore.

succeed in finding a valet, who wanted £20 per annum, and it was very doubtful whether he would eat with other servants. Mrs. Hamilton thought the terms rather high.

1708

" Dec 24. The favour of yours I received yesterday, and am of your opinion that 20£ a year is to great wages for such a servant, one that expects so much will hardly eat with other servants, or wait at table ; twelve or fifteen pounds I am willing to give ; I hope to be going towards Winchester in April, if you don't hear of one till then he must come strait from London there or els directly to the Bath.

" We are all pretty well only my Daughter is still ailing I wish your Family a merry Christmas

and am Sr

Your humble sevrt

A. Hamilton.

My son presents his service to you and hopes you will excuse the trouble he has given you.

To Dr Sloan at his house in Great Russell Street, London "

The tale of woes is resumed two years later.

1710

" Sept 4. I have followed your directions for a fortnight I bless God I have had no return of the cramp but the . . . after I was bleed I found a numbness in both my arms which went of with a pricking as when ones foot is asleep, since that night I have feelt nothing of that kind but a numing pain sometimes in one shoulder sometimes in another and a tingling or pricking through my veins and a weakness in my arms and legs, but that which is most uneasy to me is the hot flushing which comes often in the day and is so violent when I goe to Bed I can get very litle sleep. When I doe slumber I wake in a sweet all over my face and head : this day I feel such a disorder in my head a straitness as if 'twas bound about that I resolve to Blister this night.

" If you think the Bath waters proper the season for drinking is not over, I shall be glad to hear from you next post, ... all the young ones are well. My service to your Lady.

Sr your humble servt

A. Hamilton.

For Doctor Sloane at his house near Bloomsberry Square, London."

The next two letters are occupied entirely by her son's troubles.   They are written from Oxford, where, probably, the boy was at this time a student.

> " Mar 5.   I am mightily disheartened to find the disorder continues in my son's head notwithstanding the bleeding, cupping and blistering in London, and the course of Steal & Spaw waters that he has taken since he came into the country, he complain'd so much of the pain in his head yesterday that I sent for a surgeon and had him bleed this morning ; we took between seven and eight ounces ; if this does not relieve him there must be some other method thought of.   I shall not be willing to take more blood from him, what would you think of purging him, his stomack is not so good as it usit to be, but he is chearfull and the pain goes soon of but an uneasyness or weariness continues all over him for some time.   This is the best description I can give of his disorder.   Pray let me hear from you.   I am S^r
>
> 1713

Your humble serv^t

A. Hamilton.

To Doctor Sloan at his house near Bloomsberry Square, London, with care."

> " Mar. 23.   Finding my son continues still very much oppressed and restless at nights I resolve to goe to the Bath ; if the Doctors when I come there don't advise to his drinking the waters which we shall try in a very small quantity I will God willing goe up to London.   Betty is much as she was the swelling is rather less : she and Cary presents their service to your Daughters
>
> 1713

I am S^r

your hum^{ble} serv^t

A. Hamilton."

The next is written from Tollymore.

> " Aug. 10.   I have write to my Daughter to deliver this to you which is to desire your directions in what you think may be proper to ease me of a palpitation in my Heart which has been heavy on me near three months.   I cant say I have been quite from it since
>
> 1721

last Summer but is now much increased and strikes across my stomach with an odd motion.   I have such an oppression that

I am forced to sigh deep to get a little ease ; sometimes I am chilly, other times have a flushing heat all over me have no appetite and often wake in the night a trembling or shakeing both in my Head and hands which make writing troublesome to me. Doctor Cummyng advised me to stell and spaw waters which I have taken for two months but find no benefit by it, but rather an increase of the disorder which occasions my giving you this trouble . . .

I am Sr Your friend

and humble Servt

A. Hamilton.

I would not frighten my Daughter haveing troubles enough of her own.

To Sir Hans Sloane."

A scanning of eighteenth-century accounts shows that proprietary medicines, and beautifiers of the teeth and hair, were not unknown to ladies of the period. Under the heading "Apothecary and Sundries" appear in Mrs. Upton's accounts notes of the purchases as given below. These date in 1772-3.

" For a dozen packets of James' Powders ..	2	6
A box of Dr James' Pills	4	0
3 boxes Dr James' Pills	12	0
P^d for a Quarter pound Canister of herb Snuff	1	3
3 Bottles Pearl Essence for the Teeth.. ..	7	6
2 Artificial Load-stones for the Cramp ..	7	0
Coliquintida for ye Hair		
Mrs Marsden's bill for Peppermint water ..	4	6
To Mrs Phillips for ingredients wth wch she made		
me a Tinct of Guiacum	7	0
7 oz. Palsy-Drops	7	0
1 Bottle of Scowering Drops..	1	0
2 oz Lavender Drops	2	0
Stuff to cure corns	2	0
2 pots of pomatum to thicken ye Hair ..	5	0
Pd by Molly for a bottle of Scowering Drops ..	8	0

Three things are clear from this short study of the ailments of our ancestors :—That, for the old folk, the symptomatic pain was the disease, the place where it was felt

indicating appropriate cure. That a scientific conception of
disease did not exist, among even very learned people, as
late as 1725 : witness Dr. Burnet Boyle's lecture on Sin as
the result of fermentation of the 'liquors' of the body.
That even the educated believed in the potency of charm :
witness Mrs. Upton's purchase of "two artificial load-stones
for the cramp."

CHAPTER XVIII.

Travel.

In a vague, general way, we all know that, for our ancestors, travel by sea or land was a slow, fatiguing, and often very dangerous experience. The privateer in the Channel was no rare visitor. Rev. John McBride, Belfast, writing to Principal Stirling of Glasgow, 29th May, 1704, says:

> " I had given you an account of my present state before this, had not the fear of privateers in this channel hindered the ordinary frequent passage between you and us,"

and forty-one years later, Bernard Ward (September 14th, 1745) sent to his father news of the taking of an English ship off the coast of Down.

> " Michale Echlin who was with me yesterday, told me that on Wednesday last he saw a large French ship take an English one just off ye shore of Ballyhalbert so near that they saw her take her in tow & sail towards Scotland. They judged ye French man to carry about 50 guns, she fired 5 guns at ye other ship before she struck."

But setting aside the risk of capture by the country's enemies as exceptional, the traveller's trials were numerous

and varied. A few hours' frost after rain made the journey
on horseback, in winter, a thing of dread. The urgent mail
journey might be baulked by non-arrival of the coach, or by
its arrival without vacant place. On sea, the start was not,
with high degree of certainty, followed by finish at the desired
haven. Even in the short voyage between England or Scotland and a Down port, baffling winds might cause the traveller's
return to port of departure after days of fright and discomfort
in the channel. Perhaps our fathers had a joy in movement
which we, who travel with speed and comfort and at little
risk, do not know. Possibly the discomfort of the average
journey was rudely balanced for the horseman by a rhythm
of step, or sense of partnership in effort with his steed ;—
for the traveller by mail, by society of fellows, the enlivening
roar and rumble of the lurching coach, and the excitements
of stoppings and startings on the road ;—for the sea voyager
by the near sight of great green depths, the hiss of passing
wave, the salt-tasting air, the creak of spar and rattle of
cordage ; with a glorious sense of achievement when the
journey came to end. These joys were not set down on paper
—or but rarely,—but the delays, fatigues, and dangers of the
old-time are the subjects of contemporary record, and enough
extracts from these old writings are here presented to enable the reader to feel the difference between travel in the
eighteenth and the twentieth century.

Rank, in those days, knew no safer or quicker way over
sea than did the commonalty,—although in a larger yacht, or
packet with a better cabin, it may have had a slight advantage.
Clarendon, coming to Ireland as Lord Lieutenant, tells the
Lord Treasurer of the delays, troubles, and losses of the passage
suffered by the servants having charge of his belongings.

" Jany 16. I know you will be concerned when I tell
you the condition of my family here. When I was
$1685/6$ at Chester I embarked all my coach-horses, servants
and goods in two ships there : they both set sail
from Chester on Sunday last (the winds were so bad

they could not stir before) in company with another vessel called Providence, but the storm on Sunday in the afternoon scattered them : the vessel in which were my saddle horses and plate was driven into the Skerries, twelve miles from hence, and I got my things and horses and three servants here yesterday, but the other vessel in which were several of my servants and my two sets of coach horses is not yet heard of—the Providence is cast away upon the coast of Carlingford and but one man of all the company saved."

The missing ship from Chester was driven into Strangford, as will be seen from the note three days later.

168⁵/₆

" Jany 19. No letters yet from England. My ship from London arrived well here on Sunday in the evening : and the same night I had an account that the other ship from Chester was this day sennight driven into Strangford, so that, I thank God, all my servants and horses are safe."

The ship from London which arrived at Dublin between 16th and 19th January, had sailed from London on the 16th November.

In these days a student at Glasgow, returning to his parents at Donaghadee, will leave Scotland in late evening, and after a good night's rest—some hours of it in a moored steamer at Belfast quay—will be with his own people at Donaghadee in time for breakfast. Here is the experience of his fellow of 1704—John Scott, student of Divinity,—and there is nothing in his notes to indicate that he considered the journey exceptional :—

1704

" June, Thursday yᵉ 15th I was in Carsdick & about 9 of the clock went over to Greenock to look for a Boat to Belfast but found none.

" Fraiday yᵉ 16th I left Greenock about 8 in the morning & came in a yoal (yawl) to Gourock where we gott breakfast in Skipper Scot's & about 11 we left Gourock and came over to Dunune where we meet with Joⁿ Andrew bound for Belfast wᵗʰ whom we agreed to carry us of hither (viz) Mr William Mᵗᵗ Caa & self.

" Saturday yᵉ 17th I was in Dunune p diem.

" Sunday yᵉ 18th I was in Dunune & heard Mr Walter Campbell on Isai 26 for lecture & for sermon which was in Irish, Isai 26:8. latter clause yr of and in the afternoon on same text & in English.

" Munday yᵉ 19th I left Dunune at 1 of the clock in the morning and came through Lamlash about 3 in the afternoon wind N N W we came out and gott up wᵗʰ or about 2 leagues to the S Westward of Pleda then the wind about 7 at night came to a South, we takt and came below an old castle & there dropt anchor where we roade all night, about 3 in the morning Tuesday it blew hard.

" Teusday yᵉ 20th I was at sea at anchor below an old castle near Lamlash about 3 in the morning it blew hard the wind S S W we held up anchor & came to Lamlash togither wᵗʰ 4 Barks & 3 Boats that had been crusing all night we put out boat & came ashore to Lamlash about 6—rained exceedingly hard, the wind still increased & about 5 at night came to a W & W N W blow mighty hard, our boat drove at length they gott down the main mast & so held fast, another of the Barks drove within a cable length to the shore.

" Wensday ye 21st I was in Lamlash, the wind as upon Tuesday blow mighty hard (until 6 at night) at W or W by N memorandum I then meet wth one James Brown a young man brother to Roᵗ Brown Skipper of a bark bound for Dublin wᵗʰ coals, who told me that E.C. was not yet come to Kilbride.

" Thursday ye 22nd I was in Lamlash, & about 11 went to sermon & heard Mr Mtt Clane on Joel 1:14 for sermon in the forenoon & in English, & in the afternoon & in Irish for lecture Hos. 14 & for sermon Joel 1:14 being a fast day about 9 at night I left it yᵉ wind at N W.

" Fraiday yᵉ 23rd I was at sea betwixt Lamlash & Belfast & landed at Belfast about 9 of the clock at night. Praise to God.

" Saturday yᵉ 24th I was in Belfast and about 10 of the clock gott my things (viz) Chest box & books ashore, & left it about 4 of the clock in the afternoon & came home to my father's in Donaghadee about :9 at night."

Nine days en route. Primate Boulter, in one of his letters, mentions that the Bishop of Ferns and his family have just arrived, " after being at sea four days." Mrs. Delany, wife of the Dean of Down, replying to a commiserating friend, thinks too much ought not to be made of the discomforts of the channel-crossing, seeing that the passage is seldom more than forty hours, and often not much more than half that time. But not everyone was so plucky as the Dean's wife. Lord Darnley, writing to his brother-in-law, Bernard Ward of Castle Ward, answers thus the query as to why he does not visit his relations :—

> " If the sea was as indifferent to me as it seems to be to you, I should very frequently visit Ireland. But as it is, I cannot think of a sea voyage without Horror."

The costs of a journey must have been incalculable beforehand, seeing that in winter time the delay caused at port of departure by unfavourable winds might lengthen into several weeks. On arrival, in winter, there might be another forced delay through impassability of roads, or lack of vehicle to continue the journey. If the distance between arrival port and home was not excessive, the traveller, in time of snow, who did not wish to wait for a change, had, perforce, to walk, and pay highly for porters to carry his luggage. Alexander McMinn, of Herdstown, Donaghadee, has some notes in his diary which show what the traveller in winter had to bear at times.

> " Thursday Feby. 7. Heavy snow all night.
>
> Friday Feby 8. Desperate snow all night, could not stir out.
>
> 1799 Saturday Feby 9. Snow so deep no person could stir out.
>
> Sunday. A fine morning. Walked into Belfast with F. Hull. Snow very deep. Breakfast at Sherridans. No carriage could possibly travel.
>
> Monday. The passengers from Donaghadee were obliged to walk up (to Belfast 14 miles) and have their luggage carried on men's shoulders."

An entry in his diary, eight years later, shows that life might be lost on the snowy road.

1807
" 27th Nov. Last evening between 7 & 8 o'clock,
while a chaise was going from Belfast to Donaghadee
with a gentleman and his servant in it, owing to the
ground being deeply covered with snow they missed
the road and fell into a deep moss pit. The gentleman and his servant fortunately got out of the window of the
chaise, but the driver and a pair of horses perished."

What might or could be the sufferings of a traveller on
the short passage between England and Down, in wild weather,
can be learned from the following simple account of a real
experience. It was printed over a hundred years ago (Gamble's
View of Society and Manners in the North of Ireland, 1812),
but is worthy of reprint, for nothing, in available document,
paints more vividly the possible horrors of a channel-crossing
in the old days. And this was a summer passage.

" I have all my life had a dread of the passage from Liverpool to
this country, and, guided by circumstances, have rarely come by
any other. I shall I trust be wiser for the future ; and to make
my experience of service to others, I shall give an account of
my present voyage.

" I went on board the . . . bound to Newry, about
six o'clock on the evening of the second of July, and sailed
immediately afterwards. There were three vessels in company
bound likewise to Ireland. 1 was hardly on board before I wished
myself back again : the evening was dark and lowering, the wind
every moment becoming more unfavourable and the Captain
evidently intoxicated. From that moment I had a presenti-
ment of all that was to follow.

" On getting round the rock the Captain of our little fleet had
a consultation whether to proceed, or put back—three were of
opinion that it was wisest to put back—the fourth, ours, was
obstinate and swore he would go on by himself,—the others, I
suppose, lest their courage should be called in question, resolved
to follow him.

" The first two days the weather, though rough, was not very
unfavourable, and at ten of the third morning we had a distant
view of the Mountain of Mourne, dimly seen through the dusky
vapour that gathered round its head and mocking us with a
sight of the promised land which we were doomed to view afar

off, and not to enter. I was standing, or rather endeavouring
to stand, on the deck at the time, and gazed upon it with
heart-sinking fondness ; gloomy and dreary as it appeared, I
am sure it was dearer to my imagination than the most sun-
decked hill or sheltered valley ever feigned by a writer of romance.

" About noon the wind suddenly shifted and blew a tremendous gale from the westward. At four we were driving rapidly
to the southward, the sea, in the common, but expressive, phrase,
running mountains high. As the evening advanced the horror
increased ; the gale became still more terrific, and our frail bark
laboured so much that each time she sunk we thought she would
never rise again. The sight, indeed, was so shocking that I
could witness it no longer ; I went below and threw myself into
my little berth.

" The Captain now came down and, as well as he could speak,
addressed the passengers. He told us he was at a loss to know
what to do—that the gale was so dreadful, the vessel so crazy,
and the men so exhausted, he was almost certain of foundering
if we kept to sea ; that Drogheda river, which lay a little ahead,
was, he understood, a very dangerous one, even to those who knew
it best ; that he was utterly unacquainted with it ; but as the
lesser evil, would prefer venturing if we had no objection.

" We told him we were incapable of advising, and begged him
to do whatever he thought best for the safety of the vessel and
the preservation of all our lives.

" We shaped our course (as we thought) for Drogheda river
accordingly ; the sea roaring with a violence of which it is impossible to form an idea, though the darkness hid it from our
view,—we saw nothing—we knew nothing of where we were
going ; we were ignorant of everything except that danger
surrounded us on every side ; that shoals and rocks were round
us and about us, and that little short of a miracle could save us.

" The horrors of that night can never be erased from my
recollection ; I am sure the agonies of death, ' if any sense at
that sad hour remains,' could alone equal it. It was so long—
that night—often when the gust came violent and bore down the
little bark that bore us and our hopes—when I raised myself in
the wretched berth where I lay, and by the miserable lamp that
glimmered in the cabin, making ' darkness ' visible, I observed
the slow progress of time—I exclaimed in the words of a German
poet—' Will this eternal night last to the day of judgment ? '

" At intervals the cries of the women in the hold mingled with
the blast and gave it new horrors ; more ear-piercing and heart-
rending than the others were those of a female I had noticed the
day before for her extraordinary attention to an infant she carried
at her breast . . . . .

" About two in the morning when we were beginning to flatter
ourselves with some hopes, the vessel struck,—of the scene that
followed it is as painful to think as it would be impossible to
describe.   The violence of the shock threw the vessel on one side,
and the waves beat over her in every part.   The rudder was
unshipped and the mast went by the board.   The shrieks of the
men and women passengers, the cries or rather shouts of sorrow
of the seamen, formed a perfect chorus of misery."

Contracting the narrative, it may be told that the vessel
held together, and, about six o'clock, fishermen from Skerries
rescued crew and passengers—thirty-eight souls.

CHAPTER XIX.

The Dawn of the Industrial Age

WITH the completion, in 1688, of the Long Bridge over the Lagan, the stone causeway which replaced the many-centuries-old ford at the mouth of the river as a means of communication between two counties, Belfast first set foot in Down. In the time of the ford and the long rough track over mud flats and sandbanks which was its continuation, inhabitants, calling themselves of Belfast, would have been, on the Down side, too far away from the business town for quick movement, the ford being available only at low water, and too far away for safety when Belfast's rough stone and earth-work fortifications were things of need and value. True, there were houses on the Strand, or Great Strand, in Down, a place now far away from the cabined and confined Lagan of to-day—Blair of Bangor lived there for a time after his eviction,—but these were true country houses. Beyond the swamps and levels beginning at high-water mark, there rose, half a mile away, a gentle slope of which the Pottinger family took possession, and on which they built their home, dignifying the little elevation by the title 'Mount'; and, although the Pottingers have now no connection with the city, and their house has long since disappeared, the name Mountpottinger remains, and is the twentieth-century designation of a large and populous district. Looking from the windows of the new dwelling on The Mount, the owners had a clear view of the new long stone bridge over the Down-side levels, and beyond the bridge, and the great lake-like expanse it and its long stone-built extension crossed, they saw, without obstruction, the even-then strenuous Village City of Belfast. These Pottingers were old Berkshire folk, settling in Belfast in Queen Elizabeth's time. They have left evidence of their importance on the Antrim, as well as on the Down, side of Belfast—one of the old narrow courts where, probably, they carried on trade, being still named Pottinger's Entry. In the time of James II. a member of the family, Thomas Pottinger, was Sovereign of Belfast, and his influence with the Government seems to have been considerable, for he obtained a new Charter for the town. The more liberal constitution of the town's governing body was very offensive to the upholders of the belief that all privilege belonged by right to members of the Church by law established. The author of *The Conduct of the Dissenters, etc.*, thus expresses his disgust :—

> " There was one Potinger, a Professed Presbyterian, an inhabitant of Belfast, who when King James was in Ireland, proved a zealous and avoud Jacobite and made Interest to have the Old Charter of that Town broken, and a New one granted. Upon what motives this was done I will not determine, but thus far I affirm to be Fact, That at the time when that Charter was broke there were but One or Two of the Twelve Burgesses who were Dissenters ; but by the New Charter the number of Burgesses was augmented to Thirty Four whereof by the best Computation I can make there were Eleven or Twelve Dissenters and Nineteen Papists."

The lands of the Pottingers were in the hands of the Irish chieftain Con O'Neill, after the triple division of his old territory, as described in Chapter III. But, through his improvidence, they passed speedily, with all the remainder of

his share, into other hands, and in 1624 were in possession of
Sir James Hamilton, who became, later, My Lord Claneboye.
His grandson Henry, Earl Clanbrassil, granted the Ballymacarrett property in 1672 to Thomas Pottinger in fee-farm, in
consideration of a payment of £300 and an annual rent of £30.
When the Pottinger family sold the Ballymacarrett estate
(not including The Mount) a hundred years later, they received
for it £18,113 5s. od., and the purchaser re-sold, eight years.
later, for £25,000—a striking proof of the rapidly rising value
of land in this part of Down, at a time when Belfast was so
small as to appear in our eyes a village,—which, indeed, the
Belfast of 1787 is often called.

The view of Belfast from the old Mountpottinger house
must have been very pleasing. Indeed, before the power
factory, as we know it, destroyed the amenities of the district, Belfast and its environs were charmingly beautiful,
and are so described by strangers. Even as early as 1758 the
fine character of the Down country in the neighbourhood of
Belfast, and enriched by Belfast's trade, was notable, as
evidenced by a letter to her sister from the wife of the Dean
of Down on a visit to Belvoir. The date is 1st October, 1758.

> " This place is much more finished than Hillsborough, and in a
> finer country, and much enriched with bleach yards, farm houses
> and pretty dwellings. On Friday we went in a boat on the river,
> which runs round the improvements almost, and several turnings
> of it can be seen from the house. The grounds are laid out in
> enclosures, which with the hedge rows and woods on the sides
> of some of the hills make the prospect very rich. The town of
> Belfast, Cave-hill, and the bridge of 22 arches over the river, on
> a very clear day can be seen from the windows."

Even after the steam-engine had arrived (by 1810 there
were fifteen engines in Belfast and neighbourhood), it was
long before the charm of the town's environs was adversely
affected. Hoare, the grandiloquent, writing from the Down
side in 1806, says :—

> " The city appears to great advantage on a retrospective view,
> backed by a fine range of mountains, one of which presents a

very bold rugged outline. The general face of the country bears a cheerful aspect, and very different from what we had hitherto seen ; it is thickly studded with gentlemen's seats and whitened houses."

Seven years later, Gamble, arriving by the Lagan Valley, thus expresses himself :—

" Had it not been for the lofty ridge of mountain on my left hand which seemed to move along with and accompany me, I should have thought myself in the environs of London. The country was in the highest state of cultivation—it looked like one continued garden, shadowed with trees interspersed with thickets and neat white washed houses, smiling with beauty, scented with fragrance, thrilling with harmony, delightful to the eye, ear and smell."

Inside the town, Antrim or Down side, the houses of the masses along the out-creeping roads were often replicas of the thatched and whitewashed farm buildings in which the occupants had spent their earlier lives. But the town had also in number its large and dignified houses, in streets where dwelt Earl and Bishop and merchant prince,—for Belfast had, as the eighteenth century closed,

49 persons worth from £5,000 to £9,000 stg.
14   ,,   ,,   ,,   10,000 to 14,000 ,,
9   ,,   ,,   ,,   15,000 to 19,000 ,,
5   ,,   ,,   ,,   20,000 to 29,000 ,,
7   ,,   ,,   ,,   30,000 or over,

and these figures represented much greater estate then than they do now.

The activity of the town and neighbourhood was remarkable. Of manufactured goods, needed by town and the country round, the greater part was produced in Belfast— iron-works, salt-works, breweries, tanneries (36 in operation in the last year of the eighteenth century), sugar refineries existed. There were also manufactories of linen yarn, cotton goods, ropes, paper, hats, pottery, glass, soap, candles, mustard, glue, and starch. The glass-works, the ' bottle-houses,' were on the Down side of the river.

What of the people who established these industries ?
Strenuous they were, admittedly ; but what of the manner
and mental equipment of the best of them ? The answer
supplied by the records of the time is eminently favourable.
Probably no town of Belfast's size, not being a University
town, had, at the end of the eighteenth century, a larger
number of enlightened citizens. They thought in a large
way, a scientific way, and they thought finely. The old
conception of scientific study as a wondering consideration of
uncorrelated phenomena is not discoverable in the writings
of Belfast's Antrim and Down men as the eighteenth century
closed. They founded in 1788 the Belfast Reading Society,
with, for object,

> " the collection of an extensive Library, Philosophical apparatus
> and such productions of Nature and Art as tend to improve the
> mind and incite a spirit of general enquiry."

By 1792 the Society had changed its title to that by which
it is known to-day—The Belfast Society for Promoting Knowledge ; one of the rules of which, in 1792, was, that no money
was to be spent on any

> " common novel or farce, or book of trivial amusement."

In 1792 we find the Society setting aside the sum of £100
for the purchase of The Philosophical Transactions of the
Royal Society of London. The members furnished papers
on topography, natural history, mineralogy, antiquities,
civil history, the solution of practical questions connected
with science, arts, and manufactures, on the various types of
ancient learning, on current literature, metaphysics, law,
medicine, commercial and political economy.

They were men of a liberal spirit. On 16th January, 1792,
at a meeting called in consequence of a requisition—Rev.
James Brigson in the chair—

> " A motion was made and carried on the propriety of their publicly
> declaring their sentiments on the great and important question of
> admitting the Roman Catholics to a full and immediate participa-
> tion of the rights enjoyed by their fellow citizens and countrymen."

On the next evening a series of resolutions, couched in temperate and dignified language, was agreed to unanimously, and ordered to be published.   Three of these may be given :

" 1st. Resolved—That civil and religious liberty is the birthright of every human being ; that Governments were formed to secure them in the possession of these rights, and that States should be regulated so as to protect them in the exercise of it."

. . . .

" 2nd.   That doctrines of faith and modes of worship can neither give nor take away the rights of men ; because opinion is not the Object of Government ; because the mode of expressing Religious Worship ought to be left to the judgment of God and the decision of conscience : and because persecution, however it be disguised, is destructive of the equality of men and the most sacred laws of nature."

. . . .

" 5th.   In fine, it is our most fervent wish that the nation would call for their deliverance with a voice so temperate as to excite no tumult ; so affectionate as to conciliate the hearts of all ; but so United and so powerful as to carry conviction to every source of legislation."

They built well, these pioneer scientists and philanthropists of Antrim and Down, and much of their work stands. It is true that an observer in 1813 has left it on record that the men of Belfast did not read much.   He must mean the mass of men ; for Belfast maintained its reputation, in the early nineteenth century, for men who thought as well as worked. Even this writer, however, has a good word of our manners.

" Young women appear to walk as little as the men read.   I know not whether this is a restraint of Presbyterianism or of education ; but let the cause be what it may, it is a very cruel one.   Young women have few enjoyments ; it is a pity therefore to deprive them of so innocent a one as that of walking.   I have conversed with them at parties and generally found them rational and unassuming,   . . .   They seldom played cards, nor did the elderly people seem to be particularly fond of them.   Music was the favourite recreation, and many were no mean proficients in it."

A rapid glance at the outstanding characteristics of Down and its people at the end of the second century after the Scottish settlements, shows in existence—

An aristocracy, or gentry, losing touch with the people on their lands ; tending more and more to form a class having relations with the outer world of common people through agents only. They are still, generally, resident, and active in planting, in improving breeds of cattle, and in experimenting with seeds and new farming implements and machinery.

An Established Church clergy of fair education and much more earnest and faithful than their predecessors of a century earlier, but pluming themselves too much on privilege of their order, and too ready to assume, rather offensively, a position of superiority to ordinary persons of learning and manners equal to theirs, when these persons were dissenters.

A Presbyterian ministry, plain-living and hard-working ; some of the younger looking at doctrines of their faith through New Light spectacles,—charged, perhaps not unjustly, with preaching ethics rather than spiritual truth.

A quickly-growing manufacturing and trading class, for the most part connected with linen production and bleaching, —members of a new class of gentry whose houses and ' improvements ' dot the county along main roads near towns ; a considerable percentage of them of enlightened ideas, and having scientific tastes.

A yet larger body of sharp and intelligent, but imperfectly educated, small traders, quick to earn profits by seizing opportunities furnished by the county's rapidly developing commerce. The granting of Free Trade with England, in 1780, has given them their chance. They are engaged in transport, export, and the minor industries.

A class of farmers holding from twenty to one hundred acres. Those of Scottish descent, with few exceptions, hold tenaciously to the tongue and the theology of their fathers. They are narrow in their interests, and, if somewhat illiberal in supporting their ministry, may be held excused for the hardness of their own lives. They have little idea of loveliness and none of sanitation in their dwellings. The old orchards are dying out and are not being replaced ; vegetables are cultivated, but not flowers. A hearth-taxing which allows one hearth free, but requires payment for all if more than one exists, has made the frugal farmers abandon all fireplaces save one—they sleep in rooms unventilated by chimney. And their windows are not opened,—the people believe that night air has a noxious quality, and shut it out. The turf bogs are wearing out ; but the prejudice against coal as fuel is so strong, that even near little ports where it is procurable, turf, which has been carted eight or nine miles, is burned. They are sharp-witted people—able to take care of themselves in all that relates to buying or selling,—but they are too much at the mercy of the landlord and his agent. Dubourdieu speaks of them as unexceptionable payers, the landlord suffering no deductions for repairs, so that the cost of management of estates is low. On the whole, the condition of this class is improving : since 1780 they have had good prices for their produce, and the larger holders of land are following the gentry in the use of improved farming implements and machinery.

A very much larger class of small cultivators, which divides into (a), those who depend for subsistence on the produce of a few acres, and (b), those farming a few acres, whose income is supplemented by the fruits of an industry which, over the greater area of the land, will be one connected with the linen manufacture. The holdings are, in general, far too small : in bad seasons many of the (a) section go under, and swell the ranks of the emigrants. The fences are bad—can indeed be scarcely said, in certain districts, to exist ; such as they are, they are wasteful of land.

An illiterate land-labouring class, knowing little of the comforts or even decencies of life. Their living accommodation in farmers' out-buildings, or in cottages, is extremely deficient. Wages are very low—about three guineas per half

year with food, a boy getting, for same time, one guinea and
upwards, until, arrived at man's estate, he receives three.
A higher payment rules near towns.

If there is unrest anywhere, it is due to excessively bad
handling of Irish affairs by the English Government. The
people as a whole are settled and industrious, and the alliterative
phrase " populous and prosperous," so often applied to the
Down of this time, may be considered as justified. In forty
years the number of houses in the county has doubled.

It is not a far cry in time to the end of our two-century
period. Two average lives, end to end, will stretch well into
it, and there is at least one member of an old County Down
family, happily alive and vigorous at the time of this writing,
whose father was born in 1767. But in ' atmosphere ' of our
lives and conditions of living, we are very far indeed from the
end of the eighteenth century ;—how far off will be felt by
those who know Belfast and the Down of to-day, and who will
listen to an old lady's story of a frightened rush for safety when
the ' rising ' of 1798 took place. We know how empty were
the duty entries in the diary of Anne, Countess Dowager of
Roden, but when there was anything beyond the trivial
movements of the placid life to record, her diary became a
living document, and an extract from it is here used as distance
indicator to close this story of Two Centuries of Life in Down.

1798

" Wednesday, May 23rd, Louisa, the Hutchinsons, and
I came to Tollymore Park. This day begun those
dreadful scenes in and about Dublin, which, as we
came farther north, we were ignorant of for two days :
dreadful indeed they are, but mercy has attended us,
and Oh, surely it has attended me and supported me under the
dreadful apprehension from reports yesterday that this shocking
rebellion had broke out at Belfast and Drogheda, so that all I
loved on all sides was in danger, except the single one who was
with me, and even we appeared from that report to be between
two fires, which would soon destroy us. God Almighty supported
me for some hours that I endured this misery, and at last He
granted me the mercy to know this report was false. His

protection of my beloved son in his brave undertaking against these
unfortunate rebels, is a mercy for which my heart is too narrow
to conceive or to return praise. . . . These threatenings
continued ; but the Province of Ulster was supposed to be quiet,
nor was there any danger apprehended. In this persuasion we
remained for some days, and we were enjoying ourselves as
comfortably as I could. On Thursday, June 7, Mr Moore and Mr
William Moore came to see me, and gave me some instances that
seemed to be convincing that the Province of Ulster was likely
to continue quiet. In the evening, Gray asked me if I should not
like to have some of the troops, that were at Bryansford, guard
this house. I was rather startled at the question, as I appren-
hended he might have heard some alarming account ; and he
slightly said No, and I refused the guard. In less than an hour
after, I received an express from Harriot, to inform me that there
was a rising in Larne, which they hoped would be soon got under,
but urging me most eagerly to set out for Belfast, for which purpose she had sent her horses to meet me at Saintfield, and also
an order from General Nugent that the six dragoons that were
stationed in Bryansford should escort me. This account was
most alarming. We waited for break of day, and set out in our
chaise and Miss Hutchinson's chaise. Louisa recollected that
Captain Wolseley was in the neighbourhood, and wrote to ask
him to accompany us, which he most kindly complied with ;
and we found him upon our road at Clough. We got with perfect
safety to Belfast, and saw nothing alarming. The two Miss
Hutchinsons, Louisa, my three little children and our two maids,
Davis and Miss H's footman, were all that went with us. Hammy
Gray also accompanied us as far as Belfast. When we arrived
within two miles of it, during which time we had met nothing
alarming, Captain Wolseley took his leave of me, as there were
troops from thence to the town. In his return he narrowly
escaped being taken on that road which so few hours before we
had travelled in safety. The next day Saintfield, where we had
changed horses, was in the hands of the rebels."

" June 8th. We got to Belfast about ten o'clock, and
found Harriot in a worse situation than I expected.
She had not seen Chitty for two days and nights,
during which time he had been in the Battle of
Antrim. It was a desperate one, where, by the
brave but rash intrepidity of Colonel Lumley, part of the 22nd

1798

were cut off, and the yeoman cavalry were probably saved by the
means of Chitty's coolness and recollection.   Poor Lord O'Neill
was murdered this day as he was going to a meeting of magistrates,
not at all in the act of fighting.   We were told Chitty was safe,
but I could hardly believe it, not seeing them return ; but after
some hours the troop returned, and he safe with them.   Lord
O'Neill lingered some days at Lord Massareene's, where he died.
Before we got to Belfast the only friends in whom Harriot could
have comfort were fled to Scotland, so that when I got to Belfast
she was well-nigh overcome : the only gleam of earthly comfort
she had was seeing us.   The troop had been delayed in their
returning by conveying prisoners.   They entered the town with
the greatest acclamations through the streets.   The emotion was
strong upon this sight ; but the doubt of the sincerity of these
testimonies of joy damped the luxurient feel one might have had.
When Chitty came to us he bore every mark of the most terrible
feelings, joined to the most manly firmness and tenderness to
us.   The question was this day what we were to do.   Chitty
did not seem at this moment to advise us to leave Ireland, but
we heard that General Nugent had thought it necessary to send
Mrs Nugent away.   Every hour brought accounts of increased
disturbances.   This day was passed, indeed, in a most agitated
state, and on the next,

1798
" Saturday June 9th, Chitty seemed strongly of
opinion we ought to sail.   He told me if an exceeding
large force came upon the town, they might seize
the boats, and leave us no means of escaping, and
that there was now a very good little coal boat in
which we might go.   This day was also past in suffering, seeing
him only for short minutes, when he rather wished to avoid than
to see us.   His eagerness to put us on board was very great, and
at nightfall we (those I have named above) went down to the
quay and embarked on board this little vessel (The Liberty,
Captain Cargo).   Poor Chitty put us on board, and then was
obliged to leave us.   Soon after, Harriot had the misery of
hearing the trumpet sound to arms.   The river of Belfast is
such a difficult passage, except with every favourable circumstance, that, as we had not these, we were soon a-ground, by the
fault, as the Captain said of the Pilot.   All confidence being
entirely lost in our countrymen there was no security in our minds
that this was not intended.   As we lost a tide by it, and remained

little more than a stone's throw from the land, if God had permitted us to see it, they might have made us a prey : but it was not permitted. There was an engagement near Saintfield, in which our troops were driven back, and this day, Sunday,

1798

" June 10th, the ladies upon the deck had the misery of seeing the York Fencibles flying over the bridge of Belfast, to which, as we lay a-ground, we were very near, indeed. We made very little way any part of this day, and got aground again. People were constantly coming to us from the town, by which we had the comfort of hearing that the Yeomanry Troop had not been out the night before, when that dreadful trumpet sounded. They had been so harrassed at Antrim, it was almost necessary to spare them this night if it was possible. This evening we had some prospect of sailing, but the Pilot (without whom the Captain dare not sail) did not come on board till barely time for the tide, and then half the crew had left us. All this appeared to me extremely suspicious, but as there was no mending the situation, it was needless to express my fears ; there was terror enough spread amongst our fugitives by cruel and false reports which were continually brought from the town. While we were in this situation, Mr Salmon (Mr Skeffington's clerk) brought down the King's boat, out of which he replaced our crew, and worked jointly with them and a servant of Mr Skeffington's (Denis) till twelve o'clock to get us off, which they effected, and on this day,

1798

" Monday June 11, we began to sail, and landed at Portpatrick, I think, between three and four in the evening. We brought with us a maid servant and her child, who had lived many years in the family.

" The ship was wonderfully crowded—we lay in the hold fifty three, women and children—and tedious and woeful as the time we were confined there was, I never heard a complaint from any person, except the cries of the poor little innocent children. Harriot had brought some mattresses which were very useful ; one of them, spread over some dressing boxes belonging to the passengers, was my bed for the most part of forty five hours, and I fear, I fared a great deal better than most of my companions. In one thing I fared well indeed, by the strength and spirit it pleased God to give me, never to sink at this

strange and unexpected situation. I ought to mention every
comfort it pleased God to give us, though it cannot probably
tell half : our poor Captain, who I believe to be one of the best
hearted creatures in the world, showed us such kindness and
feeling as one only could have expected from a much higher
style of education. When we landed, the town of Portpatrick
was so completely full of military, going to Ireland, and fugitives
from thence, that we had no hopes of a bed of any kind : we could
only get a dirty bed-chamber in the inn to eat our dinner : but
the regulating officer, Captain Carmichael, from whom we received every civility and assistance, found us out some rooms at
the Minister's house, Mr. McKenzie, who, with his wife, joined
in affording us every comfort in their power. Mrs. Nugent,
who had got a lodging at an ale-house, gave Harriot and her
child a bed in it."

The Countess appears to have left Longtown, near
Dumfries, on her homeward journey, on 12th September, but

" obliged to travel so slow upon account of the children,"

she did not reach Portpatrick till the 18th. On the next day
she crossed to Donaghadee, travelling to Belfast on the 20th,
and on the day following—nine days out from the neighbourhood of Dumfries,—she was at home at Tollymore in Down.

INDEX